PRESTO_ _ Hu_ _ _ in Winfield, Alabama at the time the M_ _ _ _ by _ _ beginning, and his long acquaint _ _ ith _ _ _ nd the arguments led to his interest in makin_ _ rou_ _ object _ _ dy of the origins of the TVA.

Aft_ _ _ ice with the Army _ _ ng World War II, Mr. Hubbard compl_ _ his education, receiving his Ph.D. from Vanderbilt Unive_ _ n 1955. He is at present Professor of Histo_ t Austin Peay _ _ College, Cla_ _ _ nnessee.

ORIGINS

OF THE

TVA

THE MUSCLE SHOALS CONTROVERSY, 1920-1932

PRESTON J. HUBBARD

THE NORTON LIBRARY

W·W·NORTON & COMPANY·INC·NEW YORK

FIRST PUBLISHED IN THE NORTON LIBRARY 1968
BY ARRANGEMENT WITH VANDERBILT UNIVERSITY PRESS

PUBLISHED SIMULTANEOUSLY IN CANADA
BY GEORGE J. MCLEOD LIMITED, TORONTO

Frontispiece: An aerial photograph of Wilson Dam, at Muscle Shoals, Alabama, taken over by the TVA in 1933.

(Photograph courtesy Tennessee Valley Authority Office of Information.)

Books That Live
The Norton imprint on a book means that in the publisher's
estimation it is a book not for a single season but for the years.
W. W. Norton & Company, Inc.

PRINTED IN THE UNITED STATES OF AMERICA

1 2 3 4 5 6 7 8 9 0

Table of Contents

Editorial Comment

Preface

THE CREATION OF THE Tennessee Valley Authority in 1933 by the New Deal Congress marked a decisive turning point in an important phase of American public policy. This study constitutes an attempt to ascertain the political and economic origins of the Tennessee Valley Authority through an investigation of the struggle for the control of the Tennessee River system from 1920 to 1932. The heart of that struggle was centered on Muscle Shoals, Alabama, the most important water-power site of the entire river system.

The controversy over control of Muscle Shoals resulted from an attempt by the federal government to salvage its wartime investment in the great defense project there. The National Defense Act of 1916 had provided that the facilities at Muscle Shoals were to be used by the government in peacetime for the production of nitrates for fertilizer and national defense. When the Wilson administration attempted to carry out this mandate in the postwar period, the plan became enmeshed in a dispute over public versus private operation of the plants.

The central theme of the controversy soon shifted from fertilizer to water power. The possession by the government of a huge hydroelectric dam at Muscle Shoals was important from the standpoint of both time and place. The dam was the key to successful development of the water-power resources of a great river system, and the decade following World War I was a period of rapid expansion in the electrical power industry—a development which created complicated interstate power problems. Since many of the principal factors in the national power problem were also involved in the controversy over the development of Muscle Shoals and the Tennessee River, the Tennessee Valley became one of the most important battlegrounds of the power fight during the 1920's.

During the first years of the controversy, the principal issue involved was the application of the Federal Water Power Act, primarily in connection with efforts of private parties to control the river. Before the struggle between the private contenders could be brought to a decisive conclusion, however, the advocates of public power, led by Senator George W. Norris, emerged as the most powerful group in the controversy. It was essentially the Norris plan which became the Tennessee Valley Authority in 1933.

The controversy over Muscle Shoals and the Tennessee River system during the 1920's eventually developed into one of the most significant political disputes of recent times. That debate was concerned not only with important national power policies— it affected and reflected other important aspects of American political and economic institutions. For example, it involved regional planning, the ability of a democratic society to make public policy with regard to science and economics, and the problem of relationship between federal and state government.

In the final analysis, this study indicates that the Tennessee Valley Authority was primarily the handiwork of a relatively small band of Progressives in Congress led by George W. Norris. Why did the Progressives fight so long and arduously for public development of the Tennessee River despite the fact that most of them resided in other sections of the nation? It appears that their motives sprang primarily from a desire to uphold Progressive principles regarding public welfare which called for planned multiple-purpose development of the nation's water resources. The Tennessee River offered to them a handy instrument with which to facilitate this program. To this group, more than any other, the Muscle Shoals controversy became a tool for the making of important public policy. The policy thus established in regard to the Tennessee River is no longer merely national in character, for the Tennessee Valley Authority has become a model for regional development throughout the world.

I am deeply indebted to many persons who have given me aid and comfort in the preparation of this work. I especially wish to acknowledge my gratitude to Dr. Dewey W. Grantham, my major professor at Vanderbilt University, who directed this study as a doctoral dissertation; and to Dr. Henry Lee Swint and Dr. Harold

W. Bradley, both of whom made many helpful contributions. Also I am most grateful for the aid rendered to me by the staffs of the Joint University Library, Nashville, Tennessee; Division of Manuscripts, Library of Congress; and the Technical Library, Tennessee Valley Authority, Knoxville, Tennessee.

PRESTON J. HUBBARD

Austin Peay State College
Clarksville, Tennessee
May, 1961

I

Muscle Shoals: A Postwar Problem

THE MUSCLE SHOALS CONTROVERSY, like many other postwar problems, had its origins in the nation's preparedness program during the First World War. Because of the growing intensity of the war in Europe, the attention of the United States by 1916 had been turned toward problems of national defense. One of the most important of these problems concerned the nation's munitions supply, for the country was almost completely dependent on Chilean sources for nitrogen compounds necessary to the manufacture of explosives. The dependence on Chilean nitrates jeopardized the security of the United States in at least two important respects: first, the long sea route to Chile was dangerously exposed to naval attack by potential enemies; and second, most of the great powers of the world were rapidly developing domestic synthetic nitrogen facilities while the United States continued to rely on foreign sources for nitrates.[1]

Consequently, in order to improve the nitrate situation, Senator Ellison D. Smith of South Carolina introduced a bill in March, 1916, providing for the production of synthetic nitrogen on a large scale in the United States. The Smith bill was incorporated into the National Defense Act of June, 1916, as section 124 of that historic measure.[2] Section 124 authorized the President to ascertain the most feasible method of synthetic nitrogen production and to construct and operate such plants, hydroelectric dams, and other facilities as the President might deem necessary for the production of nitrates. Section 124 also provided for the

1. *Sundry Civil Appropriations Bill for 1922*, Hearings, U. S. House of Representatives, 66 Cong., 3 Sess., 976–79.
2. Joseph S. Ransmeier, *The Tennessee Valley Authority* (1942), 41–43.

peacetime use of the nitrate plants for the manufacture of fertilizer. Since the nation's agriculture was also dependent on Chile for nitrates, it was hoped that this provision would serve to cheapen the cost of fertilizer to the American farmer. The act required that the proposed nitrate industries be operated solely by the federal government and not in conjunction with private industries. The act also authorized the President to improve inland navigation wherever necessary to implement the nitrate program.[3]

Immediately upon passage of the National Defense Act, President Wilson set in motion the administrative machinery necessary to execute section 124. During the following year, three different executive committees were created to study the nitrate problem. The entrance of the United States into the war in April, 1917, increased the acuteness of this problem. In June, 1917, the Wilson administration decided to accept the recommendations of Dr. Charles L. Parsons of the Bureau of Mines, who had spent the early months of 1917 inspecting nitrogen fixation plants in Europe. Dr. Parsons recommended experimentation with the Haber or synthetic ammonia process as a first step. A successful development of this process, which required comparatively small amounts of hydroelectric power, would avoid the necessity of constructing an expensive hydroelectric dam. This process had never been employed in a successful commercial venture in this country, although the General Chemical Company appeared to have demonstrated, through laboratory experiments, an ability to operate the process successfully. On the other hand, the cyanamid process, the only other feasible method, was at this time being employed with success commercially in nitrogen fixation in the United States, but its feasibility depended on large amounts of cheap hydroelectric power. On June 5, 1917, the War Department signed a contract with the General Chemical Company providing for the construction of an experimental Haber process plant. On September 28, 1917, President Wilson chose Sheffield, Alabama, as the site of the plant (nitrate plant no. 1). This plant,

3. U. S. Statutes at Large, XXXIX, Part 1, 215; Sundry Civil Appropriations Bill, House Hearings, 66 Cong., 3 Sess., 976–79.

which cost approximately $12,000,000, was never successful. Since the termination of the war removed the incentive for further experiments at the plant, all activities in relation to it were suspended in January, 1919.[4]

Because of the increasing need for additional supplies of nitrogen in late 1917, the War Department entered into a contract with the American Cyanamid Company on December 10, 1917, for the construction of a cyanamid-process plant capable of producing 40,000 tons of nitrogen a year. The plant was located at Muscle Shoals, Alabama, because of the great amount of potential water power available there. This plant (nitrate plant no. 2) cost approximately $68,000,000 and was ready for operation by October, 1918. A test run found the plant to have fulfilled all expectations, but it was not put into operation because of the armistice in Europe.[5]

Realizing that the hydroelectric dam at Muscle Shoals, the construction of which was authorized on February 23, 1918, could not be finished in time to coincide with the completion of nitrate plant no. 2, an auxiliary steam plant was installed, and in order further to insure a dependable supply of power immediately upon completion of the nitrate plant, a contract was made with the Alabama Power Company to supply a part of the power needed to operate the plant. This contract, which involved the War Department in an agreement providing for additional construction of power facilities by this company at Gorgas, Alabama, on the Warrior River, was to become an important item in the Muscle Shoals controversy.[6]

With the ending of hostilities in Europe, the question at once arose as to what disposal should be made of the Muscle Shoals

4. Muscle Shoals Inquiry, *Majority and Minority Reports of the Muscle Shoals Inquiry*, House Doc. 119, 69 Cong., 1 Sess. (1925), 13–15; *Sundry Civil Appropriations Bill*, House Hearings, 66 Cong., 3 Sess., 976–79; War Department Report No. 2041, U. S. Ordnance Department, *Report on the Fixation and Utilization of Nitrogen* (1922), 262–71.

5. House Doc. 119, 69 Cong., 1 Sess., 14–15. The American Cyanamid Company created a subsidiary company, the Air Nitrates Corporation, for the purpose of building nitrate plant no. 2.

6. *Ibid.*, 14–15; Jerome G. Kerwin, *Federal Water-Power Legislation* (1926), 268.

nitrate project. The nitrate plants fell idle, but there were sufficient funds remaining to continue work on the hydroelectric dam (Wilson Dam) until April, 1921.[7] The unifying forces of national defense had marshaled public opinion in support of the project during the war. Now that this force was removed, the project became an object of suspicion to those who feared that the government's position at Muscle Shoals might constitute a foothold for public ownership of business.[8] The Republicans, in preparation for the election of 1920, began to attack the project, charging that it had been a costly failure. According to Donald Davidson, in commenting on this subject: "The great Muscle Shoals project looked very sick. Its contribution to the war effort had been just about zero." [9]

Upon cessation of hostilities in Europe, the War Department attempted to carry out the fertilizer mandate of the National Defense Act. In March, 1919, Arthur G. Glasgow, who had made a study of the nitrogen situation in allied countries for the War Department during the summer of 1918, was appointed Fixed Nitrogen Administrator with instructions to formulate a plan for postwar use of the Muscle Shoals project. Glasgow spent the summer months of 1919 in a vain effort to attract private capital to the Muscle Shoals project, despite the prohibition against such a course in the National Defense Act. He probably intended, however, to obtain congressional approval before accepting any offer; this was the principle to which Secretary of War John W. Weeks adhered in 1921 when the War Department received the first Muscle Shoals offer. Glasgow tendered an extremely generous offer to the large fertilizer companies—they would be required to pay no rent until they had earned 9 per cent on their working capital, and after that whatever profit might accrue would be divided equally between the operator and the federal government. Having failed to receive an offer from the fertilizer industry, an effort was made to attract some New York financiers and "the coke-oven interests" to the Muscle Shoals project. The

7. See New York *Times*, March 26, 1921.
8. Ransmeier, *op. cit.*, 45.
9. Donald Davidson, *The Tennessee* (1946–48), II, 183.

persons and firms involved were not identified. These efforts also ended in failure.[10]

Having failed to interest private capital in the Muscle Shoals nitrate plants, Glasgow turned to government operation as a solution to the Muscle Shoals problem. In a report to the Secretary of War on October 22, 1919, Glasgow laid down a plan for such a course. This plan contemplated the operation of the nitrate plant no. 2 by the government in the manufacture of fertilizer for agriculture and nitrates for national defense. Glasgow admitted that until the completion of Wilson Dam, operation would probably be conducted at a loss, but he confidently estimated that when cheap water power from the dam became available, the government would net an annual profit of $2,900,000 from the Muscle Shoals project.

The basic justification for this plan, according to Glasgow, was the necessity of continuous operation of nitrate plant no. 2 in order to prevent obsolescence and to maintain the plant at its maximum efficiency for the sake of national defense. Glasgow reported that the best method of utilizing nitrate plant no. 1 had not been determined.[11]

Thereupon, Secretary of War Newton D. Baker drew up a bill based on the Glasgow report and asked Senator James W. Wadsworth of New York, the chairman of the Senate Committee on Military Affairs, and Representative Julius H. Kahn of California, chairman of the House Committee on Military Affairs, to introduce it in Congress. Baker's request was complied with, Kahn introducing the bill in the House on November 1, 1919, and Wadsworth presenting it to the Senate a few days later.[12]

The Wadsworth-Kahn bill provided for the organization of a corporation which would be endowed with a legal structure very similar to a private corporation except that all of the stock would be in the possession of the federal government. It would be governed by a board of directors who would be appointed by and

10. House Doc. 119, 69 Cong., 1 Sess., 17–18; War Department Report No. 2041, 310–11.
11. *Cong. Rec.*, 66 Cong., 2 Sess., 4782–83.
12. *Ibid.*, 66 Cong., 1 Sess., 7860, 8055.

hold office at the pleasure of the Secretary of War. The principal function of this government corporation would be to operate the Muscle Shoals nitrate project for the production of nitrogen products and to sell these products, after meeting the needs of national defense, to farmers and producers of fertilizer. Upon completion of Wilson Dam the surplus power not needed in the production of nitrogen and fertilizer products would be sold at the switchboard. The corporation would be permitted to enter into contracts with others and to purchase or lease patents or other property needed in carrying out the purpose of the act.[13]

In the spring of 1920, both the House and Senate held hearings on the Wadsworth-Kahn bill at which Secretary Baker strongly endorsed the provisions of the proposed legislation. Baker denied that government operation of the nitrate project would injure private development of the nitrogen industry as was contended by various members of the committees. On the contrary, he said, the research to be provided by the corporation would greatly aid private industry by ascertaining the most profitable method of nitrogen production. He stated that an uncertainty with respect to the relative merits of the various processes and a scarcity of scientific knowledge concerning the whole subject of nitrogen fixation was deterring private capital from entering the synthetic nitrogen industry. Furthermore, he declared that the need of freeing national defense and American agriculture, which he believed to be faced with an acute problem of rapid exhaustion of soil fertility, from dependence on Chilean nitrates was more important at this time than considerations of private capital. He revealed that the contemplated plan of distribution of Muscle Shoals fertilizer was through private fertilizer distributors rather than directly to the consumer. In answer to committee members who felt that Muscle Shoals should be operated by the War Department or some other existing governmental agency, Baker defended the corporate type of organization as being more advantageous in such an undertaking. Tacitly, he suggested that removing the project from the direct influence of Congress and placing it in a self-supporting, self-operating position would free

13. *Ibid.*, 66 Cong., 3 Sess., 812–13.

it from undue political interference and permit a more business-like operation.

Disturbed by reports that the Haber process of nitrogen fixation, which had been developed in Germany during the war period, had surpassed the cyanamid process in efficiency, the committees pressed Baker for a clarification of this issue. The Secretary conceded the possibility that the Germans might be operating the Haber process more economically than other processes, but he asserted that American scientists did not yet know all of the secrets of that method. He insisted that all available information demonstrated the superiority of the cyanamid process. Moreover, Baker declared that since the government had invested some $68,000,000 in nitrate plant no. 2, which was equipped with the cyanamid process, it would be extremely unwise to scrap the plant when there was no certainty of a better process in sight. Baker intimated that the failure of the experiment with the Haber method at plant no. 1 had created an unfavorable attitude on his part toward that process.[14]

Secretary Baker's position was well supported by testimony of experts. The House Military Committee heard Professor Albert H. White of Yale University, who had been associated with the nitrate division of the Army Ordnance Department during the war period, and Major David D. Gaillard of the Army Ordnance Department, testify that nitrate plant no. 2 could be operated by the government at a profit.[15] In addition, Baker presented to this committee an extract from a recent report by General John J. Pershing in which the General advocated that the federal government operate Muscle Shoals for the production of fertilizer in peacetime so that the project would be constantly available for national defense.[16]

Dr. Arthur B. Lamb, Director of the Fixed Nitrogen Research

14. *Atmospheric Nitrogen, Operation of Muscle Shoals Nitrate Plants,* Hearings, U. S. House of Representatives, 66 Cong., 2 Sess. (1920), 838–46; *Production of Atmospheric Nitrogen,* Hearings, U. S. Senate, 66 Cong., 2 Sess. (1920), 8–9, 13, 17.

15. *Atmospheric Nitrogen,* House Hearings, 66 Cong., 2 Sess., 871–78, 884, 891.

16. Extract from General Pershing's report to the War Department, March 9, 1920, reprinted *ibid.,* 854.

Laboratory of the Army Ordnance, and Major General Clarence
C. Williams, Chief of Ordnance, appeared before the Senate
Agriculture Committee to endorse Secretary Baker's program for
Muscle Shoals. They were joined by representatives of the
Farmers' National Council and the American Farm Bureau Fed-
eration who favored government operation of Muscle Shoals for
the production of fertilizer. The only discordant note, as far as
the Baker plan was concerned, resulted from the appearance of
Frank S. Washburn, president of the American Cyanamid
Company, who objected to his company's being displaced from
Muscle Shoals by a government corporation. Washburn testified
that the government could neither make a profit on nor lower
the price of fertilizer by operation of the Muscle Shoals project.
Baker called in Russell F. Bower, Washington representative of
the National Farmers' Union, for the specific purpose of refuting
Washburn's testimony.[17] But no further action was taken on the
Wadsworth-Kahn bill during this session.

During the same session the Muscle Shoals project came under
heavy attack in the House of Representatives. A subcommittee
of the House Select Committee on Expenditures in the War
Department under the chairmanship of William J. Graham,
Illinois Republican, conducted an investigation of the Muscle
Shoals project, hearings being held intermittently from January
to May, 1920. This committee not only assumed the responsibility of ascertaining the extent of waste of public funds at
Muscle Shoals but it undertook to solve the more difficult problem
of postwar utilization of the project. With the national election

17. *Production of Atmospheric Nitrogen*, Senate Hearings, 66 Cong., 2 Sess.,
25, 61–62, 416–24, 437, 455, 501.

Perhaps Washburn, in his opposition to government operation of Muscle Shoals,
was partially motivated by fear of government competition in the manufacture
of cyanamid, since that compound was the principal product of the American
Cyanamid Company as well as of nitrate plant no. 2. It was very likely that the
American Cyanamid Company desired to acquire the Muscle Shoals project,
particularly nitrate plant no. 2. This company had unsuccessfully sought to obtain
an agreement with the government whereby plant no. 2 would be given to it at
the end of the war. Failing in this effort, the cyanamid company was successful in
inserting a preferential option-to-buy agreement in the final contract. Nevertheless,
the company had made no effort to exercise this option. See New York *Times*,
Feb. 11, 1922; War Department Report No. 2041, 276; Ransmeier, *op. cit.*, 52n.

of 1920 near at hand, the Republican majority on the committee unquestionably hoped to embarrass the Democrats by revelations of waste, corruption, and inefficiency at Muscle Shoals. Furthermore, the Republicans apparently hoped to prove that since the project failed to contribute to the war effort, the completion of nitrate plant no. 2 occurring simultaneously with the armistice, the Democratic nitrate program had been a colossal blunder.

The Graham committee probed extensively into the wartime relationships between the government and the Air Nitrates Corporation, the subsidiary created by the American Cyanamid Company to construct nitrate plant no. 2, and the Alabama Power Company, which had been under contract to furnish a portion of the power for the nitrate plant. Nevertheless, the committee failed to uncover any sensational scandals, although evidence of some waste and petty graft was revealed. The contractors who built the nitrate plant, together with the minority member of the subcommittee, Finis J. Garrett of Tennessee, admitted that waste had occurred in building the plant but contended that wartime speed was the causal factor rather than dishonesty.[18]

The Republicans probably scored some political gains as a result of revelations of petty waste and graft, but they did not succeed in seriously challenging the feasibility of the wartime Muscle Shoals project itself. The loudest voice in the defense of the practicability of the project was raised by Bernard Baruch who had been chairman of the War Industries Board. Baruch testified that he assumed full responsibility for the approximately $100,000,000 which was spent on the nitrate plants. Baruch told the committee that even though the nitrate plants did not contribute directly to the war effort, the wisdom of constructing them would have become apparent had the war lasted six months longer. Moreover, Baruch claimed that these plants, even though they had produced nothing except in the test run at plant no. 2, had already paid for themselves "many times over" by forcing down the price of Chilean nitrates. He said that as the war proceeded the price of Chilean nitrates doubled but when the United States instituted the Muscle Shoals nitrate program,

18. New York *Times*, Jan. 10, 23, Feb. 4, 1920.

the price of Chilean nitrates dropped to a point which represented a saving of some $300,000,000 to the American people. With respect to the future utilization of the Muscle Shoals project, Baruch gave a somewhat qualified endorsement of government operation in the manufacture of fertilizer as a yardstick for the fertilizer industry. He was inclined, however, to be apprehensive lest the yardstick idea be perverted into outright government competition.[19]

Frank S. Washburn, president of the American Cyanamid Company, denied all charges of inefficiency and waste in connection with the construction of the plant as far as the Air Nitrates Corporation was concerned. On the other hand, he charged that the War Department had bungled the nitrate program and had wasted millions of dollars. He used these charges to oppose government operation of the plant.[20]

Despite the lack of evidence to substantiate its charges, in its report the Republican majority of the Graham committee condemned the government's entire wartime nitrate program. Bernard Baruch was described somewhat disparagingly as the "moving spirit" behind the nitrate scheme. On the other hand, the majority charged that the whole Muscle Shoals project was a scheme devised by Frank S. Washburn of the American Cyanamid Company, by which the government had been induced to build the nitrate plants and Wilson Dam with the view that they would be relinquished to Washburn's company after the war. The report accused Washburn's company of having taken advantage of the "credulity" of War Department officials by enticing them into signing a contract for the construction of nitrate plant no. 2 that was "unfair and unjust" to the United States government. The Muscle Shoals nitrate program was classed as unnecessary and it was implied that proof of this contention lay in the fact that the program contributed no nitrates to the military victory. It was alleged by the majority that President Wilson had ordered the construction of Wilson Dam when he undoubtedly knew that it could not be completed before the end of the war.

19. *Ibid.*, Jan. 11, 1920.
20. *Ibid.*, April 9, 1920.

The majority also charged that the Wilson administration had greatly exaggerated the dangers that might arise from continued dependence on Chilean nitrates, particularly the threats posed by German submarines and the possibility of unreasonably high prices of nitrates. In this report, the Republicans accused the administration of virtually having perpetrated a hoax by publicizing these alleged dangers. There were also charges of waste.[21]

The majority concluded that government operation of Muscle Shoals would be detrimental to the nation. On the one hand it was stated that such a policy would greatly retard the development of a private domestic nitrogen industry, while on the other hand the report declared that the capacity of the Muscle Shoals project would be so inconsiderable as to have no appreciable effect on fertilizer prices in this country. Consequently, the majority recommended that nitrate plant no. 2 be leased to private industry with reservations for "reasonable" regulation by the federal government of the distribution and prices of fertilizer produced there. It was recommended that plant no. 1 be kept in a stand-by condition subject to further experimentation, the majority declaring that the Haber process installed there held greater potentialities than the cyanamid process at plant no. 2. The majority further recommended the discontinuance of work on Wilson Dam pending the formulation of a definite policy toward the project by Congress.[22]

All of the majority charges were categorically denied by Representative Garrett in his minority report. Garrett vouched for the good faith of President Wilson, Bernard Baruch, and all other government officials involved in the Muscle Shoals nitrate program. He charged that the majority report had been motivated by

21. *War Expenditures—Ordnance*, House Report 998, 66 Cong., 2 Sess. (1920), 1–7.

22. *Ibid.*, 7–8. The majority report, in an attempt to justify the condemnation of government operation of Muscle Shoals, cited as evidence a written statement by Dan E. McGugin, a Nashville, Tennessee, attorney representing the Tri-State Quarrymen's Association. McGugin opposed government operation of Muscle Shoals on the grounds that "extravagant and unreasonable wages" which the government probably would pay would demoralize labor conditions in the Muscle Shoals area and that the selling of lime as a by-product of the nitrate plants would constitute unfair competition to lime quarrymen in that area. *Ibid.*, 56.

political bias. He contended that the wartime nitrate program had been essential to Baruch's plan to have absolute assurance that American armies on the front would at all times have sufficient ammunition. Regarding the majority recommendations, Garrett maintained that the Graham committee had not been charged with the responsibility of proposing legislation in this matter which, he declared, was solely under the jurisdiction of the House Military Committee.[23]

During the summer of 1920, a survey conducted by Milton Whitney, Chief of the Bureau of Soils, Department of Agriculture, aided the cause of the Wadsworth-Kahn bill immensely. Whitney addressed a questionnaire to the state commissioners of agriculture and directors of experiment stations throughout the country in an effort to ascertain the prevailing attitude among agricultural leaders toward the Muscle Shoals problem. The replies revealed that there was a general opinion among these officials that the country was confronted with a serious fertilizer shortage and that the government should operate Muscle Shoals as a means of solving the fertilizer problem.[24]

In December, 1920, the House Appropriations Committee, which was conducting hearings on the sundry civil appropriations bill, turned to consideration of the request of the Secretary of War for an additional $10,000,000 to finance further work on Wilson Dam. Here Secretary Baker and General Harry Taylor, Assistant Chief of Engineers, made a vigorous effort to convince the committee that it would be economically wise to complete the dam immediately, since a stoppage of work would entail various additional expenses relating to interruption of the labor force and deterioration of equipment and machinery. According to General Taylor the funds available for construction of the dam would be exhausted by June 1, 1921.[25]

At this hearing, the consideration of the appropriations item was secondary to another subject, the Wadsworth-Kahn bill.

23. *Ibid.*, Part 2, 73–92.

24. Whitney to Colonel James H. Burns, Sept. 27, 1920, Records of the Bureau of Plant Industry, Soils, and Engineering, Fertilizer Investigations, Muscle Shoals, National Archives.

25. *Sundry Civil Appropriations Bill,* House Hearings, 66 Cong., 3 Sess., 989–93.

Secretary Baker undoubtedly desired to keep these two subjects separated in order that the request for appropriations would not appear to be merely an attempt to implement government operation of the plant. Nevertheless, Secretary Baker was forced to defend the Wadsworth-Kahn bill. Baker emphasized that the nation's soil fertility, which he believed to be more important to national defense than military considerations, was being rapidly depleted, according to reports from agricultural leaders, and that his Muscle Shoals plan was designed to remedy this situation.

Secretary Baker again avoided an extreme position in regard to the merits of the cyanamid process and nitrate plant no. 2, stating that while evidence perhaps indicated that nitrates could be manufactured more cheaply under the Haber process, its true nature was still not fully known in America. Although the Secretary recommended further experimentation with the Haber process at plant no. 1, he still insisted that it would be wise for the government to initiate fertilizer production at nitrate plant no. 2. Baker denied that he was "wedded" to government operation in principle but asserted that public operation of Muscle Shoals as a supplement to Chilean and privately produced American nitrates would be necessary to meet the future needs of American agriculture.

Although Secretary Baker primarily emphasized the need of nitrates for national defense and agriculture, he nevertheless revealed to the House committee that he was impressed with the water-power potentialities of Wilson Dam, and he advocated that the primary power produced there be sold for general distribution in the area.[26] It was Colonel Hugh L. Cooper, consulting engineer for construction of Wilson Dam and one of the nation's outstanding hydroelectric engineers, however, who first urged that Muscle Shoals be considered primarily a water-power proposition. Colonel Cooper made his views known in a letter to General Harry Taylor in November, 1920.[27] In appearances before the Senate and House appropriations committees early in 1921,

26. *Ibid.*, 976–85.
27. Cooper to Taylor, Nov. 27, 1920, quoted *ibid.*, 998.

Cooper elaborated more fully on his plans. He recommended the completion of Wilson Dam as a water-power project, stating that the dam could not be justified on the basis of national defense and fertilizer production. He asserted that a growing need for additional power in the South plus the key position occupied by Muscle Shoals in future hydroelectric expansion in the region and the probable great cost of the Wilson Dam project justified completion of the dam by the federal government. He declared that because of the government's ability to borrow money at low rates it could net an annual profit of $2,500,000 on power receipts at Wilson Dam whereas private capital, paying higher interest rates, would be very fortunate to break even. According to Cooper's plan, the government, operating the plant through a hired firm, would sell the power at the switchboard at market rates to power companies. He strongly opposed any policy of governmental distribution of power, asserting that such a course would drive private power capital from the South.[28]

Conservative Republicans on the House Appropriations Committee vigorously maintained that there was no market for additional power in the South, although Colonel Cooper insisted that several southern power companies were eager to purchase Muscle Shoals power. Representative James W. Good of Iowa, chairman of the House Appropriations Committee, noted that only the Alabama Power Company had access to Muscle Shoals and implied strongly that Colonel Cooper was seeking to place the dam under control of that company.[29]

Dr. Charles L. Parsons, who had been closely connected with the government's wartime nitrate program and was at this time a consulting chemist for the Atmospheric Nitrogen Association, a subsidiary of the General Chemical Company, appeared before the House Appropriations Committee to oppose the completion of Wilson Dam. Dr. Parsons recommended that nitrate plant no. 2 be put in mothballs as a reserve for wartime. While admitting

28. *Sundry Civil Appropriations Bill for 1922*, Hearings, U. S. Senate, 66 Cong., 3 Sess. (1921), 3–28; *Sundry Civil Appropriations Bill for 1922*, Supplement to House Hearings, 66 Cong., 3 Sess. (1921), 21–22, 60–73.

29. *Sundry Civil Appropriations Bill*, Supplement to House Hearings, 66 Cong., 3 Sess., 21–28.

that his company was engaged in fixation of nitrogen for fertilizer by the Haber process, he insisted that he did not fear competition from the cyanamid process which, he averred, was obsolete, but rather that he opposed the principle of public operation of a commercial nitrate plant.[30]

The nation's farmers were also represented at the hearings before the Appropriations Committee. As early as May, 1920, in fact, representatives of the Farm Bureau, the National Grange, and other farm organizations began to congregate in Washington to lobby for the development of Muscle Shoals by the government as a fertilizer enterprise.[31] Also, in December, 1920, Congress received a petition signed by official representatives of the Farm Bureau, the National Grange, the Co-operative Union of America, and the National Board of Farm Organizations, which, in endorsing the Wadsworth-Kahn bill, stated: "Operating this plant does not bring the Government into competition with American manufacturers making nitrates. There is no such industry in America. Domestic production of nitrogen is entirely a by-product industry." [32]

At the hearings before the Good committee, agricultural interests were represented by Gray Silver, Washington representative of the Farm Bureau, and Russell F. Bower, Washington representative of the National Farmers' Union. They advocated the manufacture of nitrates by the government at Muscle Shoals as well as immediate completion of Wilson Dam. Silver testified that Muscle Shoals nitrates could be produced and sold profitably more cheaply than the prevailing prices of Chilean nitrates. Bower declared that the government was obligated to enter the nitrate business at Muscle Shoals in order to break the Chilean nitrate monopoly which, he said, allocated amounts and fixed prices of nitrates for each nation of the world. Bower also presented evidence purporting to show that Muscle Shoals nitrates could be sold profitably at one-half the prevailing market prices. Chairman Good, who did not appear to be greatly impressed with

30. *Ibid.*, 184–85, 198, 201, 213–16.
31. *Cong. Rec.*, 66 Cong., 2 Sess., 7259.
32. *Ibid.*, 66 Cong., 3 Sess., 863.

the farm leaders' testimony, suggested that farmers depend on crop rotation rather than Muscle Shoals nitrates to restore the fertility of their soil.[33]

In January, 1921, the Muscle Shoals problem occupied much of the attention of Congress. Besides the hearings and debate on the Wilson Dam item in the sundry civil appropriations bill, which at times occurred simultaneously, debate began in the Senate on the Wadsworth-Kahn bill. The Senate Agriculture Committee had reported this bill favorably, with only minor alterations, on May 31, 1920, but Congress adjourned a few days afterward, preventing further action on the measure until the next session, which began in December, 1920.[34] The attack on the bill was led by Senator Wadsworth, who had originally introduced it. The New York Senator had never been in sympathy with the measure and had introduced it only as a personal favor to Secretary Baker. The defense of the bill was chiefly in the hands of southern Democrats, particularly Senators Oscar W. Underwood and J. Thomas Heflin of Alabama and Ellison D. Smith of South Carolina. Wadsworth and other opponents of the bill, most of whom were conservative Republicans, attempted to have the bill recommitted to committee on the ground that the technical problems involved had been ill considered.[35]

The chief arguments of this Senate debate centered around the fertilizer aspects of the Muscle Shoals problem. In the first place, there was the question of whether the plant could be justified on the basis of additional need for fertilizer in this country. The proponents of the bill asserted that there was a rapidly expanding need of fertilizer not only in the cotton belt but in every section of the nation. They maintained that the nation's farmers were still dependent on Chile for nitrates and that operation of the Muscle Shoals plant would aid in breaking the alleged Chilean monopoly which, they claimed, was maintaining unduly high prices without any economic justification. Further, the advocates of the bill argued that the fertilizer products of nitrate plant no.

33. *Sundry Civil Appropriations Bill,* Supplement to House Hearings, 66 Cong., 3 Sess., 113–14, 129, 136–37.

34. New York *Times,* June 1, 1920.

35. *Cong. Rec.,* 66 Cong., 2 Sess., 8074; *ibid.,* 66 Cong., 3 Sess., 984.

2 could be absorbed without disturbing in the least the commercial production of fertilizer in America.[36]

The opponents of the bill argued that present and future demands for fertilizer in this country were being and would be satisfactorily met by the domestic private industry. Senator Wadsworth insisted that within the next decade domestic production from coke-oven products alone would be producing more nitrogen than the nation could consume.[37]

The second important fertilizer question involved in this debate concerned the relative merits of the cyanamid and Haber processes. Justification of the Muscle Shoals nitrate undertaking, among other factors, depended on proof that the cyanamid process was reasonably adequate, for the only plant at Muscle Shoals that was equipped for production in commercial quantities was plant no. 2, which was equipped with the cyanamid process. Opponents of the bill alleged that the cyanamid process was obsolete and that, as a consequence, passage of the proposed measure would force the government to expend more money in a worthless enterprise. On the other hand, Senator Heflin declared that this process would produce nitrates cheaper than the natural products of Chile, while Senator Pat Harrison of Mississippi concluded that the opposition of the American Cyanamid Company, which was engaged in some fertilizer manufacture, constituted ample proof of the competency of nitrate plant no. 2.[38]

The proposed entry of the government into the fertilizer business posed the problem of public competition with the private fertilizer industry, an issue which constituted the third major point of contention in the Senate debate. The opponents of the bill professed to see in the Wadsworth-Kahn bill a public subsidy of below-cost production which would surely bring ruin to the private fertilizer industry. Senators Underwood, Heflin, and Smith, who carried the burden of defense on this point, denied that passage of the measure would open the door to unfair compe-

36. *Ibid.*, 66 Cong., 3 Sess., 989, 1090–91, 1095–99.
37. *Ibid.*, 993, 1114.
38. *Ibid.*, 992, 1102, 1106–7, 1246.

tition. Underwood and Heflin declared their fidelity to the cause of private enterprise in principle, but Senator Smith asserted that a profitable private fertilizer business should come second to cheap fertilizer for farmers. Underwood, who revealed that he had interests in the coke-oven business, maintained that the coke-oven industry could abandon its profits from ammonia entirely and still carry on a profitable by-product business. He accused the Koppers and Semet-Solvay companies, which he said were fighting the bill, of being motivated in their opposition by the fact that they would not be able to collect royalties from the operation of the cyanamid process as they would from the operation of coke-ovens. Despite Underwood's professed faith in private enterprise, he declared it to be a function of the government not only to develop a source of cheap fertilizer, but to build dams, such as Wilson Dam, as a part of the multiple-purpose development of rivers which private enterprise could not afford. At this point the Alabama Senator appears to have been more strongly in favor of public operation of Muscle Shoals than at any other time during the period he was connected with the controversy.[39] Regarding the issue of public versus private enterprise, he said:

. . . unless we are going back to the old days, when this Government pottered, with moss growing on every endeavor, when it was impossible to pass progressive legislation in the interest of the American people, when the hands of the clock were set backward and governmental progress ceased and special interests sat enthroned in Washington . . . then there is no reason why an effort should not be made to determine whether this development [Muscle Shoals] can be practically carried on in the interests of the Nation's life. . . .[40]

Some senators revealed beliefs that the Wadsworth-Kahn bill was not a fertilizer measure at all but, in reality, a water-power proposition. In fact, Senator Irvine L. Lenroot of Wisconsin declared that the ultimate purpose of the bill was to deliver Wilson Dam to the Alabama Power Company which, he pointed out, had the only lines of access to the Muscle Shoals area. Lenroot's attack on the Alabama Power Company brought Underwood and

39. *Ibid.*, 1100–2, 1105, 1138.
40. *Ibid.*, 1206.

Heflin to the defense of that firm, the former declaring that the Wisconsin Senator had absolutely no evidence to support his charges and the latter warmly praising the power company as a beneficial institution.[41]

During the debate on the Wadsworth-Kahn bill, the American Cyanamid Company issued, through a New York press service firm, a series of bulletins attacking the bill. These bulletins were sent to members of Congress as well as newspapers. During the debate on this bill, some of the senators who were supporting it protested vigorously against this action of the cyanamid company. These bulletins stated that the Muscle Shoals nitrate project could not relieve farmers from the Chilean nitrate monopoly because the ingredients to be manufactured at the project could not be substituted for Chilean nitrates. In addition, the bulletins denied that Muscle Shoals nitrates would be sold directly to the farmers but contended that they would be sold only to fertilizer manufacturers. They asserted that nitrate plant no. 2 could not compete economically with the domestic by-product coke-oven industry.[42]

The Senate made some minor changes in the Wadsworth-Kahn bill before the final vote. In order to dispel the fears of Senator Smith that the bill would permit fertilizer manufacturers to purchase all of the Muscle Shoals nitrates, the Senate adopted an amendment giving preference to farmers in the sale of this product. Also, in order to allay the apprehensions of Senator Wadsworth, who feared the bill granted excessive powers to the Secretary of War and excessive rights of eminent domain to the proposed corporation, the Senate adopted amendments sharply curtailing the powers of the Secretary of War and prohibiting the corporation from acquiring additional property by condemnation proceedings.[43]

On January 14, 1921, the Senate passed the Wadsworth-Kahn bill by a vote of 34 to 29. Since the southern Democrats had provided the greater part of the defense of the bill, the vote

41. *Ibid.*, 1137–43, 1212.
42. *Ibid.*, 1186, 1306–7.
43. *Ibid.*, 1136–37, 1248, 1359, 1397–98, 1413.

appeared to be a distinct victory for the South. The victory was achieved, however, only by some timely aid from western senators.[44]

It seems highly probable that the Wadsworth-Kahn bill was destined to fail from the beginning of its existence. The Republicans, who controlled Congress, were hostile to the principle of government operation of a business.[45] Nevertheless, the bill did receive some substantial support even after it had died in the House committee. In May, 1921, a committee of the Farm Bureau, which had just completed an investigation of the whole Muscle Shoals problem, came before the new Congress advocating the manufacture of fertilizer at Muscle Shoals through a government corporation.[46] Also in May, 1921, a special committee of the Mississippi Valley Association, an economic pressure group representing various business interests in the Mississippi Valley area which had been conducting an investigation of Muscle Shoals, reached the conclusion that the Muscle Shoals project should become a public fertilizer plant.[47] In June, 1921, the Chicago League of Women Voters also endorsed the principles of the Wadsworth-Kahn bill.[48] In the following month, the principles of the bill were given strong support by important agri-

44. *Ibid.*, 1415–16, 1488. Of those voting for the bill the sectional division was as follows: twenty southern Democrats, eight western Democrats, two eastern Democrats, and four western Republicans. The term "South" hereinafter will refer to the former Confederate states and the border states except Missouri and West Virginia.

45. Ransmeier, *op. cit.*, 45–46.

46. *Muscle Shoals*, Hearings, U. S. Senate, 67 Cong., 2 Sess. (1922), 486–88. See *Report of the Muscle Shoals Committee of the American Farm Bureau Federation* (Chicago, May 31, 1921).

47. *Report of the Special Committee of the Mississippi Valley Association* (May 28, 1921), General Records of the Department of Agriculture, Correspondence of the Secretary of Agriculture, Muscle Shoals Nitrate Plant, National Archives. The Mississippi Valley Association represented "leading" business interests of twenty-seven states in the Mississippi Valley, particularly business interests in the large cities of the Middle West. One of its principal functions was to bring pressure on Congress in regard to economic legislation. Some members of Congress were members of the association. New York *Times*, Jan. 9, March 12, Nov. 6 (LX), 1921.

48. Memorandum for the Secretary of Agriculture, June 9, 1921, Correspondence of the Secretary of Agriculture, Muscle Shoals, National Archives.

cultural spokesmen in New England, including Herbert Myrick, the publisher of *Farm and Home*.[49]

The $10,000,000 Muscle Shoals item in the sundry civil appropriations bill was rejected in the House on January 4, 1921, after a bitter debate, by a vote of 207 to 144. The opposition, which consisted of conservative Republicans led by Representative William J. Graham, author of the controversial Graham report on Muscle Shoals, emphasized the "unbelievable" waste which they averred had been committed by the Wilson administration in the wartime construction of the Muscle Shoals project. It insisted either that the project be leased to private industry as it stood or that further work on it be delayed pending an investigation of its economic feasibility. The Republican leadership rejected claims by the Southerners that the project could be operated economically and charged that the true motive behind the southern support of the bill was a desire to divert federal funds to the South.[50] On this point, Representative Martin B. Madden of Illinois said:

This proposal to do something for the farmer, is a subterfuge. You are throwing sand into the farmers' eyes in order that you may be able to put your hands up to the elbows into the treasury of the United States. The time has come when we must know the facts before we impose further burdens upon the taxpayers. . . . Facts should be the basis of action here, and not fancy, and we must under no circumstances pay any more money for this iniquity until we know more about it.[51]

The Democratic defense of the Muscle Shoals project in this debate was spearheaded by Representatives Joseph W. Byrns and Finis J. Garrett of Tennessee and Edward B. Almon and

49. James R. Riggs to Bert M. Fernald, Jan. 19, 1920, and Herbert Myrick to Henry C. Wallace, July 15, 1921, *ibid*.

50. *Cong. Rec.*, 66 Cong., 3 Sess., 819, 844–49, 854, 858. On January 8, 1921, James R. Howard, president of the Farm Bureau, was summoned to appear before a House committee to explain his charges that the proposed appropriations for Muscle Shoals had been defeated in the House through the influence of large fertilizer interests. Howard told the committee that he had no intention of impugning the integrity of Congress, but he still insisted that it was evident to farmers that the appropriations item had been defeated through the influence of the "Fertilizer Trust." New York *Times*, Jan. 9, 11, 1921.

51. *Cong. Rec.*, 66 Cong., 3 Sess., 950.

William B. Bankhead of Alabama. Garrett gave an eloquent presentation of the fourfold plan for development of the Tennessee Valley—nitrates for national defense, fertilizer for agriculture, and development of navigation and water power—which he insisted was to be inferred from the National Defense Act. Byrns disputed Republican assertions that there was no market in the South for the surplus power at Muscle Shoals; Almon attempted to prove the feasibility of fertilizer production at Muscle Shoals; and Bankhead endeavored to use alleged farm support for the Muscle Shoals fertilizer plan as a club to hold over the heads of midwestern Republicans.[52]

Consideration of the appropriation item for the Wilson Dam came up in the Senate on February 5, 1921, where, after a short debate, it was passed, 36 to 27. During this debate Senator Reed Smoot of Utah proposed that the Muscle Shoals project be sold for scrap and asserted that the underlying factor motivating the construction of Wilson Dam was a scheme by the southern states to promote the distribution of cheap water power throughout that region. He predicted that Congress would soon be called on to build transmission lines. Senator Underwood, citing the recent testimony of Colonel Hugh L. Cooper before a congressional committee, declared that there was an acute need for more water power in the South. Senator Kenneth D. McKellar of Tennessee accused the Utah Senator of attempting to throw Muscle Shoals into the arms of private power interests.[53]

On February 9 the appropriations proposal returned to the House where a bitter debate ensued as a result of charges by the Republican leadership that the Alabama Power Company was covertly financing literature advocating the immediate completion of Wilson Dam. The specific literature in question had been printed and distributed under the name of the Muscle Shoals Association, an organization in the Tennessee Valley area. Two of its officials, Edward B. Stahlman, publisher of the Nashville *Banner,* and Claudius H. Huston, the association's treasurer,

52. *Ibid.,* 832, 838–40, 856–57, 863.
53. *Ibid.,* 2645–49.

denied that the publicity material had been financed by the power company.[54]

The House refused to concur in the Senate's action, and the issue was not settled until March 3, when the Senate capitulated by eliminating the proposed appropriation for continuation of work at Wilson Dam.[55]

The death of the Wadsworth-Kahn bill together with the defeat of the proposed appropriation for continuation of work on Wilson Dam appeared to have stifled any chances for government operation of the Muscle Shoals project. In fact, this turn of events seemed to have sounded the death knell of any further development of Muscle Shoals, public or private. It soon became evident, however, that the new Republican administration under President Harding had not yet decided to scrap the project. Late in March, 1921, just a few days before the cessation of work on Wilson Dam, the new Secretary of War, John W. Weeks, announced that if any industrial organization would guarantee the federal government a fair return on the investment in Muscle Shoals, he could recommend to Congress that Wilson Dam be completed and that the entire project be leased. Weeks declared that this course was prompted by several industrial leaders who had urged that the Muscle Shoals venture be completed.[56] *Electrical World*, one of the principal voices of the electric power industry, advised completion of the dam on the grounds that the government investment would otherwise be a total loss and the nation needed the great potential water power of Muscle Shoals.[57]

Secretary Weeks followed this by instructing the Chief of Engineers to seek bids for Muscle Shoals in order to ascertain the feasibility of completing the dam.[58] Several of the southern power companies were approached by the Chief of Engineers but the response was discouraging. None of these companies, except the Alabama Power Company, displayed any perceptible interest

54. *Ibid.*, 3873, 3877–78, 4505.
55. *Ibid.*, 4430.
56. New York *Times*, March 26, 1921.
57. "Facing a Dilemma with Very Sharp Horns," in *Electrical World*, LXXVII (March 12, 1921), 577.
58. House Doc. 119, 69 Cong., 1 Sess., 19.

in the proposition, and one of them, the Southern Power Company, recommended that the project be scrapped, describing it as worthless and impractical. Thomas W. Martin, president of the Alabama Power Company, while refusing to tender a definite offer, indicated that his company might be interested if the government would charge most of the expenses of the enterprise to war loss and navigation.[59]

The unsuccessful effort by Secretary Weeks to attract the interest of the southern power companies marked the end of the first phase of the Muscle Shoals controversy. Although nothing positive toward solving the Muscle Shoals problem was accomplished during this period, important steps had been taken toward formulating a policy concerning the project. In the first place, the failure of the Wadsworth-Kahn bill in the House meant congressional rejection, for the time being at least, of the policy of public operation of Muscle Shoals. As far as the Republican leadership in Congress was concerned, the policy of governmental operation of Muscle Shoals was rejected from the standpoint of both principle and practicability. Thus, as the first phase of the controversy drew to a close, it appeared that the desire of many Southerners for a public fertilizer plant at Muscle Shoals was doomed to failure as long as the Republicans controlled Congress. The fact, however, that an alliance of farm states in the Senate had been able to pass a public operation bill despite the Republican control of that body provided a bright spot in an otherwise dark future for the supporters of governmental operation of the Muscle Shoals enterprise.

The desire of Secretary Weeks to negotiate a successful lease of the Muscle Shoals properties perhaps presaged continued governmental participation in the enterprise, for its completion would require an enormous outlay of capital, part of which probably would have to be provided by the federal government. The results of attempts by the Wilson and Harding administrations made it appear unlikely that private interests would be

---

59. *Cong. Rec.*, 67 Cong., 2 Sess., 3698; Martin to John W. Weeks, May 28, 1921, quoted in *Muscle Shoals Propositions,* Hearings, U. S. House of Representatives, 67 Cong., 2 Sess. (1922), 38–40.

willing to risk sufficient capital to complete the project. At any rate, the action of the newly installed Harding administration definitely insured that the Muscle Shoals project would not be consigned to the scrap heap, although the credit for this development was later attributed to Henry Ford by supporters of his Muscle Shoals offer. In turning from public to private operation of Muscle Shoals, the Harding administration clearly proposed to set aside a major principle of the National Defense Act, the provision prohibiting private control and operation of Muscle Shoals. As events later proved, Secretary Weeks did not intend actually to violate the law but instead envisaged congressional approval of this course of action.

During this first period, the Muscle Shoals controversy became tainted with partisan and sectional politics. The South, the section chiefly interested in the development of the Muscle Shoals enterprise, contributed the majority of the Democrats who held seats in Congress. Also, the close association of Secretary Baker with the Wadsworth-Kahn bill helped to put the controversy on a partisan basis because his action identified public operation as a goal of the Wilson administration. This state of affairs permitted the Republicans to link Muscle Shoals, to a great extent, with party, pork-barrel, and sectional politics. In all probability, the fertilizer possibilities at Muscle Shoals would have had a great deal of national appeal had fertilizer been used in great amounts in sections outside the South. Some of the farm organizations did perhaps create a favorable sentiment toward Muscle Shoals in scattered and isolated areas around the country outside the South.

During the immediate postwar phase of the Muscle Shoals controversy, the Muscle Shoals venture was primarily considered as a plan to manufacture nitrates for national defense and fertilizer for agriculture. Although the potentialities of Muscle Shoals as a water-power development were realized by Secretary Baker and Colonel Cooper, the issue of water power was not important at this time. Yet an important development in the nation's water-power policy, which was destined to play a major role in the Muscle Shoals controversy in its later phases, occurred during this period. This was the passage of the Federal Water Power Act of 1920. This measure was the result of a twenty-year struggle over the nation's water-power policy. It was essentially a compromise between conservationists and the power companies. The former group had been appalled by the lack of governmental regulation of water-power development in the United States. On the other hand, the water-power acts of 1901 and 1910 failed to provide the security that was needed to protect the huge investments required for water-power developments, principally because of the issuance of revocable licenses. As a consequence the development of the nation's water-power resources had been exceedingly slow until the First World War, when the stress of the emergency stimulated growth in this field. This wartime expansion forced the passage of the Water Power Act of 1920. The insurgent Republicans of the Middle West led the fight for stronger federal regulation of water-power development, although some of them refused to vote for the final compromise that emerged from conference. The electrical industry, which had for the most part fought vigorously against increased federal regulation, capitulated in 1917 and opened negotiations with congressional leaders. The final product of these parleys was the compromise Water Power Act of 1920 which pleased none of the interested groups entirely.[60]

The Federal Water Power Act of 1920 created the Federal Power Commission, composed of the secretaries of War, the Interior, and Agriculture, which was empowered to issue licenses for power developments on navigable streams and on public lands, the terms of the leases not to exceed fifty years. The act required that the licensee must pay to the federal government reasonable annual charges for administrative costs, for rent on public property, and for expropriation by the government of excess profits. It also required that the licensee must pay for increased value of dam sites resulting from the construction of reservoirs by others upstream and must provide navigational

60. Philip Wells, "Our Federal Power Policy," in *Survey Graphic* LI (March, 1924), 572–73; O. C. Merrill, "The Federal Water Power Act of 1920," undated memorandum in the Conservation of Water Power section of the Papers of Gifford Pinchot, Library of Congress.

facilities at dam sites if needed. The act also provided for regulation of power rates and distribution policies by the states whereever state regulatory bodies existed; otherwise, the licensee would be subject to regulation by the Federal Power Commission. The act further provided that rates charged by the licensee would be based on actual investments. It required that the licensee keep the hydroelectric properties in good repair and provided that at the termination of the lease period these properties would revert to the federal government upon payment to the licensee of their original cost less the amount of the depreciation and amortization funds.[61]

The second phase of the Muscle Shoals controversy began in the summer of 1921 when Henry Ford became involved in it. In June, following an inspection of Muscle Shoals by Ford, rumors that the Detroit industrialist was extremely interested in acquiring the project began to be circulated. Late in that month, Secretary Weeks announced that he was ready to negotiate with the automobile magnate. Consequently, it came as no great surprise when on July 8, 1921, Henry Ford submitted a bid for Muscle Shoals.[62]

61. *U. S. Statutes at Large*, XLI, Part 1, 1063–67.
62. House Doc. 119, 69 Cong., 1 Sess., 19.

II

The Ford Offer: The Early Stages

IN THE COURSE of executing the order of Secretary Weeks to seek
bidders for Muscle Shoals, Major General Lansing H. Beach,
the Chief of Engineers, who had written to several large industrialists about the matter, received a reply from Henry Ford
which indicated interest in the project. General Beach became
highly interested in the possibility of disposing of the government's properties at Muscle Shoals to Ford. Accordingly, he
sought the services of J. W. Worthington, executive secretary of
the Tennessee River Improvement Association, who for many
years had been promoting the development of the Muscle Shoals
area. Worthington approached Ford (as the agent of General
Beach) and succeeded in stimulating the automobile magnate's
interest in the Muscle Shoals enterprise. Following consultation
with Ford, Worthington drew up a proposal which was endorsed
by Ford and which became the original Ford offer.[1]

Ford's offer consisted of three principal parts. First, if the
government would complete construction of Wilson Dam and
dam no. 3 (later the site of Joe Wheeler Dam), including the
installation of the necessary hydroelectric equipment, he would
lease them for a period of one hundred years. Ford's proposed
rental payments on this property would consist of 6 per cent
annually on the additional funds to be expended in completing
the project, these additional funds not to exceed $20,000,000 for
Wilson Dam and $8,000,000 for dam no. 3. Ford's rental payments
would amount to less than 6 per cent for the first six years, and

---

1. *Muscle Shoals*, Hearings, U. S. Senate, 67 Cong., 2 Sess., 317–18; Chicago
Tribune, July 28, 29, 1921; Judson C. Welliver, "The Muscle Shoals Power and
Industrial Project," in *American Review of Reviews*, LXV (April, 1922), 381–82.

the offer did not provide for payments on the $17,000,000 already expended on the project. The offer provided for the establishment of a fund which Ford claimed would amortize the entire cost of the power facilities. This amortization would be accomplished by paying to the federal government an annual sum of $46,547—a sum which Ford asserted would produce, if invested at 4 per cent interest compounded semi-annually for a period of one hundred years, the amount needed for amortization. In addition, Ford agreed to pay to the United States an annual sum of $55,000 for which the government would assume responsibility for repair and maintenance of the dams, power facilities, and navigational structures.

Second, Ford offered to purchase outright both nitrate plants, with all lands and other properties belonging thereto, including two steam electric plants, for $5,000,000. This property had cost the government some $82,000,000.[2] Moreover, to be included in the nitrate properties were a steam plant at Gorgas, Alabama, and a transmission line connecting that plant with Muscle Shoals, the total original cost of which was approximately $5,000,000.[3]

Third, Ford agreed, as consideration for acceptance of his lease and purchase terms, to operate nitrate plant no. 2 at its approximate maximum capacity in the production of "nitrogen and other fertilizer compounds" with the special objectives of determining by research whether fertilizer of better grades and lower prices could be produced at Muscle Shoals and of maintaining nitrate plant no. 2 in readiness for national defense. Ford agreed to limit his profits on fertilizer to 8 per cent. To investigate costs and profits for public information and to supervise the territorial distribution of the fertilizer, Ford suggested the creation of a board to be manned by representatives of farm organizations, the Department of Agriculture, and the company which Ford would organize to operate Muscle Shoals. Disputes between the board and the Ford Muscle Shoals Company would be referred for arbitration to the Federal Trade Commission.[4]

2. *Cong. Rec.*, 67 Cong., 2 Sess., 1641–42.
3. *Ibid.*, 1642; New York *Times*, Sept. 26, 1923.
4. *Cong. Rec.*, 67 Cong., 2 Sess., 1641–42.

The Ford offer was characterized by an extreme vagueness and indefiniteness which later gave rise to many controversies. The offer contemplated the operation of Muscle Shoals by a company, the nature of which was not revealed. The company's preference rights at the termination of the lease appeared to be of such a paramount nature as to give it an option to renew the lease. What the Ford offer meant in terms of a financial transaction was not clear because of lack of knowledge as to the real value of the properties. It did mean that should the offer be accepted, Ford would have at his disposal all of the surplus power at Muscle Shoals, but the amount of this excess power was a subject of debate. Estimates of power potentialities at Muscle Shoals were complicated by such technical aspects as seasonal variations in the flow of water, the question whether the fertilizer operation would utilize primary or secondary power, and the possibilities of the future increase of primary power through use of the three steam plants and by reason of further water-power development upstream.[5] For this indefinite amount of power Ford offered to pay a total of about $1,700,000 annually. The value of the nitrate plants to Ford would depend on his ability to compete with fertilizer and chemical companies already in the field.[6] This subject was further complicated by speculation as to the value of the offer to the country at large. Ford's supporters declared from the first that his offer was made entirely in the interest of the American farmer and national welfare and

5. According to a report of the Corps of Engineers, the estimated available water power at Muscle Shoals, based on a fifty-year record, ranged from 87,000 horsepower 99½ per cent of the time to 600,000 horsepower 21 per cent of the time. Memorandum for the Secretary of War, Dec. 13, 1924, Records of the Office of the Judge Advocate General, Muscle Shoals Correspondence File, 1918–34, National Archives.

6. The nitrate plant properties contained some personal property, especially building supplies, which Senator George W. Norris estimated to be worth at least $5,000,000, and several thousand acres of land from which, Norris asserted, Ford could realize millions of dollars through real estate development. General Clarence C. Williams, Chief of Ordnance, estimated that the personal property was worth about $2,000,000. Senator Edwin F. Ladd, a strong supporter of the Ford offer, denied that Ford had any intentions of real estate speculation. George W. Norris, "Shall We Give Muscle Shoals to Henry Ford?" in *Saturday Evening Post*, CXCVI (May 24, 1924), 54, 56; Edwin F. Ladd, "Why I am for Henry Ford's Offer for Muscle Shoals," *ibid.*, CXCVII (Nov. 22, 29, 1924), 68, 86.

that its acceptance would constitute a sacrifice by and impose a burden on the great industrialist.[7]

The first public reaction to the Ford offer inside government circles came from Herbert Hoover, the Secretary of Commerce. Hoover praised Ford for his "courage" in making the offer and declared that it proved that the Muscle Shoals project should be completed. The New York *Times* interpreted Hoover's remarks as an endorsement of the Ford offer.[8] Secretary of War Weeks, on whom fell the burden of handling the Ford offer, made no immediate comment. On July 25, 1921, following consultations with other members of the Harding cabinet and the staff of the Federal Power Commission, Secretary Weeks announced that the Ford offer was unsatisfactory and could not be accepted because it was based on the assumption that the government would guarantee 600,000 horsepower at Wilson Dam, an obligation which the Secretary said the government could not undertake because of the irregular flowage of the Tennessee River. Weeks also stated that other provisions of the offer were not entirely satisfactory though it was likely that they could be easily modified. At this time Weeks announced that he would hold a conference with Ford as soon as Secretary Hoover and Secretary of the Treasury Andrew W. Mellon, together with the staff of the Federal Power Commission, had completed their studies of the offer.[9] Two days after Weeks's rejection of the Ford offer, General Lansing H. Beach, the Chief of Engineers, advised its acceptance in principle, his recommendations stipulating only a few minor changes.[10]

Outside government circles, there were also differences of opinion regarding the Ford proposal. The New York *Times* conditionally endorsed the offer, although the editor reserved his opinion as to the adequacy of Ford's proffered payments. At first, the press as a whole appears to have mildly approved the Ford offer without analyzing its terms. Typical of the newspapers

7. New York *Times*, July 20, 1921; *Cong. Rec.*, 67 Cong., 2 Sess., 1541, 2929, 9354, 9845.
8. New York *Times*, July 15, 16, 1921.
9. *Ibid.*, July 26, 1921.
10. *Ibid.*, July 28, 1921.

that commented editorially on the subject was the Philadelphia
Record which saw in the Ford offer a chance for the government
to rid itself of a white elephant. The Birmingham *Age-Herald,*
reflecting the more enthusiastic pro-Ford press of the South,
praised Ford as the savior of Muscle Shoals. *Electrical World* and
the Chicago *Tribune* led the early press opposition to the Ford
offer. The former publication, reflecting the attitude of the power
industry, declared that the Ford offer would cost the government
$1,203,000,000 because of inadequate rental payments and
pointed out that it would violate the Federal Water Power Act
by removing Muscle Shoals power from general distribution to
the public and, hence, from control by public authority. The
Chicago *Tribune,* within a fortnight after Ford submitted his
offer, published summaries of correspondence of J. W. Worthington and Gray Silver, Washington representative of the Farm
Bureau, with Claudius H. Huston, Assistant Secretary of Commerce, who was formerly associated with Worthington as an
official of the Tennessee River Improvement Association. These
summaries appeared to show that almost as soon as the Ford offer
was formulated, plans had been made by these three men to
drive the Ford offer through Congress under the sponsorship of
farm organizations whose support would be based on a claim by
farm leaders that Ford would deliver cheap fertilizer to the
farmers. This claim would be based on the fertilizer provisions
of the Ford proposal. The newspaper summaries also indicated
that Worthington regarded Huston as a valuable contact man
inside the government who would be able to gain the ear of
the administration. Worthington warned Silver that Ford's "plan
to manufacture aluminum" at Muscle Shoals must be kept secret
for fear that Secretary Mellon, who purportedly controlled the
aluminum industry in America, would hear of it and bring the
wrath of the administration down on the Ford offer. These summaries also showed that Ford planned to gain control of a large
share of the water-power resources of the upper Tennessee
River.[11]

11. Birmingham *Age-Herald,* July 15, 1921; New York *Times,* July 16, 1921;
Philadelphia *Record,* July 27, 1921; Chicago *Tribune,* July 27, 28, 29, 1921;

Immediately following the advent of the Ford offer, officials of the Mississippi Valley Waterway Association met in conference with Secretary Weeks to urge acceptance of the Ford offer. They declared that Ford's development of Muscle Shoals would result in incidental navigational benefits which would open up lands rich in minerals along the upper Tennessee River to profitable exploitation. The Water Power League of America, which emphatically endorsed the Ford offer in its infancy, took the position that the monetary return to the government was a minor consideration since Ford would operate the project "for the greatest good of the greatest number." [12]

The most severe critic of the Ford offer was the eminent conservationist, Gifford Pinchot, who demanded that the bid, if accepted, be modified to conform more closely to the Rooseveltian conservational ideals. Pinchot felt that the offer, besides violating numerous provisions of the Federal Water Power Act, did not nearly reflect the value of the project in its rental provision. He saw in the offer only a suggestion rather than an assurance that Ford would produce fertilizers for American farmers. What perturbed Pinchot most was his belief that even if Ford permanently operated nitrate plant no. 2 to its full capacity, he would still have a vast amount of excess power at his own disposal.[13] Pinchot's criticism forced the New York *Times* into an outright endorsement of the Ford offer, which was announced in an editorial critical of the fiery Pennsylvania conservationist. The *Times* concluded that

His [Ford's] offer to take this white elephant off the Government's hands astonished everybody. . . . The question for the Government is whether it shall reject Mr. Ford's offer on the grounds set forth by Mr. Pinchot—that it does not conform to the Rooseveltian program— therefore assuming the very considerable risk that down to the end of recorded time it will never have another offer from anybody on any terms; or whether it should make the best bargain it can with Mr. Ford, and so get some return on the great expenditure at Muscle

"Government Moves Slowly on Muscle Shoals Offer," in *Electrical World*, LXXVIII (Aug. 13, 1921), 337; "Ford's Muscle Shoals Offer and Public Policy," *ibid.* (Aug. 20, 1921), 353.

12. New York *Times*, July 16, 17, Sept. 6, 1921.

13. *Ibid.*, Aug. 29, 1921.

Shoals. It seems to us it is first of all a matter of Government business; that it has about as much to do with the Rooseveltian conservation program as it has with the inclination of the ecliptic.[14]

Another source of vigorous criticism of the Ford offer in its early phases was the Merchants Association of New York which sent a committee to Washington advising against acceptance of the offer. The merchants termed it "an undisguised subsidy" to be used for "strictly private purposes to the detriment of competing unsubsidized industries." [15] Secretaries Hoover and Weeks announced early in August, 1921, that the Ford offer was the only bid received that the government could possibly accept, the other "one or two" offers being from entirely irresponsible sources. The two secretaries added, however, that they were expecting an offer "from a substantial source" in the near future.[16]

On September 6, Secretary Weeks wrote Ford suggesting a conference to be held at the latter's convenience. The next day the report came from Detroit that Ford would arrive in Washington immediately "with a chip on his shoulder" and an "aroused ire" to defend his offer and prove to Weeks that it was liberal. Ford was said to have characterized criticisms of his offer as "an insidious Wall Street movement to injure him." It was reported that Ford had recently sent a group of engineers to Muscle Shoals to resurvey the project so that he would be in a sound technical position to talk with Weeks. Ford decided not to attend the conference himself, and it was not until September 19 that the Ford negotiators, William B. Mayo, Ford's chief engineer, and J. W. Worthington, the Muscle Shoals promoter, arrived in Washington. As a result of the first meeting, the difficulty regarding government guarantee of minimum horsepower at Wilson Dam was solved, but new problems arose, the most serious being that while Ford's engineers estimated that it would cost $28,000,-000 to complete the hydroelectric projects at Muscle Shoals, the Corps of Engineers calculated that the construction would require twice that amount. This point of dispute was quite important because it was on the cost of completion, not to exceed

14. *Ibid.*, Aug. 30, 1921.
15. *Ibid.*, Sept. 4, 1921.
16. *Ibid.*, Aug. 7, 1921.

$28,000,000, that Ford's power rentals would be paid in the event of acceptance of the offer.[17]

By mid-November the conferees had failed to make substantial progress. Ford himself arrived in Washington on November 18 to attempt to break the deadlock. Upon his arrival, the Corps of Engineers offered to revise their figures for the estimated cost of completion downward by allocating a portion of it to navigation, but Ford refused to budge from his original estimate of $28,000,-000. After a single conference with administration officials, Ford suspended negotiations and announced that he and Thomas A. Edison would make a personal inspection of Muscle Shoals. The Ford office announced, according to the New York *Times*, that the purpose of the visit to Muscle Shoals was to restudy on the spot the water-power potentialities of the Shoals and probable cost of completion of the power projects in order "to obtain data to convince the United States Government that Mr. Ford's offer . . . is liberal." [18] Even though Edison was no hydroelectric engineer, there is little doubt that the country at large viewed him as a universal genius.

The Ford inspection tour of Muscle Shoals was very dramatic. On December 2, following the arrival of Edison in Dearborn from his New Jersey home, the Ford party, which included several engineers and high officials of the Ford company, departed for the Southland in Ford's private car, the *Fair Lane*. The Ford special was scheduled nonstop to Muscle Shoals despite hundreds of invitations from chambers of commerce and other civic organizations along the route. En route, Ford told reporters that his attempt to acquire Muscle Shoals was based primarily on his desire to provide cheap fertilizer for the American farmers. He said Edison's main function on the tour would be to ascertain the true status of the nitrate plants at Muscle Shoals. Ford revealed at this time that he was contemplating the use of the excess power at Muscle Shoals for the manufacture of one or more of several products, including aluminum, cloth, steel, and automobile parts.[19]

17. *Ibid.*, Sept. 8, 20, 21, 1921.
18. *Ibid.*, Oct. 25, Nov. 1, 19, 24, 1921.
19. *Ibid.*, Dec. 2, 3, 4, 1921.

When Ford arrived in Florence, Alabama, the largest city in the Muscle Shoals area, on December 3, he was accorded a great ovation by an enthusiastic crowd of local citizens. Here, Ford made a spectacular appeal for nation-wide grass-roots support of his bid for Muscle Shoals by injecting into the issue anti–Wall Street themes. In answer to questions regarding his Muscle Shoals offer, Ford said that the principal factor underlying his bid was his desire to eliminate war from the world. This could be accomplished, not by producing nitrates for national defense, but by using the Muscle Shoals project to demonstrate a new method of financing which Ford called the "energy dollar." Ford declared that his new financial system would eliminate the one cause of war—gold:

It is very simple when you analyze it. The cause of all wars is gold. We shall demonstrate to the world through Muscle Shoals, first the practicability, second the desirability of displacing gold as the basis of currency and substituting in its place the world's imperishable national wealth. . . .

According to Ford, the international bankers of Wall Street, becoming dissatisfied with the low rates of interest prevailing in peace time, created wars from time to time in order to raise interest rates. These "money sellers" and dealers in human misery, Ford said, through their control of the world's supply of gold, had acquired sufficient control of most of the nations of the world to have gold established as national monetary standards, giving them enormous powers over the economic and political life of these nations. Ford's proposed solution of this alleged international financial problem was for the federal government to finance the completion of the Muscle Shoals project by issuing paper money based on the potential wealth of Muscle Shoals. This method of financing, Ford predicted, would become so overwhelmingly and amazingly successful "that the government would never again need to borrow interest-bearing bonds for internal improvements but instead it would merely issue currency against its imperishable national resources." Ford said he had formulated a specific "plan of values" which would be available for the use of Congress.[20]

20. *Ibid.*, Dec. 4, 1921.

The next day the Detroit industrialist added flavor to his proposed financial reforms by identifying Wall Street and financial capitalism with international Jewry. All of the evils he had attributed to the international bankers on the previous day were now saddled on the Jewish race, including the deliberate creation of wars for monetary profit. Ford declared that not only were these Jewish financiers responsible for World War I, they also constituted the causal factor in the American Civil War. Although this was not Ford's first attack on the Jews—he was currently engaged in a five-year program to "educate" the American people about the evils of international Jewry—it was a sensational event. Apparently, Ford had found a pragmatic use for his anti-Semitism in the promotion of his Muscle Shoals bid.[21]

Samuel Untermyer, noted Wall Street lawyer, immediately assumed the role of defender of both Wall Street and the Jewish race. He said:

The man [Ford] is so densely ignorant on every subject except automobiles and so blinded by a depth of bigotry that belongs to the dark ages from which he has not emerged, that he is fool enough to publicly exploit this madhouse bug of his about the international bankers owning the gold of the world. He imagines that the great international bankers of the world are Jews, which is not true. . . .

Why can't the people realize that a cheap, petty, ignorant man who has grown rich can get just as crazy as any poor devil of an inmate of a lunatic asylum? The only difference is that the one is locked up for the public safety, while the other is permitted to roam at large to the great peril of the public.[22]

Another stalwart champion of the gold standard who arose to defend Wall Street was the editor of the New York *Times*. He asked:

How can Mr. Ford doubt . . . [the value of the prevailing financial system] as he looks around the world today, or as he reads his history? . . . [But] Mr. Ford does not read history, and flouts its teachings. It is only a few weeks since he said "history is bunk. What difference does is make how many times the ancient Greeks flew their kites?"

---

21. *Ibid.*, Dec. 5, 1921. For an account of Ford's anti-Semitic program see William C. Richards, *The Last Billionaire* (1948), 87–102.

22. New York *Times*, Dec. 5, 1921.

So many kites like his present currency kite have been flown by Americans that there is no danger to them in this particular kite-flying proposal. Still, the "energy dollar" is likely enough to be made the basis of a new currency system proposed by the Agricultural bloc in the House.[23]

The next day the *Times* launched a blistering, sarcastic attack on Thomas A. Edison, who, in the meantime, had endorsed Ford's "energy dollar" plan for Muscle Shoals. Although Edison struck a blow at gold-standard capitalism, he did not resort to anti-Semitism. Edison described Ford's monetary plan as being "flawless" and predicted that should Congress adopt it, a dynamic era of progress and prosperity would result "such as never could have come otherwise." He predicted that should the American people ever begin to think about the nature of the country's monetary system, "the game is up" for the "interest collectors" of Wall Street. Although Edison did not believe that Congress had the "imagination" to adopt the Ford plan, he did feel that the masses of the people, sensing something wrong, were beginning to reawaken to another "outbreak of common sense" such as in the days of Greenbackism. In its editorial spanking of Edison, the New York *Times* declared that he rivaled Ford in his impracticability and contempt for history, but relented somewhat by stating that the great inventor was "a less ridiculous person than Mr. Ford." [24]

On the eve of his departure from Muscle Shoals, Ford made another dramatic bid for public support. He assured the citizens of that area who had gathered at the railroad station to see him off that he was motivated by a desire to serve the public welfare rather than by an expectation of high profits, "which others would demand." More important, he stated that congressional acceptance of his offer would mean the creation of the greatest prosperity in the South that this economically blighted region had ever known. His promise of prosperity was reinforced by his expressions of awe regarding the mineral and water-power possibilities of the Muscle Shoals region. Then Ford threw the re-

23. *Ibid.*, Dec. 6, 1921.
24. *Ibid.*, Dec. 6, 7, 1921.

sponsibility for making this wonderful dream of prosperity come true into the lap of Congress. "We have made our offer. . . . All I ask of Congress is to give me the opportunity. And I am going to leave that to you, if you wish me to come down here, to see that Congress does." [25]

Ford's visit to Muscle Shoals created tremendous support in his behalf in the South.[26] In early January, 1922, his popularity was further increased in this area by an astonishing news release from his office which stimulated much excitement in the Tennessee Valley. According to this Associated Press story, Ford planned, in the event his offer was accepted, to build a great city, seventy-five miles long, in the Muscle Shoals district, which would become one of the great industrial centers of the nation. In fact, the report stated that this great metropolis would be larger than Detroit and would be planned so as to protect the health and social welfare of the workers and their families. According to the report, Ford had "bent the greater part of his energies" since his inspection of Muscle Shoals, to the formulation of plans for the great Muscle Shoals city on which he would begin construction immediately following congressional approval of his offer. Furthermore, this fabulous report from Detroit stated that Ford planned eventually to turn the completed project over to the people of that area, or to the federal government, "in such a way" that no one in the future, including Ford and his heirs, would be able to make a personal profit from real estate speculation. Perhaps, however, the most important item of this news release was the intimation that the Muscle Shoals undertaking was only the first of a whole series of such projects which Ford planned eventually to build in various sections of the country.[27]

25. *Ibid.*, Dec. 6, 1921.
26. See editorials in Nashville *Tennessean*, Dec. 6, 1921, and Chattanooga *News*, Dec. 7, 1921.
27. New York *Times*, Jan. 12, 1922. Also see "City All Main Street," in *Literary Digest*, LXXIII (April 8, 1922), 72–74. Ford's proposed city would not be built in the form of a compact mass, but instead would be composed of a group of small towns. According to the New York *Times*, "this is in line with the manufacturer's view that men and their families should live in small communities where benefits of rural or near-rural life would not be entirely lost." New York *Times*, Jan. 12, 1922.

Although the Ford offer had from the beginning stimulated an expanding atmosphere of excitement in the Muscle Shoals district, the story about the new Detroit seized the imagination of the people in that area and greatly increased their concern for the Ford plan for Muscle Shoals. For many residents of the Tennessee Valley, Ford had indeed become the economic savior of the South. Donald Davidson describes the situation in the Muscle Shoals area thus:

The Ford offer was like commutation of a death sentence. It offered new life, in terms that the Alabama people had been teaching themselves to hold productive of good. . . . God's infinite blessing, the Alabama people felt, were about to be showered upon them. . . . At long last southern enterprise would compete with northern or eastern enterprise on something like equal terms. They had hardly dared hope for such bliss.[28]

Ford's promise of a bonanza for Muscle Shoals stimulated a real estate boom in that area, and the Tri-Cities district was suddenly overrun with speculators and adventurers. In early February, 1922, real estate in the region was reputed to be changing hands almost hourly. Old ante-bellum estates were divided into lots and sold. In the North Alabama area, cotton farmers began to plan the conversion of their land to truck farms and orchards in order to supply Ford's great city with fruits and vegetables.[29] Unfortunately, the Muscle Shoals boom encouraged speculation in Muscle Shoals land by real estate speculators in various parts of the country, especially in New York, and the ruthless exploitation that resulted eventually brought much adverse publicity to Muscle Shoals.[30] This speculation which continued throughout the Ford period of the Muscle Shoals controversy, is discussed further in a subsequent chapter.

As was to be expected, Thomas A. Edison, after his inspection of Muscle Shoals, announced that he would advise Congress to accept the Ford offer. He said he based his decision on three principal factors. First, the nation must maintain the great nitrate plant no. 2, which had apparently impressed Edison greatly, in

28. Donald Davidson, *The Tennessee* (1946–48), II, 184.
29. New York *Times*, Feb. 12 (VI), 1922.
30. Davidson, *op. cit.*, II, 184.

readiness for national defense—the Ford offer provided for that. Second, Ford was the "one logical man" in the nation who could operate this huge and complex project successfully. Third, the entire nation had an "abiding faith" that Ford would not ruthlessly exploit the project for his own profit but would efficiently and patriotically force it to work for the public welfare.[31]

With Edison's backing and with the plaudits of southern farmers ringing in his ears, Ford arrived in Washington on January, 13, 1922, to renew the conferences with Secretary Weeks. The very first day the automobile manufacturer unexpectedly modified his offer regarding the cost of completion provision which had been the chief obstacle preventing an earlier agreement. Now Ford proposed to pay a rental of 4 per cent annually on the cost of the remaining construction at Muscle Shoals regardless of the amount. Weeks insisted that this modification would not result in any material changes in the amount Ford would pay, based on the lowest estimates of cost of completion by the Corps of Engineers. Weeks demanded that Ford pay 4½ per cent on the remaining cost of construction and $8,500,000 for the nitrate plants. Nevertheless, the Secretary agreed to end the negotiations and submit the Ford offer to Congress, but he would not agree to endorse it. On the next day, January 14, as the legal staff of the War Department began to draft Ford's modified offer, Weeks reiterated that this action did not imply his endorsement of the proposal. Already there were predictions that the Ford offer would split Congress across party lines with the farm bloc supporting the bid. Already southern Democrats appeared to be forming an almost solid pro-Ford bloc.[32]

31. New York *Times*, Dec. 6, 1921. The Chattanooga *News* of Dec. 6, 1921, intimated that the Ford offer was no longer subject to criticism from a technical standpoint now that Edison, the "creative genius," had placed his stamp of approval on it.

32. New York *Times*, Jan. 13, 14, 15, 1922. The fact that Ford had been a Democratic candidate for the United States Senate in 1918 probably influenced the attitude of some members of Congress toward the Ford offer, particularly conservative Republicans who had vehemently opposed his candidacy. On the other hand, his Democratic affiliations probably increased the popularity of his offer in that party.

The term "pro-Ford" as used in this study indicates merely support of the Ford offer, and not an endorsement of Ford's other activities.

Simultaneously with Weeks's agreement to submit the Ford offer to Congress, Ford began a campaign designed to accelerate action on his bid. The Detroit industrialist charged that the "fertilizer trust, the power and chemical interests of Wall Street, the money brokers, and other interests that fear to have Muscle Shoals developed along lines that will serve all the people most, are deluging Weeks and Congress with literature that grossly misrepresents the facts." It is highly probable that Ford's principal object in this attack was to force Secretary Weeks to endorse the offer before submitting it to Congress. In this regard Ford said:

This is not a political matter to be jockeyed and juggled about. Why doesn't Secretary Weeks take it or leave it, "yes" or "no," as he would a private business matter? I mean that now, after six months, he is still asking what appear to me as irrelevant questions and delaying the settlement of this matter.[33]

Ford implied that his alleged desire to render a public service through his offer placed it in a special category not subject to criticism:

We didn't want Muscle Shoals for selfish purposes in the first place. Hanged if we care very much whether or not we get it now. We did not make the Government a selfish business proposition. It was an industrial philanthropy which we offered—an offer based on a desire for great public service.[34]

The Detroit manufacturer also implied that since the government had invited him to make the bid without prior encouragement of such action on his part, the administration and Congress were estopped from rejecting it, particularly so in view of the alleged patriotic motives behind it. In this drive against Weeks, Ford made extensive use of the support previously given him by Thomas A. Edison and General Beach, Chief of Engineers. Ford answered charges that he could not make cheap fertilizer at Muscle Shoals by shifting the burden of responsibility to Edison. He said that Edison was at this time working out Muscle Shoals fertilizer problems in his East Orange, New Jersey, laboratory, and that the great inventor had already informed him that "we

33. *Ibid.*, Jan. 15, 1922.
34. *Ibid.*, Jan. 15, 1922.

can give the American people a better fertilizer at a much lower price than they have ever had before." Referring to the support of General Beach, Ford said his opponents "would climb the Washington monument rather than consult the chief engineer's calculations." [35]

Secretary Weeks promptly retorted that Ford's charges that action on the offer had been unnecessarily and deliberately delayed were "unjust and unwarranted." Weeks considered it strange that although no complaints about delay had been voiced by either Ford or his representatives during the conference on January 13, Ford made his charges to the press in less than an hour after he emerged from this meeting. Weeks insisted that had the charges of deliberate delay been raised during the conference, he could have easily demonstrated their invalidity. [36]

On January 20, the War Department completed the draft of the new Ford offer in contract form, and it was forwarded to Detroit where Ford signed it on January 25. The principal modification found in the new offer was Ford's agreement to base rental payments on the remaining cost of construction without limitations, the rate to be 4 per cent annually. There were minor modifications, the most important of which required the Ford company to bear the expense of maintenance of the power houses at the dams and enabled Ford's engineers, rather than the Corps of Engineers, to complete construction of the dams. An attempt was made to clarify the nature of the farm board which was to prevent Ford's Muscle Shoals corporation from earning in excess of 8 per cent profit on fertilizer, but its powers were still ill defined. The lease renewal provision was altered, taking from the Ford company the absolute right of renewal but still leaving it a residue of preferred rights in the matter. In addition, provisions were made for termination of the lease in the event of violation of the terms of the contract by the lessee. [37]

35. *Ibid.*

36. *Ibid.*, Jan. 18, 1922.

37. *Ibid.*, Jan. 21, 27, 1922; War Department, *The Henry Ford Muscle Shoals Offer*, House Doc. 167, 67 Cong., 2 Sess. (1922), 6–8. In reality, the latter provision did not commit Ford's proposed company to any particular obligations but merely granted to the federal government the right to institute proceedings

Immediately following the announcement that the revised
Ford offer was completed, Secretary Weeks and the Harding administration were subjected to a great deal of pressure from pro-
Ford men in Congress and from other sources. Senator McKellar
declared that acceptance of the Ford offer meant cheap fertilizer
for American farmers and economic progress for the South. Nine
of the eleven members of the Wisconsin delegation in the House
signed a petition to Weeks endorsing the Ford offer. The petition
informed Weeks that the farm interests of the nation demanded
acceptance of the Ford plan and that Ford's ability to render a
great service to the farmers by operation of Muscle Shoals had
been proved by his record of performance in the industrial world.
Two delegations of farm and civic leaders, including a number of
editors of agricultural publications, called on Weeks and urged
him publicly to endorse the Ford offer. One of the delegations
was led by Gray Silver, Washington representative of the Farm
Bureau, who already was engaged in lobbying for the Ford
proposal. Weeks replied that he could not endorse any offer that
did not guarantee the manufacture of fertilizer, the apparent
implication being that he doubted the presence of such an assurance in the Ford plan. Weeks also chilled the ardor of these
delegations by offering the doubtful consolation that in the event
of rejection of the Ford offer, he would go ahead and recommend
the completion of Wilson Dam. Following the intervention of
these delegations in behalf of the Ford offer, Senator Underwood,
who apparently had not been discouraged by the seemingly
unfavorable attitude of Weeks toward the proposal, optimistically
stated that he believed the Secretary of War would openly endorse the Ford plan upon submitting it to Congress.[38]

Amidst these attempts to enlist the support of Weeks for the
Ford offer, Senator William J. Harris of Georgia embarrassed
Weeks and the administration by introducing a resolution in the
Senate calling for an investigation of the alleged fertilizer and

in a federal court should the lessee appear to violate the terms of the contract.
Significantly, this provision required that the court of original jurisdiction in this
matter be the Federal District Court for the Northern District of Alabama.

38. New York *Times*, Jan. 25, 26, 28, 1922; *Cong. Rec.*, 67 Cong., 2 Sess., 1858.

power trusts which Ford had pointed out as being responsible for delaying the consideration of his offer. Harris said he was confident that the fertilizer and power interests were seeking to prevent an agreement between the Detroit manufacturer and Weeks. The Georgia Senator vouched for the integrity of Secretary Weeks and the Corps of Engineers but implied that they were being duped by special interests. Despite the vigorous support of Senator Heflin, the resolution failed.[39]

On January 31, Secretary Weeks personally submitted his report on the Ford offer, which he intended to send to Congress, to the White House for presidential inspection. What developed at his conference with the President was not revealed, but obviously the subsequent action of the Secretary of War had the approval of the Chief Executive. Thereupon, Weeks submitted the report to Congress, the House receiving it on February 2 and the Senate two days later.[40]

Secretary Weeks's comments accompanying the submission of the Ford offer to Congress constituted, in effect, a recommendation that the offer be rejected.[41] It brought gloom to the Ford camp.[42] The only merit that the Secretary saw in the Ford bid was that the modifications made by Ford in his revised offer made it more favorable to the government than the original one. Otherwise, he found faults. In the first place, he doubted that the offer could be legally accepted because of the provision of the National Defense Act prohibiting the sale or lease of the nitrate projects to private operators. He warned Congress that acceptance of the offer would also raise legal problems regarding the option to purchase nitrate plant no. 2 and the Gorgas steam plant held by the Air Nitrates Corporation and the Alabama Power Company, respectively, although he admitted that the Judge Advocate General had recently held these options to be null and void. More important, Weeks pointed out that the offer violated the terms of the Federal Water Power Act. That Muscle Shoals

39. *Cong. Rec.*, 67 Cong., 2 Sess., 1750.
40. New York *Times*, Feb. 1, 3, 7, 1922.
41. House Doc. 167, 67 Cong., 2 Sess., 1–11.
42. Nashville *Banner*, Feb. 3, 1922.

water power would not be subject to regulation by a public body
if the offer were accepted was of particular concern to the Secretary. Weeks recommended that the offer be revised to conform
to the national water-power policy in every respect, including
limitation of the lease to fifty years; regulation of power rates, if
any power should be sold, by a public agency; and compelling
the lessee to bear the entire cost of maintaining the dams. The
Secretary of War expressed doubt that the offer obligated Ford,
or the company to be formed by the industrialist, to manufacture
fertilizer. He strongly recommended that should Congress accept
the offer, an unconditional guarantee of fertilizer production be
included in it. Weeks also called the attention of Congress to
official estimates of the War Department which placed the scrap
value of the property to be purchased by Ford for $5,000,000 at
a median of $12,000,000.

Secretary Weeks recommended that, should the Ford offer
be rejected, funds be appropriated for the completion of Wilson
Dam. This course of action, he stated, would put the government
in a better bargaining position and would provide some allevia-
tion of the acute unemployment problem then prevailing.[43]

Although the Ford offer, because of the fertilizer provisions,
vitally affected the country's agricultural interests, the Secretary
of Agriculture, Henry C. Wallace, refused definitely to commit
himself on the proposal. In a memorandum allegedly giving the
views of the Department, the Secretary stated that if the terms
were sufficiently definite and binding as to leave no doubt of
Ford's legal obligations to produce fertilizer, the Department
would "look with favor" on acceptance of the offer.[44] Andrew W.
Mellon, the Secretary of Treasury, was apparently affected personally by the Ford offer. It was said that the American Aluminum
interests, which were reported to be under Mellon's control, were
actively opposed to the proposal of Ford, apparently because of
the fear of possible competition in aluminum production by Ford
at Muscle Shoals and because it was believed that Ford intended

43. House Doc. 167, 67 Cong., 2 Sess., 1–11.
44. Memorandum of the Department of Agriculture, Feb. 14, 1922, Correspondence of the Secretary of Agriculture, Muscle Shoals, National Archives.

to gain control of the water power of the upper Tennessee basin, some of which the aluminum interests were already utilizing. Nevertheless, it was reported that Mellon himself had assumed a neutral position in regard to the Ford offer and had refused actively to oppose it.[45]

The submission of the Ford offer to Congress relieved Secretary Weeks and the administration, temporarily at least, of the heavy responsibilities relating to that proposal. At this point Congress had to assume the duty of solving the problem resulting from Ford's bid, a problem involving principles which were important to the welfare of the nation.

45. "Whole Country Should Back Ford-Edison Scheme for Muscle Shoals Development," in *Manufacturers' Record*, LXXXI (Jan. 19, 1922), 53. See also Carl M. Loeb, *Aluminum* (1950), 51; "More Power for Bomber Production," in *Engineering News-Record*, CXXVIII (Feb. 26, 1942), 334.

III

The Ford Offer in the Sixty-seventh Congress

As soon as the Ford offer was received in Congress, it became a subject of contention. The proposal precipitated a discussion on the Senate floor as to the proper committee to consider it. Immediately following the receipt of the offer by the Senate, Senator Oscar W. Underwood moved that it be referred to the Agriculture Committee. The Alabama Senator declared that the primary purpose of the Muscle Shoals project was the production of fertilizer for agriculture, and he pointed out that the Wadsworth-Kahn bill had been under the jurisdiction of the Agriculture Committee. The reaction to Underwood's motion showed that some of the conservative Republicans in the Senate were not in harmony with the Alabama Senator with respect to this subject.

Senator Wesley L. Jones of Washington asserted that the primary purpose of the Muscle Shoals project was the improvement of navigation and development of water power; hence, he insisted that the Ford offer be referred to the Commerce Committee of which he was chairman. He declared that the Ford proposal involved basic water-power policies. Senator Francis E. Warren of Wyoming contended that since the proposal involved federal expenditures and legal problems, it should be referred to either the Appropriations Committee or Judiciary Committee. Senator James W. Wadsworth of New York suggested that the offer be sent to the Appropriations Committee. Senator George W. Norris of Nebraska, chairman of the Agriculture Committee, supported the Underwood motion, declaring that the fundamental purpose of the Muscle Shoals project was the production of fertilizer for farmers. The conservative Republicans did not persevere in their opposition, thus permitting the Underwood motion to be adopted by a voice vote.[1]

The Memphis *Commercial-Appeal* described the adoption of the Underwood motion as a victory for the farm bloc over administration forces in the Senate. According to this newspaper, the Republican leaders "wanted it [the Ford offer] sent to the Appropriations Committee, on which the farm bloc is barely represented." [2] This dispute over committee jurisdiction resulted in an apparent victory for the Ford offer because it was resolved in favor of Senator Underwood, one of the principal supporters of the Ford proposal. Underwood's actions indicated that he believed that the Agriculture Committee would be friendly to the offer. This seemingly minor incident proved to be one of the most important events in the whole course of the Muscle Shoals controversy. As a result of the decision to refer the Ford offer to the Agriculture Committee, Muscle Shoals came into the sphere of Senator Norris and his fellow Progressive Republicans who dominated the committee and who were friendly toward public power, which later proved to be the most important issue in the controversy.[3]

Upon receipt of the Ford offer by the House, the Speaker, Frederick H. Gillett, referred it to the House Military Committee which had considered the Wadsworth-Kahn bill in the previous Congress. The House Agriculture Committee, however, voted unanimously to ask the Speaker to withdraw the bill from the Military Committee and refer it to the Agriculture Committee because of the importance of fertilizer in the Muscle

1. *Cong. Rec.*, 67 Cong., 2 Sess., 2208–12.
2. Memphis *Commercial-Appeal*, Feb. 8, 1922.
3. The term "Progressive" as used in this study is not intended to denote a particular political party but instead refers to a group of Republicans, mostly western senators, who, during the 1920's, referred to themselves from time to time as "Progressives" and were often thus described by the press. Although their political philosophy varied according to the individual, in general they subscribed to the creed of the Theodore Roosevelt Progressives. Among their most important objectives were aid to farmers and public power. This group included such Republican senators as George W. Norris, Robert M. LaFollette, Hiram W. Johnson, Robert B. Howell, Smith W. Brookhart, William E. Borah, Charles L. McNary, Peter Norbeck, and Lynn J. Frazier.

Shoals problem. Some members of the Agriculture Committee threatened a fight on the House floor if the Speaker did not accede to their request, but after discussing the subject with Julius H. Kahn, chairman of the House Military Committee, they agreed to let the Ford proposal remain in the Military Committee.[4]

The House Military Committee began hearings on the Ford offer on February 8, 1922. The committee had anticipated that Ford himself would appear to testify, but despite the special invitation of Chairman Kahn, Ford declined, saying he was too busy to come to Washington. At the outset, the automobile manufacturer and his aides attempted to avoid the hearings altogether, implying that the offer was self-explanatory. Within two days after the hearings began, however, Ford relented and consented to send a representative to testify.[5]

The Ford offer was given timely support at the hearings by Gray Silver who informed the committee on the first day that Ford's proposal had been endorsed by the Farm Bureau. It soon sailed into troubled waters when the chief witness, Secretary Weeks, took the stand. The committee members favorable to the proposal undoubtedly hoped to force Weeks to give it an explicit endorsement, but he still refused to do so. In fact, his testimony, like his report to Congress, constituted an indirect recommendation that the offer be rejected. In one important respect, the testimony of the Secretary of War differed from his report to Congress. In the report, he had emphasized the failure to conform to the national water-power policy as the chief fault of the offer, but in his testimony before the Military Committee, he stated that he would be inclined to endorse the bid but for his disbelief in the ability of Ford successfully to manufacture fertilizer at Muscle Shoals in the face of growing domestic production and continuing imports of large quantities of Chilean nitrates. Weeks testified that during a recent conference with Ford, the latter had explicitly replied in the negative when asked if he would continue production of fertilizer at Muscle

4. Chattanooga *News*, Feb. 8, 10, 1922; Nashville *Tennessean*, Feb. 9, 1922.
5. New York *Times*, Jan. 4, 9, Feb. 9, 10, 1922.

Shoals in the event his profit margin should fall below 8 per cent.[6]

At these hearings, Secretary Weeks did not receive unanimous support from his department. Although Major General Clarence C. Williams, Chief of Ordnance, supported his chief, Major General Lansing H. Beach, Chief of Engineers, testified in behalf of the Ford offer. General Williams insisted that the properties for which Ford had offered $5,000,000 would bring a minimum of $9,000,000 as scrap. On the other hand, General Beach praised the Ford offer as a model for water-power development and denounced the Federal Water Power Act as an obstacle to that end.[7]

The Department of Agriculture gave a cautious and conditional endorsement of the offer. Dr. Richard C. Tolman, Director of the Fixed Nitrogen Research Laboratory, a bureau of the Department of Agriculture, told the committee that he had been authorized by the Secretary of Agriculture, Henry C. Wallace, to report that the Secretary "looked with favor" on the Ford offer, providing its terms were sufficiently binding to insure the continuous operation of nitrate plant no. 2 in the manufacture of fertilizer.[8]

The chief witness testifying in behalf of the Ford proposal was William B. Mayo, Ford's chief engineer. In interrogating Mayo, the committee members were principally interested in ascertaining the nature of Ford's obligation with respect to the production of fertilizer. Some of the members expressed the belief that the Ford offer contained no such guarantee, and others were dubious. It was suggested that a personal pledge be extracted from the industrialist, guaranteeing without reservation that fertilizer would be produced under all circumstances throughout the lease period. Mayo declared that Ford intended to produce fertilizer in good faith but admitted that according to his interpretation of the offer, Ford would be required to produce fertilizer only so long as he did not sustain a loss because of the operations. Mayo refused to identify the cost factors involved in

6. *Ibid.*, Feb. 9, 1922.
7. *Ibid.*, Feb. 10, 1922.
8. *Ibid.*, Feb. 15, 1922.

Ford's proposed 8 per cent fertilizer profit limitation. Some of the committee members felt that the offer contemplated the manufacture of fertilizer ingredients only, but Mayo assured them that Ford would produce a complete commercial fertilizer. He promised that the automobile magnate would use every "known formula," while working his chemists in search of new processes, in an attempt to develop new methods of cheap fertilizer production. Mayo said it had been Ford's dream "to make fertilizer so low that everybody can use all he wants."

The committee attempted to ascertain the nature of Ford's plans regarding the use of the surplus power at Muscle Shoals. Mayo revealed that Ford intended to distribute none of it, but instead planned to utilize the whole of it at Muscle Shoals in the manufacture of automobile parts and other products. He denied that control of this great source of cheap power by Ford would result in unfair competition with other manufacturers as some of the committee members charged. Representative John F. Wise of Washington, whose constituents were vitally interested in water-power development, was particularly apprehensive of the Ford plan of water-power utilization. He declared that it was unfair to the other citizens of the country for the federal government to show partiality toward Ford to the extent of assuming the financial responsibility for his grandiose Muscle Shoals scheme. Mayo replied that since the government had invited Ford to submit the bid, Congress could take it or leave it.[9]

Representative Percy Quin of Mississippi, an ardent supporter of the Ford offer, reprimanded committee members who had criticized the Ford offer and accused them of trying to read ideas into it that were not there. In a spirited defense of Ford, Quin attempted to substitute Ford's prestige and personality in place of an analysis of the offer itself. "We have great respect for Mr. Ford in our country," said Quin, in an apparent reference to the people of his state. "We call him 'Uncle Henry,' and we believe he will give us cheaper fertilizer, just like he has given us automobiles to ride around in." [10]

9. *Ibid.*, Feb. 14, 15, 1922; *Muscle Shoals Propositions,* Hearings, U. S. House of Representatives, 67 Cong., 2 Sess., 245–55, 302–304.
10. New York *Times,* Feb. 15, 1922.

Other important pro-Ford witnesses appearing before the House Military Committee were J. W. Worthington, who was then an adviser to Ford regarding his Muscle Shoals offer, Governor Alfred A. Taylor of Tennessee, James E. Smith, a vice-president of the Mississippi Valley Association, and Theodore Swan, president of the Federal Phosphorus Company of Birmingham, Alabama. Worthington, whose long experience in lobbying had apparently sharpened his talents in that field, turned his appearance before the committee into a promotional campaign for the development of the Tennessee River based on the Ford offer. Governor Taylor, who headed a delegation of Tennesseans urging acceptance of the Ford offer, denounced the Alabama Power Company for its alleged activities in opposing the offer. The Governor declared that no person or organization opposing the Ford offer was welcome in Tennessee. Smith asserted that a majority of the directors of the Mississippi Valley Association, an organization devoted to the economic development of that area, were supporters of the Ford offer. Swan, besides outlining for the committee the possibilities of a great chemical industry at Muscle Shoals, attempted to assure the committee of the success of Ford's proposed fertilizer operations there by announcing that he had developed a new and most efficient process of fertilizer production which would be made available to Ford.[11]

Two important witnesses opposing the Ford offer at the House hearings were Colonel Hugh L. Cooper, noted hydroelectric engineer, and Dr. Charles L. Parsons, consulting chemist and former adviser to the government on nitrogen fixation. Colonel Cooper estimated that the hundred-year lease of the Muscle Shoals water-power properties would cost the federal government $1,275,000,000 "in order that Mr. Ford may secure sole unregulated possession of the greatest water power the South has." Colonel Cooper said he realized that the South was crying for acceptance of the Ford offer, but he predicted that such a course would soon be followed by a loud demand by Southerners that the lease be abrogated. Dr. Parsons, one of the nation's outstanding experts in the field of atmospheric nitrogen fixation,

11. *Ibid.*, Feb. 16, 18, 1922.

attempted to defeat Ford with science. He assured the committee that the cyanamid process, on which the success of Ford's fertilizer operations apparently would depend since the Ford offer provided only for the use of nitrate plant no. 2 in fertilizer operation, was obsolete and could not compete economically with the Haber process.[12] Parson's testimony brought down the wrath of Senator Heflin who, a few days later on the floor of the Senate, indicated a strong doubt as to both the veracity of Parson's statements and his ability as a chemist.[13]

Another important witness testifying against the Ford offer was Charles H. McDowell, president of both the National Fertilizer Association and the Armour Fertilizer Company, whose principal aim was to clear the American fertilizer industry of charges of monopolistic activities which had been leveled by Ford and his supporters. He roundly denied that the National Fertilizer Association had any price-fixing or other such monopolistic functions. He averred that Ford could not economically produce nitrate at plant no. 2, his contention being based on assertions that the cyanamid process was obsolete, that the domestic fertilizer market was already flooded, and that the domestic fertilizer industry already had an excessive capacity for production. Therefore, he declared, the fertilizer industry was not opposed to the Ford plan out of fear of competition but because the offer proposed to permit Ford to monopolize a great water-power resource contrary to the established water-power policy.[14]

Opposition by the Alabama Power Company to the Ford offer was conspicuous at the House hearings. The inclusion of the Gorgas steam plant, on which the power company held an option, in the properties to be purchased by Ford presented the company with an opportunity to play the role of a legal martyr. Colonel John Hull, the acting Judge Advocate General who had already advised Secretary Weeks that this wartime option was null and void on the ground that the War Department

12. *Ibid.*, Feb. 18, March 14, 1922.
13. *Cong. Rec.*, 67 Cong., 2 Sess., 3958.
14. *Muscle Shoals Propositions*, House Hearings, 67 Cong., 2 Sess., 519–41.

had exceeded its authority in agreeing to the option, reiterated his opinion before the committee. Nevertheless, Weeks told the committee that the government was morally, if not legally, bound to honor the full contract with the power company. Major General Williams, Chief of Ordnance, endorsed Weeks's view on this matter, but Colonel Hull remained adamant in his decision. Thomas W. Martin, president of the Alabama Power Company, testified that the option was placed in the contract at the insistence of the government in order to insure itself of a responsible buyer in the event it was decided to sell the plant. Otherwise, he explained, the government might have had to sell the plant as scrap. Martin failed to point out that the contract neither required the power company to purchase the plant nor set a minimum sale price. Representative John F. Miller of Washington insisted that the Alabama Power Company had taken advantage of the government "during the exigencies of war" in order to gain control of the disposition of this property so that it could not be used in competition against the power company after the war. This charge brought heated protests from Martin who warned that if the government did not honor its contract, the steam plant would have to be moved from the power company's land on which it was constructed. J. O. Hammit, representing the American Cyanamid Company's subsidiary, the Air Nitrates Corporation, presented that company's claims to nitrate plant no. 2 based on an option in its wartime contract with the government. Colonel Hull had also ruled this option to be null and void.[15]

The Ford offer apparently forced the southern power companies, especially the Alabama Power Company, to change their attitude toward Muscle Shoals. In 1921 they had responded to General Beach's request for bids by overtly discouraging further development of the power facilities at the project, contending that such a course would not be economically feasible. After the advent of the Ford offer these power companies showed an increasing concern regarding Muscle Shoals, and at the House hearings in 1922 on the Ford offer, officials of the Alabama Power

15. New York *Times*, Feb. 11, 12, 22, 25, 28, 1922.

Company registered vigorous opposition to the offer. According to one authority, the southern power companies saw in the Ford offer the emergence of "an aggressive and successful competitor" who could place them in an uneasy position through control of Muscle Shoals. Consequently, they hurriedly abandoned their professions of disinterest in Muscle Shoals. In fact, officials of the Alabama Power Company candidly admitted that the power company had been compelled by the Ford offer to make a bid for Muscle Shoals in order to protect the company's alleged water-power rights in that area.[16]

At first the Alabama Power Company attempted to secure control of Muscle Shoals through the Farm Bureau. An effort was made to obtain the assistance of Gray Silver, Washington representative of the Farm Bureau, in promoting a drive to lease the project to that organization in order to produce fertilizer, with an agreement that all surplus power would go to the Alabama Power Company. Silver refused to co-operate.[17] Failing in this plan, the power company, on February 15 in the midst of the House hearings on the Ford offer, formally submitted a bid for Muscle Shoals. The features of their bid differed radically from those of the Ford proposal, especially in their simplicity. The power company simply offered to lease the power site of Wilson Dam and complete construction of that project at its own expense, the lease to conform to the terms of the Federal Water Power Act including a limitation of fifty years. The company agreed to purchase all other electrical generating and transmission facilities connected with the Muscle Shoals project for $5,000,000, less an amount to be allocated to navigation, to be paid in annual installments. This property consisted of the Gorgas steam plant, the Gorgas-Muscle Shoals transmission line, and the steam plants attached to the nitrate plants.

The power company's offer contained no provision for the acquisition of the nitrate plants or the production of fertilizer,

16. Jerome G. Kerwin, *Federal Water-Power Legislation* (1926), 271; Macon (Ga.) *Telegraph*, April 22, 1922.

17. Roy E. Bishop (secretary of the Alabama Farm Bureau), to Silver, March 7, 1922, Correspondence of the Secretary of Agriculture, Muscle Shoals, National Archives.

but the company did agree to furnish free of charge a limited amount of power to the government, or agent of the government, for that purpose.[18] Officials of the power company intimated that they had already negotiated an agreement with a firm to which the nitrate plants would be leased for fertilizer production.[19]

The chief merit of the offer of the Alabama Power Company, Thomas W. Martin informed Secretary Weeks, lay in the fact that it constituted a plan through which Wilson Dam could be completed and the nitrate and fertilizer problem solved without further governmental expenditure. Furthermore, the development of the Muscle Shoals water-power project by the power company would, Martin continued, attract new industries to the Tennessee Valley. Martin said he had been assured by several industrial firms that they would build new plants in that area should Muscle Shoals power become available.[20]

Secretary Weeks presented the offer of the Alabama Power Company to Congress on February 21, 1922. Officially, he made no recommendations, but his accompanying comments were very favorable to the offer. He considered all of the principal provisions of the offer to be advantageous to the public welfare. He was particularly pleased that the power company's proposal conformed to the essential provisions of the Federal Water Power Act which would permit public regulation of the Muscle Shoals power. Furthermore, the Secretary pointed out that the offer would relieve the government of further expenditures in the matter.[21]

The presentation of the offer of the Alabama Power Company to Congress produced some rather heated complaints against that company, particularly in Alabama. On the same day Congress received the offer, the Florence, Alabama, Chamber of Commerce adopted a resolution stating that the Alabama Power Company was owned by foreign capital and warning that acceptance of that company's offer would jeopardize national defense by plac-

18. War Department, *Offer Made by the Alabama Power Company Proposing to Complete Wilson Dam,* House Doc. 192, 67 Cong., 2 Sess. (1922), 3–4.

19. New York *Times,* Feb. 28, 1922.

20. House Doc. 192, 67 Cong., 2 Sess., 3, 5–7.

21. *Ibid.,* 1–3.

ing the only domestic source of nitrogen under the control of a foreign influence. The resolution also stated that the power company already controlled most undeveloped water-power resources in Alabama and, significantly, protested that acceptance of the power company bid in lieu of the Ford offer would deprive the Muscle Shoals area of large industries.[22] There were similar resolutions adopted by various civic and economic organizations in Alabama and other sections of the South. In addition, former Governor Emmet O'Neal, president of the Alabama Farm Bureau, and Governor Thomas E. Kilby of Alabama, denounced the power company's offer. O'Neal repeated charges that the power company was foreign-owned and declared that approval of the company's offer would only serve to swell the dividends of the British stockholders. President Martin of the Alabama Power Company denied that British capitalists controlled the company. He said that since about 1914 the company had been financed largely by American capital and that only 35 to 40 per cent of its securities were currently held abroad. He admitted that in the prewar period British capital had great influence in the company.[23]

At the same time, Representative George Huddleston of Alabama delivered a blast at the Alabama Power Company on the floor of the House:

We . . . know that the Alabama Power Company is not acting for itself alone in making an offer for Muscle Shoals. The real purpose of the offer is to defeat Henry Ford's offer and the competition for the great trusts which lies in his acquisition of Muscle Shoals. The Alabama Power Company . . . has not the financial strength to put through the offer that it has made. It has received assurances from outsiders who use it as a tool with which to strike at Ford . . . the fertilizer trust . . . the chemical trust, and the great trusts . . . [controlling] nitrates, aluminum, abrasives, steel alloys, and carbide—these colossal concerns are deeply concerned in preventing Ford's development of Muscle Shoals. They . . . through their Wall Street affiliations are well able to finance any adventure which promises to further their aims. . . . Their Washington lobbyists are coordinated and in action. The

22. New York *Times*, Feb. 21, 1922.
23. *Ibid.*, Feb. 25, 1922; *Cong. Rec.*, 67 Cong., 2 Sess., 2979–81, 4111–13.

Alabama Power Company offer is obviously the fruit of a conspiracy which they have concocted.[24]

Huddleston charged that the power company had gained a monopoly over Alabama's water-power resources through control of the Alabama legislature. In reference to the alleged political machinations of that company, he declared:

It has had its State governor, its legislators, and other officials. It has had its champions in Congress. It has tainted the judgment of our courts. The slime of its trail has befouled our elections. It has its subsidized newspapers. As Ford stands for the best in American industry, so does the Alabama Power Company stand for the lowest in our industrial life.

Huddleston said there was evidence that some southern newspapers which had been supporting the Ford offer were succumbing to financial lures in the form of advertising accounts held out by the Alabama Power Company.[25]

Representative Frank James of Michigan, one of Ford's leading supporters, also vigorously attacked the Alabama Power Company. James accused it of having feigned disinterestedness with respect to Muscle Shoals in the postwar period in the hope that the property could be acquired as scrap at the company's own price.[26]

Late in February, 1922, the House Military Committee temporarily put aside the investigation of the Ford offer in order to hear testimony on the Alabama Power Company offer. The chief witness for the power company was Thomas W. Martin, who promised that acceptance of the offer would open the door to a huge hydroelectric development, based on Muscle Shoals, which would result in the industrialization of the mid-South. According to Martin, the reason the power company had changed its position with respect to the feasibility of utilizing Muscle Shoals was because of an increasing number of applications for power by industrialists in the Tennessee Valley area.[27]

24. *Cong. Rec.*, 67 Cong., 2 Sess., 2980.
25. *Ibid.*, 67 Cong., 2 Sess., 2979–80.
26. *Ibid.*, 4313.
27. New York *Times*, Feb. 25, 28, March 8, 1922.

Edward B. Almon, who represented the Muscle Shoals district in Congress, was the principal witness against the power company's offer. Almon characterized the proposal as being inadequate in monetary considerations and deliberately rigged to avoid fertilizer production. He averred that it was merely a scheme to delay development of Muscle Shoals indefinitely by defeating the Ford offer. He charged that the power company was "intertwined" with both the fertilizer and power trusts, and he repeated the charges that the company was foreign-owned and that it had encouraged abandonment of Muscle Shoals at the end of the war with the view of acquiring the project very cheaply.[28]

Electrical World reported that the offer of the Alabama Power Company had created a sentiment against the Ford Muscle Shoals plan among many people because the former promised widespread distribution of the cheap water power at Muscle Shoals, a feature not present in the Ford offer. This publication also stated that Chairman Kahn, after having entered the hearings favorably disposed toward the Ford offer, had concluded, after hearing the testimony of witnesses, that it should be rejected.[29]

Hearings on the Muscle Shoals offers were held by the Senate Agriculture Committee intermittently from February to July, 1922. Senator Norris, the chairman of that committee, was not friendly to either the Ford or the power company offer and obviously sought to prolong the hearings with the view of mobilizing opposition against the Ford scheme, the one mostly likely to be accepted by Congress. To give the power company's supporters a chance to strengthen their forces would also bring about a balance of power and a deadlock between these two powerful forces, a situation which would perhaps improve the chances that Norris's bill for public operation of Muscle Shoals would be adopted. At these hearings Secretary Weeks and some of his subordinates continued their attack against the Ford offer.

28. *Cong. Rec.*, 67 Cong., 2 Sess., 3699–3704.
29. "Alabama Power's Muscle Shoals Offer Makes Favorable Impression," *Electrical World*, LXXIX (Feb. 25, 1922), 399; "Hearings on Muscle Shoals Project Concluded," *ibid.* (March 25, 1922), 595.

As at the House hearings, Weeks emphasized the alleged lack of any substantial guarantee of fertilizer production in the Ford offer and again stated that Ford had declared to him his intention of suspending fertilizer production if he could not earn a profit on fertilizer operations. Again Weeks emphasized the failure of the offer to meet the terms of the Federal Water Power Act, the most serious consequence of which would be the placing of Muscle Shoals power outside the sphere of public regulation.

Despite the assertions of the president of the Alabama Power Company at the House hearings that there was an acute need of additional water power to meet the needs of increased industrialization in the South, Weeks severely criticized the provision of the Ford offer providing for construction of dam no. 3, the Secretary averring that there was no market in the South for such additional power. Weeks contended that the cyanamid process was obsolete and asserted that nitrate plant no. 2 could not compete with private industry, which, he said, was beginning to utilize the Haber process. In an attempt to deliver the death blow to the cyanamid process, Weeks used the services of an expert, Major James H. Burns, Chief of the Nitrate Division of the Ordnance Department, who assured the committee that it would not be economically feasible to utilize nitrate plant no. 2 in the production of fertilizer. He advised that it be kept in a stand-by condition for national defense.[30]

On the other hand the Department of Agriculture gave some technical support to the Ford offer. Dr. Richard C. Tolman, director of the Department's Fixed Nitrogen Research Laboratory, admitted the apparent superiority of the Haber over the cyanamid process except under two special conditions both of which, he said, prevailed at Muscle Shoals—cheap water power and the presence of materials and facilities for manufacturing various by-products.[31]

Despite Senator Norris's efforts to provide every opportunity for opponents of the Ford offer to voice their opinions at the Senate hearings, this group could not match the array of dis-

30. *Muscle Shoals*, Hearings, U. S. Senate, 67 Cong., 2 Sess., 52–112, 748–52.
31. *Ibid.*

tinguished personages appearing in behalf of Ford's proposal. The pro-Ford witnesses included Senator Underwood, Governor Alfred Taylor of Tennessee, former Senator Hoke Smith of Georgia, William B. Mayo, Ford's chief engineer, J. W. Worthington and W. G. Waldo, executive secretary and consulting engineer, respectively, of the Tennessee River Improvement Association, and Thomas A. Edison.

Senator Underwood testified that the Ford plan offered the best solution to the nation's problem of increasing soil exhaustion. Underwood, who had supported the Wadsworth-Kahn bill, said Ford's willingness to limit his profit and risk his capital on fertilizer production had caused him to turn from government operation to the Ford offer for a solution to the fertilizer problem.[32] Both Governor Taylor and ex-Senator Smith gave enthusiastic endorsement to the Ford offer.[33] Governor Taylor said, "I express the sentiments of every man and woman in Tennessee, without any exception, without regard to political affiliation . . . I express the sentiment of every human being in my State, when I say that they are looking and longing for Congress to pass the great measure." [34]

Worthington, Mayo, and Waldo strongly intimated that Ford contemplated a unified power-navigational development of the entire Tennessee River basin, although they were vague in their testimony on this matter. Mayo maintained that there was no market for additional power in the South, and he made it plain that Ford did not intend to distribute to the public any power that he might develop in the area but would use it in his own plants. Under sharp questioning by Senator Norris, Mayo admitted that the Haber process showed greater possibilities than the cyanamid method, but he insisted that Ford's offer did not bind him to use nitrate plant no. 2 which was equipped with cyanamid apparatus. Instead, he claimed, Ford would use a "secret process" which he had developed and which was superior

32. New York *Times*, April 11, 1922.

33. *Muscle Shoals*, Senate Hearings, 67 Cong., 2 Sess., 5; New York *Times*, May 8, 1922.

34. *Muscle Shoals*, Senate Hearings, 67 Cong., 2 Sess., 5.

to all other processes. Waldo, however, denied that Ford had a "secret process," and he insisted that Ford could lower fertilizer prices with the facilities already installed at Muscle Shoals.[35]

The testimony of Thomas A. Edison served to add further confusion to the testimony of pro-Ford witnesses. He stated that he knew of no "secret process" in the possession of Ford and that had there been such a scientific development, he would have been aware of it. He further stated, without reservations, that the Haber process was definitely superior to all other nitrogen fixation processes. Like all supporters of the Ford offer, he had no doubt regarding Ford's ability to produce cheap fertilizer at Muscle Shoals, but he felt this accomplishment depended on utilization of the Haber process. He emphasized that use of this process could free a large amount of water power for other purposes, and, in fact, his testimony implied that Ford intended to install the Haber process at nitrate plant no. 2. Edison's greatest contribution to the cause of the Ford offer was his strong intimation that he would be associated with the automobile manufacturer in the production of fertilizer and other chemicals at Muscle Shoals. In fact, he stated that he was then engaged in laboratory research on certain problems involving the production of fertilizer at Muscle Shoals including the utilization of local feldspar deposits as a source of potash.[36]

Farmers were allegedly represented at the Senate hearings by Gray Silver, Washington representative of the Farm Bureau, and his assistant, Russell F. Bower, and Benjamin C. Marsh, managing director of the Farmers' National Council. Silver and Bower lavishly praised the Ford offer. Norris and his colleagues put them on the defensive by inquiring as to motives behind the change in Farm Bureau policy toward Muscle Shoals since the debate on the Wadsworth-Kahn bill, when that organization endorsed government operation. Both witnesses replied that the Ford offer portended more benefits than could possibly have resulted from government operation, one of the principal reasons being that Ford would not be handicapped by political inter-

35. *Ibid.*, 275–76, 281–84, 299, 319–22, 799–833.
36. *Ibid.*, 701–3.

ference as would a governmental body. Norris told Silver that
the Ford plan was an "unconscionable" scheme to gain control
of Muscle Shoals for Henry Ford.[37]

On the other hand, Benjamin C. Marsh denounced the Ford
offer, his testimony marking the first time that any considerable
opposition to the offer had come from a farm organization. He
declared that Muscle Shoals should be developed as purely a
water-power project rather than as a source of fertilizer, and that
the principal issue involved in the Muscle Shoals controversy
was national water-power policy. He called for government
operation of the Muscle Shoals project. Marsh said he regarded
the officials of the Farm Bureau as "absolutely dishonest" and
implied that their activities were being directed by strong financial interests rather than by the nation's farmers.[38]

The conservationists were represented at the Senate hearings
by Oscar C. Merrill, executive secretary of the Federal Power
Commission, and by Philip Wells, an expert in the field of
conservation and former assistant to Gifford Pinchot in the
Forest Service. Both witnesses declared that the Ford offer
violated practically all of the principles of conservation embodied
in the Federal Water Power Act. Merrill termed the offer a bid
for an outright subsidy, and Wells described it as "outrageous." [39]

William McClellan, president of the American Institute of
Electrical Engineers, aided Norris's efforts to mobilize opposition to the Ford offer by recommending to the committee that the
judgment of the nation's business and technical experts be obtained before reaching a final decision on Muscle Shoals. Norris
complied by holding the hearings open for everyone of this
category who cared to testify. This maneuver was not particularly
fruitful in attracting important witnesses, although representatives of the DuPont and Pacific Gas and Electric interests appeared to testify against the Ford offer. In at least one respect,
this strategy backfired for it furnished the Ford supporters with

37. *Ibid.*, 546–47; New York *Times*, May 10, 1922.
38. *Muscle Shoals*, Senate Hearings, 67 Cong., 2 Sess., 584, 601.
39. *Ibid.*, 37–38; New York *Times*, May 14, June 21, 1922.

evidence that financial capitalism was aligned against the Ford offer.[40]

In all probability, the most effective opposition to the Ford scheme at the Senate hearings came from some of the committee members themselves, particularly Norris, whose penetrating analyses and biting innuendoes frequently dampened the spirit of pro-Ford witnesses. Norris charged that "propaganda" in favor of the Ford offer was being spread by Muscle Shoals real estate speculators, by politicians anxious to gain political power through use of Ford's great prestige, and by farm organizations which were abusing their positions of trust by attempts to indoctrinate the farmer with publicity favoring the Ford offer. He accused Ford of deliberately using farm leaders to gain control of Muscle Shoals.[41] Senators John W. Harreld of Oklahoma, Charles L. McNary of Oregon, and John B. Kendrick of Wyoming, all of whom were members of the Agriculture Committee, voiced strong opposition to the Ford offer.[42]

Among the members of the Senate Agriculture Committee, Senator J. Thomas Heflin was the chief defender of the Ford proposal. Heflin refused to enter into discussions of the details of any of the provisions of the Ford offer but instead fought the battle for Ford by repeating the latter's charges against the alleged fertilizer trust and by reciting eulogies of the automobile magnate with the intention of placing him on a pedestal above criticism.[43] As the Senate Muscle Shoals hearings were ending, Heflin insinuated that Norris had conducted the hearings unfairly and that he had resorted to unethical practices in order to defeat the Ford offer. According to Norris, Heflin "practically accused everybody who is not for Ford of being a demagogue, and almost a traitor to his country." Heflin denied that his remarks could be construed as questioning Norris's integrity.[44]

As early as March, 1922, it had become evident that both the House Military and Senate Agriculture committees were some-

40. *Muscle Shoals*, Senate Hearings, 67 Cong., 2 Sess., 561, 731–39.
41. New York *Times*, May 10, June 14, 1922.
42. *Muscle Shoals*, Senate Hearings, 67 Cong., 2 Sess., 20, 355, 362–64.
43. New York *Times*, Feb. 19, 1922.
44. *Cong. Rec.*, 67 Cong., 2 Sess., 8900.

what dissatisfied with the fertilizer provisions of the Ford offer, and particularly with the apparent failure of Ford personally to obligate himself to manufacture fertilizer, the one consideration for which he was to receive control of Muscle Shoals as well as title to a vast amount of property there. Following a conference in early March between pro-Ford members of the House Military Committee and Ford's representatives, William B. Mayo and Gray Silver jointly announced that Ford had agreed to strengthen the fertilizer guarantee in his offer.[45] Nevertheless, no changes were made in the fertilizer provisions of Ford's offer at the time. Continued criticism of the Ford offer in and out of Congress, together with a report received by Ford that the many Ford supporters in the South believed his interest in Muscle Shoals was lagging, prompted the industrialist to break a two-month period of silence concerning his Muscle Shoals offer with a withering blast at Wall Street. Ford told the press:

Tell the people of the South that Wall Street will have no part either in financing or operating Muscle Shoals if I can help it. If it's the last thing I do I'll exert every resource and influence at my command to keep the hands of Wall Street off the Shoals project and perpetuate that as a great example to the American people—a living example of what they can do if they will safeguard the country's water power and develop it. In Muscle Shoals lies the freedom of American industry.

Ford included, in this interview with the press, an implied threat of discipline to Congress:

All I have to say . . . is that I have a great faith in the sound judgment of the American people and trust they will not stand silent and let Wall Street put anything over on their representatives at Washingon.[46]

In April, Ford representatives met in executive session with the House Military Committee to discuss possible modifications of the Ford offer. By this time, some committee members favorable to the proposal had become anxious that, in addition to strengthening his fertilizer guarantee, Ford should eliminate the

45. New York *Times,* Feb. 19, March 8, 15, 1922.
46. *Ibid.,* March 18, 1922.

Gorgas steam plant from the offer in order to avoid a legal battle with the Alabama Power Company. Nothing definite developed at this time but on May 31 Ford officially submitted a revised bid which he declared was his last and final offer. He notified Congress that it must be accepted in the whole or rejected, and he warned if the latter event should occur, "that will be but the beginning of a more determined effort on my part to save Muscle Shoals for the benefit of the public." [47]

The modification contained in Ford's new offer purportedly strengthened the guarantee of fertilizer production. In the first place, Ford agreed that Muscle Shoals would be operated by a corporation having a capital stock of $10,000,000 of which Ford would have control. He agreed that this company would manufacture "nitrogen and other commercial fertilizer" and that the annual amount of fertilizer produced would contain 40,000 tons of nitrogen, the estimated capacity of nitrate plant no. 2. In addition, the revised offer provided that the company would manufacture fertilizer, in the above named amount, "continuously throughout the lease period, except as it may be prevented by reconstruction of the plant itself, or by war, strikes, accidents, fires or other causes beyond its control." None of these factors was further defined. Ford also agreed that the Secretary of War could initiate proceedings in the federal court of the northern district of Alabama for the termination of the lease should he feel that the lessee had violated the terms of the contract.[48]

Otherwise, the Ford proposal remained unaltered. Ford refused to omit the Gorgas steam plant from the offer, declaring that its auxiliary power was essential to the successful operation of Muscle Shoals. Meeting in executive session to consider the revised proposal, the House Military Committee on June 3 voted 12 to 9 to accept it with the exception of one provision—that involving the Gorgas plant. The committee excluded this property from the offer despite Ford's previous declaration that his proposal must be accepted in whole or rejected.[49]

47. *Ibid.*, April 28, June 2, 1922.
48. *Muscle Shoals Propositions*, House Report 1084, 67 Cong., 2 Sess. (1922), 33–37.
49. *Ibid.*, 1; New York *Times*, June 2, 4, 1922.

The committee's majority report, submitted by Representative John C. McKenzie of Illinois, acting chairman, stated that a majority of the committee had concluded that for the good of the public welfare, Muscle Shoals should be operated by private enterprise and that government operation under any circumstances was opposed. The Ford offer was described as the only proposal "sufficiently comprehensive in its terms" to satisfy the requirements imposed by the National Defense Act. The majority expressed the opinion that the language of Ford's most recently revised offer sufficiently defined the right and obligations of Ford and the government with respect to Muscle Shoals and that it contained a definite guarantee to produce fertilizer as well as a satisfactory formula for termination of the lease in the event of violation of the contract. The report urged that the House be given an early opportunity to vote on the proposition, pointing out that prompt acceptance meant that the government would soon begin to receive returns on its investments at Muscle Shoals and that resumption of work there would save the project from further physical deterioration. Nevertheless, it was admitted that the offer was not entirely without objectionable features, but hope was expressed that any defects in it could be easily eliminated by agreement between Congress and Ford.[50]

There were two minority reports, one by Representative William C. Wright of Georgia and the other by Representative Richard W. Parker of New Jersey. The Wright report, signed by two Republicans and six southern Democrats, demanded the acceptance of the Ford offer in full, including the Gorgas steam plant, and insisted that the omission of this property was tantamount to rejection of the offer in view of Ford's recent declaration that it must be accepted in toto or be rejected. The report suggested that inclusion of the steam plant in the offer would in no way injure the rights of the Alabama Power Company because the government would merely be transferring its rights in the plant to Ford with whom the power company could reach a settlement of the matter. Furthermore, the option on the steam plant held by the power company was described as being devoid

50. House Report 1084, 67 Cong., 2 Sess., 2, 38–46.

of either "law or morality." It charged that the Alabama Power Company was the chosen instrument being used by special interests to defeat the Ford offer. The offer itself was described as an "absolute, unqualified obligation" to produce a given quantity of fertilizer annually.

The Parker report, which carried the signatures of only two members of the committee, recommended that the Ford proposal not be accepted unless further modifications were made. It concluded that since the fertilizer agreement was "the bargain counter in the proposal," it would be unwise to accept it unless further security for performance of contract was pledged.[51]

Because of the confusion created by the Gorgas plant provision, it was impossible to determine exactly how the House Military Committee really stood on the question. How many members of the majority endorsed the Ford offer in principle could not be ascertained, since some committee members may have supported the committee version hoping that the elimination of the Gorgas plant would defeat the proposal.

The Gorgas steam plant controversy plagued the long House Military Committee hearings from beginning to end, despite the ruling by the Judge Advocate General that the wartime option clause in the government's contract with the Alabama Power Company was null and void. The option on nitrate plant no. 2 held by the Air Nitrates Corporation further aggravated this problem which was particularly annoying to pro-Ford members of the Committee.

The legal difficulty involved was perhaps the principal motive prompting Chairman Kahn to suggest, in early March, 1922, that the whole Muscle Shoals problem be turned over to an executive commission to be composed of the secretaries of War, the Treasury, and Agriculture. He declared that until these legal difficulties were solved Congress could take no action on the problem and that it might be several years before a solution could be found. Kahn denied charges that he was merely following administration instructions to remove the Muscle Shoals problem from Congress and place it with the executive branch

51. *Ibid.*, 47–53, 57.

where it would be less susceptible to pressure from Ford.[52] Senator Heflin professed to see in Kahn's proposal an attempt to delay action on the Ford offer. He asserted that both Mellon and Weeks, who would sit on Kahn's proposed commission, were predisposed against the Ford offer, Mellon because of fear of competition from Ford in aluminum production and Weeks because of an apparent commitment to support the offer of the Alabama Power Company.[53] Kahn's proposal met strenuous opposition from the pro-Ford group on the committee which took the position that Congress alone would have to assume the responsibility for solving the Muscle Shoals problem.[54] Undoubtedly, this group's opposition to Kahn's proposal stemmed more from the realization of the powerful pressure that Ford could exert on Congress than from any political principles. Kahn's commission plan died in April following a conference on the matter between Kahn and President Harding, who reportedly told Kahn that Congress and not the White House was the proper place for the settlement of the Muscle Shoals problem.[55]

A week before the House Military Committee voted to accept the Ford offer minus the Gorgas plant, Attorney General Harry M. Daugherty ruled that the option clauses in the wartime contracts with the Alabama Power Company and the Air Nitrates Corporation were null and void. Daugherty, like the Judge Advocate General, held that the inclusion of the options in the contract exceeded the power granted to the War Department by the statutes on which the contracts were based. He severely reprimanded the two companies for allegedly having taken unfair advantage of the government under the stress of war. The House Military Committee had been withholding its decision pending this ruling by the Attorney General. Then despite the fact that it appeared to pave the way for a clear title to the Gorgas plant to be granted to Ford, the majority of the committee voted to omit the Gorgas properties.

52. New York *Times*, March 5, June 6, 1922.
53. *Cong. Rec.*, 67 Cong., 2 Sess., 3657.
54. New York *Times*, June 6, 1922.
55. "Deadlock in Congress over Muscle Shoals," in *Electrical World*, LXXIX (April 8, 1922), 697.

President Martin of the Alabama Power Company was elated by the omission of the Gorgas plant from the Ford offer by the majority of the House Military Committee. He declared that this action recognized "the essential right and justice" of his company's claims, and again he insisted that the property was not properly a part of the Muscle Shoals project. Despite the elimination of the steam plant, W. B. Mayo, Ford's chief engineer, regarded the Committee's majority report as a victory for Ford. He stated that Ford would now increase the intensity of his fight for Muscle Shoals which would result, he intimated, in the restoration of the steam plant by the House.[56]

Ford had already intensified his efforts by following up the submission of his revised offer of May 31 with charges that certain Wall Street interests were behind the opposition to his offer, and he defiantly threw down the gauntlet to them:

If the selfish Wall Street interests which, behind the scenes, have been delaying and misrepresenting our proposition will come out in the open and make the government a better offer than mine, I'll fall right in and co-operate and help them and the Government in any way that I can. But if they think they can get over a less worthy private offer I notify them now that the fight for Muscle Shoals, so far, has been but a skirmish. We will exert every resource at our command to keep Muscle Shoals out of the hands of Wall Street.

Again Ford verbally disciplined Congress. He declared that he planned to begin work at Muscle Shoals during the coming summer and that there was no reason for that body to delay any longer on his offer. He again appealed directly to public opinion to prod congressmen into action. He said that

Congress is willing to spend a hundred million at Muscle Shoals for war, but in three years and six months it has not spent a nickel there for peace. The destiny of our country, agriculturally and industrially, lies at Muscle Shoals. If the project can be developed as an example of what can be done with water power, a new epoch in American agriculture and industry will be born, an epoch in which the American farmer and working man will be better off than he ever has been before.[57]

56. New York *Times*, June 4, 1922.
57. *Ibid.*, June 2, 1922.

At this time Ford assumed complete responsibility for the claims among his supporters that he would drastically reduce the price of fertilizer through operation of Muscle Shoals. He branded any assertion to the contrary as "a fraud" and declared that acceptance of his offer would mean greatly lowered fertilizer prices.[58]

Bills embodying the majority and minority reports of Representatives McKenzie and Wright, respectively, were introduced in the House soon after these committee decisions were officially reported.[59] Immediately following the introduction of the Wright bill, which provided for acceptance of the Ford offer in full, Ford announced that he was ready to begin work at Muscle Shoals on a few hours' notice. Ford's efforts to speed approval of his offer were supplemented by renewed activities of the Farm Bureau. At this time, Gray Silver began a campaign for acceptance of the offer at that session of Congress. He requested Farm Bureau officials in the various states to urge all of their members to inform Congress "in unmistakable terms" that a very favorable sentiment in regard to the Ford offer was prevalent among farmers.[60]

The introduction of the McKenzie and Wright bills was accompanied by the beginning of a great agitation by Ford's friends in the House, especially the Southerners, to have action on the Ford offer at that session. The ardor of the pro-Ford congressmen was soon dampened to a considerable extent by a prediction by Senator Norris that no Ford bill would be acted on before adjournment and by the lack of enthusiasm for the bills on the part of administration leaders in the House. The demand in the House for immediate consideration of the Ford offer precipitated a sharp debate between Frank W. Mondell of Wyoming, the Republican leader, and leading congressional exponents of the proposal, particularly Finis J. Garrett of Tennessee, the minority leader, and John N. Garner of Texas. Mondell refused to entertain any hope that the Ford bills would be placed

58. *Ibid.*
59. *Cong. Rec.*, 67 Cong., 2 Sess., 8139, 8508.
60. New York *Times*, June 12, 1922.

on the House calendar during the session. His view was that the extremely complicated nature of the Muscle Shoals problem would militate against hurried action on the matter. Furthermore, he informed the Ford supporters that appropriations for resumption of work on Wilson Dam would probably be considered before other Muscle Shoals legislation. The group supporting the Ford offer accused the administration of deliberately preventing the Ford offer from facing a test on the House floor. It was also suggested that the administration hoped a policy of continual delay would force Ford to withdraw his offer in disgust.[61]

Representative Mondell was placed in an embarrassing position by an Associated Press story of June 13 which stated that President Harding had instructed Mondell to delay action on the Ford bill until adjournment. Although Mondell admitted having briefly discussed the Muscle Shoals problem with the President, he denied that the Chief Executive ever had expressed an opinion on the subject or had given any instructions as to legislation on the matter. According to the Associated Press story, Harding did not commit himself on the Ford offer other than to state his opinion that the problem was too complex to be hurriedly considered.[62] On the other hand, the New York *Times*, on the same day, stated that President Harding told Mondell that he was opposed to the bid and that Secretary Weeks had White House backing in his opposition to it. The *Times* also stated that Harding was somewhat upset for fear that administration opposition to the Ford offer would endanger one of his favored measures—the ship subsidy bill.[63]

Meanwhile, on June 20, another minority report on the Ford offer, the Kearns report, came from the House Military Committee. It was signed by six conservative Republicans and apparently represented the viewpoint of the administration. This report declared that the country had been misled by "false" Ford propaganda which promised a drastic reduction in fertilizer prices if

61. *Cong. Rec.*, 67 Cong., 2 Sess., 8481–82, 9845.
62. *Ibid.*, 8656–57; Nashville *Tennessean*, June 13, 1922.
63. New York *Times*, June 13, 1922.

the industrialist should acquire Muscle Shoals. Contrary to the popular belief, the report stated, Ford had not bound himself legally ever to produce fertilizer in the event of acceptance of his offer, and it was pointed out that Ford himself had informed Secretary Weeks during the Ford-Weeks conferences earlier in the year that he would discontinue fertilizer production if he should fail to make a profit on the fertilizer. The report charged that the pro-Ford group was attempting to exploit the miseries of the nation's unemployed with false promises that a million men would be employed by Ford at Muscle Shoals. The report admitted that Ford himself was honest but pointed out that after his death Muscle Shoals might fall into "unconscionable hands." [64] On the other hand, Ford's honesty did not make him a superman, the report intimated. It stated: "If we were believers in fables, or had faith to believe in the pranks of fairies, then we might also think that Mr. Ford is the reincarnation of Aladdin plus his lamp. But we cannot have such childish faith." [65]

The Kearns report vigorously protested the violation of the Federal Water Power Act by the Ford offer, particularly in that Ford would be given access to cheap power, denied to others, which would give him an unfair leverage of competition to use against other manufacturers.[66]

Following the Kearns report, the pro-Ford contingent in the House intensified its efforts to bring the Ford offer to a vote. Representative Garrett of Tennessee served notice that he would utilize every parliamentary weapon at his command.[67] Representative Edward B. Almon of the Muscle Shoals district was the loudest in demanding action. He asserted that 6,500,000 American farmers were "petitioning and urging Congress to accept the Ford offer." Nevertheless, the Republican leaders insisted that the House could not act until Ford himself had passed on the changes in his offer proposed by the majority report of

64. House Report 1084, 67 Cong., 2 Sess., Part 2, 2–4.
65. *Ibid.*, 3.
66. *Ibid.*, 9.
67. New York *Times,* Aug. 11, 20, 1922.

the House Military Committee.[68] The session ended in September without further House action on the Ford offer.

In early July, the pro-Ford group in the Senate, composed mostly of southern Democrats, started a drive for the Ford bid when Senator Edwin F. Ladd of North Dakota introduced a bill for unconditional acceptance of the offer. Ladd also presented resolutions endorsing the Ford offer that had recently been adopted by the Farm Bureau, the Farmers' Union, and the American Federation of Labor. This Ford boom was short-lived, for later in the month the Senate Agriculture Committee rejected the Ford offer by a vote of 9 to 7 and spurned the power company's bid unanimously. Senator Norris and four other Progressive Republicans on the committee voted to adopt the Norris bill for government operation.[69] Senator Norris had advocated, as early as March, 1922, the creation of a government corporation to operate Muscle Shoals, a suggestion which won the approval of Senator McNary. At this time Norris refused to concede that the issue of public versus private business in any form was involved in his suggestion. He maintained that government operation at Muscle Shoals was essential to the salvaging of the government's huge investment there.

It was not until May 11, 1922, several weeks after the Senate had begun hearings on the Ford offer, that Norris introduced his first Muscle Shoals bill.[70] It authorized the completion of Wilson Dam and construction of dam no. 3. Upon completion, the project would be operated by a government corporation which would manufacture a complete fertilizer for farmers at cost and would sell the surplus power, preference to be given to states, counties, and municipalities. In regard to fertilizer the Norris bill chiefly stressed experimentation and research, the contention being that "improvements must be made if we would cheapen the production of fertilizer." This bill authorized the Secretary of War to make a survey of the Tennessee River and its tributaries to ascertain the extent of water-power resources, particularly storage

68. *Cong. Rec.*, 67 Cong., 2 Sess., 10098, 11795–96.
69. *Muscle Shoals*, Senate Report 831, 67 Cong., 2 Sess. (1922), 1.
70. *Cong. Rec.*, 67 Cong., 2 Sess., 3659-60, 6709.

reservoirs, that could be used to augment the primary power of Muscle Shoals. The Secretary of War was also authorized to construct such dams there as in his opinion would be economically feasible.[71] Although Norris claimed that his bill provided for a multiple-purpose (power, navigation, and flood control) development of the river basin, there were no specific provisions for flood control. Another major deficiency in the bill was the failure to authorize construction of transmission lines to carry the surplus power to the municipalities and other public agencies.[72]

The report of the Senate Agriculture Committee, written by Senator Norris, consisted of two parts. It was a majority report in that it recommended rejection of all private bids for Muscle Shoals, but it was a minority report in its recommendation of government operation. In this report Norris delivered a blistering attack on the Ford offer. He contended that Ford had offered no guarantee that he would even attempt to reduce fertilizer prices, and he pointed out that following Ford's death, the Muscle Shoals Corporation would be open to control by less honest and patriotic men. Referring to Ford's purchase of the nitrate properties for $5,000,000, Norris declared that if the automobile manufacturer had been buying this same property from a minor, "there is no court in Christendom but what would promptly set aside the conveyance as having been obtained for want of consideration." In regard to Ford's proposed lease of the hydro-electric properties, Norris pointed out that it would violate the Federal Water Power Act, particularly so in the case of the long lease and the special privileges it would afford Ford in competition with other manufacturers. He denied that Ford would actually pay 4 per cent on the government investment at Muscle Shoals as purportedly was the case, and contended that an analysis of the offer showed that the figure would be 2.79 per cent.[73]

Norris declared that sentiment for the Ford offer had been generated primarily by real estate speculators:

71. Senate Report 831, 67 Cong., 2 Sess., 30–33.
72. Joseph S. Ransmeier, *Tennessee Valley Authority* (1942), 55; *Cong. Rec.*, 67 Cong., 4 Sess., 175.
73. Senate Report 831, 67 Cong., 2 Sess., 12, 15, 19–21.

These real estate speculators are organizing a wonderful propaganda in favor of the acceptance of Mr. Ford's offer. . . . They have flooded the country with their letters and circulars, particularly among the farmers, in which they falsely represent that Mr. Ford has agreed to make fertilizer at one-half its present cost, and thus they have brought to the aid of their real-estate speculations thousands of honest farmers throughout the country. . . . If their propaganda is anywhere near true, there will be, if Mr. Ford gets this property, a city spring up there which will make New York look like a country village. Why a warranty deed to the capitol at Washington is not included in this great transfer of Government property . . . has never been explained. . . . Notwithstanding this apparent neglect, the transaction still remains the most wonderful real-estate speculation since Adam and Eve lost title to the Garden of Eden.[74]

In this report Norris praised his own bill lavishly. He declared that it provided for the greatest fertilizer research program ever undertaken by man, and he stressed the water-power features in his measure, claiming that they would implement widespread distribution of cheap Muscle Shoals power to both urban and rural areas throughout the South while Ford proposed to use all of the power himself at Muscle Shoals.[75]

Electrical World, expressing the viewpoint of the power industry, heaped praise upon the Norris report despite the fact that the document advised rejection of the Alabama Power Company offer and recommended government operation. This publication applauded Norris and his colleagues for having penetrated "the mass of jingoism and fanaticism" surrounding the Ford offer.[76]

Senator Ladd's minority report, which was signed by two midwestern Republicans and four southern Democrats, urged unconditional acceptance of the Ford offer. Ladd maintained that the offer bound Ford, his personal estate, and his heirs to performance of contract, including the production of a given quantity of fertilizer. The Senator insisted that Ford would reduce fertilizer prices and that evidence had been submitted showing that this

74. *Ibid.,* 15.
75. *Ibid.,* 29–32.
76. "The Rejection of Ford's Muscle Shoals Offer," in *Electrical World,* LXXX (July 22, 1922), 161.

feat was possible. He protested that if Ford were forced to give
a more absolute guarantee, it might hamstring him to the point
that it would be impossible to operate the project successfully.
According to Ladd, the Ford offer presented a plan which would
serve as an example for the development of cheap water power
all over America. In criticizing the Norris bill, Ladd, who was a
professional chemist, warned that Muscle Shoals was not the
proper place to test a policy of government operation because
of the difficulties involved in dealing with problems of commercial
chemistry which could be more readily solved by private enterprise.[77]

Following the issuance of the Senate Agriculture Committee
reports, Gray Silver of the Farm Bureau wrote to some of the
committee members who opposed the Ford offer asking that
they make clear their position on that proposal. Two of them,
Senators William B. McKinley of Illinois and John W. Harreld
of Oklahoma, replied forthrightly, the former stating that Ford
proposed to deprive thousands of people in the South of their
cheap water power for the sake of his own industry while the
latter replied that the automobile manufacturer would be getting
an enormous amount of power without adequate compensation
to the government. Silver replied with heated statements accusing
these and other anti-Ford members of the committee of hostility
to the interests of American farmers. He intimated that McKinley
was primarily interested in the welfare of private power companies. According to Silver, anyone who had read the Ford offer
should have been able to understand that it included an ironclad
guarantee to produce and distribute a certain quantity of fertilizer
regardless of whether or not a profit accrued to the operation.
Senator Thaddeus H. Caraway of Arkansas, a pro-Ford member
of the committee, joined Silver in castigating the anti-Ford committee members. He averred that his colleagues who voted against
the Ford offer had permitted the "fertilizer trust" to win a victory,
and he accused Norris of resorting to illegal and unethical practice to defeat the offer in the committee. Caraway declared that

77. Senate Report 831, 67 Cong., 2 Sess., Part 2, 5–15.

Norris had violated a committee agreement by casting a proxy vote. Norris denied the existence of such an agreement.[78]

As in the House, the session closed without further action in the Senate on the Ford offer.

One of the most bitter events of the Ford offer controversy in the Sixty-seventh Congress occurred in June, 1922, when an appropriations amendment authorizing resumption of work on Wilson Dam was considered by the House of Representatives. By this time, the stalwart Republicans had reversed their stand on this matter and were advocating completion of the dam while the pro-Ford congressmen opposed the measure, expressing fear that further governmental expenditures on the dam at the time would injure Ford's chances of acquiring Muscle Shoals. Such action, they contended, would serve to confuse the issue because it would change the amount of investments on which Ford would be paying the 4 per cent rental fees, that amount to be the total cost of completion after acceptance of the offer. The Ford adherents demanded, as a compromise, that the availability of such funds be deferred until January, 1923. A compromise was finally formulated which withheld the availability of the funds until October 1, 1922.[79] Representative William B. Bankhead admitted that the real purpose behind the Democratic strategy was to force a delay in the belief that an idle and incomplete Muscle Shoals would crystallize public opinion in favor of the Ford offer.[80]

In the Senate, the authorization of the Wilson Dam funds had already passed with a minimum of effort, southern Democrats such as Underwood and Heflin declaring that such action would not affect the Ford offer. When the House version of the amendment returned to the Senate, however, Norris attempted to defeat it because of the provision for delay in availability of funds. Norris accused the Ford adherents in the House of deliberately delaying work on the dam until the winter season so that the project would be made more expensive in order further to dis-

78. *Cong. Rec.*, 67 Cong., 2 Sess., 10313–14, 10801, 11298.

79. *Ibid.*, 9328 ff., 9337 ff., 9357.

80. *Ibid.*, 9340–41.

credit government operation of Muscle Shoals. He also accused Gray Silver of attempting to intimidate the Senate in order to force the approval of the House version of the appropriations amendment, and he intimated that some of his colleagues were taking orders from the Farm Bureau representative. .Despite Norris's forceful opposition, the Senate accepted the House version, southern Democrats and administration Republicans combining to put it over.[81]

In December, 1922, after the Sixty-seventh Congress had convened for its last session, the Ford offer precipitated a definite breach in the representation of the agricultural states, especially in the Senate. Two important farm-state leaders, Norris and Heflin, engaged in a running battle over the Ford proposal. Norris averred that his bill would aid the Alabama farmer "ten thousand times more" than the Ford offer, and Heflin retorted that the Senator from Nebraska could "tell it to the Marines." Heflin insisted that the Norris bill was a "stalking horse" for opponents of the Ford bid, and both Heflin and McKellar implied that passage of that bill would result in the Alabama Power Company's gaining control of Muscle Shoals. Senator Ladd asserted that the power company was favorably disposed toward the Norris bill, though he hastened to add that Norris was just an innocent victim who was being duped. According to these Senators, the Alabama Power Company planned to dominate the government corporation provided for in the Norris bill should that measure pass. Senator McKellar charged that various interests opposing the Ford proposal were circulating Norris's speeches throughout Tennessee and neighboring states.[82]

Senator Norris raised the ire of the Ford supporters in late February, 1923, by advocating the construction of an experimental Haber process plant at Muscle Shoals for the purpose of research with fertilizer.[83] It was objected that such a course would conflict with Ford's plans for Muscle Shoals. Norris sarcastically apologized for having forgotten to obtain the permission of Henry

81. *Ibid.*, 8305 ff., 9462 ff.
82. *Ibid.*, 67 Cong., 4 Sess., 118, 736, 740, 744.
83. *Ibid.*, 2147.

Ford before making such a recommendation. He added that "it is high time we turned the Senate over to Mr. Ford's men and Mr. Gray Silver." [84] Ladd admitted indirectly that Norris's proposal would reflect adversely on a sacred Ford dogma—that the cyanamid process was, without doubt, superior to the Haber method. Norris withdrew his motion when it became apparent that it was headed for defeat.[85]

It became evident late in February that Representative Guy E. Campbell of Pennsylvania, chairman of the Rules Committee, was blocking action on Muscle Shoals in the House. Southern Democrats instituted a last-minute effort to have action before the end of the short session by attempting to exert pressure on Campbell. It was charged that opposition to the Ford offer was being fomented by the power companies, the chemical and steel interests, and the automobile interests. Campbell refused to yield. The refusal of Campbell to permit consideration of the Ford offer at this session, which was obviously in harmony with the administration policy, came as a shock to some Ford supporters. They had interpreted an earlier speech by Representative Madden, chairman of the House Appropriations Committee, in which unconditional acceptance of the Ford offer was urged, as indicating that the administration was ready to accept the Ford offer.[86] Thus, the Sixty-seventh Congress came to an end on March 4, 1923, without a decision on the Ford offer.

The Harding administration as a whole appears to have been opposed to the Ford offer throughout the duration of the Sixty-seventh Congress though the situation was confused by the defection of General Beach and the evasive attitude of Secretaries Wallace and Hoover. In late February, 1923, after it had become obvious that no further action would be taken on the Ford bid that session, Secretary Hoover stated that he would "like to see Mr. Ford do it [acquire Muscle Shoals] if that will suit anybody." Hoover hastened to add that he did not know "whether Mr. Ford's terms are the terms Congress ought to adopt." He explained

84. *Ibid.*, 3306–7.
85. *Ibid.*, 3247.
86. New York *Times*, Feb. 4, 16, 17, 1923.

that his principal concern was the problem posed by an international nitrate monopoly, the breaking of which, he said, could
be hastened by the operation of Muscle Shoals. Representative
Joseph W. Byrns of Tennessee, a spokesman for those who favored
the Ford offer in the House, interpreted Hoover's remarks as
being an endorsement of the Ford proposal.[87]

Gray Silver continued his campaign for the Ford offer in the
name of the Farm Bureau throughout the last session of the
Sixty-seventh Congress. Bernard Baruch lent his prestige to the
aid of Silver's pro-Ford publicity. In early 1923 Silver requested
Baruch to conduct a survey of the Muscle Shoals problem and
make recommendations as to the most feasible solution. Baruch
complied. He recommended the acceptance of the Ford offer with
two important conditions: first, Ford should remove any doubt
as to his personal liability for performance of the contract; second,
Ford should clearly guarantee the production of 40,000 tons of
nitrogen annually throughout the period of the lease.[88] Silver
chose to consider Baruch's statement as tantamount to an outright
endorsement of the Ford offer as it stood, characterizing Baruch's
conditions as "minor changes of phraseology." [89]

Silver's campaign for the Ford offer consisted principally of
literature distributed to Farm Bureau leaders throughout the
nation with instructions to encourage their members to write
their congressmen and senators urging approval of the Ford
proposal. The main theme of Silver's literature was that acceptance of the Ford offer would result in a drastic reduction of fertilizer prices and widespread rural electrification. Senator Norris
continually attempted to expose Silver's "propaganda" as being
false, particularly Silver's claims that the Ford offer contained an
ironclad guarantee to manufacture a given quantity and quality
of fertilizer for the duration of the lease period and that Ford
himself was legally liable for performance of the contract. Norris

87. *Ibid.*, Feb. 23, 1923; *Cong. Rec.*, 67 Cong., 4 Sess., 4522.
88. New York *Times*, Jan. 26, 27, 1923.
89. *American Farm Bureau Weekly News Letter* (Feb. 1, 1923). Silver regarded the fact that Baruch was a Jew as being of great value to the Ford offer
since Baruch had apparently endorsed that offer despite Ford's attacks on the
Jewish race in general and Jewish financiers in particular.

insisted that Ford would relieve himself of all liability upon organization of the corporation which would operate Muscle Shoals. Secretary Weeks maintained that Norris's legal interpretation of the matter was correct, and Baruch's report to Silver on Muscle Shoals indicated a belief that Ford's liability was perhaps limited to the obligation of organizing the corporation.[90]

Congress was also subjected to publicity against the Ford offer. For example, in February, 1923, Herbert Knox Smith, formerly Commissioner of Corporations during the administration of Theodore Roosevelt, and Philip P. Wells, secretary of the National Committee for Defense of the Federal Water Power Act, launched a broadside attack on the Ford offer by showering Congress with literature. This printed matter emphasized the fact that the bid proposed to violate the Federal Water Power Act which they described as the well-established national water-power policy.[91]

In the latter stages of the Sixty-seventh Congress, an important member of the pro-Ford press deserted. The *Manufacturers' Record*, which had originally been an enthusiastic supporter of the Ford offer on the grounds that it would stimulate prosperity in the South and save Muscle Shoals from the Alabama Power Company, deserted the Ford cause in March, 1923, declaring that Ford's fertilizer guarantee was not adequate. By May, 1923, the *Record* was clamoring for widespread general distribution of Muscle Shoals power by private power companies and was

90. New York *Times*, Jan. 27, 30, 1923; *Nitrate*, Hearings, U. S. House of Representatives, Series HH, 2nd Supplement, 67 Cong., 4 Sess. (1923), 17–50. An example of the results of Silver's mobilization of Farm Bureau sentiment in order to press Congress for acceptance of the Ford offer was the attempt by members of the Idaho Farm Bureau to apply pressure on Senator Borah with letters and petitions. Borah remained steadfast in his opposition to the Ford offer. Letters to Borah, Aug. to Dec., 1922, Papers of William E. Borah.

Wallace's Farmer, edited by Henry C. Wallace, Secretary of Agriculture, severely criticized the publicity activities of the Farm Bureau in regard to Muscle Shoals and accused that organization of grossly exaggerating any benefits that farmers might receive from the Ford offer, particularly midwestern farmers. Editorial in *Wallace's Farmer*, Dec. 29, 1922.

91. "Defenders of the Water Power Act Attack Ford Plan," in *Electrical World*, LXXXI (Feb. 17, 1923), 411.

beginning to attack Ford for his desire to concentrate and control this power for his own use.[92]

The struggle over the Ford offer in the Sixty-seventh Congress demonstrated that the Muscle Shoals problem was no mere business matter to be solved by a financial transaction in the market place. The debates and hearings in the Sixty-seventh Congress had demonstrated that Muscle Shoals was a political as well as an economic problem.

92. "The Muscle Shoals Situation," in *Manufacturers' Record*, LXXXI (March 2, 1922), 75; "The Muscle Shoals Situation Again," *ibid.*, 62; "Henry Ford and Muscle Shoals," *ibid.*, LXXXIII (March 1, 1923), 80–81; "One Million Primary Horsepower Could Be Developed at Muscle Shoals," *ibid.*, 81–82.

IV

The Prelude to the
Sixty-eighth Congress

A T THE BEGINNING of the second session of the Sixty-seventh
Congress, it had appeared that the Ford offer would achieve
victory. During the course of the session the actual strength of
the proposal was not tested on the floors of Congress because of
the opposition of the Harding administration and the Progressive
Republicans. During the session, the only vote on any phase of
the Muscle Shoals problem was that involved in authorization of
funds for completion of Wilson Dam, but this did not constitute
a test of the strength of the Ford offer because sentiment for
completion of the dam was not necessarily congruent with sentiment for Ford's proposal. The offer won a victory in the House
Military Committee but suffered a defeat in the Senate Agriculture Committee. During the course of the session much opposition to the scheme developed. Consequently, the Ford offer,
instead of achieving a quick victory, suffered a setback during
the session.

Despite its failure to win the approval of the Sixty-seventh
Congress, the future of the Ford proposal looked bright when
Congress adjourned in March, 1923. This favorable outlook was
based on the great amount of support that the offer still commanded throughout the country—support that to a large extent
had been created by the campaign for the proposal which was
being conducted by a group of its devoted advocates in and out
of Congress. The final adjournment of the Sixty-seventh Congress
found them very much on the offensive, and by that time their
campaign for the proposal had acquired some rather definite
characteristics. There were a limited number of points on which

they concentrated their efforts, and, in most cases, each point of attack had been developed by a repetitive use of certain allegations and slogans.

There were two principal aspects of the Muscle Shoals offer—fertilizer and water power. By March, 1923, Ford unquestionably held a commanding lead over his combined opposition in both of these categories as far as public opinion was concerned. For a number of reasons the supporters of the Ford offer concentrated their publicity efforts on the fertilizer aspect, perhaps the most important being that the proposal did not specifically provide for any general distribution of power. Moreover, the Ford group believed that farmers were more desirous of obtaining cheap fertilizer than electric power. In addition, the National Defense Act specifically had provided for production of fertilizer at Muscle Shoals during peacetime.

One of the principal objectives of the Ford group, with respect to fertilizer, was to convince the farmer that he was the victim of a "fertilizer trust" which had routed all competition within the fertilizer industry, paving the way for monopolistic prices. Pro-Ford congressmen were joined by the Farm Bureau and the pro-Ford press in the battle against the alleged "fertilizer trust." Senator Norris, as well as officials of the National Fertilizer Association, denied the validity of the "fertilizer trust" charges. Norris asserted that no evidence that such a combination existed had been presented to Congress. In May, 1922, at the Senate hearings on Muscle Shoals, a representative of the Federal Trade Commission testified that there was no "fertilizer trust." [1]

Along with the drive to convince the farmer that the fertilizer industry was dominated by monopoly, the proponents of the Ford offer promoted the idea that operation of Muscle Shoals by Ford would result in a drastic reduction of fertilizer prices. Many of his supporters claimed he would cut prices by one-half, and this became the standard figure used by Ford partisans to indicate

1. See Cong. Rec., 67 Cong., 2 Sess., 1642–43, 1750, 2687, 3631, 8771–72, 8895, 8900, 9343, 9353, 13179; Muscle Shoals, Hearings, U.S. Senate, 67 Cong., 2 Sess., 671–88, 741–76; Nitrate, Hearings, U.S. House of Representatives, 67 Cong., 4 Sess., 8, 13, 25.

the extent of price reduction that would result from acceptance of Ford's offer. The Ford opposition, particularly the Progressive Republicans, protested that many farmers were being led to believe that the Ford offer actually contained a provision guaranteeing a reduction of fertilizer prices by one-half.[2]

Since the Ford offer provided for use of the cyanamid-equipped nitrate plant no. 2 only and in view of the fact that the opposition claimed the Haber process to be the only economically possible method, it became necessary for the Ford adherents to prove the superiority of the cyanamid process. In this argument, scientists became politicians and politicians became scientists. The argument soon lost all reality and merged into a world of pseudo-science where the elements and compounds were identified by political rather than physical characteristics. Each side averred that its favorite process was outdistancing the other in American and European industry.

At the conclusion of the hearings on Muscle Shoals in 1922, Norris concluded that the consensus of experts indicated that the cyanamid process was obsolete and that any further developments in nitrogen fixation would come through the Haber process. Norris insisted that the government should engage in sufficient research to ascertain the most efficient method of production, but Senator Underwood contended that there already had been too much research on the problem. He declared that it would be unwise to devote funds to such a purpose when the government already possessed an up-to-date plant like nitrate plant no. 2.[3]

There was some disagreement among Ford partisans themselves with respect to fertilizer processes. Not everyone in that group had faith in the cyanamid process. The leading advocate of the Haber process among Ford supporters was Thomas A. Edison. Representative W. Frank James of Michigan, an ardent sup-

2. See *Cong. Rec.*, 67 Cong., 2 Sess., 3654, 3658–59, 3700, 8895–98, 9343–49; *ibid.*, 67 Cong., 4 Sess., 172–76, 491, 1859, 3298; *Muscle Shoals*, Senate Hearings, 67 Cong., 2 Sess., 20; *Muscle Shoals Propositions*, House Report 1084, 67 Cong., 2 Sess., 49; New York *Times*, June 18, 1922; "Editorial Views on the Ford Offer," in *Congressional Digest*, II (Oct., 1922), 22.

3. See *Cong. Rec.*, 67 Cong., 2 Sess., 3658–59, 8900; *ibid.*, 67 Cong., 4 Sess., 1859, 3297–3300.

porter of the Ford offer, admitted in early 1923 that he believed
the cyanamid process was obsolete. James attempted to capitalize
on his admission by declaring that the federal government was
fortunate in being able to sell an obsolete plant to Ford.[4]

The claim of William B. Mayo, Ford's chief engineer, at the
Muscle Shoals hearings before the Norris committee in 1922 that
Ford possessed a "secret process" gave the Ford group an important argument. In particular, most Ford partisans who had
never approved the cyanamid process relied on this claim in their
attempts to justify the fertilizer provisions of the Ford offer. In
early 1923 Senator Edwin F. Ladd utilized the claim of a "secret
process" as a means of attacking Norris's proposal to appropriate
funds for research with the view of ascertaining the most appropriate nitrogen-fixation method. According to Ladd, who hinted
that he was familiar with the chemical composition of Ford's
"secret process," there was no need for further research because
the new Ford process would solve the nitrate problem.[5] Norris
described the "secret process" as Ford "propaganda." He said:

If we will credit him with the ordinary amount of the milk of human
kindness that there is in the heart of any honest citizen, we certainly
will not say that he has a secret process by which he can cheapen the
cost of fertilizer and that he will not divulge it for the American farmer
unless he is given Muscle Shoals. . . .

.   .   .   .

. . . we will not ascribe to Mr. Ford such unphilanthropic principles
as those. We will not charge Mr. Ford . . . with considering the poor
farmer so little, that he will carry in his brain a secret process by
which he can cheapen fertilizer and not give the farmer the benefit of
it unless we pay him a bonus from the treasury of the . . . United
States.[6]

The Ford adherents maintained that Ford's principal motive
for acquiring Muscle Shoals was his philanthropic desire to
produce cheap fertilizer for farmers, while the opposition insisted that Ford was deliberately exploiting the cheap fertilizer
theme in order to gain control of the vast water-power resources

4. *Ibid.*, 1859, 4314; *Muscle Shoals*, Senate Hearings, 67 Cong., 2 Sess., 703.
5. *Cong. Rec.*, 67 Cong., 4 Sess., 1859, 3254.
6. *Ibid.*, 3307.

at Muscle Shoals after which he would likely curtail sharply or drop entirely the manufacture of fertilizer. Thus the nature of the obligations and guarantees embodied in the Ford offer became exceedingly important. Most Ford supporters interpreted the offer as guaranteeing the production of commercial fertilizer in annual quantities not less than the full capacity of nitrate plant no. 2. According to the Ford supporters, the alleged fertilizer guarantee in the offer was actually written by representatives of the leading farm organizations. The opposition maintained that the fertilizer provisions, particularly the clause permitting suspension of fertilizer production for causes beyond control of the corporation, offered Ford easily accessible loopholes through which to abandon his fertilizer obligations in case he failed to realize a profit on the fertilizer operations.[7]

The provision of the Ford offer limiting profits on fertilizer to 8 per cent above costs were greatly publicized by the Ford group as evidence of Ford's philanthropic motives. Nevertheless, no accounting procedure for determining the costs of fertilizer production was outlined in the offer, giving substance to charges by the opposition that Ford could, through various bookkeeping devices, manipulate the costs and profits as he chose. Ford's defenders pointed out the provisions in the offer which apparently gave some farm representatives the right to examine the fertilizer accounts, but any complaint by this farm group could be heard only in the federal district court which embraced the Muscle Shoals area.[8]

In general the Ford supporters did not stress the monetary return which the government would realize from the Ford offer, although Arthur Brisbane, noted Hearst writer, declared that "once in its life the government would get some real money for a war investment." [9] Instead, Ford advocates emphasized the alleged value of the Ford offer as an instrument of economic

7. *Ibid.*, 67 Cong., 2 Sess., 9348, 12117; *ibid.*, 67 Cong., 4 Sess., 1858, 1860, 3306–7, 5175–79; *Muscle Shoals,* Senate Hearings, 67 Cong., 2 Sess., 748.

8. *Cong. Rec.*, 67 Cong., 4 Sess., 1861; Jerome C. Kerwin, *Federal Water-Power Legislation* (1926), 278.

9. "Henry Ford's Bid for Muscle Shoals," in *Literary Digest*, LXXII (Jan. 28, 1922), 10.

reclamation of the South and as a pattern for the economic development of the nation as a whole. It was even suggested by the Ford group that the nation would benefit by giving the entire Muscle Shoals properties to Ford without any compensation to the government. Nevertheless, Ford's opponents, particularly Norris, attempted to show that the Ford offer proposed to relinquish tremendously valuable properties to Ford for a very scant consideration. Norris described Ford's proffered payments as a "mere bagatelle." Ford's supporters countered with the claim that these payments would compare favorably with the amounts received by the government in salvaging other war projects.[10]

Ford's admirers hailed his amortization plan for Muscle Shoals as an ingenious arrangement which would result in breaking the shackles of Wall Street from America's water-power resources. According to their calculations, the annual amortization payments of some $46,000 by Ford would, at the end of the lease period, reach a total sum in excess of the entire cost of the two dams at Muscle Shoals. They arrived at this conclusion by compounding the Ford payments, which were to be paid in six-month installments, semi-annually at 4 per cent interest.[11]

On the other hand, Ford's opponents united in agreeing that Ford's amortization plan amounted to little more than a government subsidy. These critics pointed out that the amortization plan in reality meant that Ford would pay an interest but no principal for the use of government funds in completing the dams. The Ford opponents protested that he was proposing to extinguish a debt of some $50,000,000 by actually paying only about $4,500,000. In addition, there was the original $17,000,000 investment at Wilson Dam on which Ford did not contemplate amortization payments.[12]

10. *Cong. Rec.*, 67 Cong., 2 Sess., 2768, 8900; *ibid.*, 67 Cong., 4 Sess., 2114–15, 4057, 4315, 5174; Chattanooga *News,* Dec. 6, 1921.

11. *Cong. Rec.*, 67 Cong., 2 Sess., 2769, 9352, 12116.

12. *Ibid.*, 1091, 8901–2, 9347; *ibid.*, 67 Cong., 4 Sess., 495, 4056. Oscar C. Merrill, executive secretary of the Federal Power Commission, stated that Ford's amortization plan was "only good if the United States goes into the money loaning business, because the fund can accumulate the interest only if the United States takes these payments every six months, as they come, and finds somebody who will bank them—pay 4 per cent interest compounded semi-annually for 100 years

It was stated by some Ford supporters that he planned, in conjunction with his contemplated Muscle Shoals industrial center, a unified power-navigational development of the entire Tennessee River system. J. W. Worthington, who was personally close to Ford during this period, informed the Senate Agriculture Committee in May, 1922, that "Mr. Ford has stated that he felt a river ought to be taken up as a whole and completed in its entirety" and that Ford intended "to make Muscle Shoals and the Tennessee River an example of what our power resources on our rivers will do for the people of this country." [13] W. B. Mayo, Ford's chief engineer, also told this committee at about the same time that "Mr. Ford assumes if he gets the project and he creates a demand for the greater part of this power, he will then turn his attention toward other reservoirs to increase his primary power." [14] Senator Ladd hinted that he had knowledge of a Ford plan for full development of the Tennessee River. No concrete evidence was uncovered that would substantiate these intimations. Senator Norris challenged the Ford group to point to any provision of the Ford offer or any official statement by Ford that indicated a unified development of the river. The challenge was not accepted.[15]

Prominent pro-Ford businessmen and congressmen from the Tennessee Valley emphasized the alleged navigational benefits which would result from approval of the Ford offer. They professed to see in the Ford offer the opening of the Tennessee to navigation all the way from Knoxville to the Ohio. It was even hinted that Ford intended to connect the Warrior River in Alabama with the Tennessee. Thus the great agricultural and mineral wealth of the Tennesse Valley would become accessible to cheap navigation.[16]

and turn it back principal and interest." *Muscle Shoals,* Senate Hearings, 67 Cong., 2 Sess., 637–38.

Ford's critics asserted that his proposed payments for maintenance of the Muscle Shoals dams were insufficient while his supporters declared them to be unduly generous. *Cong. Rec.,* 67 Cong., 2 Sess., 8903, 12116; *ibid.,* 67 Cong., 4 Sess., 495.

13. *Muscle Shoals,* Senate Hearings, 67 Cong., 2 Sess., 321–22.
14. *Ibid.,* 282.
15. *Cong. Rec.,* 67 Cong., 4 Sess., 738, 743, 3255.
16. *Ibid.,* 67 Cong., 2 Sess., 2770, 9346, 9349.

Although there was no provision in the Ford offer for general distribution of power, many defenders of the offer held that one of Ford's primary aims was to provide cheap electric power to the South. The opposition of the southern power companies was cited as proof of the validity of this contention, fear of competition being assigned as the ulterior motive behind the Alabama Power Company's offer. Ford's supporters also asserted that acceptance of the Ford offer would be the first step in the creation of a nationwide network of cheap electric service which Ford had planned for the country.[17] Nevertheless, there was a great deal of contradiction and confusion within the Ford camp as to the nature of Ford's ultimate plans regarding possible distribution of Muscle Shoals power. W. B. Mayo testified before the Senate Agriculture Committee in May, 1922, that ultimately Ford intended to absorb all Muscle Shoals power in industrial enterprises at Muscle Shoals. In early 1923 Gray Silver told a House committee on two different occasions that Ford would utilize all of the power at Muscle Shoals in fertilizer and chemical industries. Yet at the same time Silver was distributing literature to Farm Bureau members which boldly proclaimed that in the event of acceptance of the Ford offer, Ford would furnish the farmers with cheap power in order to relieve farm families from laborious farm and household tasks.[18] Senator Norris protested that Muscle Shoals real estate speculators were engaged in directing propaganda toward the rural areas to the effect that approval of the Ford offer would mean cheap power to relieve farm wives of their drudgery. The Nebraska Senator declared that acceptance of this offer meant that "not a single washerwoman will get a kilowatt of power."[19]

17. *Ibid.*, 8903, 12117–18; *ibid.*, 67 Cong., 4 Sess., 494. James E. Smith, an official of the Mississippi Valley Association, busily propagated the idea that Ford intended to distribute cheap Muscle Shoals power throughout the Mississippi Valley. *Ibid.*, 8903.

The Memphis *Commercial-Appeal* announced authoritatively that Ford intended to furnish 300,000 horsepower of Muscle Shoals power for distribution in North Alabama, West Tennessee, North Mississippi, and "elsewhere." Memphis *Commercial-Appeal*, June 4, 1922.

18. *Muscle Shoals*, Senate Hearings, 67 Cong., 2 Sess., 281, 299; *Nitrate*, Hearings, U. S. House of Representatives, Series HH, 1st Supplement, 67 Cong., 4 Sess., 131, 147; *ibid.*, 2nd Supplement, 29, 31.

19. *Cong. Rec.*, 67 Cong., 2 Sess., 8903.

During the period of the Sixty-seventh Congress and the interim following the adjournment on March 4, 1923, the fertilizer and power aspects of the Ford offer controversy were overshadowed at various times by the proposed development of a gigantic industrial center at Muscle Shoals. The intense excitement that pulsated through the Tennessee Valley and adjacent areas following Ford's spectacular promise in January, 1922, to build a huge metropolis at Muscle Shoals was further stimulated in the succeeding months by various incidents which pointed to a vast industrial expansion in that area. In March, 1922, Dr. Robert Calvert, a University of California chemist, predicted that Ford's proposed nitrogen-fixation development and related chemical industries at Muscle Shoals would become one of the largest industrial units in the nation. The following June, Walter Glaesner, an executive of a large chemical firm, proclaimed the glad tidings that potash could be extracted from feldspar in the Muscle Shoals area sufficiently inexpensively to permit competition with the German product. This information appeared to confirm the testimony of Thomas A. Edison a month earlier when he revealed to a Senate committee that he had been experimenting with the extraction of potash from southern feldspar and that very favorable results had given him great hope that America would soon be able to compete with Germany in potash production. Within the next few months pro-Ford congressmen strengthened the country's belief in the potash story and added the exploitation of nearby phospate and bauxite deposits as being among Ford's aims at Muscle Shoals. It was stated that Ford intended to improve the country's transportation industry by producing aluminum parts for automobiles, tractors, and railway cars while at the same time providing competition for the Mellon aluminum monopoly.[20]

According to a sensational news item in December, 1922, Ford's principal purpose in seeking control of Muscle Shoals was to process the mineral alunite from which enormous quantities of aluminum and other products would be obtained. There were

20. New York *Times*, March 5 (VII), 1922; *Muscle Shoals*, Senate Hearings, 67 Cong., 2 Sess., 775–87; *Cong. Rec.*, 67 Cong., 2 Sess., 9345, 12117.

other stories related by the press and the pro-Ford group that
Ford intended to electrify all railroads in the Muscle Shoals area,
that he intended to curb the steel "trust" through the use of
electric furnaces at Muscle Shoals, and that the International
Harvester Company feared possible competition from Ford's
proposed project at Muscle Shoals. In addition, Ford's promise
of a new Detroit seemed near to fruition when it was authoritatively reported in September, 1922, that he had developed the
idea for a great model city before he had contemplated making
a bid for Muscle Shoals, that area being selected because it
fulfilled the qualifications desired by Ford.[21]

Both Norris and the Harding administration protested that the
Ford partisans, in order to gain support for the Ford offer, were
attempting to exploit the alarm and distress caused by increasing
unemployment during 1922. The Alabama delegation in Congress
led all others in this respect. Senator Heflin assured his colleagues
that Ford would hire 100,000 men within ten days after acceptance of the Ford offer. Representative Almon stated that Ford
would eventually employ 1,000,000 men at Muscle Shoals, affecting the lives of 5,000,000 people.[22] Ford himself stated that on
the basis of past experience he believed that he could furnish
employment for 1,000,000 men at Muscle Shoals.[23]

In view of the indefinite and seemingly confused language of
the Ford offer, as well as its apparent inconsistencies and omis-
sions, the Ford partisans felt it necessary to direct public attention
toward the personality of Ford himself rather than to the provisions of his offer. Fortunately for the pro-Ford leaders, the masses
appeared to have a resolute faith in Ford. This faith served the
Ford offer in two ways: first, there were those who believed that
Ford's verbal statements, which he had delivered from time to
time, provided sufficient guarantee for performance of contract;
second, there were those who believed the offer contained rigid

21. *Ibid.*, 9354; *ibid.*, 67 Cong., 4 Sess., 3205; New York *Times*, Dec. 31 (VIII),
1922, Jan. 18, 1924; "Why Henry Ford Wants the Muscle Shoals Property," in
Current Opinion, LXXII (Feb., 1922), 262–4; Littel McClung, "The Seventy-
Five Mile City," in *Scientific American*, CXXVII (Sept., 1922), 156.

22. *Cong. Rec.*, 67 Cong., 2 Sess., 3658, 3661, 8635, 9346, 9353.

23. Nashville *Banner*, Feb. 21, 1922.

and absolute guarantees simply because Ford had not denied such assertions by pro-Ford leaders. Norris, protesting bitterly, placed the majority of the Ford supporters in the latter category. Nevertheless, it was evident that the former class was quite large.[24]

In commenting on the faith of the people in Ford, Representative George Huddleston of Alabama said:

> The people of Alabama trust Henry Ford. They believe in him. . . . He is no ruthless dollar grabber. He holds to honorable competition and not to monopoly gained through corrupt methods and oppressive practices. He does not grind the face of labor and take advantage of every extremity to extort the greatest possible amount of toil for the least possible return. He is not an oppressor of the poor. He has some higher ideal than the worship of the dollar made god.[25]

Representative Clarence W. Turner of Tennessee attested that

> The masses have faith in Henry Ford and believe that should he acquire this property he will in a reasonable time be giving the farmers all the fertilizer they need at one-half the price they have paid heretofore; that he will employ thousands of laborers at remunerative wages; that he will build factories, furnaces, and railroads to develop the latent resources . . . [of the Tennessee Valley].[26]

Many Ford partisans in and out of Congress professed their faith in Ford. Petitions and resolutions adopted by pro-Ford groups contained expressions of faith in him. In some quarters it was said that their faith was based primarily on Ford's business acumen or his reputation as an anti-monopolist. In others it was said to have been created by Ford's reputation for honesty and integrity, and still others attributed it to his intense patriotism.[27] Charles S. Barrett, president of the National Farmers' Union, stated in March, 1922, that he believed that 98 per cent of the people of the South, if not the entire nation, had sufficient faith in Ford's honesty and ability to accept his offer without further guarantee.[28]

---

24. *Cong. Rec.*, 67 Cong., 2 Sess., 3660; Judson C. Welliver, "The Muscle Shoals Power and Industrial Project," in *American Review of Reviews*, LXV (April, 1922), 384–85.
25. *Cong. Rec.*, 67 Cong., 2 Sess., 2979.
26. *Ibid.*, 67 Cong., 4 Sess., 1541.
27. *Ibid.*, 67 Cong., 2 Sess., 9341, 9354, 9845, 12587.
28. *Ibid.*, 4111.

Pro-Ford leaders in the Sixty-seventh Congress attempted to establish for Ford certain *a priori* rights which, they felt, would virtually stop the opposition from criticizing the Ford offer. First, there was the assertion that Ford had special rights to Muscle Shoals because he had first recognized its value and saved it from being scrapped. It was said that Ford, by tendering his offer, broke up a plot between the Harding administration and the Alabama Power Company to deliver Muscle Shoals to the latter for little or no consideration. The Ford adherents claimed that since the government invited Ford to make an offer in the first place, there was a particularly heavy obligation on the government to aid him in acquiring it. Furthermore, there was the assertion that Ford's bid should be accepted because it was not a business proposition but an act of charity on the part of Ford. Lastly, the Ford group formulated a major premise that the Ford offer was superior to all other bids—consequently, the burden of proof was upon Ford's opponents who were challenged to "produce a better proposition." [29]

Supporters of Ford's bid exerted a great amount of overt pressure on the Sixty-seventh Congress in an attempt to force acceptance of the offer. On the other hand, pressure on Congress from the opposition groups was much less in evidence, though Secretary Weeks attempted to influence Congress in behalf of the Alabama Power Company. One of the chief sources of pro-Ford pressure on Congress during this period was that generated in rural areas by the Farm Bureau and other farm organizations. There were, in addition, many attempts by various other organizations and groups to influence Congress in behalf of Ford, particularly in the South. Several state legislatures, mostly southern, addressed resolutions to Congress endorsing Ford's bid.[30] Another instrument of pressure was the mass meeting. Huge crowds gathered at various cities in the South to rally support behind

29. *Ibid.*, 2769, 8899; *ibid.*, 67 Cong., 4 Sess., 87, 737, 744, 2029, 3306.

30. *Ibid.*, 67 Cong., 2 Sess., 10291; New York *Times,* Jan. 6, 16, 1922, Jan. 17, 1923. Interestingly enough, the state legislature of Nebraska, in an apparent attempt to bring pressure to bear on Senator Norris, urged Congress to accept the Ford offer. Norris refused to budge from his opposition to the Ford plan. *Cong. Rec.,* 67 Cong., 2 Sess., 4056.

Ford and to memorialize Congress to accept his offer. Congress received pro-Ford petitions from industrial promotion associations, and civic and business clubs.[31] Labor and service organizations also aided the Ford cause. At the annual convention of the American Federation of Labor in 1922, that organization's Washington representatives were instructed to direct their efforts toward securing approval of the Ford offer. The Maine State Federation of Labor and various locals throughout the nation urged Congress to accede to Ford's Muscle Shoals plan. The legislative committee of the American Legion adopted a resolution in 1922 which was tantamount to an approval of Ford's bid and numerous local Legion posts endorsed it. Ford himself appealed directly to ex-servicemen to support his offer by announcing in early 1922 that this group would be given preference in employment at Muscle Shoals.[32] In addition, many public officials and private citizens, especially Southerners, wrote letters and signed petitions to Congress imploring that body to look with favor on the Ford offer.[33]

Religion was utilized in the fight for acceptance of the Ford offer. The Reverend George Stanley, general secretary of Methodist Men's Clubs and pastor of the First Methodist Church of Sheffield, Alabama, issued an appeal in December, 1921, for all Christians to come to the support of the Ford offer in the name of humanitarianism and in the interest of the unemployed. This message, which was widely distributed to the secular and religious press as well as to members of Congress, carried with it endorsements of the Ford offer by prominent educators and clergymen.[34]

There is little evidence of any attempt by the Ford group to organize Negroes. In January, 1923, however, the Annual Conference of Negro Farmers, consisting of delegates from all southern states, endorsed the Ford offer for the stated reason that

31. *Cong. Rec.*, 67 Cong., 2 Sess., 3705, 4111, 6093, 8193, 8890–93.

32. *Ibid.*, 1983, 3373, 3705, 4111, 4537; *ibid.*, 67 Cong., 4 Sess., 1840–41; New York *Times*, June 21, 1922.

33. *Cong. Rec.*, 67 Cong., 2 Sess., 1857, 3705–7, 4111, 12587.

34. J. Thomas Heflin to William E. Borah, April 3, 1922, Borah Papers; Associated Press dispatch, Dec. 29, 1921, Correspondence of the Secretary of Agriculture, Muscle Shoals, National Archives.

it would provide cheap fertilizer for the Negroes' cotton crops.[35]

Thus stood the Ford offer in the summer of 1923. The proposal had suffered some reverses, but its supporters hoped to carry it to victory in the Sixty-eighth Congress.

Meanwhile, the Gorgas steam plant controversy continued lethargically in Congress throughout the summer of 1922 and subsided almost to the point of disappearance in the latter stages of the Sixty-seventh Congress.[36] It appeared, by the summer of 1923, that the Gorgas problem was a dead issue and no longer posed an obstacle to acceptance of the Ford offer. As later events proved, this appearance was deceptive.

President Harding died on August 2, 1923, and was succeeded by Calvin Coolidge. About one month later the issue of the Gorgas plant was precipitated anew by the Alabama Power Company, which served notice that the government must either sell the Gorgas plant to that company or vacate the company's properties by October 14, 1923. Ford hurried to Washington for a conference with Coolidge and Weeks in an attempt to checkmate this move. There Weeks warned Ford that the power company's threatened action in the Gorgas plant matter was legal, and both Coolidge and Weeks warned Ford voluntarily to eliminate the Gorgas properties from his offer. As an inducement to Ford, Coolidge and Weeks promised that the full amount of the Alabama Power Company's purchase price for the property would be credited to the purchase price offered by Ford for certain of the Muscle Shoals properties. Emerging from the conference, Ford announced that he had taken the Coolidge-Weeks counsel under advisement. A few days later, the Alabama Power Company announced that it had granted the government an extension of time in which to formulate a policy toward the Gorgas plant. It appeared at this juncture that the issue would be settled peacefully.[37] There was a widespread belief in the press at this time that the new administration stood ready to support the Ford

35. R. R. Moton to Martin B. Madden, Jan. 22, 1923, Papers of Calvin Coolidge.
36. *Cong. Rec.*, 67 Cong., 2 Sess., 8902, 9343–44, 12116–17.
37. New York *Times*, Sept. 7, 12, 1923.

offer if Ford would consent to the exclusion of the Gorgas properties from his offer.[38]

Within a few days, however, the Gorgas volcano erupted
again, pouring forth a stream of exceedingly acrid controversy.
As late as July, 1923, Major General Walter A. Bethel, the Judge
Advocate General, reaffirmed earlier decisions by the legal division of the Harding administration that the Alabama Power
Company's option on the Gorgas plant was null and void. Then on
September 14, 1923, a few weeks after the inauguration of
Coolidge as successor to Harding, Attorney General Daugherty,
who in 1922 had ruled the power company's option null and
void, reversed himself by declaring it to be valid. He declared
that the government must either sell the Gorgas properties to
the power company or remove them from the company's property.
Then on September 24 came the bombshell—Weeks sold the
Gorgas plant to the Alabama Power Company, the purchase price
being $2,472,000 while the property had originally cost $4,750,000.
The next day a spokesman for the President defended the transaction and stated that the receipts would be applied as credit to
the proposed purchase price in the Ford offer.[39]

The sale of the Gorgas plant produced a violent reaction among
the Ford supporters. Senator Edwin F. Ladd bitterly protested
directly to Weeks. Gray Silver, to whom the alleged necessity of
the Gorgas plant for the operation of the Muscle Shoals project
had been sacred dogma, accused Weeks of deliberately selling
the property at this time to forestall congressional action and
possibly incite Ford to withdraw his offer. This turn of events led
to consternation within the ranks of the Ford partisans in the
South. The Alabama Senate adopted a resolution urging Ford
to revise his offer to meet the new conditions. Rumors that Ford
was abandoning his offer flowed freely.[40] Much of the gloom

38. "Ford Politics in Muscle Shoals," in *Literary Digest*, LXXIX (Oct. 27,
1923), 15. *Electrical World* denied that the administration had any intention of
endorsing the Ford offer under any circumstances. "Officials not Backing Ford," in
Electrical World, LXXXII (Sept. 22, 1923), 618.

39. New York *Times*, Sept. 15, 25, 26, 1923.

40. New York *Times*, Sept. 26, 27, 1923; Ladd to Weeks, Sept. 18, 1923,
Records of the Office of Chief of Engineers, Alabama Power Company, Muscle
Shoals, National Archives.

was soon dispelled by W. J. Cameron, the editor of Ford's newspaper, the Dearborn *Independent,* who on September 26 brought
joy and hope again to the Ford faithful by advising them to be
"cautious in accepting reports that are based upon the desires of
exploiters." [41]

Ford himself announced on October 11 that his offer would
remain before Congress, but its status seemed confused since the
offer called for property which the government no longer possessed.[42] Instead of further clarifying the issue, Ford accompanied
his announcement with statements in which he launched one of
the most bitter and relentless attacks against Weeks that occurred
during the whole course of the Muscle Shoals controversy.
Ford said:

... I have a very strong conviction that, while we have been negotiating with Mr. Weeks, we have not been negotiating with the United
States Government. John W. Weeks's repeated assertions that Henry
Ford would never get Muscle Shoals, neither with the Gorgas plant
nor without it, is evidence that the parties to this matter are not the
bidder and the government, but other parties best known to the man
who is at present Secretary of War.

Long ago Mr. Weeks matured in his mind the plan to break up
Muscle Shoals and dispose of it piecemeal. When he sold the steam
plant at Gorgas he pulled the first stitch in unraveling the greatest
single prospect ever held out to the American farmer and manufacturer. ...

This plan was formed by John W. Weeks for the purpose, as he
thought, of injuring Henry Ford. Which shows how much a Boston
bond broker, in politics for a pastime, knows about industrial problems.

But the injury has shot past Henry Ford and has landed on the
farmers. I was willing to demonstrate at Muscle Shoals that power and
fertilizer could be produced at much lower cost than now, and that
the Government could be assured an adequate supply of war nitrates.
...

The Ford Motor Company has never needed Muscle Shoals. ... The
only thing I could do at Muscle Shoals which I am not able to do
elsewhere would be to make fertilizer for the farmer. And that is the
sole reason why John W. Weeks and scores of corporation lawyers have

    41. Chattanooga *News,* Sept. 26, 1923.
    42. New York *Times,* Oct. 12, 1923; "Ford Politics in Muscle Shoals," *loc. cit.,*
15.

exerted their cunning to prevent me. The same influences that prevented a vote in the House last spring are responsible for the sale of the Gorgas plant to prevent a vote on Gorgas. . . .

It would be well worth while for the water power and fertilizer financiers who control this situation to pay $100,000,000 if thereby they can retain the endless millions which they now make through exorbitant prices of power and fertilizer. The demonstration which we could make at Muscle Shoals would be a death blow to all such exploitation.

My offer is still before Congress. I shall not withdraw it. . . .

It is not to me that John W. Weeks has anything to explain. I know how much value to attach to his explanations. Let him explain to the farmers.[43]

Ford also took notice of critics who had been attacking the water-power policy embodied in his offer, and promised that if his offer were accepted he would "run power lines 200 miles in every direction from Muscle Shoals." [44]

Secretary Weeks was highly provoked by Ford's attack. He retorted that he would lay the facts in the case before the "proper tribunal." The next day, when his anger had subsided somewhat, he denied that he had any intention of bringing a libel suit against Ford, as his remark was generally interpreted, but identified the "proper tribunal" as being Congress. In his reply to Ford, Weeks denied that he had opposed the Ford offer for any reason other than the lack of a sufficient guarantee of fertilizer production. He interpreted Ford's announcement that his offer was still before Congress as admitting that the Gorgas plant was not necessary to the operation of Muscle Shoals. Indirectly, Secretary Weeks accused Ford of duping the farmers through a promise of cheap fertilizer.[45]

Soon after Ford's quarrel with Weeks, Senator Ladd came to the aid of the automobile manufacturer with a threat that the forthcoming Sixty-eighth Congress would conduct an investigation of the government's wartime contract with the Alabama Power Company. He declared that the sale of the Gorgas plant by Secretary Weeks appeared to be a "feverish effort" to put the

43. New York *Times,* Oct. 12, 1923.
44. *Ibid.*
45. *Ibid.,* Oct. 13, 14, 1923.

property in possession of the power company before Congress would have an opportunity to prevent it.[46]

In his reply to Ford, Secretary Weeks charged that the Ford attack on him was, in reality, a manifestation of Ford's presidential aspirations.[47] From all indications it appeared that Ford was a strong presidential darkhorse at this time. He had been mentioned from time to time since 1916 as a possible presidential candidate, but such talk consisted of mere gestures for the most part. The serious Ford-for-President movement began in May, 1922, when the Ford Muscle Shoals offer was being considered by two congressional committees.[48] Whether the timing of the movement was coincidental is not clear. The first Ford-for-President club was organized by Ford's friends at Dearborn on May 23, and it was announced that this club was to be the nucleus of a nationwide organization composed of similar clubs to be organized in every congressional district in the nation.

The movement grew apace. The Ford clubs began to spring up around the country. Photographs and biographies of Ford were sent out by the Ford Motor Company to dealers throughout the nation for distribution. In May, 1923, William Randolph Hearst announced his support of Ford for President and threw the influence of the Hearst papers behind the Ford presidential campaign. Some prominent politicians from both major parties declared that Ford possessed great political strength. With the exception of a few southern Democrats, however, they did not believe that the automobile magnate was likely to win the Presidency because they did not think that he could obtain the nomination of either major party.

Ford's radical economic theories and attacks on Wall Street gave rise to predictions that he would be the standard bearer of the La Follette Progressives in a third party. La Follette himself

46. *Ibid.*, Oct. 18, 1923.

47. *Ibid.*, Oct. 13, 1923.

48. For the highlights of the Ford-for-President movement prior to the Ford-Weeks dispute of October, 1923, see the New York *Times*, May 24, 30; June 25 (VII); July 31; Aug. 21; Nov. 29, 1922; Jan. 7 (VIII), 24; March 2, 17; April 9; May 3, 15, 27, 28; June 12, 19, 21, 24, 27, 30; July 4, 8 (VII), 21, 28; Aug. 1; Sept. 12, 21; Oct. 12, 1923.

admitted that Ford had great strength among the Progressives. Without doubt the Ford presidential boom was a source of serious concern to both major parties, particularly the Republicans. There was evidence of widespread grassroots support for Ford in the Middle West, Far West, and South.

Ford never positively stated whether he was a presidential candidate, and he disclaimed any official connection with the Ford-for-President clubs. Yet, his statements in respect to this matter, together with assurances from close friends and high-ranking officials of the Ford Motor Company that he was seriously considering a race for the Presidency, gave the implication and led his followers to believe that he looked with favor on the Ford-for-President movement. Furthermore, his failure to have his name removed from the ballot of the Nebraska Progressive party in the Nebraska presidential preferential primary in early October, 1923, was interpreted in most quarters as meaning a silent approval of such political efforts in his behalf.

In short, by October, 1923, it was taken for granted in most Washington political circles that Ford was definitely a presidential candidate. In fact, Ford's slashing attack on Weeks was believed to be, in reality, an attempt to embarrass the Coolidge administration politically, the Secretary of War merely serving as a convenient target. It was reported that Coolidge placed that interpretation upon the Ford-Weeks episode.[49] Many newspaper editors and correspondents around the country agreed that the Gorgas dispute had precipitated a first-class political issue, and there was a widespread belief in this group that Ford's attack on Weeks indicated that he had definitely decided to run for President. Several editors suggested that the combination of Muscle Shoals and cheap fertilizer would make a potent national political issue with Ford playing the role of defender of the farmers against the villains of Wall Street.[50] On the other hand,

49. *Ibid.*, Oct. 13, 1923.
50. "Ford Politics in Muscle Shoals," *loc. cit.*, 14. The violent reaction to the sale of the Gorgas plant apparently caused Coolidge some concern, for on October 29 Weeks sent a message to the White House reassuring the President that the Gorgas plant was not necessary to the operation of Muscle Shoals. Weeks to C. B. Slemp, Oct. 29, 1923, Coolidge Papers.

the Chattanooga *News* interpreted Ford's attack on Weeks as a
successful effort to put the War Department and the Congress
"in a dilemma" with respect to public opinion in order to hasten
action on his offer.[51]

By this time confidence was so strong among the Ford-for-
President leaders that on October 23 a conference of all Ford
clubs was scheduled to be held in Dearborn on the following
December 12 in order to chart a more definite course for the
campaign of 1924. The proclamation announcing the Dearborn
conference vibrated with a rather radical tone. The leadership
of both major parties was characterized as being the servant of
special interests and America was said to be "fast declining into
a land of exploiters and exploited." Ford was extolled as the only
man who possessed the "vision and courage" safely to lead the
American people. Ford refused to comment with respect to the
forthcoming conference, but instead launched another attack
against Wall Street and the international bankers. His remarks
were accepted by his followers as conclusive proof that he was
a candidate.[52]

Meanwhile, congressional supporters of the Ford offer began
to meet in Washington under the leadership of Representative
Byrns of Tennessee to attempt to solve the problem created by the
sale of the Gorgas plant. By November 5 a new plan was formulated which provided for governmental construction of a new
steam plant to replace the Gorgas plant in the Ford offer. In late
November, after conferences with President Coolidge, who was
said to be in harmony with the new plan, Representative Madden
drafted a bill, embodying the new plan, to be presented to the
Congress in December.[53]

On December 3, Ford conferred with President Coolidge regarding the plan to duplicate the Gorgas plant. What transpired
at the conference was not revealed. On the next day Ford was
badly beaten in presidential preference contests in both the
Democratic and Farm-Labor conventions in South Dakota. The

51. Chattanooga *News*, Oct. 12, 1923.
52. New York *Times*, Oct. 24, 26, 28 (IX), Nov. 21, 25, 26, 1923.
53. *Ibid.*, Nov. 5, 6, 18, 24, 1923.

Ford cause there was greatly hampered by the vagaries of local politics, but, nevertheless, the loss was a heavy blow to the Ford cause nationally. Two days later Ford himself cancelled the scheduled Dearborn Ford-for-President conference, although it was denied by Ford-for-President leaders that the reversal suffered in South Dakota was the cause of this action. On the same day, December 6, President Coolidge, in his first message to Congress, outlined a plan for Muscle Shoals which, as was suggested in some quarters, could conceivably have fitted the new Ford offer bill drafted by Representative Madden. The President recommended that the Muscle Shoals property "with a location for auxiliary steam plant and right of way be sold." He also advised that a joint committee be established to conduct negotiations with Muscle Shoals bidders.[54]

On December 16, George Fort Milton, Jr., Chattanooga newspaperman, reported that "there is a strong intimation that the present Congress will be told by the leaders to accept Ford's offer as the best way to eliminate him as an aspirant for the presidential nomination." Milton pointed out that Claudius H. Huston, an associate of J. W. Worthington in promoting the development of the Muscle Shoals area and a close friend of Ford, was now chairman of the Ways and Means Committee of the Republican National Committee, a position which would enable him to exert pressure on the administration to support the Ford offer.[55]

Three days later, December 19, Ford issued the death warrant for the Ford-for-President movement—he declared himself to be emphatically and unconditionally in support of President Coolidge for re-election. He flatly stated that he would not run on any ticket against President Coolidge. On the same day the President dispatched a message of thanks to Ford for his support. Administration Republicans were overjoyed by this turn of events. In some quarters, including some Ford-for-President workers, the immediate conclusion was that Ford had traded his endorsement of Coolidge in return for a promise of administration support of the

54. *Ibid.*, Dec. 4, 5, 6, 7.
55. *Ibid.*, Dec. 16 (VIII), 1923.

Ford offer.[56] In fact, Senator Hiram Johnson, in a statement to the press questioning Ford's motives in endorsing Coolidge, strongly implied a belief that Coolidge and Ford had reached such an agreement at their conference on December 3. Johnson pointed out that the recent presidential message to Congress was "not inimical" to the ideas expressed in the newly drafted Madden bill which provided for replacement of the Gorgas plant. Johnson expressed the belief that the Madden bill was an administration measure. He felt that Coolidge's tax-reduction proposals, which he described as being favorable to big business, also influenced Ford toward a better understanding with Coolidge. The New York Times, which strongly reprimanded Johnson and termed his speech a "political outrage," denied that there was any evidence of a Ford-Coolidge deal.[57] Administration leaders disclaimed any uneasiness as a result of Johnson's statements, asserting that Ford's endorsement of Coolidge was evidence of the decline of radicalism throughout the nation.[58]

The relationship between the Ford presidential boom and Muscle Shoals is not clear. As early as May, 1922, Benjamin C. Marsh, an official of the Farmers' National Council, asserted that Democrats in Congress were using the Muscle Shoals issue to groom Ford for the presidential candidacy on the Democratic ticket in 1924.[59] At the time of the Gorgas dispute in the early autumn of 1923, the consensus of the press was that Ford was utilizing Muscle Shoals, particularly the cheap fertilizer aspect of

56. Ibid., Dec. 20, 21, 1923. After Ford's endorsement of Coolidge, the Ford-for-President movement rapidly disintegrated. Robert M. Pointer, a Progressive and a leader of the movement, who was greatly disillusioned by Ford's action, angrily implied that the ill-fated movement had been initiated and nourished by E. G. Liebold, Ford's secretary, in order to promote the selfish interests of Ford. Ibid., Dec. 23, 1923, Jan. 5, 31, July 19, 1924.

57. Ibid., Dec. 23, 24, 1923. Garet Garrett, an admirer and biographer of Ford, declares that "there was no trade." Garrett bases his conclusion on a belief that Ford "was not a man to trade away his heart's desire." On the other hand, Upton Sinclair, a biographer but no admirer of Ford, assumes that the alleged Ford-Coolidge deal was negotiated at their conference on December 3, 1923. Garrett, The Wild Wheel (1952), 166–67; Sinclair, The Flivver King (1937), 131.

58. New York Times, Dec. 23, 1923. For the Norris investigation of the alleged Ford-Coolidge deal see Chapter V.

59. Muscle Shoals, Senate Hearings, 67 Cong., 2 Sess., 601–2.

it, to promote his presidential candidacy.[60] In November, 1923, Senator James Couzens of Michigan, a former business partner of Ford, stated that Ford was using the Muscle Shoals issue to augment his political popularity. On the other hand, Democratic leaders meeting at French Lick, Indiana, in November, 1923, were confronted with a report from a Democratic leader in Michigan to the effect that the Ford-for-President boom "was merely an adjunct to propaganda carried on by his agents with a view to obtaining him a long-term lease of Muscle Shoals." In the summer of 1923 it was reported that many Ford partisans in Tennessee believed the Ford-for-President movement was an attempt to insure the success of the Ford offer by putting Ford in the White House.[61] One of Ford's biographers concludes that whether Ford really desired to be President is debatable but that he "had his heart set" on acquiring Muscle Shoals.[62]

The Ford offer faced the first session of the Sixty-eighth Congress, which met in December, 1923, under auspicious circumstances. At the very beginning it was endorsed by an informal organization of some Southerners in Congress called the "cotton bloc." Furthermore, the growing popularity of the Ford offer in the South had completely welded southern congressmen into a solid pro-Ford bloc in which it was not enough to be merely a lukewarm advocate of the offer: in order to satisfy their constituents, most southern members of Congress assumed the pose of militant crusaders for the Ford bid. A feeling by Southerners that the lack of action on the Ford offer in the Sixty-seventh Congress was typical of Republican discrimination against the South and gross favoritism to the financial interests of the East had by this time elevated the Muscle Shoals issue in the South to a position of importance comparable to prohibition. Practically every candidate for public office in the South, from Congress to constable, felt it necessary to proclaim fervid support of the offer. It was reported that many candidates for Congress in the South were making it their sole issue.[63]

60. "Ford Politics in Muscle Shoals," *loc. cit.*, 14.
61. New York *Times*, July 6, Nov. 1, 16, 1923.
62. Garrett, *op. cit.*, 164.
63. New York *Times*, Dec. 2, 16 (VII), 1923.

There followed on December 19 the Ford-Coolidge reconciliation which appeared to portend a friendly attitude of the Coolidge administration toward the Ford offer. Representative Carroll Reece, newly elected Republican from Tennessee, expressed a belief on December 24 that barring the appearance of another offer with a stronger fertilizer guarantee, the administration would support the Ford offer.[64] *Electrical World* reported at this time that the administration was drafting a bill which that publication believed to be a compromise under which Muscle Shoals would be leased to Henry Ford under the terms of the Federal Water Power Act. The Chattanooga *News* observed a "much more marked friendliness in administration circles toward the Ford offer." [65] Senator McKellar attempted to create a more favorable environment for the Ford proposal in Congress by offering a resolution to authorize an investigation of the government's wartime contract with the Alabama Power Company.[66]

Despite the signs indicating possible administration support of the Ford offer in the Sixty-eighth Congress, Secretary Weeks did not appear to have relented in his opposition to the offer. The War Department announced early in December, 1923, that a new offer was in prospect which was as comprehensive in nature as the Ford offer. Weeks thereupon announced that he would recommend to Congress the acceptance of any reasonable offer from a responsible source containing a guarantee of production of nitrates and fertilizers as prescribed by the National Defense Act, the implication being that the Ford offer did not contain sufficient guarantees of fertilizer production.[67] Weeks was not alone in his continued opposition to the Ford offer. Oscar C. Merrill, the executive secretary of the Federal Power Commission, advised the Secretary of Agriculture at this time that the Ford offer should not be accepted unless it was revised to provide for public

64. *Ibid.*, Dec. 25, 1924.
65. "Bill Leasing Muscle Shoals to Ford Strongly Backed," in *Electrical World*, LXXXII (Dec. 22, 1923), 1284; Chattanooga *News*, Jan. 12, 1924.
66. *Cong. Rec.*, 68 Cong., 1 Sess., 93.
67. New York *Times*, Dec. 8, 1923.

distribution of water power under the Federal Water Power Act.[68]

Merrill already had begun negotiations with certain southern power companies several weeks before the Sixty-eighth Congress assembled. As a result of these negotiations, nine southern power companies, including the Alabama Power Company, submitted a joint bid for Muscle Shoals on January 15, 1924. The Associated Power Companies' bid provided for the leasing of the Wilson Dam and dam no. 3, if and when completed by the government, under the terms of the Federal Water Power Act. As consideration, the power companies agreed to annual rentals of $2,000,000 for Wilson Dam and not more than $1,200,000 for dam no. 3, the latter rental to be determined after construction of the dam. These rentals, however, represented a maximum which would not be reached for a number of years. In addition, the offer provided for the purchase of the steam plant at nitrate plant no. 2 for $4,500,000. The offer contained no provisions for fertilizer production.[69]

Representative Harry E. Hull of Iowa, who helped Merrill negotiate the power companies' offer, declared that since the offer did not provide for fertilizer production, there was "nothing in this plan which would debar Mr. Ford from carrying out his often expressed desire for doing something for the farmers by the manufacture of fertilizer at Muscle Shoals." Hull declared that a widespread distribution of Muscle Shoals power, which would be accomplished by acceptance of the bid of the power companies, would result in the growth of southern industry.[70]

The offer of the power companies was subjected to a heavy attack by southern Democrats in Congress who demanded quick action on the Ford offer. Representative Almon, who led the opposition to the power companies' bid, declared that it was concocted by the Alabama Power Company as a "smoke screen" to

68. Federal Power Commission, Memorandum for the Secretary of Agriculture, Nov. 30, 1923, Correspondence of the Secretary of Agriculture, Muscle Shoals, National Archives.

69. *Cong. Rec.*, 68 Cong., 1 Sess., 1228-30.

70. *Ibid.*, 813–15, 1229–30.

confuse and delay the Muscle Shoals issue now that it had become apparent that "the Ford offer will be accepted by this Congress." In the Senate, Senator McKellar led the attack on the power companies' offer. He repeated the charge that the Alabama Power Company, which he termed the principal bidder, was British-owned and warned his colleagues that the next American war might be with England.[71]

Meanwhile, President Coolidge, at the insistence of Secretary Weeks, authorized the Secretary of War to urge the passage by Congress of a bill creating a governmental agency or designating some person with authority to negotiate with bidders and deal with all other phases of the Muscle Shoals problem. Weeks did not make clear at this time the extent of authority desired for the proposed Muscle Shoals agency, but previously he had taken the stand that the problem should be taken entirely out of the hands of Congress.[72]

The failure of the power companies to provide for fertilizer production probably placed their offer at a disadvantage insofar as popular support was concerned. The National Defense Act as well as the debate on the Wadsworth-Kahn bill had undoubtedly established Muscle Shoals in the thinking of the public as primarily a fertilizer proposition—as an instrument to control fertilizer prices by the production of cheap fertilizer. In turn, Henry Ford based his offer—at least the publicity aspects of it— on this cheap-fertilizer concept. First Norris and later the power companies began to attempt to refute this cheap-fertilizer idea with the claim that Muscle Shoals would not afford any unusual cheapness in fertilizer production and that the project was primarily, from an economic standpoint, a water-power rather than a fertilizer proposition. Nevertheless, in early 1924, the cheap-fertilizer idea was dominant and consequently the power companies' offer appeared to violate public policy.[73] To counter-act the adverse public opinion, the power companies, on January 24, 1924, added to their offer provisions for producing fertilizer.

71. *Ibid.*, 825, 921.
72. New York *Times*, Jan. 11, 12, 1924.
73. Chattanooga *News*, Jan. 12, 1924.

The revised offer provided for an initial production of fertilizer containing 5,000 tons of nitrogen to be increased to 50,000 tons "as there may be a commercial demand therefor." This constituted a less definite and rigid guarantee than that contained in the Ford offer. As in the Ford offer fertilizer profits were limited to 8 per cent. The power companies also provided that the fertilizer would be produced in a new plant in which the Haber process would be installed.[74]

The power companies' revised offer was followed by a bid by the Union Carbide Company for lease of the nitrate plants at Muscle Shoals. Apparently this company contemplated operating the nitrate plants in an agreement with the power companies. As a consideration for the production annually of 100,000 tons of fertilizer, containing 20 per cent nitrogen, the carbide company proposed that it would acquire for its own use 50,000 horsepower of Muscle Shoals power at a very low rate. Secretary Weeks passed the offer on to Congress without comment.[75]

On the eve of the beginning of hearings on the Muscle Shoals problem in the Sixty-eighth Congress, Henry Ford, at the insistence of Gray Silver, notified Congress that his offer still stood, and he still insisted that it must be accepted in full. He again declared that patriotic motives were the only reason for his desire to acquire Muscle Shoals. At this time, Gray Silver declared that never before had there been such a powerful combination of special interests as that which had banded together to defeat acceptance of the Ford offer.[76] Meanwhile, Senator Norris was indicating that the Ford offer would not have smooth sailing in the Senate Agriculture Committee. Speaking at a meeting of the Public Super-Power Conference in January, 1924, the Nebraska Senator advocated a nationwide development by the federal government of all potential water-power resources, linked together in one huge public power system.[77]

74. War Department, *Additional Offer Made by the Tennessee Electric Power Company to Manufacture Nitrogen and Fertilizer at Muscle Shoals*, House Doc. 173, 68 Cong., 1 Sess., 2–3.

75. War Department, *Offer of Union Carbide Company for Muscle Shoals*, House Doc. 166, 68 Cong., 1 Sess., 1–6.

76. New York *Times*, Jan. 20, 1924.

77. *Ibid.*, Jan. 17, 1924.

V

The Ford Offer: Victory and Defeat

AT THE Muscle Shoals hearings before the House Military
Committee, which were held in late January, 1924, the Ford
adherents had little new to offer. Henry Ford was requested to
testify, but he refused to comply and would not permit any of
his representatives to appear before the committee. He declared
that "further hearings would only serve to delay action and
unnecessarily consume the time of a busy and important committee of Congress already in possession of the facts." He reminded
the committee that his offer had been before it for two years.[1]
Representatives John C. McKenzie of Illinois, Percy E. Quin of
Mississippi, Lister Hill of Alabama, and Finis J. Garrett of Tennessee, all of whom were members of the House Military Committee, were the chief defenders of Ford at the hearings.
Essentially, the pro-Ford strategy here was to attack the offer of
the power companies as being merely a water-power proposition
and, hence, in violation of the fundamental purposes of the
Muscle Shoals project, nitrate for defense and cheap fertilizer for
agriculture. The Ford defenders claimed that the Ford offer was
a proposal to perform unselfish public service, especially in the
production of cheap fertilizer. This argument was countered by
Oscar C. Merrill, executive secretary of the Federal Power Commission, who contended that the production of fertilizer by the
power companies would constitute as great a public service as the
production of fertilizer by Ford. Merrill again denounced the
Ford bid as a proposed violation of the national water-power

1. New York *Times,* Jan. 27, 1924.

policy, especially in its failure to provide for public regulation of rates and the distribution of power.[2]

At the hearings, representatives of the Alabama Power Company emphasized the need of great amounts of additional power to meet the demands of an alleged growing power market in the South. Representatives of the other companies asserted that in their respective areas of the South, there was a great need for additional electric power. Engineers representing the power companies countered the cheap fertilizer publicity of the Ford group by declaring that the power companies, through the use of the Haber process, would produce fertilizer at less than half the cost Ford would incur in operating nitrate plant no. 2.[3]

The most significant factor about these House hearings was the disclosure of the beginnings of an apparent revolt in the South, outside the Muscle Shoals area, against the Ford offer. The rebels were particularly numerous among southern manufacturers. Many representatives of this group appeared before the committee protesting that Ford himself intended to absorb all of the cheap Muscle Shoals power in his own industries, which would not only deny to other southern manufacturers access to this source of cheap power but would place Ford in a competitive position that would be totally unfair to competing producers in the area. One of the most prominent representatives of southern manufacturers appearing before the committee was Dan E. McGugin, an attorney of Nashville, Tennessee, who testified in behalf of the Tennessee Manufacturers' Association. McGugin declared that more and more Tennesseans were turning against the Ford offer as they became aware that its acceptance would deprive Tennessee industries of cheap Muscle Shoals power.

2. *Muscle Shoals Propositions*, Hearings, U. H. House of Representatives, 68 Cong., 1 Sess. (1924), 31–33, 67–69, 72. Secretary Weeks remained adamant in his opposition to the Ford offer. In January, 1924, during the House hearings on Muscle Shoals, he informed Senator Norris that his past criticisms of the Ford offer still stood. Weeks to Norris, Jan. 30, 1924, Judge Advocate General, National Archives.

3. *Muscle Shoals Propositions*, House Hearings, 68 Cong., 1 Sess., 67, 94, 101, 140–43, 179–82.

Representatives of the Carolina textile industry also appeared
with a plea for a share of cheap Muscle Shoals power.[4]

Significantly, the major opposition to the Ford offer at these
hearings came from the manufacturing interests in central and
southern Alabama. Richard V. Taylor, the mayor of Mobile,
delivered a slashing attack on the Ford offer and declared that
cheap Muscle Shoals power was essential to the industrial growth
of Mobile. Representatives from Selma, Troy, Birmingham, and
other Alabama cities, including Huntsville in the Tennessee
Valley, appeared before the committee to protest against the
Ford offer.[5]

Benjamin C. Marsh, managing director of the Farmers' National Council, testified in behalf of the Norris bill for government
operation. Marsh claimed that his organization represented
800,000 farmers, over one-third of whom were farm laborers.[6]

Despite the domination of the witness chair at the House
Military Committee hearings by opponents of the Ford offer and
the avowed hostility to it by Republican leaders on the committee, it was obvious that the large bloc of Ford supporters in
the committee, composed of southern Democrats and midwestern
Republicans, were determined to bring out a report favorable to
Ford. None of the Ford adherents on the committee was impressed by the arguments, advanced by witnesses opposing the
offer, that the South would be best served by acceptance of a
proposal guaranteeing the widest possible distribution of power.
In executive session, the committee decided by a vote of 14 to 6
that Ford would not be required to comply with the Federal
Water Power Act. In addition, attempts by Republican leaders to
make Ford's personal obligations more definite and rigid and to
require him to pay interest on the $17,000,000 expended at Wilson
Dam before the advent of the Ford offer were beaten down. By
a vote of 14 to 5, the committee reported favorably on the
McKenzie bill, as modified by the Madden amendment, which

    4. *Ibid.*, 161, 182–83, 187, 195–201.
    5. *Ibid.*, 150–52, 157–58, 209–30.
    6. *Ibid.*, 184–87. See also "Farmers' National Council," in *Nation*, CVIII
(March 15, 1919), 400.

authorized acceptance of the Ford offer in full, including replacements for the Gorgas properties. The bill also contained an amendment which required that the securities of the corporation to be established by Ford to operate Muscle Shoals must remain in the hands of American citizens in order to prevent foreigners from gaining control of an important segment of national defense.[7] The votes in the Military Committee showed that the Ford plan for Muscle Shoals had gained considerable strength in that committee since the adjournment of the Sixty-seventh Congress. In fact, the number of committee members advocating unconditional approval of the proposal had increased by six. Three of these were the result of Democratic gains in the elections of 1922. Of the five Republicans voting with the Democrats to report the bill favorably, two were new to the committee while, in the Sixty-seventh Congress, two had advocated unconditional acceptance of the Ford offer and the third had voted to accept the offer minus the Gorgas properties.[8]

In its report to the House on February 21, 1924, the majority declared that fidelity to the National Defense Act had been its principal guide in reaching its decision. In the light of that act, the majority reported, the Ford offer was found to be satisfactory in all respects. The majority was particularly pleased, the report stated, that the Ford offer was a responsible, comprehensive bid which adequately would dispose of both the fertilizer and power aspects of the Muscle Shoals problem and at the same time provide for national defense. The majority's chief criticisms of the power companies' offer were that it lacked an adequate guarantee for the production of nitrates for national defense and fertilizer for the farmers, and that it provided for a larger fertilizer profit than the Ford offer by inclusion of more cost factors. In answer to the criticisms of the hundred-year lease period in the Ford offer, the majority declared that the power companies' offer, in reality, provided for a perpetual lease but

7. New York *Times*, Feb. 2, 1924; "Committee for Ford Offer," in *Electrical World*, LXXXIII (Feb. 2, 1924), 248; *Muscle Shoals,* House Report 143, 68 Cong., 1 Sess. (1924), 3–7.

8. New York *Times*, Feb. 2, 1924.

contained no provisions for amortization of government investments as did the Ford proposal.[9]

The minority report, submitted by administration Republicans
on the committee, stated that there was no longer any need to
grant Ford a heavy subsidy as an inducement to obtain production of fertilizer at Muscle Shoals, since the power companies
had come forward with an offer which would accomplish this
goal as well as pay the government a reasonable return for use
of the hydroelectric properties. The report asserted that the Ford
offer did not contain a sufficient guarantee of fertilizer production.[10] It severely attacked the Ford offer because of its failure
to conform to the Federal Water Power Act and noted the
"large amount of evidence [which] was brought before the committee to show the widespread demand in the South for hydroelectric power and the concern which is felt in that section lest
the Muscle Shoals power be entirely withdrawn from public
service." [11]

Opponents of the Ford offer in the House decided not to oppose
consideration of the McKenzie bill but rather to wage a vigorous
fight against it on the floor. Thus, on March 4, 1924, the Ford
offer reached the floor of Congress for the first time.[12]

In the House debate on the McKenzie bill practically all of
the old Muscle Shoals issues which had arisen since the war were
reconsidered. The principal targets of the opponents of the Ford
offer were its failure to conform to the principles of the Federal
Water Power Act and the apparent indefinite guarantee in the
production of fertilizer. Representative Theodore E. Burton of
Ohio led the administration forces in attacking the water-power
features of the proposal, but it was a Norris supporter, Representative William Williamson of South Dakota, who most aggressively
assaulted the Ford bid in respect to this issue. Williamson warned
that the Federal Water Power Act, which he described as being
the product of a long, hard struggle in response to an insistent

9. House Report 143, 68 Cong., 1 Sess., 47–48, 51, 56–58, 60–61.
10. *Ibid.*, part 2, 1, 16–20.
11. *Ibid.*, 19.
12. *Cong. Rec.*, 68 Cong., 1 Sess., 3556.

pressure by public opinion, would be forfeited by acceptance of the Ford offer. He predicted that such a course would result in the seizure of all of the nation's water-power resources by private monopolies unbridled by regulations. Even Representative Harry M. Wurzbach of Texas, a lukewarm Ford supporter, admitted that the Ford offer conflicted with the basic national water-power policy. On the other hand, Representative Almon of Alabama argued that the Ford offer did not violate the basic water-power policy, his interpretation being that Ford's verbal promise of October, 1923, to construct transmission lines for a distance of two hundred miles in every direction from Muscle Shoals was sufficient to qualify the offer under the terms of the Water Power Act. Representative W. Frank James of Michigan, another ardent Ford supporter, branded the Federal Water Power Act as a product of a private power lobby.[13]

Pro-Ford congressmen attempted to sidetrack the water-power arguments of the opposition with contentions that Muscle Shoals should properly be regarded as a fertilizer rather than a water-power proposition. They professed to see the United States as a nation with a rapidly growing population, faced with a dwindling capacity to produce food because of the declining soil fertility. They predicted that fertilizer needs in other sections of the nation would soon be as acute as in the South.[14]

In the House debate, the Ford adherents continued strongly to assert the claim that the Ford offer would result in a sharp reduction of fertilizer prices. The opposition just as stoutly denied the validity of this claim and added the counter-assertion that no reasonable evidence had been shown to prove that Ford even guaranteed to produce fertilizer. The opposition borrowed a point from Senator Norris's repertory of anti-Ford arguments by asserting that upon formation of the corporation, as outlined in

13. *Ibid.*, 3565, 3568–80, 3635, 3640–42. Specifically, three points in which the Ford offer violated the Water Power Act received most of the criticism of the opposition to the offer; the failure to provide for distribution and public regulation, and the hundred-year lease period. In respect to the latter, Representative Williamson declared that it would set a precedent which would "leave future generations bound hand and foot, utterly unable . . . to work out their destiny along the lines of the greatest good to the greatest number." *Ibid.*, 3583.

14. *Ibid.*, 3556–59.

the Ford offer, Ford's obligations would cease. It was implied by the opposition that Ford had deliberately provided for utilization of nitrate plant no. 2 with the view of later using its state of obsolescence as a pretext for abandoning fertilizer production.[15]

The Teapot Dome scandal crept into the Muscle Shoals controversy during the House debate. A few days prior to the debate, an item in the Washington *Herald* reported that the Teapot Dome scandal had produced a more cautious attitude in Congress toward disposal of Muscle Shoals to private interests.[16] The opponents of the Ford offer seized the initiative in this matter and declared that the Ford proposal loomed as an even greater scandal than the Teapot Dome affair. Representative Charles C. Kearns, a stanch administration supporter, stated that probably Edward L. Doheny and Harry F. Sinclair, like Ford, had flattered themselves that they had acted in good faith and that in reality the Ford offer, like the Teapot Dome episode, was inimical to the national interest. Representative Fiorello LaGuardia asserted that Ford's bid relegated the Teapot Dome scandal to the rank of "petty larceny." [17]

The offer of the power companies was bitterly censured by the Ford party in the House. The power companies were accused of acting in bad faith in tendering their offer since their only purpose, it was charged, was to delay congressional consideration of the Ford proposal. The Alabama Power Company was designated the motivating force behind the power offer. Furthermore, it was asserted by the Ford party that Thomas W. Martin, the president of the Alabama Power Company, was the real author of the

15. *Ibid.*, 3559–64, 3584, 3588, 3710–11. Representative LaGuardia was apparently the only congressional opponent of the Ford offer who felt that Muscle Shoals possessed significant possibilities for fertilizer production as well as water power for distribution. Like the Ford adherents, he expressed concern about the ability of the nation to produce food for a growing population. His professed concern for the American farmer was challenged by a pro-Ford colleague who declared that the New York Congressman had not a single farmer in his constituency. LaGuardia admitted the point but added that numerous consumers resided in his district. *Ibid.*, 3709.

16. Washington *Herald*, Feb. 10, 1924, quoted in *Cong. Rec.*, 68 Cong., 1 Sess., 3579.

17. *Cong. Rec.*, 68 Cong., 1 Sess., 3584, 3709; New York *Times*, March 6, 1924.

recent minority report of the House Military Committee as well as a House bill based on that report, both of which advocated acceptance of the power companies' offer.[18]

One of the principal arguments that had been used by the Ford partisans against the Muscle Shoals offer of the Alabama Power Company was that acceptance of the proposal would jeopardize national defense because, it was alleged, the company was foreign-owned. During the House debate, this charge was turned against Ford by Representative LaGuardia. The New York Congressman declared that if Muscle Shoals, on which the army would depend for munitions in time of war, were turned over to Henry Ford, every treaty made by the United States with a foreign government would have to be submitted to Ford for his approval.[19]

In this debate the Ford group was able effectively to utilize Ford's attack on Wall Street, but his anti-Semitism served as a weapon for the opposition. In a heated exchange between Representative John J. McSwain of South Carolina and LaGuardia, the former inquired of the latter:

Does not the gentleman admit that Henry Ford is the one conspicuous man in this Nation who has defied the combined powers of Wall Street and licked them to their knees, and that is the reason they are now fighting him?

And do not they hate Henry Ford more than they hate Government public-utility ownership?

LaGuardia, long a champion of public power, opposed the Ford offer in principle, but his reply revealed in addition a deep hostility to Ford's anti-Semitic activities:

The only man who has hatred in his heart is Henry Ford, based on his ignorance of history, literature, and religion. And Henry Ford has done more, I will say, owing to his bigoted hatred, to create strife and hatred in this country among the races than any man in the United States.

And I will say that the wealth and ignorance of Henry Ford combined has made it possible for vicious men to carry on a nefarious

18. *Cong. Rec.*, 68 Cong., 1 Sess., 3567, 3631, 3633, 3841-42.
19. *Ibid.*, 3708.

warfare against the Jews, not only of America, but of the whole world. . . .[20]

Some outside pressure was exerted on the House during the debate on the Ford offer by both Ford and power company supporters. At that time, Edward B. Stahlman, publisher of the Nashville *Banner,* was conducting a poll among *Banner* readers as to whether they preferred the offer of Ford or the power companies. Returns from this poll, which showed an overwhelming majority for Ford, were wired to Washington as they were being tabulated and were read at frequent intervals in the House by members of the Tennessee House delegation during the Muscle Shoals debate. Also, during the debate, the House was the recipient of messages from various local Farm Bureau chapters and other organizations imploring acceptance of the Ford offer. On the other hand, members of the Alabama delegation in the House received several telegrams from citizens of Alabama deploring the attacks being made in Congress on the Alabama Power Company and praising that company as a laudable and progressive institution.[21]

Ford received opposition at this time from three eminent national figures—Governor Gifford Pinchot of Pennsylvania, former Governor Leslie M. Shaw of Iowa, who served as Secretary of the Treasury in Theodore Roosevelt's cabinet, and Newton D. Baker, former Secretary of War. Pinchot declared that the Ford offer violated six of the seven features of the Federal Water Power Act designed to protect the public interest.[22] Shaw, who implied that his past association with Roosevelt qualified him as an expert on the subject of disposal of natural resources, described the Ford offer as a sneak attack on the Federal Water Power Act as well as on Rooseveltian conservation principles.[23] Baker opposed both the Ford and the power offers. Clinging steadfastly to

20. *Ibid.,* 3708.
21. *Ibid.,* 3660, 3829, 3839, 3852–55, 3908. The validity of Stahlman's poll was challenged by Dan McGugin, a leading opponent of the Ford offer. *Muscle Shoals,* Hearings, U. S. Senate, on S. 139, S. 2372, S. 3214, and H. R. 518, 68 Cong., 1 Sess. (1924), 246.
22. New York *Times,* March 6, 1924.
23. *Cong. Rec.,* 68 Cong., 1 Sess., 3820.

the policy which he pursued in the immediate postwar period, Baker advised Congress to adopt a policy of public operation of Muscle Shoals and declared that "it would be a great public calamity to have this great national asset come into private hands upon any terms now possible to be secured." [24]

Pro-Ford House leaders depended heavily on the alleged farm support of the Ford offer to exert pressure on all congressmen from agricultural areas. The Ford group insisted that the great majority of farmers throughout the nation were strongly in favor of the Ford proposal. On the other hand, the opposition contended that farm support of the Ford proposal was mainly confined to the activities of Gray Silver, Washington representative of the Farm Bureau, who was attempting to exert heavy pressure on Congress.[25]

Representatives LaGuardia and Williamson, who were Progressive Republicans and supporters of the Norris Muscle Shoals bill, were unconditionally opposed to the disposal of Muscle Shoals to private interests on any terms. Williamson used the occasion to advocate the principle of public power in general; LaGuardia confined himself to the advocacy of government operation at Muscle Shoals, but he made it plain that he considered that project to be a symbol of the public power fight.[26]

On one factor practically all of the chief combatants agreed—that Muscle Shoals was a national problem. Nevertheless Senator Heflin injected a note of sectionalism into the debate. He attempted to gain the support of New England congressmen by promising that cotton prices, which he said were so high that New England textile mills were being forced to close, would be lowered as a result of cheap fertilizer to be produced by Ford.[27]

The opponents of the Ford offer dominated the debate; the Ford group, confident of victory, was mainly interested in terminating the verbal struggle so that the issue could be brought to a vote. Furthermore, the Ford group was handicapped by the

24. New York *Times,* March 8, 1924.

25. *Cong. Rec.,* 68 Cong., 1 Sess., 3582, 3588, 3837; New York *Times,* April 20 (IX), 1924.

26. *Cong. Rec.,* 68 Cong., 1 Sess., 3584–85, 3706–8.

27. *Ibid.,* 3556–59, 3579.

nature of the opposition. The administration spokesmen, who favored the power companies' offer, carefully refrained from attacking LaGuardia and his fellow public-power exponents. Although the latter group did not return fully this courtesy it did confine itself mainly to criticism of the Ford offer. Since the Ford plan contemplated the lease of Muscle Shoals to private industry, as did the power offer, the LaGuardia group was able to utilize many of the same arguments in attacking the Ford offer that the Ford partisans were using against the power offer.

Opponents of the Ford proposal offered a flurry of amendments in an attempt to force Ford to provide for general distribution and public regulation of Muscle Shoals power. This was obviously a delaying action and was regarded as such by the Ford group. All major amendments were rejected and the bill emerged practically intact with only a few minor alterations.[28] Thus on March 10, 1924, the McKenzie bill, authorizing unconditional acceptance of the Ford offer, passed the House by a vote of 227 to 143. It was a victory for southern Democrats with some substantial aid from midwestern Republicans.[29] Thus the Ford group tasted victory the first time their bill was brought to the floor.

The passage of the Ford offer by the House was a joyful event for the Muscle Shoals area. The elation of the people there was signified by bonfires and the ringing of bells throughout North Alabama. They happily recalled Ford's promise to build a great new Detroit, and now that unimaginably bold dream was about to be realized. Gray Silver hailed the passage of the McKenzie bill as a victory over a "formidable array" of Wall Street and fertilizer interests.[30]

According to Jerome G. Kerwin, the success of the Ford offer in the House could be attributed to the following factors: the

28. New York Times, March 9, 11, 1924; Cong. Rec., 68 Cong., 1 Sess., 3927–28.

29. Cong. Rec., 68 Cong., 1 Sess., 3927-28. Voting for the bill were 170 Democrats and 57 Republicans, and voting against it were 122 Republicans and 19 Democrats. Of the 57 Republicans voting for the bill, 30 were from the Middle West, the remainder being distributed about equally among the other sections of the nation. Southern Democrats voted practically as a solid bloc.

30. New York Times, March 11, 1924; Silver to Farm Bureau members (form letter), March 13, 1924, Norris Papers.

tremendous prestige of Ford, who had enjoyed "such phenomenal success in identifying his industrial achievements with the welfare of the people"; the promise of cheap fertilizer for the farmer; the activity of real estate speculation; and the opposition of the "great power trust." [31] The *New Republic* declared that the nature of the opposition contributed greatly to the Ford victory:

It is unfortunate that the only serious offer which has been made in addition to Ford's is that of the Southern power companies. It gives the automobile man's supporters the cheap and easy argument that whoever criticizes his offer is a henchman of "big business." [32]

Around the country the press as a whole appears to have sounded a note of disappointment in its reflections on the Ford victory. Newspapers opposing Ford's bid professed more concern about the basic principles of government involved in the matter than about the quality of the offer itself. The editorial consensus among these publications was that the placing of such a great amount of power and trust into the hands of one man, as provided by the McKenzie bill, was an exceedingly dangerous precedent to set in a democratic society. Congress was accused of having betrayed the public interest. As for the offer itself, the opposition press felt it to be a questionable bargain for the government. It lamented the violation of the basic water-power policy proposed in the offer and protested that there was no guarantee of fertilizer production.

Yet the Ford offer was not without considerable press support. A large number of newspaper editors throughout the country expressed pleasure at the Ford victory. They described the Ford offer as the only bona fide Muscle Shoals bid, the general implication being that the power companies' proposal was merely an attempt to confuse the issue. Furthermore, they felt that Ford's honesty, integrity, and ability merited some such reward, and

31. Jerome G. Kerwin, *Federal Water-Power Legislation* (1926), 279. Kerwin states that the McKenzie bill had the "definite approval of President Coolidge." He does not document this statement nor does he take into consideration the fact that administration leaders in the House waged a most vigorous and energetic fight against the bill. *Ibid.*, 279n.

32. "Muscle Shoals: A Scandal in the Making?" in *New Republic*, XXXVIII (April 23, 1924), 221.

they asserted that the South was in great need of Ford's brains and money.[33]

After the passage of the McKenzie bill in the House, President Coolidge referred it to various members of his official family with instructions to study it in the light of public interest. This action revealed that Henry C. Wallace, the Secretary of Agriculture, had apparently taken a definite stand against the Ford offer, although there was still a division among his subordinates. Dr. Frederick G. Cottrell condemned the offer but Dr. Milton Whitney continued to support it. Whitney advised the President that the Muscle Shoals problem should be considered from the standpoint of fertilizer, and he declared that the cyanamid process was the most practical method of fertilizer production. Thereupon, Secretary Wallace disavowed Whitney's contentions, asserting that the cyanamid process was obsolete.[34]

Alarmed by the Ford victory in the House, Senator Norris set about to prevent the Ford partisans from storming the Senate.[35] Upon his request the American Engineering Council appointed a committee to study "the general economic phases of the Muscle

33. "Ford Winning Muscle Shoals," in *Literary Digest* LXXX (March 29, 1924), 10. Typical of the more radical pro- and anti-Ford press were the Birmingham *Age-Herald* and the Chicago *Tribune*, respectively. The former identified the Ford victory in the House as merely another step in the "inevitable acceptance" of the Ford offer while the latter described the episode as a conspiracy against the public interest made possible by fear of Ford's financial power. The *Tribune* also published a cartoon entitled "The Rape of Muscle Shoals." Birmingham *Age-Herald*, March 13, 1924, and Chicago *Tribune*, March 15, 1924.

34. Whitney to Wallace, March 14, April 3, 1924; Wallace to Coolidge, March 14, 17, 1924; Wallace to Senator Smith W. Brookhart, April 7, 1924, Records of the Bureau of Plant Industry, Soils, and Agriculture Engineering, Correspondence of Bureau of Soils, Muscle Shoals, National Archives.

35. Senator Norris introduced his second Muscle Shoals bill in February, 1924. It provided for complete separation of the power and fertilizer functions of Muscle Shoals. The nitrate plants would be placed under the authority of the Secretary of Agriculture while the hydroelectric facilities would be operated by a government corporation which was authorized to construct adequate transmission lines through which the surplus power was to be transported and sold to municipalities and other public agencies in the area. Perhaps the most significant aspect of the second Norris bill was the fact that it authorized the Secretary of War to survey the Tennessee River system and to construct there as many dams as he considered to be "advisable and practical" for the purposes of increasing primary power, flood control, and navigational improvements. *Muscle Shoals*, Senate Report 678, 68 Cong., 1 Sess. (1924), 1–5.

Shoals problem," with the view of rendering a report to the Norris committee at the forthcoming hearings. Almost simultaneously one of Norris's Progressive colleagues, Senator Smith W. Brookhart of Iowa, announced that he intended to offer a resolution for an investigation of alleged lobbying for the Ford offer. At this time, Norris revived the ghost of the alleged Ford-Coolidge deal with the implication that important evidence bearing on the subject had been uncovered. Meanwhile, two of the most adamant administration opponents of the Ford offer, Representatives Theodore E. Burton and Harry E. Hull, came to the aid of Norris. Burton, a conservative Republican, averred that though he was opposed to public power in principle, he would support the Norris bill rather than agree to the approval of the Ford offer. Hull took to the stump against the Ford offer, warning the nation that Ford proposed to violate the basic water-power policy.[36]

As the hearings before the Norris committee got under way, Ford supporters in the Senate demanded that the investigation be speedily concluded so that a vote could be had on the Ford offer in the Senate without delay. Although Norris promised that the committee, which was dominated by Progressive Republicans, would not attempt to prevent a Senate vote on the Ford bid, he nevertheless made it clear that he intended to prolong the hearings until the Muscle Shoals problem had been thoroughly aired. At this juncture political observers were divided as to the probable outcome of the Ford offer at that session. In general, it was believed that should the offer reach the floor of the Senate it would be accepted, but it was also felt that Norris would make a mighty effort to keep it bottled up in the committee. The opinion was expressed in some quarters that Norris would be aided in this effort by some senators opposing the proposal who would feel compelled to vote for the Ford bill, should it reach the floor, because of Ford's popularity with their constituents.[37]

36. New York *Times,* April 15, 16, 18, 1924.
37. *Ibid.,* April 18, 1924; Edwin Dakin, "Henry Ford—Man or Superman?" in *Nation,* CXVIII (March 26, 1924), 336.

On the eve of the hearings, Robert L. Duffus, a veteran political analyst, observed that the Ford offer had become the testing ground of the Federal Water Power Act. He wrote:

Thus the Ford issue in Congress strikes deep. It involves a difference in theory as wide as that between Pinchot and Ballinger. . . . Many of those who support his [Ford's] Muscle Shoals proposal do so because they believe he knows how to develop a great industry, whereas the Government does not. They use precisely the same arguments which led honest men at one time to accept the Teapot Dome leases as legitimate.[38]

The hearings on Muscle Shoals before the Senate Agriculture Committee began on April 16, and it soon became obvious that Norris intended to extend them as long as possible by giving everyone who desired an opportunity to testify. The first week for the most part was devoted to examination of witnesses concerning a minor offer which had not previously received serious consideration and which had absolutely no chance of being accepted. In addition, various individuals appeared for the purpose of attacking the Ford offer. Indicative of Norris's attitude at this time was his agreement to support a proposal by Senator Samuel M. Ralston of Indiana to postpone the hearings so that Congress might have more time in which to adopt a more definite policy toward Muscle Shoals. This plan failed.[39]

During the second week of the hearings, Norris began an investigation of the alleged Ford-Coolidge deal of December, 1923, when Ford had endorsed Coolidge's candidacy for President. Norris had been delaying this phase of the hearings until an answer could be had from Ford regarding the committee's request that he appear in person to testify. Upon receipt of Ford's refusal to appear, Norris went ahead with the investigation, declaring that Ford's reluctance to testify before the committee indicated that he feared embarrassing questions might be asked regarding his relations with Coolidge.[40] The committee considered

38. New York *Times*, April 20 (IX), 1924.

39. *Ibid.*, April 17, 18, 19, 20, 22, 1924; *Muscle Shoals*, Senate Hearings, 68 Cong., 1 Sess., 31–163.

40. *Muscle Shoals*, Senate Hearings, 68 Cong., 1 Sess., 70, 165.

the subpoenaing of Ford but instead ordered the attendance of E. G. Liebold, Ford's private secretary.[41]

Norris learned that following a conference on October 12, 1923, between Coolidge and James Martin Miller, a Ford biographer who was part-time Washington correspondent for the Ford newspaper, the Dearborn *Independent,* telegrams had been exchanged between Miller and Ford officials. Thereupon, the Norris committee ordered Western Union to produce copies of these messages.[42] Upon compliance by that company on April 26, it was found that one of the telegrams contained the following message addressed jointly to E. G. Liebold and William J. Cameron, the editor of the Dearborn *Independent:*

In private interview had with President Coolidge this morning he said incidentally: "I am friendly to Mr. Ford, but wish someone would convey to him that it is my hope that Mr. Ford will not do or say anything that will make it difficult for me to deliver Muscle Shoals to him, which I am trying to do." While President didn't say so, am sure Weeks has been in consultation with President this morning in view of Mr. Ford's reported interview today's papers.[43]

Miller testified before the Norris committee that the telegram was correct, but he stated that so far as he knew Ford had concluded no Muscle Shoals agreement with the President. He stated that he had been engaged by Ford as a political observer in Washington in connection with the Ford presidential boom. He asserted that Ford employed large "propaganda" and "secret service" forces.[44]

A round of denials followed the revelation of the Miller telegram. President Coolidge denied the validity of the Miller message and solemnly stated that there had been no White House deal with Ford. He added that his mind "was made up when Mr. Ford called on me December 3, and at that time my message [to Congress] was already written and printed." [45]

Secretary Weeks was caught in an embarrassing position. For

41. New York *Times,* April 26, 27, 1924.
42. *Muscle Shoals,* Senate Hearings, 68 Cong., 1 Sess., 382.
43. *Ibid.,* 531.
44. *Ibid.,* 679–80.
45. *Ibid.,* 457.

once, he was forced to agree with Ford. In testifying before the Norris committee, Weeks was led by the Nebraska Senator through the entire labyrinth of events surrounding Ford-Coolidge relations during 1923, in the hope of uncovering evidence that would lead to conclusive proof of a Ford-Coolidge swap of Muscle Shoals and the presidency. Weeks vehemently denied that the President had made any commitment to Ford in respect to Muscle Shoals, and he insisted that his disputes with Ford had no bearing on the relationship between Ford and Coolidge.[46]

E. G. Liebold told the committee that the Miller telegrams had never reached Ford. Norris, obviously doubting the veracity of Liebold's testimony, believed messages more important than the Miller telegrams had been exchanged between Ford and Coolidge. Liebold testified that no such messages were in the Ford files.[47]

Although nothing further concerning this matter developed, Norris maintained that the Miller telegrams in possession of the committee, together with Ford's apparent abrupt change in attitude in 1923 toward the Coolidge administration, tended to incriminate both Ford and Coolidge. He felt that they were, at least, guilty of unethical actions in relation to Muscle Shoals. He insisted that the President, in his message of the previous December, had prescribed a disposition of Muscle Shoals which could have applied only to the Ford offer.[48]

The hearings before the Norris committee developed into a campaign to save the water-power law. Gifford Pinchot told the committee that the absorption of all Muscle Shoals power by Ford's proposed factories at Muscle Shoals would hamstring industrial development in the South. James R. Garfield, who as Secretary of the Interior under Theodore Roosevelt had worked closely with the Rooseveltian conservation program, warned that it was unsound policy to set aside a general law such as the Water Power Act for the sake of one man. Newton D. Baker, who had come to believe that recent developments in technology had

46. *Ibid.*, 390.
47. *Ibid.*, 529–38.
48. New York *Times*, May 7, 1924.

rendered Muscle Shoals useless as a nitrate project, pleaded that Muscle Shoals power be made available for general distribution to the public.[49]

The Muscle Shoals hearings before the House Military Committee in January had produced evidence of an apparent revolt against the Ford offer among certain elements in the South, especially manufacturers and civic leaders. The hearings before the Norris committee confirmed the revolt and indicated that it was widespread. It appeared that there were two principal causes of this dissatisfaction with the Ford offer: firstly, the fear of unfair competition that might be conducted by Ford should he obtain a monopoly of the cheap power at Muscle Shoals, and, secondly, the desire by various southern industries and areas for a share of the Muscle Shoals power bonanza. The fear of unfair competition had been stimulated by remarks by Ford, his officials, and his supporters, who from time to time had mentioned various products that Ford might produce at Muscle Shoals. The cumulative effect was sufficient to frighten a large number of southern manufacturers.

Representatives of southern industrial firms, civic organizations, and industrial development associations flocked to the hearings to voice their protests. All demanded that any lessee of Muscle Shoals be required to distribute the surplus power as provided by the water-power law. They emphasized the vital need of cheap water power for the growth of southern industry; they accentuated the desirability of widely dispersed local industries in the South to process local raw materials, to furnish a local market for agricultural products, and to supply jobs for the surplus farm population. All denied having any connections with southern power companies, but the majority favored the lease of Muscle Shoals to private power companies rather than public operation. Yet they were almost unanimous in stating a preference for public power as an alternative to the Ford offer. Although all of the witnesses paid lip service to cheap fertilizer, it was obvious that they regarded Muscle Shoals as primarily a water-

49. *Muscle Shoals,* Senate Hearings, 68 Cong., 1 Sess., 329, 334, 371, 425–26, 436–37.

power proposition. All condemned Ford and the people of the Muscle Shoals area for their desire to keep Muscle Shoals power in that area, and most of them attributed Ford's desire to acquire the project to selfish rather than altruistic motives.[50]

Three sections were particularly well represented at the hearings—the Carolina textile district, Mississippi, and Tennessee. From the Carolinas came assertions that the water power of that region, which possessed no coal, was approaching maximum development; thus, future growth of the textile industry depended on tapping the rich water-power resources of the Tennessee Valley. Already, this region was receiving some power by relay from the steam plant at Muscle Shoals.[51] The Mississippi witnesses testified that pro-Ford sentiment in Mississippi was rapidly dissipating as the average citizen became aware that Ford's offer did not provide for general distribution of Muscle Shoals power. Many organizations in that state, including the state Chamber of Commerce, they stated, had deserted the Ford cause. It was emphasized that Mississippi was devoid of both coal and water power; hence, her industrial growth would depend on equalization of the water-power resources of the South.[52] Witnesses from Tennessee testified in much the same vein. The belief was expressed that the trend of public opinion in Tennessee also was turning against Ford as it became clear that the Ford offer would deprive the state of Muscle Shoals power.[53]

50. See *ibid.*, 230–500.
51. *Ibid.*, 176, 291–99, 373–75.
52. *Ibid.*, 305–24, 344–50.
53. *Muscle Shoals*, Senate Hearings, 68 Cong., 1 Sess., 229–60, 775–83. A private feud, occasioned by the Ford offer, was injected into the hearings by two Tennessee witnesses, Edward B. Stahlman, publisher of the Nashville *Banner*, and Dan McGugin, attorney for the Tennessee Manufacturers' Association and Vanderbilt University football coach. McGugin, appearing before the committee to attack the Ford offer, asserted that a public opinion poll on the Muscle Shoals offers, which Stahlman was conducting among readers of the *Banner*, was so heavily weighted in favor of Ford that it did not merit consideration. Thereupon Stahlman appeared before the committee and severely castigated McGugin. Besides accusing McGugin of engaging in dishonest and unethical activities against the Ford offer, Stahlman characterized him as being a servant of the power companies which were, he said, seeking to throttle the Ford offer because of the potential threat to their power monopoly. Stahlman expressed faith that Ford would distribute most of the Muscle Shoals power not needed for fertilizer

These hearings before the Norris committee revealed widespread anti-Ford sentiment in the southern press in the first quarter of 1924. Dan McGugin presented to the committee editorials from approximately sixty southern newspapers, the majority of which were large dailies—all denouncing the Ford offer. Most of the editorials explicitly endorsed the offer of the power companies, none of them giving outright approval of public operation of Muscle Shoals. Practically all of them had been published soon after the power companies' offer was presented to Congress in January. They rated distribution of Muscle Shoals power at least as important as the production of fertilizer; they protested that giving Henry Ford a monopolistic control of Muscle Shoals would place too much economic and political power in the hands of one man, besides depriving other southern industries of a just share of cheap water power. Editorials from South Alabama, the Mississippi Delta region, and West Tennessee pointed out the acute need of imported water power in those regions because of the lack of swift streams and coal deposits.[54]

At the same time, the Tennessee Manufacturers' Association issued a pamphlet containing excerpts of editorial comment on the Ford offer from some 280 American newspapers, dailies for the most part. Practically all of these editorials, most of which were published from January to March, 1924, criticized the Ford offer on at least one of the following counts: it violated basic water-power policy and unjustly gave Ford special privileges; it contained insufficient consideration for property and rights to be acquired; it was inferior to the power companies' offer; and it threatened to become another Teapot Dome scandal.[55]

The American Engineering Council aided Norris in his obvious attempt to create a strong tide of public sentiment against the

production. He accused McGugin and members of the Tennessee Manufacturers' Association of being afraid that high wages paid by Ford might spoil the labor supply in the Tennessee Valley area. *Ibid.*, 305–24, 344–50, 452–55, 466–67, 469, 486–93, 506.

54. *Ibid.*, 260–82.

55. Tennessee Manufacturers' Association, *The Muscle Shoals Situation as Viewed by the Press of America*, Series 1 and 2 (Nashville, Tenn., 1924), in Correspondence of Secretary of Agriculture, Muscle Shoals, National Archives.

Ford offer. A special committee of that organization, appointed at the request of Norris and headed by Fred R. Low, president of the American Society of Mechanical Engineers, conducted a study of the Muscle Shoals problem and reported to the council on May 3, 1924. The committee recommended the establishment of a joint committee to handle the problem and advised that Muscle Shoals be leased only under the terms of the Federal Water Power Act. It found no evidence that fertilizer could be produced more cheaply at Muscle Shoals than it was being produced by the existing fertilizer industry, and it described the cyanamid process as obsolete. These findings, which were approved by the administrative board of the council, were reported with some fanfare to the Norris committee by Lawrence W. Wallace, executive secretary of the council.[56]

John A. McSparran, Master of the Pennsylvania State Grange, who was an opponent of the Ford offer, contended that the extent of agricultural support of that proposal had been exaggerated by the Ford group. He testified that the National Grange had never endorsed the Ford offer despite reports by Ford supporters to the contrary. He insisted that a majority of neither the nation's farm organizations nor the farmers was supporting the Ford offer.[57] The Grange leader offered no evidence to corroborate his contentions.

---

56. *Muscle Shoals,* Senate Hearings, 68 Cong., 1 Sess., 417–24; "A. E. C. Wants Muscle Shoals under Water-Power Act," in *Electrical World,* LXXXIII (May 3, 1924), 895. During the hearings, the American Society of Civil Engineers and the American Institute of Electrical Engineers adopted resolutions entreating Congress to lease Muscle Shoals under the Federal Water Power Act only. Also, an official of the Mississippi Valley Waterway Association, an organization representing business interests in the upper Mississippi Valley north of St. Louis, appeared before the committee to denounce the Ford offer. *Muscle Shoals,* Senate Hearings, 68 Cong., 1 Sess., 156, 310–24.

57. *Muscle Shoals,* Senate Hearings, 68 Cong., 1 Sess., 282–84. McSparran was correct in saying that the National Grange had not endorsed the Ford offer. During the period of the Ford offer controversy, the Grange consistently followed a policy of advocating the use of Muscle Shoals for fertilizer production without endorsing any specific proposal. Thomas C. Atkeson to Edwin F. Ladd, July 7, 1922, and Thomas C. Atkeson to Theodore E. Burton, March 5, 1924, quoted in *Cong. Rec.,* 67 Cong., 2 Sess., 10098; *ibid.,* 68 Cong., 1 Sess., 3800.

Prior to these hearings before the Senate Agriculture Committee, Senator Norris received information to the effect that McSparran was "utterly amazed" to learn of a great effort by Gray Silver to "tie the Grange" with the Farm Bureau

The "fertilizer trust" charges by the Ford adherents were discussed again at the committee hearings. Gustavus Ober, Jr., president of the National Fertilizer Association, vehemently denied that any sort of trust or monopoly existed within the American fertilizer business. He contended that the industry was ruled by the "fiercest kind of competition." He declared it to be economically impractical to produce fertilizer at Muscle Shoals and branded the Ford offer as being socialistic.[58]

Although Secretary Weeks repudiated the allegations of a Ford-Coolidge agreement on Muscle Shoals, he continued to be unfriendly to the Ford offer. He defended the sale of the Gorgas plant and brought along Major General Williams, Chief of Ordnance, to help substantiate his statements.[59]

W. G. Waldo, consulting engineer of the Tennessee River Improvement Association, was the chief witness for the Ford offer. His principal aim was to demonstrate to the committee that the potential power of Muscle Shoals was only an insignificant part of the total available water power in the South; hence, the absorption of all Muscle Shoals power by Ford's industries would not create a power shortage in the South. He said that despite the automobile manufacturer's statement that he would build transmission lines from Muscle Shoals, there would be no general distribution of power under the Ford offer except for a short while during the preliminary period when Ford would be constructing his factories.[60]

Norris pushed his own Muscle Shoals bill at these hearings more energetically than ever before. For the first time since the failure of the Wadsworth-Kahn bill, there was considerable discussion of the subject of public operation of Muscle Shoals. The most prominent witnesses endorsing the Norris bill were Newton D. Baker and A. E. Bowen, the latter representing the Public Super-Power League.[61] In addition, Robert R. Pointer, former

in a scheme to achieve acceptance of the Ford offer by Congress. H. Bancroft Miller to Norris, Feb. 29, 1924, Norris Papers.

58. *Muscle Shoals,* Senate Hearings, 68 Cong., 1 Sess., 687–706.

59. *Ibid.,* 388–95, 544–55.

60. *Ibid.,* 560 ff., 626.

61. *Ibid.,* 33–38, 89–97, 784–88.

friend of Ford and a leader of the Ford-for-President movement, in a letter to the editor of the New York *Times* called for the adoption of the Norris bill. Pointer, who subscribed to the creed of the Progressives, had believed, prior to the Ford-Coolidge reconciliation of late 1923, that he and Ford had a common political philosophy.[62] In an attempt to gain the support of Norris for their Muscle Shoals bid, the Associated Power Companies, in May, 1924, approached the Nebraska Senator with an offer to support public operation of Muscle Shoals providing that he would agree to the sale of the power at the switchboard to these power companies. Norris ignored the power offer.[63]

Despite demands by Ford's friends for quick action, the Norris committee continued the hearings until May 26.[64] Practically every issue involved in the Muscle Shoals question was discussed before the committee. Concerning the fertilizer phases of the problem, the testimony of the experts overwhelmingly condemned Muscle Shoals as being unsuitable for fertilizer production. As a whole, fertilizer production was greatly minimized in importance as compared to the water-power possibilities of Muscle Shoals. The anti-Ford testimony, which dominated the hearings, was unanimous in condemning the Ford offer on the grounds that it violated the nation's basic power policy and that it contained no guarantee that fertilizer would be produced. Thus, these hearings definitely increased the importance of Muscle Shoals as a water-power project and decreased its apparent potentialities as a source of cheap fertilizer. Norris asserted that the hearings had presented the nation with "the greatest amount of useful evidence and testimony on the question of water-power that has ever been gotten together anywhere since the dawn of civilization." [65]

62. New York *Times*, May 11, 18 (VIII), 1924.
63. *Ibid.*, May 16, 1924.
64. "Effort to Report Ford Bill Fails," in *Electrical World*, LXXXIII (May 24, 1924), 1099.
65. *Cong. Reg.*, 68 Cong., 1 Sess., 8501. Norris's attempt to demonstrate that Muscle Shoals was more suitable for a water-power project than a fertilizer development was aided by the Department of Commerce, which, during the hearings, released a report on the nitrogen situation in the United States. In this report Muscle Shoals was condemned as a fertilizer project on the ground of

Meanwhile, sparked by reports that the interest of the southern power companies in Muscle Shoals was lagging and by the apparent prospects of defeat of the Ford offer as a result of the attack it was undergoing at the hearings, the Union Carbide Company came forward in May with a new offer. The essence of this bid was that the carbide company would be guaranteed 50,000 horsepower continuously at a low price with the remainder of the power to be divided between that company, which would produce fertilizer for farmers, and general distribution to the public. Although this offer was obviously less favorable to the government than either the Ford or the power offer, Norris nevertheless pretended to have great interest in it.[66]

On May 27, the Senate Agriculture Committee voted 11 to 4 to report the Norris bill favorably.[67] The majority report, written by Senator Norris, made it appear that the fight had simmered down to a struggle between the Ford offer and the Norris bill. In effect, Norris, who perhaps exaggerated the possibility of passing a public power bill in Congress at this time, appeared to assume that the Muscle Shoals controversy was now primarily a struggle between exponents of public and private power development. Concerning fertilizer, Norris declared that Ford had no "secret process" and that costs could not be reduced until more efficient methods were developed; hence, the Muscle Shoals nitrate plants should be utilized for fertilizer research under the direction of the Secretary of Agriculture. With respect to water power, he emphasized the benefits to be derived from a

alleged obsolescence of the cyanamid process. The report contended that much research lay ahead before fertilizer prices could be reduced, but added that future improvements were likely to be in the Haber process. It was admitted that the Chilean Nitrate Producers' Association was engaged in world-wide price fixing of nitrogen, but added that perhaps this monopoly was beneficial since the interest of its chief member, the Chilean government, lay "obviously less in the selling price of nitrate than in the total quantity of nitrate moved." This report was of added significance since the Secretary of Commerce, Herbert Hoover, was presumed to be a friend of the Ford offer. Department of Commerce, *A General Review of the Nitrogen Situation in the United States*, Senate Doc. 88, 68 Cong., 1 Sess. (1924), 2, 44–52.

66. New York *Times*, April 30, May 5, 11, 1924; *Muscle Shoals*, Senate Hearings, 68 Cong., 1 Sess., 719–25, 747–59.

67. New York *Times*, May 24, 1924.

carefully planned multiple-purpose development of the Tennessee
Valley watershed. He declared that in view of the great danger
that a complete national power monopoly might develop because
of recent technological and organizational developments in the
private power business, the government ought to operate Muscle
Shoals as a yardstick for measuring fair rates.[68]

In the report, Norris protested that "propaganda" for the Ford
offer was being circulated by Muscle Shoals real estate speculators
and Gray Silver of the Farm Bureau. He declared that Muscle
Shoals speculation had already taken millions of dollars from
"unsuspecting people all over the United States." As for the
alleged Ford-Coolidge deal, Norris hinted that Ford had re-
nounced his presidential aspirations in favor of the Coolidge
candidacy in exchange for "certain considerations" involving
Muscle Shoals.[69] Senator Heflin, aided by Senator Caraway, reprimanded the Republican members of the Senate for not defending
Coolidge from the charges made and implied in the Norris report
which, Heflin asserted, "practically accuse him of making a deal
with Henry Ford." Heflin declared:

There was no positive evidence before the committee that tended to
show that the President made a deal with Henry Ford, but if he did
promise Henry Ford Muscle Shoals, it is about the only thing he has
done for the farmer since he has been President.[70]

The minority report, written by Senator Ladd of the pro-Ford
group, protested that "the Ford offer has been made the subject
of the most savage attacks which we have ever seen in any
legislation." [71]

Since adjournment was near at hand, further Senate action on
Muscle Shoals was deferred to the fall session, when, it was
agreed unanimously, the Senate Muscle Shoals bill, as reported
by the Agriculture Committee, would have first place on the
Senate calendar. Senator Heflin blamed Norris for the failure
of the Senate to act on the Ford offer during the present session

68. Senate Report 678, 68 Cong., 1 Sess., 10–12, 29–31.
69. Ibid., 14, 26–28.
70. Cong. Rec., 68 Cong., 1 Sess., 10496.
71. Senate Report 678, 68 Cong., 1 Sess., Part 2, 3.

and accused him of deliberately prolonging the hearings in order to defeat the Ford proposal.[72]

In the months following the Ford victory in the House, Ford and his offer received much unfavorable attention by the press throughout the country. Influential editors averred that Ford was losing support. In some quarters, it was observed that the widespread belief that Ford's offer was motivated by patriotism and philanthropy, on which much of the support of the offer was undoubtedly based, was weakening. As the Muscle Shoals hearings before the Norris committee came to an end, the Charlotte, North Carolina, *Observer* predicted that within a year the country would be amazed that the Ford offer had ever received serious consideration. In addition, the press was directing more attention to the alleged merits of the power companies' offer. The Ford offer, however, still commanded the loyalty of many editors, especially in the South. The southern editors at this time were concentrating on efforts to prove that the Ford offer was the only bona fide Muscle Shoals bid by showing that the others were merely smoke screens covering attempts by the fertilizer and power monopolies to defeat Ford's proposal.[73]

Muscle Shoals was not an issue in the presidential campaign of 1924. The Democratic platform advocated the utilization of Muscle Shoals for the production of cheap fertilizer but did not mention the water-power aspect of the problem. The Republican platform did not specifically refer to Muscle Shoals, but it did demand that the federal water-power law remain inviolate. Robert M. La Follette's Progressive party of 1924 advocated "public ownership of the nation's water power and creation of a public superpower system."[74] Despite the great amount of publicity which had been given to Muscle Shoals and water power by the Norris committee, neither competed successfully with older issues in this campaign. Although the rapid growth of the power

72. *Cong. Rec.*, 68 Cong., 1 Sess., 10473-74, 10493.

73. "The Rival Bids for Muscle Shoals," in *Literary Digest*, LXXXI (May 10, 1924), 10–11.

74. New York *Times*, June 12, 29, 1924; Kenneth C. McKay, *The Progressive Movement of 1924* (1947), 270.

business at this time was forcing power to the front as one of
the major factors in the lives of millions of Americans, it had not
yet become an important national issue. Furthermore, the Ford-
Coolidge reconciliation of late 1923 helped to keep the Ford
offer out of national politics in 1924.

The Ford offer had undoubtedly become an important issue
in many localities, particularly in the South. Senator Heflin asserted that the Ford offer was an issue in 101 congressional races
in 1922. He attributed the Democratic gains in the House that
year to the party's support of the Ford offer. On the other hand,
Senator Brookhart of Iowa interpreted the June primaries of
1924 in his state as a repudiation of the Ford offer. Brookhart,
an opponent of the Ford proposal who handily won the Republican senatorial nomination that year, insisted that in the senatorial
and ten congressional campaigns in the Republican primary in
Iowa, Ford's Muscle Shoals bid was an important issue supported
by the losing candidate in each instance.[75]

In the early autumn of 1924, supporters of the Ford offer expressed confidence that the proposal would win acceptance in
the forthcoming second session of the Sixty-eighth Congress.
They were perhaps unduly optimistic in view of the brevity of
this lame duck session which would, in all probability, permit
the opponents of the Ford offer to delay action. Despite the
enthusiasm prevailing in the Ford camp, the Detroit manufacturer
suddenly withdrew his offer in October. According to *Electrical
World*, the principal reason for Ford's withdrawal was that he
had become convinced that the nation was committed to the
Federal Water Power Act and would not violate it by accepting
his Muscle Shoals offer. His announced reason for the withdrawal
was that "a single affair of business which should have been
decided by anyone within a week has become a complicated
political affair." [76] Yet, seemingly, he did not completely close
the door on Muscle Shoals—he challenged the government to
make him a better offer. In some quarters there was the feeling

75. *Cong. Rec.*, 68 Cong., 1 Sess., 10491, 10496.
76. "Ford Withdraws Offer for Muscle Shoals," in *Electrical World*, LXXXIV
(Oct. 18, 1924), 827.

that the Ford withdrawal was merely a shrewd move calculated to force action in Congress.[77]

As Ford withdrew his plan, he again struck a blow at Wall Street. He blamed that financial center once more for the major opposition to acceptance of his offer:

Wall Street doesn't care to have the power trust's strangle-hold broken. If we had obtained Muscle Shoals, we would quickly have exposed the present profiteering and greatly reduced the cost of power.[78]

Ford also took a parting shot at Congress, declaring that it was controlled by Wall Street, and he averred that the La Follette–Norris Progressives, who had fought his Muscle Shoals offer, "played Wall Street's game, knowingly or unknowingly." He diagnosed the Progressives as being troubled by the inability "to distinguish between big business and the money interests." [79]

The withdrawal of the Ford offer came as a surprise, particularly in view of the great amount of support it still apparently commanded both in and out of Congress. On the eve of the withdrawal, the Ford partisans had been girding their loins in preparation for a fight to victory in the Senate where they believed they held a majority. In view of the great margin by which the offer had been accepted by the House, they had sound grounds for this optimism.[80]

On the other hand, it could not be denied that the Ford star had dimmed somewhat since the House victory in March. The subsequent hearings by the Norris committee not only revealed a growing anti-Ford sentiment, they did much toward crystallizing this sentiment by bringing to the attention of the country the alleged defects of the Ford offer. The public apparently was beginning to get tired as well as suspicious of the continuous and repetitive line of attack sustained by the Ford supporters. One observer stated: "It is, in fact, small wonder that as the first

77. New York *Times*, Oct. 14, 1924; "What Next at Muscle Shoals?" in *Literary Digest*, LXXXIII (Nov. 8, 1924), 11.

78. New York *Times*, Oct. 19 (II), 1924.

79. *Ibid.*

80. Charles Merz, "Muscle Shoals," in *Century Magazine*, CVIII (Sept. 1924), 616.

thrill of turning it over to Henry wears off, and the actual en-
tanglements of the proposal become more generally understood,
the Ford bid should meet with rising opposition." [81]

In summary, there were several factors involved in producing
the increasing resistance to Ford's plan and, ultimately, the withdrawal of Ford from the contest. As Norris and his colleagues
continued to subject the alleged philanthropic aspects of the
Ford offer to critical analysis, it began to appear that Ford was
chiefly interested in acquiring a vast source of cheap electricity
rather than in helping the farmer.[82] For example, one editor
observed at the time of the withdrawal that "the country, once
it understood that the Ford bid was a mere fraction of the worth
of the property, showed no desire to make the richest man in
America an object of government charity." [83]

Perhaps the most important factor behind the opposition to
the Ford offer was the fact that the proposal clearly violated the
Federal Water Power Act. Senator Norris and his fellow Progressives, as well as the power companies, took advantage of every
opportunity to publicize the alleged benefits, especially to small
communities, to be derived from development and "equitable"
distribution of cheap water-power resources under the Federal
Water Power Act.[84] In defense the Ford proponents termed the
Water Power Act a subterfuge for protecting the interests of the
power companies, and they asserted that cheap water power
could be most economically utilized in supplying power for large-
scale industries located at the site of generation.[85]

Additional reasons for the loss of popularity of the Ford offer

81. Ibid., 618.

82. Cong. Rec., 67 Cong., 2 Sess., 108, 8897; Dakin, "Henry Ford—Man or
Superman?" loc. cit., 336–37; "Ford Mesmerism and Muscle Shoals," in Current
Opinion, LXVI (May, 1924), 626; St. Paul Pioneer Press, Oct. 13, 1923.

83. "Henry Gets Right at Last," in Independent, CXIII (Oct. 25, 1924), 300.

84. Senate Report 678, 68 Cong., 1 Sess., 8–12; William Hard, "Mr. Ford Is
So Good," in Nation, CXVIII (March 26, 1924), 340–41; "Weakness of the
Federal Water-Power Act," in Farm and Home, June, 1924, quoted in Kerwin,
op. cit., 274–76.

85. Cong. Rec., 67 Cong., 2 Sess., 9339, 9350–52; Muscle Shoals, Senate Re-
port 831, 67 Cong., 2 Sess., 19; House Report 143, 68 Cong., 1 Sess., 60; Muscle
Shoals, Senate Hearings, 67 Cong., 2 Sess., 362–64; George W. Norris, "Why
Henry Ford Wants Muscle Shoals," in Nation, CXVII (Dec. 26, 1923), 738.

include the following: Ford's consistent refusal to include an ironclad guarantee of fertilizer production; the Teapot Dome scandal; and sectionalism and partisan politics. Ford's failure to guarantee fertilizer production made it appear that he himself did not have faith in the fertilizer potential of Muscle Shoals.[86] Many editors who opposed the Ford proposal named the Teapot Dome scandal as a causal factor in the downfall of Ford's plan for Muscle Shoals, and in some quarters it was suggested that the tide of public opinion began flowing against the Ford offer as a result of the notorious oil-lease scandal.[87] Interest in the water-power aspects of the Ford offer controversy was national in scope, but the fertilizer issue was subjected to some sectional dispute. The opponents of the Ford offer consistently asserted that the South was the only region that stood to benefit directly from fertilizer production at Muscle Shoals.[88]

Although the pro-Ford leaders generally declared the issue of the Ford offer to be bipartisan, most of the opposition to the proposal came from within the Republican party, while pro-Ford sentiment was generally associated with the Democratic party However, several Republican members of congress, mostly from the Middle West, were important supporters of Ford. The administration Republicans accused the Democrats of attempting to utilize the great prestige of Ford to better the fortunes of their party.[89]

Another factor which greatly impaired the original high repute of the Ford offer was the bad odor generated by the activities of Muscle Shoals land speculators. The feverish speculation in land at Muscle Shoals which began immediately following the announcement of Ford's plan for a huge city at Muscle Shoals

86. Hard, "Mr. Ford Is So Good," *loc. cit.*, 340–41; Merz, "Muscle Shoals," *loc. cit.*, 11.

87. "Muscle Shoals: A Scandal in the Making?" *loc. cit.*, 220; "Ford Mesmerism and Muscle Shoals," *loc. cit.*, 626.

88. *Cong. Rec.*, 67 Cong., 2 Sess., 3660, 8773; *ibid.*, 67 Cong., 4 Sess., 874, 3296, 4524–25; *Nitrate*, Hearings, U. S. House of Representatives, 2nd Supplement, 67 Cong., 4 Sess., 3–7; George F. Milton, Jr., "The South and Muscle Shoals," in *Independent*, CXII (Jan. 19, 1924), 39–41.

89. *Cong. Rec.*, 67 Cong., 2 Sess., 8037–38, 9348, 11795–97, 13021; *ibid.*, 67 Cong., 4 Sess., 173.

in January, 1922, continued with varying degrees of intensity throughout the entire period of the Ford offer controversy. These speculators were well organized; they established a school in New York to train agents; and they had offices in all of the principal cities of the United States. Norris asserted that thousands of Americans lost their entire savings to these unscrupulous land speculators. Opponents of the Ford offer insisted that Muscle Shoals real estate speculators were responsible for much of the publicity given the Ford offer, especially the promise of cheap fertilizer.[90]

It would be difficult to assess the effect of Ford's anti-Semitism on his Muscle Shoals offer. After his anti-Semitic remarks of December, 1921, in Alabama, he continued his attack on Jews, but it was not again directly related to the Muscle Shoals controversy.[91]

Ford's endorsement of the conservative Coolidge and repudiation of the Ford-for-President movement were elements in the downfall of the Ford offer in that these events tended to blunt one of his sharpest weapons—his fight against Wall Street. According to Donald Davidson, his antipathy to Wall Street was one of the main factors that "made him popular with farmers and little businessmen everywhere." [92] The pro-Ford group portrayed the controversy over the Ford offer as a struggle between industrial capitalism as represented by Ford and financial capitalism as represented by Wall Street and the power companies. According to the Dearborn *Independent*:

The Muscle Shoals controversy means more than water power and fertilizer, more than the opening of the South's new era; it means that two systems of business are colliding, head on. The contest is production versus profits. Service and spoils confront each other.

If nothing else comes out of this controversy, this at least has been achieved—the system of exploitation has been drawn out from its cover into public view. All its American and foreign tentacles have

90. *Ibid.*, 67 Cong., 2 Sess., 8898, 8900; *ibid.*, 68 Cong., 1 Sess., 5747–49, 6603, 6869; George W. Norris, *The Fighting Liberal* (1945), 256–59.

91. For highlights of this subject during this period see New York *Times*, Jan. 6, 7, 17, Oct. 29, 1922, Feb. 8, June 23, 1923, Jan. 12, May 13, June 3, 1924; William C. Richards, *The Last Billionaire* (1948), 97.

92. Davidson, *The Tennessee*, II, 183–84.

been disclosed. Its pressure methods have been studied in all sections of the country and in all lines of business.[93]

Senator Norris played an important role in the failure of Ford to obtain Muscle Shoals. Jerome G. Kerwin, an authority on water-power legislation, felt that the wide adverse publicity given to the Ford offer by the Norris committee in 1924 made senatorial approval of the Ford proposal impossible. Norris himself felt that his chief contribution to the fight against the Ford offer was the alleged demonstration by his committee that the cyanamid process, and, hence, nitrate plant no. 2, was obsolete. Norris admitted that the Ford offer was not definitely defeated when it was withdrawn.[94] Doubtless, Norris, under the pretext of being fair to all parties involved, deliberately prolonged the Muscle Shoals hearings in 1924 in order to prevent a Ford bill from reaching the floor.

The Norris bill for government operation of Muscle Shoals never attained any considerable success during the Ford period of the Muscle Shoals controversy except within the Senate Agriculture Committee. The principle of government ownership and operation of public utilities was, at this time, in disfavor in Congress. The issue of private versus public power was never very prominent nationally during this period of the controversy and was completely overshadowed by the struggle between Ford and the power companies.[95]

Southern members of Congress, in supporting the Ford offer, deserted their former position advocating government operation of Muscle Shoals which they had held during the debates on the Wadsworth-Kahn bill. Nevertheless, practically all of the Southerners preferred public operation of Muscle Shoals to acceptance of the power companies' bid. They varied considerably in their respective attitudes toward the sacred dogmas of private enterprise which then prevailed, ranging from the extremist position of Senator Heflin, who vied with New England Republicans in

93. Dearborn *Independent*, May 11, 1924, quoted in *Cong. Rec.*, 68 Cong., 1 Sess., 9822–23.
94. Kerwin, *op. cit.*, 282; Davidson, *op. cit.*, II, 186; Norris, *op. cit.*, 255, 261–62.
95. Norris, *op. cit.*, 251.

denouncing public power projects, to the policy of expediency advocated by Senator Smith of South Carolina, whose loyalty to the private operation of Muscle Shoals was lukewarm.[96] Whether the Southerners were conscious of any philosophical basis for the great elasticity of their economic ideology which they had demonstrated thus far in the controversy they never fully explained; it is obvious that they followed a policy of expediency designed to bring economic aid to the South.

Next to Norris, Senator McNary and Representative LaGuardia were the most outspoken advocates of government operation of Muscle Shoals. These three Progressives vigorously attacked the theory, expounded by opponents of the Norris bill, that it was impossible for a government to operate a business successfully because of the lack of a profit incentive. They contended that profit was not the only motive for business and that men could be found who would operate a government power enterprise efficiently and successfully while earning a fixed salary.[97]

To some degree, perhaps, the Muscle Shoals controversy during this period was a test of the power and duty of Congress to formulate a national economic policy. The Republican administration made it plain that it did not trust the ability of Congress to solve the Muscle Shoals problem, and it was suggested that it be turned over to an executive commission. Also, southern Democrats as a whole strongly questioned the capacity of Congress to deal with such a problem. Ford himself seriously berated Congress for not rendering a speedy decision on his offer and declared, upon withdrawing it, that "productive business cannot wait on policies." [98] On the other hand, Ford's haughty attitude toward Congress in this respect was considered in some quarters to be a factor in the growing reaction against the Ford bid in its latter stages.[99]

96. *Cong. Rec.*, 67 Cong., 2 Sess., 3064, 9338; *ibid.*, 67 Cong., 4 Sess., 172–73, 3300.

97. *Ibid.*, 67 Cong., 4 Sess., 3298; *Muscle Shoals*, Senate Hearings, 67 Cong., 2 Sess., 20, 219–22, 341–42.

98. *Cong. Rec.*, 67 Cong., 4 Sess., 3300; New York *Times*, March 5, 1922, Oct. 14, 1924.

99. "What Next at Muscle Shoals?" *loc. cit.*, 11.

Why did the Muscle Shoals controversy occupy such an important place in the United States between 1921 and 1924? The answer lies in the fact that the problem of disposing of the war surplus Muscle Shoals properties became entangled with at least two of the most important problems challenging American policy-makers in the postwar period—the water-power problem and the problem of protecting the public interest in government-owned natural resources. Muscle Shoals also became the cornerstone of an attempt to free America from dependence on foreign sources of nitrogen for the sake of national defense and agriculture, although, this aspect of the controversy was greatly confused by apparent attempts to use it as a subterfuge to gain other ends. In addition, the controversy over the fate of Muscle Shoals was intensified and perhaps exaggerated by the involvement of the dynamic personality of Henry Ford.

Some observers saw in the Muscle Shoals project itself factors of great importance. Wilson Dam was heralded as the key to a new era of power development in the southern Appalachian region, which would be characterized by a definite change of American policy toward river development—the beginning of an era of multiple-purpose dam construction. The construction of the gigantic Wilson Dam, which was described by one observer as "the most significant effort in construction undertaken by the Government since building the Panama Canal," captured the imagination of many American people.[100]

The finest tributes to the importance of Muscle Shoals were paid by Newton D. Baker and Senator Norris. The former Secretary of War asserted, "If I were greedy for power over my fellow-men I would rather control Muscle Shoals than to be continuously elected President of the United States"; and Senator Norris declared that should the Ford offer be accepted, the property transferred to the automobile magnate by that action would con-

100. Littel McClung, "Building of the World's Largest Monolith," in *Scientific American*, CXXIX (July, 1923), 8–9; K. C. McMurray, "The Geographic Setting of Muscle Shoals," in *Bulletin of the Geographical Society of Philadelphia*, XXII (July, 1924), 10–23.

stitute "the greatest gift ever bestowed on mortal man since salvation was made free to the human race." [101]

According to the press, the withdrawal of the Ford proposal was an occasion of deep disappointment for the supporters of the offer who lived in the Muscle Shoals area as well as in the Tennessee Valley as a whole. Nevertheless, they were not despondent. Instead, this group of Tennessee Valley residents together with the opponents of the Ford bid in the region expressed strong faith that the great water-power resources of Muscle Shoals would be developed by either the government or some private party. Thus it was obvious that Ford's supporters in the valley, unlike the Detroit industrialist, had no intention of withdrawing from the Muscle Shoals controversy. They made it clear that Ford's withdrawal had not removed the fundamental issues of the controversy, and their attitude indicated that the struggle over the future of Muscle Shoals would continue unabated.[102]

---

101. "Muscle Shoals—Ours," in *Nation,* CXIX (Dec. 17, 1924), 668; Senate Report 831, 67 Cong., 2 Sess., 28.

102. Chattanooga *Times,* Oct. 14, 1924; Chattanooga *News,* Oct. 14, 1924; Nashville *Banner,* Oct. 14, 1924; Nashville *Tennessean,* Oct. 14, 1924; and Memphis *Commercial-Appeal,* Oct. 14, 1924.

VI

The Underwood Bill

THE WITHDRAWAL OF Henry Ford from the Muscle Shoals controversy left the Norris Progressives and the power companies as the principals in the struggle. With the removal of the enigmatic Ford offer, the issue for the first time appeared to become clear. According to Norris:

> With withdrawal of Mr. Ford's offer, the struggle over Muscle Shoals simplified itself to an issue between those who believed in public ownership and development of the power at Muscle Shoals and throughout the entire Tennessee Valley, and the "power trust," seeking to prevent everything of the kind.[1]

The press across the country presented a divided opinion as to the relative strength of the remaining combatants. Some editors foresaw a trend toward public development and operation of Muscle Shoals while others believed that with Ford's withdrawal, the last obstacle to the success of the offer of the power companies had been removed. Asserting that the fertilizer and power "trusts" had now accomplished their aim by forcing the Ford offer from the field, some of the more rabid pro-Ford editors in the South predicted that the other offers, which the Nashville *Banner* described as "bogus bids," would be dropped.[2] At any length, the president of the Alabama Power Company announced, immediately following the Ford withdrawal, that the offer of the power companies still stood.[3]

As the Ford supporters in Congress recovered from the shock

1. George W. Norris, *The Fighting Liberal* (1945), 260.
2. "What Next at Muscle Shoals?" in *Literary Digest*, LXXXIII (Nov. 8, 1924), 10–11.
3. Memphis *Commercial-Appeal*, Oct. 15, 1924.

of the Ford withdrawal, they began to complicate the Muscle Shoals issue. On the eve of the new session of Congress, some of the former Ford partisans approached the Norris supporters seeking a compromise government-operation plan, but Norris replied that he would press for passage of his bill, which had been favorably reported by the Agriculture Committee during the previous session. Norris stated that sufficient opportunity had been extended to private enterprise to come forth with a suitable offer for Muscle Shoals and that it was time for Congress to act since no reasonable offer had been submitted.[4]

The withdrawal of the Ford offer temporarily removed the fertilizer issue from Muscle Shoals since the only two significant contending groups remaining—the power companies and the Norris group—agreed that the project was primarily a water-power issue. Nevertheless, the Muscle Shoals fertilizer question again became important as a result of President Coolidge's message to Congress on December 3, 1924, in which he declared that "the support of agriculture is the chief problem to consider in connection with this property." In his message, Coolidge rejected government operation of Muscle Shoals, although he recommended that if none of the private offers were found to be suitable, the government should temporarily continue the development of Muscle Shoals with the view of producing fertilizer materials. He also recommended that the government dispose of the power and fertilizer facilities separately, a feature which was pleasing to the power companies because they had not been enthusiastic about producing fertilizer at Muscle Shoals.[5]

As late as November 30, 1924, administration Republicans in the Senate expected to follow a policy of delay on Muscle Shoals, and Senator Charles Curtis, the Republican Senate leader, announced that the Muscle Shoals problem would be referred to the Agriculture Committee with the possibility of remaining

4. New York *Times*, Nov. 20, 27, 1924. In late November Senator Borah notified his Idaho Farm Bureau constituents, who had been demanding that he support the Ford offer, that he would continue to support the Norris bill. Paul V. Nast to Borah, Aug. 14, 1924; Borah to Nast, Nov. 26, 1924, Borah Papers.

5. New York *Times*, Dec. 4, 1924.

there until adjournment because of the brevity of the short session. Nevertheless, President Coolidge apparently decided to attempt to dispose of the problem immediately by working out a compromise with southern senators. A few days later Senator Underwood conferred at length with Secretary Weeks regarding a Muscle Shoals bill on which Underwood was working, and the resulting measure, which was introduced on the day before the President's message to Congress, contained essentially the same principal recommendations as those embodied in Coolidge's message, especially in that it provided for a private lease with government operation as a last resort. Underwood more closely identified his bill with the Coolidge message by stating that the chief difference between his plan and that of Senator Norris was that the latter was primarily a water-power bill whereas his was fundamentally a bill to produce fertilizer for agriculture.[6]

The debate on the Norris bill, which had been reported favorably by the Senate Agriculture Committee at the end of the previous session, began on December 4. Republican leaders in the Senate were expected to give an outright endorsement to the Underwood bill, but Secretary Weeks revealed that the administration was not yet quite satisfied with that proposal. The administration's main objections, according to Secretary Weeks, were that it required the lessee to produce too much fertilizer in the early years of the lease in the face of uncertain market conditions, that it placed too many limitations on the lessee's freedom of disposal of the surplus power, and that it failed to provide for sufficient time in which the project could be leased before resorting to government operation. Following a week-end cruise on the presidential yacht with President Coolidge and two additional conferences with Secretary Weeks, Underwood announced on Monday, December 8, that no serious differences existed between himself and the Republican administration with regard to Muscle Shoals and that he would make the necessary alterations in his bill to meet the objections of the administration. Accordingly, Underwood amended his bill to fit administration

6. *Ibid.*, Nov. 30, Dec. 5, 7, 8, 1924.

specifications, giving rise to the prediction that it would hurdle the Senate within a week.[7]

The Underwood bill as amended authorized the Secretary of War to lease the Muscle Shoals project for a period not to exceed fifty years, and in the event no satisfactory lessee could be found by September, 1925, the project would be operated by a government corporation. In either case, it was required that production of fertilizer begin the third year of operation and be increased to an annual amount containing 40,000 tons of nitrogen by the fifth year and thereafter. The lessee would be required to pay an annual rental of 4 per cent of the total cost of construction of Wilson Dam and in return would have at his disposal all of the power not needed in the production of fertilizer.[8]

Thereupon, on December 8, Underwood offered his newly amended bill in the form of an amendment as a substitute for the Norris bill, an action which placed the Underwood bill on the floor for immediate consideration.[9]

As the debate got underway, it soon became apparent that the solid southern bloc, which had supported the Ford offer, had cracked, thus weakening the administration-Underwood coalition. On December 12, Senator McKellar dramatically announced that he had reached a decision to support the Norris bill. He stated that his only objection to that measure had been removed

7. *Ibid.*, Nov. 30, Dec. 5, 7, 8, 9, 1924; *Cong. Rec.*, 68 Cong., 2 Sess., 254, 259–60; Weeks to Coolidge, Dec. 6, 1924, Judge Advocate General, National Archives.

8. *Cong. Rec.*, 68 Cong., 2 Sess., 259–60. The Underwood bill also authorized the construction of dam no. 3 which, when completed, would be leased or operated in conjunction with Wilson Dam. In case of a lease, the amount of the rental payments was to be determined later, but it was certain that the lessee under the Underwood bill would also receive the power benefits from this dam.

The Underwood bill did not specify which process would be used in fertilizer production but implied that both plants 1 and 2 would be employed for this purpose.

9. *Ibid.*, 258–59; New York *Times*, Dec. 8, 1924; Joseph S. Ransmeier, *The Tennessee Valley Authority* (1942), 49. *Electrical World* protested that Underwood's failure to place restrictions on the disposal of the power by the lessee might result in allowing Muscle Shoals to fall under the control of chemical interests who would absorb the power at the expense of the public. "Consideration of Muscle Shoals Deferred," *Electrical World*, LXXXIV (Dec. 5, 1924), 1219.

when Norris had agreed to accept an amendment obligating the government to produce 40,000 tons of nitrogen at Muscle Shoals annually. McKellar asserted that this added provision would make the Norris bill a genuine fertilizer proposition. Norris confirmed the fact that he had made such an agreement with the Tennessee Senator. Despite the fact that McKellar was severely reproved by the pro-Underwood Southerners, especially Heflin, who interpreted the McKellar move as a betrayal of a sacred cause of the South, the Tennessean was soon followed by a host of southern senators who turned their backs on the Underwood bill and began to drift into the Norris camp. The principal members of this group were Senators Ellison D. Smith of South Carolina, William J. Harris and Walter F. George of Georgia, Furnifold M. Simmons of North Carolina, Duncan U. Fletcher of Florida, Earle B. Mayfield and Morris Sheppard of Texas, and Joseph E. Ransdell of Louisiana.[10]

As the Underwood bill reached the floor, the Norris group attempted to kill it with a flurry of amendments. Except for a few minor changes which were unopposed by Underwood and which did not alter the meaning of the bill in the least, the amendments were unsuccessful. The most important of these defeated proposals were the Harris amendment to authorize the Secretary of Agriculture to regulate the sale and distribution of fertilizer manufactured at Muscle Shoals; the McNary amendment to require that any power development at Muscle Shoals conform to the provisions of the Federal Water Power Act; and the Smith amendment to strike out the private leasing provisions of the Underwood bill, leaving only the sections providing for government operation. The Smith amendment placed the question of government versus private operation of Muscle Shoals squarely before the Senate, and the former alternative was rejected, 49 to 32, the vote being a fairly good indication of the strength of the Underwood coalition. Underwood declared that this vote proved that victory for his bill was assured.[11]

The leaders of the administration-Underwood coalition had

10. *Cong. Rec.*, 68 Cong., 2 Sess., 513, 515, 1669, 1736, 1795, 1805–8.
11. *Ibid.*, 301–5, 307, 314, 516–25, 656.

anticipated an early vote, but they failed to obtain it because of the determined opposition of the Norris group, which was accused by coalition leaders of conducting a filibuster. Administration Republicans began to show signs of nervousness regarding the remaining legislative program, and on December 16, Senator James E. Watson, a Republican leader, announced immediately after a visit to the White House that he favored referring the whole Muscle Shoals problem to a commission. Other administration leaders, however, declared that they intended to bring the Underwood bill to a vote soon.[12]

On December 19, the Norris group, over the heated protests of the leaders of the Underwood coalition, obtained the adoption of amendments providing for interstate regulation of Muscle Shoals power, prohibition of subleases of Muscle Shoals property, and preference to farmers in the sale of fertilizer produced at Muscle Shoals. The latter two amendments were based on the alleged fear of Senator Harris that the Underwood bill might deliver Muscle Shoals to the power "trust" through a sublease and his assertion that the bill would permit the lessee to wholesale all Muscle Shoals fertilizer to the fertilizer "trust." [13]

Approaching the Christmas holidays, the outlook for the Underwood bill became more gloomy as several Republican senators began to waver in their loyalty to it, and reports from the White House indicated that President Coolidge had definitely given up hope of its passage. There was now strong talk among Republican leaders of referring the problem to a commission. When Congress reconvened after Christmas, the White House staff announced that the President would not interfere with further congressional deliberation on the Muscle Shoals problem but would sign the Underwood bill if passed.[14]

An agreement to vote was finally reached on January 7, 1925, and on the next day the Underwood bill, in the form of an amendment, was adopted as a substitute for the Norris bill by a vote of 48 to 27. It appeared that victory for Underwood was in sight.

12. New York *Times,* Dec. 13, 17, 19, 1924.
13. *Cong. Rec.,* 68 Cong., 2 Sess., 823–24.
14. New York *Times,* Dec. 21, 22, 31, 1924.

Administration senators voted almost solidly for the Underwood amendment, but the Southerners favored the Norris bill by a small majority. At this point, several administration Republicans deserted Underwood's measure in favor of an amendment offered by Senator Wesley L. Jones of Washington which proposed to refer the problem to a commission. Since the proposed commission would be endowed with no power other than advising Congress, the Norris group was willing to accept the commission plan in preference to the Underwood bill. Consequently, the Norris forces, which by that time included a considerable number of Southerners, joined with administration senators to adopt the Jones amendment as a substitute for the Underwood amendment by a vote of 46 to 33. Immediately afterward Norris offered his own bill as a substitute for the Jones amendment, and his motion was successful by a vote of 40 to 39. The temporary Norris victory was made possible by the fact that all southern Democrats who voted, except Underwood and John K. Shields, supported the Norris bill. The pro-Underwood Southerners demonstrated that they had rather have the Norris bill than nothing, and they had some consolation in the fact that the Norris plan now contained the McKellar amendment requiring that a fixed amount of nitrogen be produced regardless of the course that Norris's proposed fertilizer research program might take.

The Norris victory was short-lived for again Underwood offered his bill as a substitute for the Norris measure, and again it was adopted, 46 to 33. Again Senator Jones offered his compromise plan as a substitute for the Underwood bill. Norris, agreeing not to offer his bill again if the Jones amendment should win, threw his support behind the Jones plan which would at least defer a final decision. Thus the issue boiled down to a clash between the Jones commission plan and the Underwood bill, the latter emerging triumphant, 43 to 38. Then, on January 14, the Underwood bill was passed by the Senate, 50 to 30. Ten administration Republicans who had deserted the Underwood bill in favor of the Jones plan came back to the Underwood fold in these final two contests.[15]

15. *Cong. Rec.*, 68 Cong., 2 Sess. 266, 1454, 1724–41, 1795–1808.

In the complicated political maneuvering during these debates, a group of administration Republicans had deserted the Underwood bill and turned to the Jones plan, after which the pro-Underwood Southerners flocked to the support of the Norris bill. The Southerners preferred government operation to no operation. Consequently, in order to prevent passage of the Norris bill which embodied an economic and political philosophy completely alien to orthodox Republican principles, the Coolidge forces consolidated their position and hurriedly swung back in full support of the Underwood bill.[16]

Although the administration-Underwood forces hailed the victorious Underwood bill as primarily a plan to produce cheap fertilizer, the final measure contained much less rigid restrictions in this respect on the lessee than did the original proposal. It contained a provision permitting the lessee to cease production of fertilizer by the sixth year or after if he decided it could not be done without loss, but in such an event he would retain the power facilities on the same terms. Thus there was no guarantee in the Underwood bill that fertilizer would be produced for the farmers. Furthermore, the lessee was limited to 1 per cent profit on fertilizer, a provision which would provide an incentive for the lessee to abandon fertilizer production; and by permitting separate leases of the power and fertilizer facilities, the bill violated a time-tested dogma of the fertilizer adherents that the project should be operated as a unit. Before passing the bill the Senate had eliminated the amendments tacked on to it in December by the Norris bloc, which provided for interstate regulation of Muscle Shoals power, prohibited subleasing, and gave preference to farmers in the sale of fertilizers.[17]

In the heated Senate debate precipitated by the clash of the Underwood and Norris bills, the basic issue of public versus private operation of power utilities permeated most of the discussion, although most of the conservative southern senators who were supporting the Norris bill contended that this factor

16. "The Dance on Muscle Shoals," in *Outlook*, CXXXIX (Jan. 28, 1925), 129–31.

17. *Cong. Rec.*, 68 Cong., 2 Sess., 1809.

was not properly a part of the Muscle Shoals question since the government did not construct that project with the intent to compete with private power companies. These Southerners contended that the primary purpose of Muscle Shoals under the Norris bill would be the promotion of research and experimentation with fertilizer products, a legitimate function of the government. On the other hand, supporters of the Coolidge-Underwood coalition, as well as some of the Progressive Republicans, believed the issue of public versus private power to be one of the principal issues involved in this struggle. Senator Hiram Johnson, an ardent supporter of the Norris bill, stated that he considered this Muscle Shoals debate to be fundamentally "a question of two warring philosophies of government," while Senator Heflin called the Norris bill "socialistic" and "Bolshevistic." [18]

Although Norris had consistently maintained that the Muscle Shoals controversy did not clearly present the issue of public versus private power, he utilized this debate to promote the principle of public power. He described in detail the public-owned power system of Ontario province, Canada, quoting numerous statistics purporting to show that power development in Ontario had greatly extended rural and urban power service and drastically reduced rates without the resort to uneconomic practices. He also attempted to prove that these Canadians were enjoying much lower power rates than their American neighbors who were served by private power companies.[19]

Supporters of the Underwood bill maintained that agriculture and national defense would be better served by private rather

18. *Ibid.*, 186–87, 192–96, 268, 455–56, 763, 831, 1670, 1673.

19. *Ibid.*, 869–76. Norris had been using the Ontario public power system as a weapon in his fight for public operation of Muscle Shoals for some time. In January, 1925, the power companies counter-attacked with a pamphlet allegedly proving that the Ontario system depended on government subsidies and that it rendered inferior service. This pamphlet, which was published under the imprint of the Smithsonian Institution, was described as an unbiased study by that government agency. In 1929, the Federal Trade Commission disclosed that this publicity piece was financed by private power companies and that its author, Samuel S. Wyer, was a professional propagandist for power companies instead of an employee of the Smithsonian Institution. Samuel S. Wyer, *Niagara Falls: Its Power Possibilities and Preservation*, Smithsonian Institution's Study of Natural Resources, Publication 2820 (Jan., 1925). Also see Chapter X.

than public operation of Muscle Shoals, their contention being that political interference and inelasticity of government rules made it impossible for a government to operate a business successfully. They maintained that public power enterprises violated various scientific principles of economics such as the profit incentive. The Norris bloc countered with the assertion that it was a legitimate function of the government to operate power projects such as Muscle Shoals as yardsticks in order to regulate the private power industry, although some of the Southerners in the Norris group were careful not to defend public power in principle. The Norris bloc insisted that it would be unsafe to permit a national defense project as important as Muscle Shoals to fall into private hands.[20]

The fertilizer issue furnished the focal point of much of this Muscle Shoals debate, and because of shifting alliances, the fertilizer question became more complicated. Norris still insisted that with respect to fertilizer the principal duty of the government at Muscle Shoals was to conduct research and experimentation, but as a concession to his new-found allies from the South he agreed that a part of the power at Muscle Shoals should be used in the production of commercial fertilizer if possible. Most of the southern Democrats who joined Norris continued to insist that Muscle Shoals was primarily a fertilizer proposition, but they now agreed with Norris that further research and experimentation were necessary. Senator Smith led the way in harmonizing these two opposing theories now brought together in the Norris camp. Furthermore, some of these Southerners, particularly McKellar, Simmons, Harris, and George, inadvertently revealed a great concern about the question of distribution of Muscle Shoals power. Norris's Progressive colleagues continued to regard the project as wholly a source of water power for general distribution and the cheap-fertilizer theme as a mask to cover other purposes, such as the concentration of the power within the Muscle Shoals area in order to build up a large industry there.[21]

20. Cong. Rec., 68 Cong., 2 Sess., 113, 192, 208, 719, 763–69.
21. Ibid., 113, 267, 454, 511–12, 525, 650–51.

The Underwood Democrats stood squarely against the Norris-Smith plan for fertilizer research and asserted that the cyanamid process at nitrate plant no. 2 already had been established as the most feasible method that could be employed at Muscle Shoals. They also protested that the Norris-Smith formula would tie up the nitrate plants in research for perhaps the next generation, thus denying fertilizer to the farmer.[22]

The fertilizer provisions of the Underwood bill, like those of the Ford offer, were subjected to severe criticism by supporters of the Norris bill who insisted that they contained no guarantee of fertilizer production and intimated that loopholes had been deliberately injected in order to permit the lessee to abandon fertilizer production after the consummation of the lease.[23] On the other hand, the Underwoood Democrats declared the Underwood proposal to be the true fertilizer bill. During the debate, Oscar E. Bradfute, president of the Farm Bureau, and Louis J. Taber, Master of the National Grange, jointly endorsed the Underwood bill, the two farm leaders basing their action on their assertion that only Underwood's measure would bring cheap fertilizer to the farmer. The Underwood coalition, pointing to the farm leaders' approval, now claimed to have conclusive proof that the American farmer was looking to the Underwood bill for relief from excessive fertilizer prices.[24]

During this debate, Senator Heflin continued his war on the fertilizer "trust," declaring that this elusive economic institution was bending every effort to defeat the Underwood bill. The fact that the National Fertilizer Association was at this time distributing publicity material describing the Underwood bill as a menace to the fertilizer industry gave substance to Heflin's charges. The

22. *Ibid.*, 267, 272, 653, 1524.
23. *Ibid.*, 267, 272, 1524.
24. Bradfute and Taber to Senator Frank B. Willis, Jan. 12, 1925, quoted in *Cong. Rec.*, 68 Cong., 2 Sess., 1685. Edwy B. Reid, acting Washington representative of the Farm Bureau, had already given the blessings of the Farm Bureau to the Underwood bill. *Ibid.*, 654. At the end of the session on March 4, after the failure of the Underwood bill, Bradfute wrote Coolidge reaffirming the faith of the Farm Bureau that the measure would provide cheap fertilizer for American agriculture. Bradfute to Coolidge, March 4, 1925, Coolidge Papers.

Norris forces now possessed a valiant warrior against the fertilizer "trust" in the person of Senator William J. Harris who had vied with Heflin in the attack on this alleged monopoly. Harris, pointing to the loopholes in the fertilizer clauses of the Underwood bill, pronounced that measure a permit for the fertilizer "trust" to gain control of Muscle Shoals. Incidentally, this debate showed that the fertilizer industry had little influence in Congress. Senator William C. Bruce of Maryland, the avowed protector of the American fertilizer industry, a large portion of which was located in the Baltimore area, received very little support from his colleagues in his attempts completely to hamstring the fertilizer clauses of both the Norris and Underwood bills.[25]

Despite Senator Underwood's assertion that, under his bill, practically all Muscle Shoals power would be consumed in the manufacture of munitions and fertilizer, the Norris-southern bloc contended that the Underwood measure was designed to make Muscle Shoals primarily a water-power rather than a fertilizer development. The criticism from the Norris ranks in this matter ranged all the way from outright accusations that Underwood was camouflaging his bill with the fertilizer issue in order to deliver Muscle Shoals to private power companies to mere observations that the language of the bill could open the way to abandonment of fertilizer production at Muscle Shoals in favor of other uses of the power to be generated there.[26]

Reference to Muscle Shoals as a water-power project inevitably led to a precipitation of the issue of concentration versus distribution of Muscle Shoals power. Norris and southern senators in his camp warned that the Underwood bill would pave the way for the absorption of all Muscle Shoals power by industries concentrated at Muscle Shoals much to the detriment of neighboring regions and states which would be deprived of this cheap energy. Senator Joseph E. Ransdell admitted that his support of the Norris bill was based almost solely on an assumption that it would deliver cheap power to Louisiana which at that time was in dire

25. *Cong. Rec.*, 68 Cong., 2 Sess., 300–1, 450, 522, 650–51, 1092–93.
26. *Ibid.*, 715, 774–75, 1521, 1800, 1803, 1807.

need of a source of cheap energy because of lack of water power or coal.[27]

The Federal Water Power Act was an issue in this debate. The Norris forces made a vigorous but unsuccessful effort to bring the Underwood bill under the terms of that act, especially in the matter of regulation of rates and distribution. The Underwood Democrats, using a shield of state rights for defense, denied that the federal government had authority to regulate water-power developments in the states but insisted that the states had the power to tax federal water-power projects. The pro-Underwood Republicans, who had so vehemently defended the Water Power Act from the challenge posed by the Ford offer, remained silent.[28]

Despite the fact that the anti-Underwood forces declared the Underwood bill to be a scheme for concentration and absorption of Muscle Shoals power in North Alabama, they also attempted to prove that the Underwood bill was designed to deliver Muscle Shoals to the power "trust." These two charges were apparently but not necessarily contradictory in that the power companies were very much opposed to the direct utilization of water power by an industry because such a course would eliminate the need of the power distributing business. Substance was given to the power "trust" charges by Underwood himself when he admitted that in writing his bill he had contemplated the sale of the surplus power not needed in fertilizer production to the power companies; he assured his colleagues, however, that the amount of power so distributed would be too small for other methods of disposal.[29]

27. *Ibid.*, 508, 652, 824, 1368.

28. *Ibid.*, 309–14, 656–70, 760, 765–66.

29. *Ibid.*, 301–3, 506; New York *Times,* Dec. 11, 1924. In the attempt to saddle the Underwood bill with the power "trust," McKellar became embroiled in a quarrel with the Alabama Public Service Commission which the Tennessee Senator charged with being under the control of the Alabama Power Company. In denying this accusation, this commission dispatched a message to Washington which was couched in such strong terms that Senator James A. Reed of Missouri called it an insult to the Senate and upbraided Heflin for having allowed it to be read there. The Birmingham *News,* while admitting that power rates in Alabama were unduly high, exonerated the Public Service Commission. The *News* declared that the blame lay with the state legislature, which was "perhaps" under the influence of the Alabama Power Company, because of its failure to

The effort to tie the Underwood bill to the power "trust" was principally the work of Norris and McKellar. As McKellar bent his efforts toward proving the existence of unethical relations between the Alabama Power Company and the Underwood bill, Norris assumed the larger task of identifying an alleged nation-wide power trust to which the Alabama Power Company was said to belong. In late December, 1924, Norris conducted an unofficial investigation upon his own responsibility, and a few days later he reported to the Senate that his short inquiry had revealed that the Alabama Power Company was controlled by a gigantic power trust headed by the General Electric Company. Norris used power "trust" charges made by pro-Underwood Southerners as a pretext for his miniature probe. Thereupon, he introduced a resolution calling for a sweeping investigation of the General Electric Company by the Federal Trade Commission.[30] The very next day the General Electric Company, much to the surprise of Wall Street brokers, announced that it was disposing of its holdings in public utilities; this was to be accomplished by dissolving the concern's utility holding company, the Electric Bond and Share Company, and transferring the stock to the General Electric stockholders. Company officials denied that the Norris resolution had any connection with the proposed reorganization, but Norris declared that the alleged withdrawal of that firm from the power business would not deter his effort to initiate an investigation by which he hoped to ascertain what influences had been brought to bear in behalf of private control of Muscle Shoals.[31]

Despite the determined opposition of administration Republicans, who declared that the Norris resolution would have an unwholesome effect on the stock market, Norris persisted in his plan to investigate the General Electric Company. Administration Republicans and many businessmen alike were greatly disturbed by the vast scope of authority which the resolution would grant

grant adequate regulatory authority to the commission. *Cong. Rec.*, 68 Cong., 2 Sess., 660, 662, 703, 1669.

30. *Cong. Rec.*, 68 Cong., 2 Sess., 706, 910.

31. New York *Times*, Dec. 31, 1924.

to the Federal Trade Commission; in fact, Norris proposed virtually to hand the commission a free rein in conducting the investigation. The administration forces, after delaying the progress
of the resolution for several weeks, eventually were able to modify
it to the extent that the commission would be denied authority
to investigate the ownership of the General Electric Company.
This group, led by James E. Watson of Indiana and Simeon D.
Fess of Ohio, attempted further to restrict the authority of the
commission but failed. The Norris resolution as passed on
February 9 directed the Federal Trade Commission to investigate
the nature of ownership and control exercised by the General
Electric Company in the field of public utilities, in order to ascertain whether that company held a monopoly in restraint of trade.
Electrical World described the resolution as a desperate attempt
by the "radicals" to achieve public operation of Muscle Shoals.[32]

In the debate on the Underwood and Norris bills, as well as
the Norris power-trust resolution, there was evidence of a growing concern, especially within the ranks of the Progressive Republicans, about the fate of the regulatory principle of the
Federal Water Power Act, particularly because of the mush-
rooming super-power systems which by 1925 were becoming
the dominant trend in the electric power business. These doubting
Thomases felt that these interstate power developments were
threats to the morale and efficiency of the state regulatory bodies
on which the water-power law had laid the burden of regulating
most of the nation's power rates, and they further believed that
these state regulating commissions were rapidly being brought
under the influence of the power companies.[33] The Chattanooga
News put it this way: "The question is whether we shall regulate
it [the power companies] or whether it shall regulate us. . . .
The question is one that may not be much longer avoided. The
issue is upon us." [34]

32. *Cong. Rec.*, 68 Cong., 2 Sess., 1073–86, 3219, 3281–3303; New York *Times*,
Jan. 17, 1925; "Again the Bugaboo of a Power Trust," in *Electrical World*, LXXXV
(Jan. 10, 1925), 83.
33. *Cong. Rec.*, 68 Cong., 2 Sess., 1073–88, 3281–3303.
34. Chattanooga *News*, March 27, 1925.

During the Muscle Shoals debate, Norris vigorously attacked President Coolidge because of White House support of the Underwood bill. Norris accused the President of exceeding his constitutional authority in his alleged efforts to push the Underwood bill through the Senate, and the Nebraska Senator declared that the administration-Underwood coalition was an unholy alliance conceived for the purpose of giving Muscle Shoals to Wall Street.[35] Norris said:

This great legislative ship with the American flag at the mast has upon its bridge as the commander no less a personage than the President of the United States. At his right stands the second in command, the Senator from Alabama. Down in the hold of that mighty ship, under the command of the boatswain, the Senator from Kansas [Curtis], are the Coolidge Republican Senators tugging away at the oars as common sailors. That ship . . . is headed straight for Wall Street, and carries a deed of conveyance to the electric water power trust of America for one of the greatest inheritances of unborn generations of American citizens.

At another point he declared:

This has been really a wonderful combination of the two great political machines. There are Silent Cal at the head, Smiling Oscar [Underwood], Happy Pat [Harrison], Jovial Joe [Robinson], and "me too" Tom [Heflin], all bound up together by the sacred ties of fertilizer . . . five hearts that beat as one. . . . what a glorious banquet they could have. Going into the banquet hall, the dinner would be furnished by the Electric Trust . . . the seasoning for the meats [would be] . . . fertilizer by the Alabama Power Company, the liquid refreshments given to them by the Republican National Committee. What a glorious jubilee they could have.[36]

The administration Republicans remained silent while Oscar Underwood and Joseph T. Robinson defended Coolidge from the relentless Norris attacks. These two Southerners were somewhat handicapped in their defense of the President because much of Norris's criticism came almost verbatim from Democratic campaign literature left over from the presidential race of 1924.[37]

Senator Robinson, the Democratic leader in the Senate, de-

35. *Cong. Rec.*, 68 Cong., 2 Sess., 703, 712–13.
36. *Ibid.*, 703, 1507.
37. *Ibid.*, 1507.

creed it to be the duty of Democratic senators to support the Underwood bill. The Arkansas Senator based this party edict on the fact that the Democratic platform of 1924 advocated that Muscle Shoals be used primarily for fertilizer production, his contention being that only the Underwood bill would fulfill that prescription. Norris delivered a ringing denunciation of Robinson for attempting to coerce Democratic senators in this matter; he declared that Robinson was abusing his power and prestige in the party, and he accused Underwood of using his Muscle Shoals bill to promote his presidential candidacy.[38]

Since the Underwood bill was in part an administration measure, Norris believed that it would have clear sailing in the House. As the bill emerged victorious from the Senate, Norris conceded defeat for the first and only time during the entire Muscle Shoals controversy. He admitted openly to his Senate colleagues that his Muscle Shoals bill was a lost cause.[39] A few days later he wrote to a friend that while his group had lost the Muscle Shoals fight, it had at least succeeded in forcing the two powerful political machines openly to combine, bringing the fight into the open.[40] To another friend he wrote:

Since I have been in Congress . . . I have never been in a controversy that has so engrossed my time as the Muscle Shoals fight. It may be

38. *Ibid.*, 1449–50, 1504, 1507, 1509.

39. *Ibid.*, 1808. Senator Borah too apparently felt that the Norris Muscle Shoals bill was lost. He predicted, however, that the Underwood bill would lead to "deep regrets in the future." Borah to Paul V. Nast, Jan. 30, 1925.

Despite Norris's pessimistic attitude at this time, Judson King, director of the National Popular Government League, of which Norris was a charter member, issued a pamphlet calling the Progressives to arms against the Underwood bill. King declared that the bill had been framed with the purpose of delivering Muscle Shoals to the power "trust" and warned that such a course would set an unwholesome precedent for the development of the Colorado, Columbia, and other river valleys. He protested bitterly that agencies of the federal government were being used liberally to influence public opinion. King charged that anti-public power speeches by Oscar C. Merrill, executive secretary of the Federal Power Commission, were being circulated by federal agencies, and he cited the Wyer pamphlet on the Ontario power system as another example of the use of a federal office to disseminate private power publicity. Judson King, *Shall Coolidge and Congress Railroad the Underwood Bill and Deliver Muscle Shoals to the Power Trust?* National Popular Government League, Bulletin No. 96 (Jan. 20, 1925).

40. Norris to J. D. Ream, Jan. 18, 1925, Norris Papers.

that I am wrong, but I early reached the conclusion that the issue involved in that controversy was much more important than appeared on the face of things. The people of the country do not fully realize or appreciate the fundamental principles that were involved in it. To me the giving away of Muscle Shoals is surrendering to monopoly and greed the inheritance of unborn generations.[41]

Upon passage of the Underwood bill, there was definitely a feeling in political and governmental circles in Washington that the Muscle Shoals problem had at last been solved and that a definite policy had been established—that Muscle Shoals was to be a fertilizer instead of a water-power project and that it would be subject to private rather than public operation.[42]

A survey of the press reveals that some editors believed the fate of Muscle Shoals had been definitely determined, but the majority felt that the Underwood bill had achieved nothing and that the problem probably would have to be referred to a commission. Some editors interpreted Underwood's bill as a water-power measure while others believed it primarily designed to promote fertilizer production. Many editors asserted that the bill proved the incompetence of Congress to deal with the problem. The extreme vagueness characterizing the bill led some editors to admit that they did not know how to interpret it. Nearly all agreed that public operation of Muscle Shoals was definitely rejected and that public power in general had received a heavy blow.[43]

The arrival of the Underwood bill in the House posed a problem, for this measure was technically the same piece of legislation as the McKenzie bill which had passed the House in March, 1924, authorizing the acceptance of the Ford offer. Despite the great gulf that separated the House and Senate versions, the administration leaders in the House decided to send the bill to conference because the approaching end of the Sixty-eighth

41. Norris to C. H. Boyle, Jan. 18, 1925, *ibid.*
42. "The Senate Navigating the Shoals," *Outlook*, CXXXIX (June 21, 1925), 86–88.
43. Some of the most important newspapers examined were: Cleveland *Plain Dealer*, Jan. 14, 1925; Atlanta *Constitution*, Jan. 15, 1925; Boston *Herald*, Jan. 15, 1925; Chicago *Daily News*, Jan. 15, 1925; Kansas City *Star*, Jan. 15, 1925; St. Paul *Pioneer-Press*, Jan. 15, 1925; and New York *Herald Tribune*, Jan. 16, 1925.

Congress made them fear that a recommittal to committee would mean the death of the bill. Bertrand H. Snell, chairman of the House Rules Committee, declared the Underwood bill to be in general conformity with House policy on Muscle Shoals. The former Ford partisans in the House joined the administration in approving the Underwood bill and in demanding that it be sent to conference, although a few Southerners had mild complaints about the fertilizer clauses of the bill. Representative LaGuardia and a small band of his Progressive colleagues vigorously resisted the move to send the bill to conference. LaGuardia, who declared that he would never consent to a private lease of Muscle Shoals, interpreted the Underwood bill as being a scheme, thinly disguised with fertilizer, to turn the Muscle Shoals project over to the private power industry. The Underwood coalition was triumphant and the bill went to conference.[44]

Meanwhile a sharp controversy was precipitated in the Senate when Senator Underwood proposed to violate Senate tradition by by-passing the ranking members of the Senate Agriculture Committee, Norris, McNary, and Smith, in the selection of the Senate conferees. Normally, these three opponents of the Underwood bill would have been selected for conference duties since the Underwood bill was properly under the jurisdiction of the Agriculture Committee, but Underwood feared that they would deliberately wreck the bill in conference. This led to a sharp, bitter, and heated exchange of charges and innuendoes. Norris and his two colleagues interpreted Underwood's move as an accusation of dishonest intent on their part, but they did not contest Underwood's action—instead, they played the part of martyrs, all three performing excellently in this role. McKellar forced the issue with the result that the three senators were duly appointed; they then resigned, permitting Underwood to make appointments more to his political taste.[45]

In order to facilitate the passage of the Underwood bill before the adjournment on March 4, President Coolidge sent his secretaries of War and Commerce, Weeks and Hoover, to aid the

44. *Cong. Rec.*, 68 Cong., 2 Sess., 2537–44.
45. *Ibid.*, 2552–63.

conference committee. In connection with this development, it
was reported that the administration had decided to report a bill
which would be attractive to Henry Ford.[46] In answer to an inquiry by William Randolph Hearst about this matter, Ford announced that he was not interested. Furthermore, he advised that
the federal government operate Muscle Shoals to produce nitrates
for agriculture and national defense and not for the purpose of
distributing power. Then he delivered a blow at President
Coolidge's economic philosophy:

> It is a mistake to say the government cannot run the nitrate plant
> as well as any private party. This is the very kind of business the
> Government ought to engage in. . . . The Government has as good
> men as there are in the field.[47]

The Hearst papers declared that Ford had now made the situation clear—the responsibility was now on the doorsteps of the
White House, and "should Muscle Shoals go to the power
monopoly, that concern will be directly indebted to President
Coolidge." [48]

Despite the insistence of southern Democrats in the House
that the fertilizer provisions in the Underwood bill be strengthened, the bill that emerged from the conference was weaker in
its fertilizer aspects than the Underwood Senate bill. The amount
of fertilizer the lessee was required to produce, as well as other
fertilizer requirements, was sharply reduced, and the provisions
permitting separate leases of power and fertilizer were removed.
Dam no. 3 was made an integral part of the property to be leased,
and the amount of annual rental payments would be 4 per cent
of the cost of construction of the two dams, less an amount to be
determined by the President that would be charged to navigation costs. Also, additional time for finding a lessee was permitted.[49]

46. New York *Times*, Jan. 31, Feb. 6, 1925.
47. Washington *Herald*, Jan. 31, 1925, quoted in *Cong. Rec.*, 68 Cong., 2 Sess.,
3120.
48. *Ibid.*
49. Conference Committee, *Muscle Shoals*, Senate Doc. 196, 68 Cong., 2 Sess.
(1925), 1–11. *Manufacturers' Record* believed that the Underwood bill as originally passed was a water-power measure, but it interpreted the conference report to

When the conference report reached the Senate, Norris raised a point of order charging that it contained new matter. The Underwood forces insisted that the report was substantially the same as the Underwood bill. The failure of the Senate majority leaders to hold the administration Republicans in line permitted the Norris contention to be sustained; then, the bill went back to conference.[50] A second conference report reached the Senate on February 26, Norris again charging that it contained new matter. Furthermore, he organized a filibuster against the bill, and since the administration had other important legislation on the calendar, the Underwood bill was allowed to die without further consideration.[51]

The Muscle Shoals controversy, which seemed at the outset of the Sixty-eighth Congress to be near a settlement, was as persistent an issue as ever at the adjournment even though it had dominated the Senate proceedings during the session. Had not administration support wavered at the last moment, the Underwood bill might have passed, but it had been clear since December that several administration senators had been lukewarm in their support of the bill, preferring instead to refer the problem to a commission. The Muscle Shoals problem became even more complicated during this session because the administration supported proposals for the manufacture of fertilizer at Muscle Shoals, a position it had vehemently opposed all during the Ford offer period. The sincerity of the new administration position was open to question because administration leaders demonstrated an acute interest in reducing the fertilizer require-

mean that Muscle Shoals would be turned over to chemical interests. This interpretation was partially based on a clause dedicating Muscle Shoals to the production of fertilizer and "other useful products" which was also a feature of the Underwood bill as passed. "The Conference Report on Muscle Shoals Should Be Defeated," in *Manufacturers' Record*, LXXXVII (Feb. 19, 1925), 62.

It is interesting to note that the changes made in the Underwood bill in conference were almost identical with those suggested to the conference committee by the Department of Agriculture. Memorandum of the Department of Agriculture to Senator Henry W. Keyes, Feb. 5, 1925, Correspondence of the Secretary of Agriculture, Muscle Shoals, National Archives.

50. *Cong. Rec.*, 68 Cong., 2 Sess., 4400–3.

51. *Ibid.*, 4408–10, 4708; New York *Times*, Feb. 27, 1925.

ments of the Underwood bill. Furthermore, pro-Underwood Democrats were less vehement in demanding rigid fertilizer requirements than formerly. Nevertheless, what the intentions of Underwood and Coolidge were in respect to this matter was never clearly revealed. Senatorial opponents of the Underwood bill were in general agreement that it was designed to lease Muscle Shoals to the power industry, although some of them charged that it would place Muscle Shoals under the control of the chemical industry, thereby absorbing all of the power near the site of generation. There is reliable evidence that President Coolidge and Secretary Weeks had in mind government operation of the project under the alternative plan offered by the Underwood bill, a solution which would permit the sale of the power to the private power companies.[52]

An interesting sidelight to the debate on the Underwood bill was a dispute between Senator Underwood and Edwin J. Clapp, editor of the New York *Journal-American,* a Hearst newspaper. On December 13, 1924, soon after the Muscle Shoals debate began in the Senate, an editorial concerning Underwood that was written by Clapp appeared in the Hearst morning newspapers. According to the editorial:

He [Underwood] is an able man, capable of high statesmanship, but since his entrance into Congress, his ability and his statesmanship have often been at the service of the railroads and other great corporations seeking public privileges without paying for them. Just now his talents and ability are working in the interest of the central figure in the Electric Power Trust—the General Electric Company. It owns the Electric Bond and Share Company, which has stock ownership and its own directors in Mr. Underwood's Alabama Power Company, to which the Senate of the United States is asked to give away the

52. Lieutenant Colonel Joseph I. McMullen to "Colonel Spaulding," Jan. 21, 1925, Judge Advocate General, National Archives. It is interesting to note that while administration leaders in Congress joined with southern Democrats during this debate in proclaiming the necessity of Muscle Shoals to national defense, Major General Williams, Chief of Ordnance, was telling America that Muscle Shoals was rapidly becoming useless for military preparedness. He declared that the solution of the nitrate problem for both war and peace lay with the private chemical industry. Ernest Greenwood, "The Myth of Muscle Shoals," in *Independent,* CXIV (Feb. 28, 1925), 232.

second most valuable property of the Nation, second only to the Panama Canal.[53]

Underwood vehemently denied that his bill had any connection with the Alabama Power Company, and he insisted that the power companies would not be interested in his bill since it was a fertilizer measure. At the request of the Alabama Senator, the Senate Judiciary Committee conducted an inquiry into the Hearst editorial. Clapp denied that he had intended to impugn the integrity of Underwood. The committee reported that the honor of the Alabama Senator was completely vindicated.[54]

The debate on the Underwood bill proved to be a period of transition. Prior to that time, the Ford group had dominated the controversy. During the debate on the Underwood bill, no group emerged as the strongest contender, and the issue appeared to be hopelessly deadlocked. Within the next few months, however, the power companies would become, temporarily, the dominant party in the controversy.

53. Washington *Herald,* Jan. 13, 1924, quoted in *Cong. Rec.,* 68 Cong., 2 Sess., 833.

54. *Newspaper Charges Against Senator Underwood in Connection with the Muscle Shoals Project,* Hearing, U. S. Senate, 68 Cong., 2 Sess. (1925), 15–56; *Investigation of Editorial Charges Against Senator Underwood,* Senate Report 823, 68 Cong., 2 Sess. (1925), 1–4.

VII

Referral to a Commission and Joint Committee: Climax of the Effort for Private Power Development

THE LONG AND FRUITLESS DEBATE on the Underwood bill resulted in increased support for the theory, held by many administration leaders and conservative Southerners, that the Muscle Shoals problem could be more readily solved by a small group than by Congress. The debate on the Underwood bill was described by some observers both in and out of Congress as a splendid example of congressional ineptness in handling a highly technical problem, and they demanded that Congress lay down the broad lines of a policy, such as whether the project should be operated publicly or privately, and leave all of the details to a commission.[1] A referral of the issue to a commission would probably favor the power companies because such a course would tend to emphasize the technical rather than the political aspects of the problem. The scientific evidence available at that time indicated that any technical examination of the Muscle Shoals problem would result in stressing water power at the expense of fertilizer.

When it became evident that no action was likely on the conference report on the Underwood bill, the administration-Underwood coalition sponsored a House resolution by Representative Martin B. Madden requesting the President to appoint a commission of three men to study the problem of Muscle Shoals in order to ascertain the best available means for producing nitrates

1. "Muscle Shoals as a Hot Air Plant," in *Current Opinion,* LXXXVIII (Feb., 1925), 142; *Cong. Rec.,* 68 Cong., 2 Sess., 5178.

and the most favorable conditions under which the project could be leased. The resolution laid down the broad policy that Muscle Shoals should be dedicated to agriculture and national defense and that it should be leased to private enterprise with adequate regulations to safeguard the public interest.[2]

In the short House debate on the resolution, which was favorably reported with no dissenting votes by the House Military Committee, Madden called on all of those who desired to use Muscle Shoals for fertilizer production and those loyal to the President to support the commission plan. He gave the assurance that the President would never permit Muscle Shoals to become a "mere cog" in a super-power system. Representative LaGuardia, who led the attack on the resolution, replied that this proposal was merely another attempt to deceive the farmers and to deliver Muscle Shoals to the power companies. On the other hand, pro-Underwood Democrats accused the Norris-LaGuardia group of being in combination, perhaps unknowingly, with the fertilizer and power "trusts" to prevent action on Muscle Shoals. The resolution was passed on March 2, two days before adjournment.[3]

President Coolidge complied with the request embodied in the Madden resolution. On March 27, following a conference with Senator Underwood, the President announced that he had appointed a Muscle Shoals Commission of Inquiry. Instead of a three-member body, however, Coolidge appointed a commission composed of five members. The members of the new commission were former Representative John C. McKenzie of Illinois, chairman; former Senator Nathaniel Dial of South Carolina, a conservative Democrat known to be strongly opposed to public operation of Muscle Shoals; Harry A. Curtis, professor of chemical engineering, Yale University; William McClellan, noted electrical engineer who was a past president of the American Institute of Electrical Engineers; and Russell F. Bower, who was appointed at the request of Senator Underwood and officials of the Farm

2. *Cong. Rec.*, 68 Cong., 2 Sess., 5178.
3. *Ibid.*, 5178–81; *Muscle Shoals Commission*, House Report 1627, 68 Cong., 2 Sess. (1925), 1; New York *Times*, March 3, 1925.

Bureau and the National Grange.[4] Although he warned of the
evils of socialism, Coolidge was reported to have given the commission a free rein. Oscar C. Merrill of the Federal Power Commission suggested, however, that the commission recommend
separate leases of the power and nitrate facilities at Muscle Shoals
and that the power facilities be leased to a group of southern
power companies under the Water Power Act.[5] Senator Norris
declared that he had very little faith in the integrity of the
commission, especially in view of the presence of McKenzie and
Dial, who, Norris said, would not permit an independent report
by the technicians on the commission.[6]

The Muscle Shoals Commission of Inquiry began its studies in
early April, 1925, but, since its meetings were closed, it received
little publicity until the late fall. Throughout the year, however,
the commission was being subjected to pressure by various groups.
The National Fertilizer Association tried to influence the commission to reject Muscle Shoals as a fertilizer proposition while the
Farm Bureau bombarded the commission with the opposite recommendation.[7] Supporters of the Norris plan, including the National
League of Women Voters and the American Federation of Labor,
as well as lesser labor unions, brought pressure to bear upon the
commission in favor of public operation.[8] Most of the pressure,
however, came from friends of the private power industry. At
first this group attempted to minimize the water-power potential
of Muscle Shoals by asserting that the project could not furnish
adequate primary power for either independent distribution or
an industry; hence, Muscle Shoals power could be economically

4. New York Times, March 8, 10, 14, 28, 1925; Underwood to Coolidge,
March 5, 1925, and William M. Jardine to Coolidge, March 21, 1925, Coolidge
Papers.

5. "President Gives Free Hand to Muscle Shoals Commission," in Electrical
World, LXXXV (April 11, 1925), 781–2; "Muscle Shoals Commissioners Confer
Informally," ibid. (May 9, 1925), 992; "Merrill on Muscle Shoals," ibid., LXXXVI
(July 4, 1925), 31.

6. New York Times, April 2, 1925.

7. Circular by Charles J. Brand, executive secretary of the National Fertilizer
Association, Oct. 19, 1925, Papers of Thomas J. Walsh, Division of Manuscripts,
Library of Congress; Chester H. Gray to John C. McKenzie, Oct. 29, 1925,
Coolidge Papers.

8. New York Times, June 3, 1925.

utilized only by leasing it to a private power system.[9] By this time, however, a continuing survey of the Tennessee River system by the Corps of Engineers was beginning to reveal the great water-power possibilities that would result from a unified development of the river basin. Major General Harold C. Fiske, Corps of Engineers, declared that over 3,000,000 primary horsepower could easily be produced from such a development. Consequently, various power companies became extremely interested in acquiring the right to develop the whole river or at least a large share of it, so that the stream could be utilized to its maximum efficiency.[10]

9. *Ibid.*, June 7 (II), 1925; Alfred P. Lane, "Muscle Shoals—Bonanza or White Elephant?" in *Scientific American*, CXXXII (May, 1925), 293–95. Dan E. McGugin, representing the Tennessee Manufacturers' Association and the Tennessee Municipal League, wrote to President Coolidge after the creation of the Muscle Shoals Commission with the plea that any lessee of Muscle Shoals be forced to distribute equitably the power generated there. He praised the administration's actions in removing the problem from Congress. McGugin to Coolidge, March 14, 1925, Coolidge Papers.

In February, 1925, the Mississippi Development Board, which had vigorously opposed the Ford offer, began an attempt to force Senator Pat Harrison to cease supporting the Alabama group's effort to keep Muscle Shoals power at home, and instead to fight for equitable distribution of that power. "The Muscle Shoals Situation as Viewed in Mississippi," in *Manufacturers' Record*, LXXXVII (Feb. 19, 1925), 70–71.

10. "Developing the Tennessee," in *Electrical World*, LXXXV (May 2, 1925), 940; New York *Times*, Oct. 2, 1925. During the summer of 1925, while the Muscle Shoals Commission of Inquiry was making its study of the Muscle Shoals problem, Samuel S. Wyer, the publicist for private power companies who had attempted to refute Norris's contentions that the public power system of Ontario, Canada, was superior to private power systems in the United States, issued a report on Muscle Shoals. He described his report as an independent study of the power possibilities at Muscle Shoals, but his primary purpose was to demonstrate that the Tennessee River contained a large amount of potential power that should be developed only by private power companies. In his report, Wyer condemned Muscle Shoals as a fertilizer proposition on the grounds of obsolescence and contended that Muscle Shoals power could be used most economically by tying it to the existing private power systems in the South. Charles D. Walcott, director of the Smithsonian Institution, obtained permission from President Coolidge early in February, 1925, for Wyer to make the study under the auspices of the Institution. In March, Senator Norris demanded that Walcott be removed from his post because he had permitted Wyer to use the seal of the Smithsonian Institution on the Wyer pamphlet dealing with the Ontario power system. When the Wyer report on Muscle Shoals appeared in June, 1925, it did not purport to be a product of the Smithsonian Institution, as in the case of the Ontario report. Samuel S. Wyer, *Power Possibilities at Muscle Shoals,* presented at the annual convention of the American Institute of Electrical Engineers, Saratoga Springs,

The revelations at this time by the Corps of Engineers with respect to water-power development on the Tennessee River apparently made Muscle Shoals more attractive to the American Cyanamid Company. At any rate that firm began to show an unusual interest in the project. William B. Bell, president of the company, utilized the services of Claudius H. Huston, former Assistant Secretary of Commerce and a friend of Herbert Hoover, in an attempt to gain administration support for his company's proposed Muscle Shoals bid. Secretary Hoover openly encouraged the cyanamid company's move to capture control of Muscle Shoals but when pressed for an explicit endorsement, he retreated, declaring that he could not speak for the administration. The cyanamid company also had the support of the Farm Bureau. Important Farm Bureau officials warned President Coolidge that their organization would support the Norris bill for government operation if the President did not approve the American Cyanamid Company's proposal instead of that of the power companies.[11]

During the summer of 1925, while the Muscle Shoals Commission of Inquiry was conducting its study, the Alabama Power Company gained temporary control of Muscle Shoals power. Secretary Weeks had announced late in 1924 that he desired to negotiate a short-term lease of the power to be generated in testing the generators at Wilson Dam, the first unit of which was scheduled to begin operating in July, 1925. Weeks's plans were temporarily halted when it appeared that the Underwood bill would pass, but following the failure of that measure, the Secretary renewed his plans to lease the Wilson Dam test power. Again the action by Weeks on this matter was held up, this time by President Coolidge who desired that the leasing project be cleared with his Muscle Shoals Commission before being executed. In June, 1925, the commission gave its approval on the condition that only power resulting from tests would be involved, and, thereupon, the War Department asked for bids. The

New York, June 22–26, 1925; Walcott to Coolidge, Jan. 31, 1925, and Coolidge to Walcott, Feb. 2, 1925, Coolidge Papers.

11. Memorandum (author unknown), July 6, 1926; Chester H. Gray to Coolidge, Nov. 12, 1925; R. F. Bower to Coolidge, Nov. 12, 1925; E. B. Reid to Coolidge, Nov. 11, 1925, Coolidge Papers.

Alabama Power Company, which was the only company having transmission lines in the Muscle Shoals area, was the sole and successful bidder. The test power from Wilson Dam performed valuable service during the great drought in the South in the summer of 1925, particularly in the Carolina textile districts.[12]

The Muscle Shoals Inquiry Commission reported to the President on November 14, 1925. By a majority of 3 to 2, with the two scientists comprising the minority, the commission recommended a disposition of Muscle Shoals in a manner similar to that proposed by the Underwood bill. The principal recommendation was that Muscle Shoals should be devoted primarily to the manufacture of nitrates for agricultural fertilizer and for munitions for national defense. The commission proposed that the Muscle Shoals project should be operated by the federal government in the event no suitable lessee could be found within a reasonable time. It suggested that the power and fertilizer facilities be leased as a unit rather than separately, with the lease limited to a period of fifty years to conform with the maximum length of lease periods stipulated in the Federal Water Power Act. The majority felt that the lessee should be required to pay an annual rental of 4 per cent of the actual cost of the hydroelectric facilities, less an amount properly chargeable to navigational improvements.

The commission also advised that the lessee's profit on fertilizer be limited to 8 per cent and that he be required to conduct research and experimentation in the fertilizer field in order to reduce the costs of production of that product. Moreover, the lessee should be required to produce a stipulated amount of fertilizer periodically. The only major difference between the report of the Muscle Shoals Commission of Inquiry and the Underwood bill was that the former provided that the properties

12. New York *Times,* Nov. 20, 21, 1924, March 31, April 17, June 11, 28, July 4, 18, Aug. 29, 1925. According to *Electrical World,* the real motive behind the desire of Weeks to lease the test power at Wilson Dam was to demonstrate how efficiently a private power company would utilize the large amount of secondary power produced there in the hope of impressing Congress sufficiently to win acceptance of the power companies' offer at the next session of Congress. "Muscle Shoals Power Soon a Reality," in *Electrical World,* LXXXV (March 28, 1925), 651.

be leased as a unit rather than separately. As in the case of the Underwood bill, it could clearly be discerned that the commission's report had been modeled largely upon the Ford offer.[13]

The two scientists on the commission, Curtis and McClellan, dissented and filed a minority report. They recommended the utilization of Muscle Shoals primarily as a project to generate water power for general distribution but they advised that under no circumstances should the federal government operate the enterprise. It was suggested by the minority that the power and nitrate facilities be leased separately, the former to a chemical company and the latter to a power company. The minority further suggested that should fertilizer production at Muscle Shoals be seriously contemplated, a Haber process plant, which would consume a small amount of electrical energy as compared to the cyanamid process installed at nitrate plant no. 2, be installed so that more power would be released for general distribution. The two minority members advised that, because of uncertainty of market conditions, no lessee should be required to produce a stipulated amount of fertilizer. They criticized the proposed profit limitation on fertilizer as likely to stifle the incentive to produce and proposed that a Cove Creek dam and dam no. 3 be made a part of the Muscle Shoals project.[14]

It was alleged in some quarters that the Coolidge administration was embarrassed by the inclusion of the alternative of public operation in the majority report, the contention being that the commission was expected unanimously to proclaim that private operation was the only satisfactory solution to the problem.[15]

Following the issuance of the report of the Inquiry Commission, any designs by private power companies to acquire the choice power sites on the Tennessee River were frustrated when the Federal Power Commission complied with a request by the House Military Committee to continue a suspension of action on

13. Muscle Shoals Inquiry, *Majority and Minority Reports of Muscle Shoals Inquiry,* House Doc. 119, 69 Cong., 1 Sess. (1925), 3–5. The Muscle Shoals Commission of Inquiry did not make any public reports during its period of deliberation, and apparently held no public hearings.

14. *Ibid.,* 73–82.

15. "Norris' Power Fight," in *Nation,* CXX (March 26, 1928), 338.

applications for power sites on the river. The suspension order had gone into effect by executive order when the Coolidge Commission of Inquiry had begun its studies in April.[16]

Since the majority report embodied in substance the Underwood bill, it was generally believed that the Alabama Senator would reintroduce his plan in the coming session, and that belief was strengthened when Underwood and Coolidge met in conference immediately preceding the President's annual message to Congress. In his message to Congress, however, Coolidge stressed the minority report rather than that of the majority. Although he agreed with the majority that Muscle Shoals should be operated primarily for fertilizer production, he nevertheless asserted that the project should not be placed under the management of a public authority under any circumstances. More important, the President came forward with a definite recommendation for settling the Muscle Shoals issue—he suggested that a small joint congressional committee be appointed to receive bids and recommend to Congress the most suitable offer "upon which a law should be enacted effecting a sale to the highest bidder who will agree to carry out these purposes." Coolidge confessed an inability to understand why Muscle Shoals had created such a problem:

The problem of Muscle Shoals seems to me to have assumed a place all out of proportion with its real importance. It probably does not represent in market value much more than a first-class battleship, yet it has been discussed in the Congress over a period of years and for months at a time.[17]

President Coolidge was severely scored by some Southerners for belittling the importance of the Muscle Shoals project. Nevertheless, Representative Finis J. Garrett of Tennessee, the ranking Democrat on the House Rules Committee, described Coolidge's plan for a joint committee as the best avenue of approach under

16. *Muscle Shoals,* Hearings, U. S. House of Representatives, on H. R. 16396 and H. R. 16614, 69 Cong., 2 Sess. (1927), Part 1, 248.

17. *Cong. Rec.,* 69 Cong., 1 Sess., 462. Despite the fact that Coolidge continued to advocate the use of Muscle Shoals for fertilizer production, the Department of Agriculture, less than a week before the President delivered his message, reported that the Muscle Shoals project would be unable to compete with the private fertilizer industry. Memorandum, Department of Agriculture, Dec. 3, 1925, Bureau of Plant Industry, Fertilizer, National Archives.

existing conditions. He warned that if the President's plan did not succeed the only alternative left was government operation. On the other hand, George Fort Milton, editor of the Chattanooga *News* and a public power advocate, believed that complete development of the Tennessee River by private companies was imminent and inevitable since he felt that sufficient sentiment to promote and sustain public power projects in the Untied States did not then exist.[18]

Soon after Coolidge's message to Congress, the administration forces in the House sought to carry out the President's plans, although they refused to accept his recommendation of outright sale of Muscle Shoals. They sponsored a resolution by Representative Bertrand H. Snell, which was approved by the President, to authorize the creation of a joint committee to be composed of three representatives from each house. The duty of the proposed committee would be to seek bids for Muscle Shoals and report its findings together with recommendations to Congress.[19]

In the House debate on the Snell resolution, the administration-Underwood coalition lined up almost solidly in support of the measure, with conservative Republicans vying with southern Democrats in declaring that their support of the Snell plan was motivated by a desire for cheap fertilizer for the farmers. Only Representative George Huddleston of Alabama broke ranks; he denounced the resolution as an instrument of the power companies.[20] Outside this coalition, the resolution was strongly assailed by Fiorello H. LaGuardia of New York and William Williamson of South Dakota. LaGuardia implied that the lessee had already been selected and protested that "This resolution is only a conscience easer. They are bringing in one resolution after another so that they will finally justify themselves in turning over this plant to private operation." [21] Williamson insisted

18. "Snell and Garrett to Confer," in *Electrical World*, LXXXVI (Dec. 26, 1925), 1321; "Facts and Fancies About Muscle Shoals," in *Outlook*, CXLII (Feb. 3, 1926), 165–66; Milton to Norris, Jan. 6, 1926, Norris Papers.

19. New York *Times*, Dec. 10, 20, 1925, Jan. 5, 1926; *Cong. Rec.*, 69 Cong., 1 Sess., 1522.

20. *Cong. Rec.*, 69 Cong., 1 Sess., 1513–23.

21. *Ibid.*, 1520.

that the administration's professed loyalty to fertilizer operations at Muscle Shoals was the "sheerest kind of bunk" intended to cover up a transfer of Muscle Shoals to the power industry. Nevertheless, on January 5, 1926, the Snell resolution passed the House by a one-sided vote of 248 to 27.[22]

After the passage of the Snell resolution by the House, the Senate Agriculture Committee, headed by Senator Norris, scheduled hearings on the measure. Norris ringingly denounced the resolution and declared that it was common gossip around the capitol that a lessee for Muscle Shoals already had been selected by the administration. He described the emphasis on fertilizer in the resolution as a subterfuge to hide other intentions. The Nebraska Senator made it plain that in the forthcoming hearings he intended to give the resolution the same treatment he had given the Ford offer in 1924.[23]

Despite the suspicion of some opponents of the Snell resolution that it was designed primarily to benefit the private power industry, representatives of the power companies vigorously opposed the measure at the hearings before the Norris committee. On the other hand the chemical interests and their supporters endorsed the resolution. The power companies opposed the measure because it did not provide for general distribution of power, while the chemical interests supported the resolution because it specifically stated that the primary purpose of Muscle Shoals would be production of nitrates. The principal defenders of the resolution were Chester H. Gray, Washington representative of the Farm Bureau, and Leonard H. Davis, a spokesman for the Union Carbide Company.[24]

Those opposed to the Snell resolution were numerous, but the most important witnesses who testified against it were Colonel Hugh L. Cooper, representing the power industry, and Dan McGugin, representing the Tennessee Manufacturers' Association. Numerous other persons from the southern states, particu-

22. *Ibid.*, 1521–23.
23. New York *Times,* Jan. 22, 1926.
24. *Muscle Shoals,* Hearings, U. S. Senate, on H. Con. Res. 4, 69 Cong., 1 Sess. (1926), 14, 15–64.

larly Tennessee, Mississippi, and Louisiana, either appeared
before or communicated with the committee in opposition to the
resolution. All of the opposition made the same plea—amend the
Snell resolution to provide for general distribution of all Muscle
Shoals power not needed in fertilizer production.[25] John A.
Switzer, professor of engineering at the University of Tennessee,
who appeared in behalf of a group of power companies, revealed
that a gigantic struggle was taking place in East Tennessee
between the power companies and the chemical industry, the
rich water power of the upper Tennessee to be the reward to
the winner.[26] A representative of the American Federation of
Labor came before the committee to testify in behalf of public
operation of Muscle Shoals.[27]

After only two days of hearings, President Coolidge invited
various members of the Senate Agriculture Committee to the
White House, where he personally requested that they speedily
adopt a favorable report for the resolution. This strategy was
successful, for later on the same day a majority of the committee
complied with the President's request. It was the first time during
the Muscle Shoals controversy that Norris had lost control of the
committee. Although the Nebraskan bitterly assailed the President's action, he consoled himself by optimistically declaring
that "it is probably remarkable that the President did not control
more votes than he did." Although the Norris group continued to
dominate the Agriculture Committee during the Sixty-ninth
Congress, the two new Republican members of the committee,
Charles S. Deneen of Illinois and Frederic M. Sackett of
Kentucky, increased the strength of the administration forces
in that body. Furthermore, the Democrats had lost a member
of the committee as a result of the elections of 1924.[28]

The Republican Steering Committee in the Senate gave the
Snell resolution a preferred status, but because of the necessity

25. *Ibid.*, 9–14, 32–33, 39–56, 79–84, 99–100.
26. *Ibid.*, 27–29.
27. *Ibid.*, 64–66.
28. New York *Times*, Feb. 4, 1926; *Congressional Directory*, 68 Cong., 2 Sess.
(Dec., 1924), 184; *ibid.*, 69 Cong., 1 Sess. (Dec., 1925), 190.

of disposing of legislation already scheduled, it did not reach the floor until March 1, 1926. When the Senate finally began consideration of the resolution, Norris attempted to stifle the proceedings with a point of order charging that the Snell measure was illegal in that it proposed to repeal a law of Congress, the National Defense Act, by providing for private operation of Muscle Shoals. Since the measure was only a concurrent resolution, declared Norris, the repeal of an existing law was beyond its legal scope. The point of order was not sustained.[29]

The chief feature of the Senate debate was the intraparty strife among southern Democrats. The leading performers were McKellar and Heflin who frequently resorted to hurling personal insults at each other. McKellar charged that the purpose of the resolution was to give Muscle Shoals to either the fertilizer or the power "trust," and he intimated that large chemical interests had already made a deal with the Alabama Power Company to divide the profits from the project. Heflin insisted that these "trusts" were fighting against the Snell resolution. McKellar accused Heflin of promoting plans of the chemical interests to acquire Muscle Shoals so that all Muscle Shoals power would be absorbed in North Alabama, thus depriving adjacent states of their just share of this resource. Heflin denied that he was opposed to equitable distribution of Muscle Shoals power. Some Southerners who previously had supported Underwood showed signs of breaking away from his leadership because of the distribution of power issue. But they were mollified when Senator Thaddeus Caraway's amendment requiring equitable distribution of Muscle Shoals power was adopted over the heated protests of Heflin, who pleaded for the adoption of the resolution as reported, since it had the approval of President Coolidge. Since Underwood abstained from voting on the Caraway amendment, which definitely made the resolution a power proposition, Heflin stood almost alone with a group of Republicans in defending the sanctity of Muscle Shoals as a fertilizer proposition.[30]

Senator Robert M. La Follette, Jr., who recently had been

29. New York *Times*, Feb. 17, 1926; *Cong. Rec.*, 69 Cong., 1 Sess., 4763–68.
30. *Cong. Rec.*, 69 Cong., 1 Sess., 4772–75, 4833–35, 5101–2, 5148–51, 5217.

elected to fill the unexpired term of his father, raised the issue of public versus private power, and advocated the use of Muscle Shoals as a yardstick to regulate private power companies. Senator Ellison D. Smith brought this issue to a head by offering a government-operation bill as a substitute for the Snell resolution, but the Senate clearly demonstrated that it was in no mood to entertain such a proposal.[31]

The passage of the Snell resolution by the Senate on March 8 by an overwhelming majority seemed to indicate that the Norris forces were losing ground in the upper house. The most significant aspect of the Senate action on the Snell measure, however, was the adoption of the Caraway amendment requiring equitable distribution of power. This action, although the product of an alliance of southern Democrats and Progressive Republicans, made a lease to the power companies the only possible alternative since public operation had been rejected. Nevertheless, the administration-Underwood coalition was restored to pass the resolution over the opposition of the Norris bloc despite the fact that it carried the Caraway amendment.[32]

When the Snell resolution was returned to the House, it was defended by the administration-Underwood alliance despite the fact that it contained the Caraway amendment. The resolution was again assailed by LaGuardia. He declared it to be the most important item of legislation facing the Congress at this session, and professed to see in it the making of American water-power policy. Despite LaGuardia's plea for more time in which to study the problem, the House hurriedly passed the resolution although not before tacking on another amendment, permitting the lessee to produce "fertilizer ingredients" other than nitrates. The resolution passed the Senate without further changes on March 12. The members chosen for the joint committee were Senators Charles S. Deneen, Frederick M. Sackett, and J. Thomas Heflin, and Representatives John M. Morin, Frank W. James, and Percy E. Quin.[33] All of the committee members except James had been

31. *Ibid.*, 4902–15, 5218.
32. *Ibid.*, 5219.
33. *Ibid.*, 5438–39, 5518, 5586.

loyal supporters of the administration-Underwood coalition, but the adoption of the Caraway amendment appeared likely to cause a rift in this alliance.

Although the *New Republic* repeated the charges that the Snell resolution was intended as a means of turning Muscle Shoals over to the power companies, the press of the country in general considered the congressional action on the resolution as real progress toward a solution of the problem. Specifically, the provisions in the legislation for a private lease and the rejection of the Smith amendment for public operation appeared to the press as a formulation of a definite policy toward the project. The editors did not accept wholeheartedly the claim of the proponents of the resolution that its chief purpose was to implement the administration's alleged desire to devote the project to agriculture with power production as an incidental purpose. The fact that the measure as finally passed permitted separate leases of the power and nitrate facilities, plus the adoption of the Caraway amendment, made it clear to the press as a whole that this piece of legislation officially recognized Muscle Shoals as primarily a water-power proposition.[34] As the Montgomery *Advertiser* put it:

The original theory that "cheap" fertilizers . . . should be the prime consideration is less popular now than it was. . . . The States near Alabama have become more interested in getting cheap and abundant electricity for their industries and rural homes than in getting fertilizers, and their Senators and Congressmen, feeling the force of this increasing demand, are getting cool toward the fertilizer scheme. They are rendering the latter a mere lip service.[35]

During the consideration of the Snell resolution, the principal source of pressure on Congress was the Farm Bureau. Chester H. Gray addressed letters to the Senate members protesting the adoption of the Caraway amendment as being inimical to the best interests of the farmers.[36] On the other hand, the legislatures of Georgia and South Carolina adopted resolutions petitioning

---

34. "Muscle Shoals Open for Bids," in *Literary Digest*, LXXXVIII (March 27, 1926), 11–12; "Muscle Shoals Again," in *New Republic*, XLVI (March 10, 1926), 60.

35. "Muscle Shoals Open for Bids," *loc. cit.*, 12.

36. Gray to William E. Borah, March 8, 1926, Borah Papers.

Congress to adopt an amendment providing for equitable distribution of Muscle Shoals power.[37]

Immediately upon passage of the Snell resolution by the Senate, President Coolidge advised Congress that the joint committee should make the production of nitrates the principal stipulation of any lease of Muscle Shoals. He declared that the production of power at Muscle Shoals was secondary and of importance only to the contiguous states while nitrates were a necessity both to American agriculture and national defense. The President thereupon held a conference with Representative Snell and urged speedy action in negotiating a lease.[38] Coolidge's continued insistence that Muscle Shoals should be dedicated to fertilizer coupled with a press report at this time that Henry Ford would submit a new bid made it appear that perhaps the Republican administration was not committed to the acceptance of a power company offer as had been widely reported.[39]

During the hearings held by the joint committee, only three bids from large industrial firms were received, those being offers by a power combine, the American Cyanamid Company, and the Union Carbide Company. Only the power and cyanamid bids were seriously considered, all others being rejected on the ground that they failed to comply with the Snell resolution. According to Stephen Raushenbush, the power companies making the offer were controlled by the Electric Bond and Share Company.[40] The bid of these companies was submitted by Thomas W. Martin, president of the Alabama Power Company. The companies composing the power group as well as the provisions of their offer were practically the same as in the case of the joint power bid of 1924. This time, however, the companies proposed to form separate corporations to handle the power and fertilizer divisions of the project. The cyanamid company's offer called for practically giving to that company control of the entire Tennessee River. It provided for the leasing of Wilson Dam, dam no. 3, and

37. *Cong. Rec.,* 69 Cong., 1 Sess., 5135–37.
38. New York *Times,* March 10, 11, 13, 1926.
39. *Ibid.,* March 13, 1926.
40. Stephen Raushenbush, *The Power Fight* (1932), 185.

the Cove Creek dam site whose great storage capacity made it the key to the water-power development in East Tennessee if not of the entire river, and it included an option on several other dam sites between Muscle Shoals and Cove Creek. In regard to fertilizer, the cyanamid company offered to produce only that amount which would satisfy market demands, the company to be permitted 8 per cent profit on fertilizer operations. The fertilizer would be produced in a Haber process plant to be constructed at Muscle Shoals. In summary, both offers made fertilizer production contingent on market demand, but the power companies contemplated a total payment of some $200,-000,000 for the fifty-year lease as compared to $86,000,000 which would be paid under the cyanamid offer.[41]

At the hearings before the joint committee, Chester H. Gray and R. F. Bower, Farm Bureau representatives, and J. W. Worthington were the most important witnesses appearing in behalf of the cyanamid offer. The Farm Bureau officials, despite the obvious fact that the fertilizer provisions of the cyanamid bill were as weak as, if not weaker than, those of the power companies, insisted that the cyanamid offer constituted a definite guarantee of fertilizer production, although their testimony was more in the nature of a criticism of the power companies' offer. Several government officials testified in behalf of the power companies, including General John A. Hull, the Judge Advocate General, and Dr. Frederick G. Cottrell of the Department of Agriculture. General Hull expressed a strong belief, allegedly based on his study of the offers, that the cyanamid company was deliberately planning to suspend fertilizer production once its bid was accepted, and he pointed out that the offer proposed to give that company control of the Tennessee River. Dr. Cottrell, who defended the fertilizer provisions of the power companies' offer because they were based on use of the Haber process, also accused the cyanamid company of trying to avoid responsibility for producing fertilizer, his theory being that the company planned to use the obsolescence of nitrate plant no. 2

41. *Muscle Shoals,* Senate Report 672, 69 Cong., 1 Sess. (1926), 19–57.

as an excuse for abandoning that end of the bargain. Dr. Samuel C. Lind, a colleague of Dr. Cottrell, and Major James H. Burns of the Ordnance Department voiced substantially the same opinions.

The other important issues at the hearings involved distribution versus concentration of Muscle Shoals power, and the question whether the power and fertilizer facilities would be leased separately or as a unit. The former proposition in each case was supported by the power companies while the advocates of the cyanamid bid endorsed the latter. Also, the cyanamid company witnesses insisted that Muscle Shoals was still vital to national defense while the power companies took the opposite view.[42]

The joint committee was advised in its deliberations by Secretary of Commerce Herbert Hoover, Secretary of War Dwight F. Davis, Secretary of Agriculture William M. Jardine, Secretary of the Interior Hubert Work, and representatives of the Federal Power Commission and the Corps of Engineers, as well as lesser government officials. Herbert Hoover was the only cabinet member to commit himself at the hearings; he sided with the power companies in their argument that Muscle Shoals was no longer vital to national defense. The committee was also advised by a board of experts, composed of scientists and engineers from the various executive departments, which unanimously reported that the power companies' offer was superior to that of the cyanamid company on the grounds of a more rigid fertilizer guarantee and more liberal financial returns to the government.[43]

The joint committee accepted the advice of the advisory board, and on April 26, in its majority report to Congress, recommended the acceptance of the power companies' offer. Heflin voted for acceptance of the cyanamid bid while James, who abstained entirely, was satisfied with neither. The majority held that the power companies' bid was superior in practically every category,

42. *Leasing of Muscle Shoals*, Hearings, Joint Committee on Muscle Shoals, 69 Cong., 1 Sess. (1926), 33–73, 150–55, 210–94, 345, 483–85, 501, 611, 686–91, 713–37.

43. *Ibid.*, 114; J. A. Switzer, "The Muscle Shoals Question," in *Manufacturers' Record*, XCI (Jan. 13, 1927), 64–66. See also Senate Report 672, 69 Cong., 1 Sess., 1–3.

especially in that it provided for greater rental payments and for equitable distribution of power. Nevertheless, it was admitted that both offers were weak in their fertilizer guarantees, but no recommendations were made to remedy this defect.[44]

A minority report by Representative James ridiculed the power companies' offer. He reported that

Their offer is a power proposition disguised as a fertilizer proposal, and the disguise is so apparent that I can see no excuse why any member of Congress should be deceived for a moment. There is no guarantee that the farmer will get one pound of fertilizer. On the contrary the offer is cleverly worded to avoid that responsibility.

. . . .

Furthermore, the people of the country can now understand that the Power Trust . . . is really in control of the situation. When the people ask us just when we are going to use our property to free the country from its dependence upon Chile for nitrates, and when we are really going to have some cheaper fertilizers made at Muscle Shoals for the farmers . . . we can reply, "Not till the Power Trust permits us to do so." [45]

The majority report of the joint committee was immediately introduced as a bill by two administration Republicans, Senator Deneen and Representative Morin, but the measure did not fare well in Congress. In the Senate it was sidetracked with Senator Deneen's consent after having been sharply attacked by Norris who demanded more time to learn what had happened at the secret session of the joint committee. Moreover, Senator Heflin put up a spirited defense of the cyanamid bid, especially its fertilizer provisions. In the House the bill was referred to the Committee of the Whole House on the State of the Union but did not reach the floor for consideration before the session ended.[46] Thus the power companies failed to obtain Muscle

44. Senate Report 672, 69 Cong., 1 Sess., 2–6, 62–65; Minutes of the Joint Committee on Muscle Shoals, April 26, 1926, Records of the United States Senate, National Archives.

45. Senate Report 672, 69 Cong., 1 Sess., Part 2, 1, 15.

46. *Cong. Rec.*, 69 Cong., 1 Sess., 8205–9, 9590, 11693–94. While the Deneen-Morin bill was in Congress, the power companies' offer was aided by a report of the Ordnance Department which described the cyanamid process and nitrate plant no. 2 as obsolete. Memorandum by Major David P. Gaillard, May 13, 1926, Bureau of Plant Industry, Fertilizer, National Archives.

Shoals despite the fact that their offer had won the approval of
the joint committee.

A few days after the Senate consideration of the Deneen-Morin
bill, Senator Underwood announced his support of the cyanamid
bid while Senator Harrison deserted the Underwood fold to join
with Senator Ransdell, erstwhile Norris supporter, in endorsing
the power companies' bid.[47] It appeared that the Deneen-Morin
bill had split the administration-Underwood coalition and perhaps injured the Norris plan.

Outside of Congress, the power companies' offer was the object
of considerable criticism. Henry Ford's newspaper, the Dearborn
Independent, called it a victory of the power "combine" over
agriculture and national defense and declared that "the power
combine has succeeded in putting it over on President Coolidge." [48] Judson King, director of the National Popular Government League, assailed the power companies' offer and predicted
that control of the Tennessee River by the power "monopoly"
would retard industrial growth in the South. Late in May, the
South Carolina State Democratic Convention condemned "the
effort of the Republican administration, aided by the tools of big
business disguised as Democrats, to give the Muscle Shoals
development to the power trust." [49] At about the same time,
Chester H. Gray issued an official Farm Bureau statement condemning the power companies' offer.[50]

47. *Cong. Rec.,* 69 Cong., 1 Sess., 10245; Paul Wooton, "Chances for Muscle
Shoals Bill Improve," in *Electrical World,* LXXXVII (May 8, 1926), 1019.

48. Dearborn *Independent,* June 5, 1926, quoted in *Cong. Rec.,* 69 Cong.,
1 Sess., 10101–2.

49. *Cong. Rec.,* 69 Cong., 1 Sess., 8484–86, 9882.

50. "Farm Bureau Federation Decries Muscle Shoals Bill," in *Electrical World,*
LXXXVII (May 22, 1926), 1159. The cyanamid company leveled an attack on
the power companies which apparently was not made public. It accused these
companies of being a part of the "General Electric Trust," and it asserted that
Coolidge had been led to support their offer by Herbert Hoover, "who has lied
right and left on this Muscle Shoals project" and who "has lied to the President
and pulled the wool over Mr. Coolidge's eyes." The cyanamid officials further
asserted that Hoover had deserted the cyanamid bid because "the power interests
offered their support for his presidential aspirations in return for his aid." Undated
anonymous document entitled "Memo of What the Cyanamid People Have to Say
of the Situation," in papers dealing with the Muscle Shoals Joint Committee, 1926,
Coolidge Papers.

In late May, 1926, the Senate adopted a resolution by Senator McKellar requesting the joint committee to report on the ownership of capital stock in the two corporations set up by the power companies through which to make their bid for Muscle Shoals. At about the same time a resolution by Senator Pat Harrison was adopted requesting the joint committee to report on a rumored arrangement between the cyanamid company and the Union Carbide Company involving Muscle Shoals. The existence of this agreement had been admitted by representatives of the two companies before the joint committee but was imperfectly understood in Congress because of the secrecy of the joint committee hearings. The report, which was made on June 21 by Senator Deneen, chairman of the joint committee, revealed that the two corporations established by the power companies were separate in name only, both being wholly owned by the power companies making the offer. As for the cyanamid-carbide deal, Deneen revealed that an agreement had been made by the two companies providing that in the event the cyanamid offer was accepted, the Union Carbide Company would assign to the American Cyanamid Company its patent rights on the urea process, a method for converting cyanamid into a more suitable fertilizer than cyanamid itself. In return, the cyanamid company would provide 50,000 primary horsepower from Muscle Shoals to the carbide company and would furnish a location for that firm's plant at Muscle Shoals.[51]

The Muscle Shoals controversy during this session was intensified by a rash of state rights arguments. Bills were introduced by Senators Norris, Smith, and McKellar which would authorize the federal government to regulate rates of Muscle Shoals power. These bills brought a vigorous reaction from the Alabama Public Service Commission whose president, A. C. Patterson, notified Congress that Alabama was sovereign in this matter and that the Alabama commission had the sole authority to regulate rates regardless of whether the federal government or private operators were selling the power. He declared that no transmission lines

51. *Cong. Rec.*, 69 Cong., 1 Sess., 10359, 10563; *Leasing of Muscle Shoals*, Joint Committee Hearings, 69 Cong., 1 Sess., 294, 688.

could be constructed from Alabama to another state without the permission of the Alabama Public Service Commission. Patterson asserted that Alabama held the ultimate authority over Muscle Shoals, and Senator Heflin defended Patterson's claims.[52]

Another incident involving the local interests of states was precipitated by a resolution offered by Norris in January, 1926, which would have suspended by law the jurisdiction of the Federal Power Commission over the Tennessee River until Congress had taken final action on Muscle Shoals, despite the fact that issuance of power permits on that river was at this time under suspension by agreement between the Federal Power Commission and the House Military Committee.[53] This course was suitable to Heflin and others who were supporting the cyanamid bid because they wanted all power sites on the Tennessee to be co-ordinated with and subordinated to the Muscle Shoals project, but the resolution brought a stream of protests from Tennessee and western North Carolina. The Tennessee congressional delegation and a large number of businessmen from North Carolina appeared before the Senate Agriculture Committee to protest against the Norris resolution, all asserting that there was an acute need for additional power in the upper Tennessee River area. On the other hand, the Union Carbide Company sent a witness to support the Norris resolution. Senator Norris insisted that piecemeal development of the Tennessee River basin, such as he contended was about to take place, would not permit the maximum development of the potential power of the area. The resolution did not reach the floor for consideration.[54]

The Underwood bill, the Coolidge Inquiry Commission, the Joint Committee on Muscle Shoals, and the Deneen-Morin bill all constituted obvious attempts by the Coolidge administration to bring a speedy solution to the Muscle Shoals problem within the framework of the Coolidge economic philosophy. The anxiety

52. *Cong. Rec,*. 69 Cong., 1 Sess., 4603.
53. *Ibid.*, 1393.
54. *To Suspend the Jurisdiction of the Federal Power Commission*, Hearings, U. S. Senate, on S. J. Res. 35, 69 Cong., 1 Sess. (1926), 3–11, 21, 27, 47–48, 78–83, 91–96, 111–119.

of the administration to consummate a private lease undoubtedly was heightened by the completion of Wilson Dam, for it would have been a political disadvantage for the administration to have power going to waste at Muscle Shoals. Although these efforts for a permanent solution failed, the administration, in July, 1926, some two weeks after the adjournment of Congress, negotiated a new revocable contract with the Alabama Power Company by which the latter could take any amount of the available power at Wilson Dam that it desired at a price of two mills per kilowatt hour.[55]

The evidence indicates that during the period from December, 1924, to the summer of 1926 the administration favored the leasing of Muscle Shoals to the power industry rather than to the chemical industry, although it is not certain that this was the intent in the case of the Underwood bill. Possibly Underwood and the administration had different goals in mind but critics did not appear to believe so, nearly all opponents of the bill classifying the Underwood bill as purely a power company bill.[56] Why the administration favored the power companies over the chemical interests is not clear, and neither is it clear why the administration professed to support the dedication of Muscle Shoals to fertilizer production when, in fact, it pursued the opposite policy. In a speech in 1926, Senator La Follette expressed the Progressive Republican distrust of the fertilizer issue by declaring that the administration had shrouded all of its actions toward Muscle Shoals from the Underwood bill to the Deneen-Morin bill in a counterfeit fertilizer issue in order to deliver the project to the private power companies.[57] The administration put forth its greatest effort in creating the joint committee, but the recommendations of that body, embodied in the Deneen-Morin bill, were doomed from the start because Underwood and Heflin bolted to the cyanamid camp, breaking the administration's alliance with Underwood Democrats. The Farm Bureau, which

55. Major General Edgar Jadwin, Chief of Engineers, to the Alabama Power Company, July 15, 1926, Judge Advocate General, National Archives.

56. Joseph S. Ransmeier, *The Tennessee Valley Authority* (1942), 49, 51.

57. *Cong. Rec.*, 69 Cong., 1 Sess., 4908.

still had influence with several congressmen from agricultural states, opposed the Deneen-Morin bill. Also, a number of Republican congressmen were known to be friendly to the cyanamid offer. The failure of the Deneen-Morin bill, in the judgment of Joseph Ransmeier, brought to an end "the last serious effort to turn Muscle Shoals over to the privately owned power companies." [58]

The struggle between the power and chemical companies during 1925 and 1926 opened a new era in the Muscle Shoals controversy by focusing attention on the development of the entire valley rather than Muscle Shoals alone. According to Stephen Raushenbush,

Their bids illustrated a certain truth which had been neglected or underemphasized during the first discussions of Government policy in regard to Muscle Shoals. This truth was that while the Government dam and powerhouse and steam plant had a very considerable value by themselves, they increased in value enormously if they could be operated as part of a larger waterpower system, developing the other waterpowers on the Tennessee River.[59]

Thus, the controversy from this point on largely revolved around the idea of Muscle Shoals as the keystone of a unified development of the entire Tennessee River system. The realization brought home by the investigation of the joint committee that probably 3,000,000 to 4,000,000 potential horsepower in the Tennessee Valley lay within easy accessibility made it difficult to keep the fertilizer issue alive.[60]

The failure of the joint committee to solve the Muscle Shoals problem brightened the prospects of the Norris bill, for it had been demonstrated from time to time that a majority of the Underwood wing of the southern Democrats preferred government operation to no operation and it had been further shown that solid southern support of the Norris bloc could put the Norris plan across. Nevertheless, the third Norris bill received scant attention in the first session of the Sixty-ninth Congress,

58. Ransmeier, *op. cit.*, 52.
59. Raushenbush, *op. cit.*, 185.
60. *Ibid.*, 185–88.

principally because the attention of the legislators was focused
on the power-chemical struggle. The third Norris bill was
practically identical with the two previous Norris bills except in
two important respects: for the first time in a bill relating to
Muscle Shoals or the development of the Tennessee River, a
provision was included for allocating both navigation and flood
control benefits to the total costs of the project, and for the first
time flood control was given equal rank with power and navigation as a goal to be attained in the development of the river.[61]
Before these ideals could be realized, however, Norris would have
to wait for the private bids to run their course, particularly the
offer of the American Cyanamid Company.

61. Ransmeier, *op. cit.*, 207–8.

VIII

The Cyanamid Bid, 1927–28

THE FAILURE OF MUSCLE SHOALS legislation in the first session of the Sixty-ninth Congress made it appear that the Muscle Shoals controversy would continue indefinitely without a settlement. When Congress reassembled for the second session in December, 1926, the prospects for a solution of the problem seemed to be better. This brighter outlook resulted from the election of 1926, the results of which probably would have a strong influence on the Sixty-ninth Congress, which, however, would not be directly affected since it was meeting in a lame duck session. In that election, farm relief had been an important issue in both the West and the South, and the farm bloc had increased its strength in Congress. Consequently, chances were excellent that the West and South, because of common interests in farm problems, might reach a compromise agreement on Muscle Shoals. Many conservative Southerners, however, were opposed to the McNary-Haugen farm bill, which was popular in the West, because they believed it to be too radical. Moreover, Norris and other Progressive Republicans probably would be reluctant to entangle the Muscle Shoals problem with farm relief. These factors, together with the possibility that administration leaders would be willing to offer the South concessions on Muscle Shoals in order to defeat the farm relief program of the farm bloc, made possible the resurgence of an administration-southern coalition strong enough to pass a Muscle Shoals bill.[1]

The farm relief issue involving Muscle Shoals was further accentuated in November, 1926, when Oscar E. Bradfute, former

1. New York *Times,* Dec. 5 (IX), 1926.

president of the Farm Bureau, told President Coolidge that cheap Muscle Shoals fertilizer was the key to the farm relief problem. According to Bradfute, the depressed farm conditions then prevailing were largely the result of excessive production costs which could be greatly reduced by putting Muscle Shoals to work.[2]

Added to this was the apparent disgust prevailing throughout the country as a result of the failure of Congress to solve the Muscle Shoals problem during the previous session; this appeared likely to spur that body onward to greater efforts in the forthcoming session. Throughout the summer and fall of 1926, a large segment of the American press demanded that Congress stop playing politics with Muscle Shoals and immediately devise a practical solution. In fact, many editors flatly stated that if Congress did not arrive at a solution to the Muscle Shoals controversy in the coming session, the incompetence of that body to handle the problem would be proved and there then would be no excuse for not transferring responsibility for solution of the Muscle Shoals question to an executive commission.[3]

Despite the failure of the power companies' bill in the previous session, Senator Deneen, apparently with the backing of the administration, began an attempt early in the new session to secure acceptance of the offer of the power companies by reactivating the bill proposed by the Joint Committee on Muscle Shoals. Deneen emphasized the great amount of water power available in the Tennessee River basin that could be considered as surplus to fertilizer production needs at Muscle Shoals and thus available for general distribution. Opponents of the bill, particularly members of the Alabama delegation in Congress, asserted that the importance of the Tennessee River to the South from the standpoint of electrical power had been exaggerated and that there were many other undeveloped southern rivers.[4]

Henry Ford's Dearborn *Independent* continued to oppose the

2. *Ibid.*, Nov. 27, 1926.

3. Press comments compiled by the Associated Power Companies, 1926, Correspondence of the Secretary of Agriculture, Muscle Shoals, National Archives.

4. *Cong. Rec.*, 69 Cong., 2 Sess., 354–63, 1130–31, 2025, 2027.

bid of the power companies. Early in January, 1927, it argued that
the joint committee bill was, in reality, the key with which a
great power "combine" hoped to monopolize the water power of
the entire Tennessee Valley.[5] Despite the fact that the bill to
accept the offer of the power companies had the backing of some
influential southern Democrats, especially Senator Harrison and
Representative Quin, the ranking minority member of the House
Military Committee, there was a singular lack of enthusiasm for
the measure on the part of most congressmen in the early stages
of the new session. The lethargic atmosphere which seemingly
prevailed in the camp of the power companies made Norris
suspicious; consequently, he predicted that this group was delaying its action until near the end of the session when it would
attempt to put over the bill with a burst of energy.[6]

The renewed emphasis on farm relief gave the cyanamid bid a
considerable boost, for it was backed by the Farm Bureau and its
supporters fervently declared it to be the true fertilizer plan.
Furthermore, adherents of the cyanamid bid had been busy
during the summer of 1926 in an effort to create a more favorable
congressional atmosphere for the proposal. During that time
officials of the Tennessee River Improvement Association made
an energetic attempt to gain the support of New England congressmen for the cyanamid plan. That association distributed
literature to various important persons in New England warning
that acceptance of the power companies' offer would provide
additional power to attract textile and other New England industries to the South. On the other hand, it was pointed out that
under the cyanamid bid all of the power of the Tennessee Valley
would be concentrated at Muscle Shoals for use by the chemical
industry and thus would not lead to competition with New
England. Furthermore, the claim that cheap Muscle Shoals
fertilizer would provide cheaper cotton for New England's mills
was repeated. To reinforce these arguments, the association

5. New York Times, Jan. 5, 1927.
6. Ibid., Jan. 6, 1927; Stephen Raushenbush, The Power Fight (1932), 186;
"Senator Harrison Optimistic on Muscle Shoals Bill," in Electrical World,
LXXXVIII (Aug. 14, 1926), 339; "Congressman Quin Still Favors Muscle Shoals
Bill," ibid. (Oct. 30, 1926), 931.

sent W. G. Waldo to New England to conduct a personal campaign. During his stay there, Waldo's entourage consisted primarily of the agriculture commissioners of the New England states who appeared to be highly interested in the fertilizer provisions of the cyanamid offer.[7]

The farm support of the cyanamid bid was further strengthened when the National Grange adopted a resolution in November, 1926, which, in effect, endorsed the proposal. In addition, President Coolidge, in his message to Congress in December, 1926, promised that Muscle Shoals would be used to furnish the farmer with low-cost fertilizer. The President's emphasis on fertilizer made the Muscle Shoals section of his message more favorable to the cyanamid bid than to the offer of the power companies.[8]

The bill to authorize acceptance of the cyanamid bid was introduced in the House on January 24, 1927, by Representative Martin B. Madden of Illinois, who had been one of the leading supporters of the Ford offer. His great prestige within the inner sanctum of the Republican party placed him in an excellent position to serve as a bridge between administration Republicans and southern Democrats. The Madden bill received the blessings of the Farm Bureau's Chester Gray, who described the measure as "the answer to the power trust." Gray professed to be jubilant over the fact that the maximum amount of fertilizer promised in the Madden bill was 20 per cent more than that of the original cyanamid offer, but he failed to mention the fact that the production of fertilizer under the terms of the offer was contingent on market demand at a price to be set by the cyanamid company. Upon the introduction of the Madden bill, Gray immediately addressed a form letter to all members of Congress asking their support of the measure.[9]

7. "A Contemptible Effort to Arouse Hatred in New England to the South," in *Manufacturers' Record*, XC (Sept. 2, 1926), 75; "New England and the South's Interests in Muscle Shoals," *ibid.* (Sept. 23, 1926), 53–56.

8. New York *Times*, Nov. 19, Dec. 8, 1926.

9. *Ibid.*, Jan. 25, 1927; *Disposition of Muscle Shoals*, House Report 2303, 69 Cong., 2 Sess. (1927), 31; *Cong. Rec.*, 69 Cong., 2 Sess., 2194.

The introduction of the Madden bill was followed by resolutions adopted by the legislatures of North Carolina and Arkansas memorializing Congress to reject the cyanamid plan. Both resolutions expressed fear that acceptance of this bid would mean concentration of most of the Tennessee River water power at Muscle Shoals for the benefit of the chemical interests and to the detriment of the industrial growth of the South. At the same time a spokesman for Tennessee power interests expressed the same sentiment.[10]

Despite the fact that the Deneen-Morin bill authorizing acceptance of the power companies' offer was already on the House calendar, the cyanamid group was sufficiently strong to obtain a hearing on the Madden bill before the House Military Committee. This committee made another important concession to the cyanamid adherents—it virtually agreed that the amount of return to the United States Treasury was not to be a determining factor in selecting a lessee for Muscle Shoals. The cyanamid group, in order to counterbalance the advantage held by the power companies' offer because of its provision for greater rental payments, had argued that the only factors important enough to consider were the health of agriculture and national defense. The House Military Committee had generally adhered to this policy during the Ford period.[11]

The Military Committee hearings were held intermittently from January 25 to March 1, 1927. The chief witnesses were William B. Bell, president of the American Cyanamid Company, and Chester Gray. Bell denied that his company was using fertilizer as a subterfuge to obtain control of Muscle Shoals, and insisted that his company would realize a neat profit from fertilizer operations at Muscle Shoals. He admitted that under the terms of the cyanamid offer, his company could abandon fertilizer production entirely without losing any of its water-power privileges. He refused to agree to distribute any water power,

10. *Cong. Rec.*, 69 Cong., 2 Sess., 1829–30, 3007, 3933–34.
11. Paul Wooton, "Cyanamid and Farmers' Bids Rejected," in *Electrical World*, LXXXIX (Feb. 5, 1927), 314.

thereby implying that his company planned to utilize all of it in the production of chemicals.[12]

Chester Gray appeared before the committee armed with numerous endorsements of the cyanamid bid, the most important of which was a resolution by several professors (mostly chemists or other technical experts) at Michigan State College and Ohio State University which asserted that Muscle Shoals power could be more economically used if concentrated at one place than if subjected to widespread distribution. Gray also presented pro-cyanamid resolutions adopted by numerous state Farm Bureaus and Granges as well as an endorsement of the bid by a group of state agricultural commissioners in New England.[13]

Perhaps the most significant development of the hearings was the fact that the Secretary of Agriculture, William M. Jardine, and one of his chief scientists, Dr. Frederick G. Cottrell, endorsed a semi–government-operation bill. They recommended that the government either operate or lease the power facilities at Muscle Shoals, consigning the proceeds to the Secretary of Agriculture for the purpose of conducting a program of fertilizer research in which the Haber process would be used. This research program would not necessarily be connected with the Muscle Shoals project. They condemned the cyanamid bid on the ground that the cyanamid process was obsolete. Secretary Jardine admitted that he saw "quite a bit of merit" in the Norris plan which also contemplated a program of fertilizer research.[14] In his attitude toward Muscle Shoals, Jardine appeared to be out of step with the administration.

Representatives of various business interests in Tennessee, North Carolina, Mississippi, and Arkansas came to the hearings to protest that the Madden bill did not provide for equitable distribution. The Tennessee witnesses also complained that the cyanamid company intended to subordinate Cove Creek to the Muscle Shoals project which they declared would deal a stunning blow

12. *Muscle Shoals,* Hearings, U. S. House of Representatives, 69 Cong., 2 Sess., 162–69, 176–77, 186–87.
13. *Ibid.,* 460–62, 523–38.
14. *Ibid.,* 926–68, 1044–45.

to industry in Tennessee. Besides robbing Tennessee of Cove Creek power, such a development, they pointed out, would mean that Cove Creek would produce much less power since it would be used primarily as a reservoir to regulate water flow at Muscle Shoals.[15]

During the hearings, Oscar C. Merrill, executive secretary of the Federal Power Commission, prepared for the committee a memorandum on the cyanamid bid which constituted a ringing denunciation of that proposal. According to Merrill, the power projects contemplated in the bid would generate 1,220,000 horsepower, which would be equal to 55 per cent of the power capacity of all hydroelectric projects in the six southern states of Alabama, Georgia, the Carolinas, Tennessee, and Kentucky. Merrill estimated that this great amount of energy would be four times the probable requirements for the production of the maximum amount of fertilizer specified in the Madden bill. He warned that control of this huge volume of cheap water power would enable the American Cyanamid–Union Carbide combine to "establish an industrial dictatorship in the electrochemical field and put every competition out of business." Merrill pointed out that this danger was made even more acute because of small rental payments and absence of public regulation of power, factors which would enable this combine to obtain the power at a very low cost.[16]

One of the most severe critics of the cyanamid bid at the hearings was Representative B. Carroll Reece, Republican member of the Military Committee, who at this time was the author of a Muscle Shoals bill that was also being considered by the Military Committee. This bill proposed the lease of Muscle Shoals to the Farmers' Federated Fertilizer Corporation, an organization recently established by a group of New York financiers through which to bid for Muscle Shoals. The Reece bill would, in effect, give to this corporation, which was to engage in the power distributing business, a perpetual lease on all dam

15. *Ibid.*, 411–13, 428, 440, 446–47.
16. Federal Power Commission, *Revised Offer for Muscle Shoals,* Senate Doc. 209, 69 Cong., 2 Sess. (1927), 1–3, 14–15.

sites in the Tennessee River system. The sole financial obligation of the lessee under the Reece bill would be cash payments to the government for power actually distributed to the consumer, and these payments would constitute a fertilizer fund which would be used to finance fertilizer production by the corporation for farmers. The Reece bill was condemned by the secretaries of War, the Treasury, and Agriculture, the former two describing it as a request for a government subsidy. At the Military Committee hearings, Reece accused the cyanamid company of planning to suspend fertilizer production once the company's offer had been accepted.[17]

The House Military Committee rejected both the Madden and Reece bills on the ground that they did not conform to the established policy laid down by that committee, that Muscle Shoals should be devoted primarily to agriculture and the national defense. In the committee's report, which was issued on March 3, 1927, the last day of the Sixty-ninth Congress, two important recommendations were made: that the Secretary of War be directed to make a survey of the Cove Creek area so that the power and other potentialities of that place could be ascertained, and that the policy of not granting any power permits on the Tennessee River be continued until after the expiration of the next Congress. This policy had been in effect since 1925 at the insistence of the House Military Committee, which had feared that the power industry might obtain sufficient permits to control the river and prevent Congress from solving the problem in its own manner. At the hearings, Oscar C. Merrill showed signs of revolting against this form of congressional control. Some of the members of the committee believed that Merrill was on the verge of granting permit for the Cove Creek site, which had become very important as a result of the struggle between the power and chemical interests. At first Merrill was somewhat defiant and hinted that the Federal Power Commission would no longer

17. *Muscle Shoals*, House Hearings, 69 Cong., 2 Sess., 219–23; House Report 2303, 69 Cong., 2 Sess., 6–20; War Department, *Muscle Shoals*, Senate Doc. 189, 69 Cong., 2 Sess. (1927), 63; *Cong. Rec.*, 69 Cong., 2 Sess., 3639; New York *Times*, Oct. 9, 1926, Jan. 25, 1927.

subject itself to dictatorial control by the House Military Committee, but he soon receded from this position and agreed to conform to the committee's desires when he found that the committee would not make any concessions on the matter.[18]

The recommendations of the Military Committee with respect to the withholding of power permits on the Tennessee River were made in the face of the known opposition of some members of the Tennessee delegation in Congress. In fact, as early as December, 1926, Representative Finis J. Garrett of Tennessee began an effort to have the "navigable stream" clause of the Federal Water Power Act redefined so that the upper Tennessee would be classed as non-navigable. This would remove these waters from the jurisdiction of the federal government. Failing this, Representative Cordell Hull and former Senator John K. Shields of Tennessee made a legal study of the water-power law, both concluding that it was unconstitutional in that it usurped the rights of the individual states to their water resources. On January 15, 1927, Hull reported their conclusion to the Military Committee with the hope that it would force the committee to remove its ban on further developments on the Tennessee River, but the committee report showed no indication of having been influenced by their arguments.[19]

A few days after Hull's appearance before the House Military Committee, the Alabama state rights issue flared up again. In his inaugural address in January, 1927, Governor Bibb Graves

18. House Report 2303, 69 Cong., 2 Sess., 1–2; *Muscle Shoals,* House Hearings, 69 Cong., 2 Sess., 227–47. In regard to the move by the Military Committee to block further issuance of permits on the Tennessee River, Representative Frank James of Michigan, who led the movement and who was not committed to any Muscle Shoals bill, raised a charge of collusion between the Corps of Engineers and the Electric Bond and Share Company. This charge was based on an attempt by the engineers to solicit funds from this power holding company to finance additional surveys on the Tennessee River. James documented his charge with official records from the files of the Corps of Engineers, and General Edgar Jadwin, Chief of Engineers, made no attempt to deny it. Instead, Jadwin insisted that such a practice was not only ethical but that "under the law contributions are frequently accepted to expedite work." James did not agree, and he threatened to instigate court-martial proceedings against Jadwin and the engineers who asked for contributions. *Muscle Shoals,* House Hearings, 69 Cong., 2 Sess., 239, 256–61.

19. *Cong. Rec.,* 69 Cong., 2 Sess., 5786; *Muscle Shoals,* House Hearings, 69 Cong., 2 Sess., 979–87.

requested the Alabama legislature to create a commission to ascertain the nature and extent of Alabama's rights at Muscle Shoals. The legislature complied, and late in February, the Alabama Muscle Shoals Commission, accompanied by Governor Graves and other distinguished Alabama citizens, journeyed to Washington to make its report directly to the President and Congress.[20] Upon arriving at the capital, the Alabama group presented to President Coolidge and the appropriate executive departments and legislative committees the following statement:

Subject only to the authority of the United States relative to navigation and war purposes, the State of Alabama claims absolute title to and ownership, jurisdiction, and control of that portion of the Tennessee River which is within the State of Alabama, its waters, banks, beds, and soils, including the power in the water and the value thereof, and all other property rights in any wise incident thereto or arising therefrom. . . .

The Alabama group also stated that

It is submitted that there has been established the contentions of the State of Alabama that the State owns an equity in Wilson Dam and power plant, and that it is entitled to an equitable share of any proceeds realized from the sale or lease of hydroelectric power there generated.[21]

Thereupon, Governor Graves appeared before the Senate Agriculture Committee to press Alabama's claims. In his testimony before the committee, Graves emphasized that the State of Alabama would not press its claims to Muscle Shoals if the federal government would use that project for the production of fertilizer. This emphasis on fertilizer production made it appear that the primary purpose of the Alabama claims was to speed congressional action on Muscle Shoals, particularly the Madden bill. Also, Graves revealed that Alabama leaders hoped that should the offer of the power companies be accepted Alabama would be able to share in the profits realized from the sale of Muscle Shoals power. Many people in northern Alabama, however, frowned on the Graves claim because of the fear that it

20. Legislative Doc. 28, State of Alabama, Session of 1927, 3–31.
21. *Muscle Shoals,* House Hearings, 69 Cong., 2 Sess., 1320, 1344.

would injure the chances of obtaining desired congressional action on Muscle Shoals.[22]

Meanwhile, late in February, 1927, administration leaders in the Senate, displaying a last-minute burst of energy as Norris had predicted, managed to bring the Deneen-Morin bill to the floor, but during the brief debate which followed, its supporters were decidedly on the defensive in the face of the combined opposition of the Norris and cyanamid supporters. Democratic Senator Harrison shared the defensive chores with his Republican colleague, Senator Deneen. Significantly, Harrison, who heretofore had emphasized the fertilizer issue, minimized that factor in this short debate, though he did not go so far as to admit the primacy of water-power distribution. Underwood and Heflin led the cyanamid forces in the debate, but their insistence that the Madden measure was the best Muscle Shoals fertilizer plan was undermined by Smith of South Carolina who, while extolling the merits of the Norris fertilizer plan, continually called attention to the loopholes in the cyanamid offer that would permit that company to abandon fertilizer operations. The administration leaders who were supporting the Deneen bill secured a time limit on the debate with the hope that a vote could be had without delay, but the Norris group sponsored a motion which sent the Deneen-Morin bill back to the Norris committee, from which it never emerged.[23] The Senate debate demonstrated that

22. *Muscle Shoals,* Hearings, U. S. Senate, on S. J. Res. 163, 69 Cong., 2 Sess. (1927), 3–8; R. M. Sims to Attorney General John G. Sargent, April 30, 1927, Judge Advocate General, National Archives. In July, 1927, the Alabama legislature levied a tax on the Wilson Dam power which was being sold by the War Department to the Alabama Power Company, and in the following October, the Alabama Tax Commission presented the War Department with a claim for accrued taxes on that power. The War Department refused to pay this tax, asserting that a state could not lay and collect taxes on federal property. The War Department was upheld by John G. Sargent, the Attorney General of the United States. New York *Times,* Oct. 11, Nov. 8, 1927; Department of Justice, *Legal Rights of the United States and Alabama in Muscle Shoals Project,* Senate Doc. 31, 70 Cong., 1 Sess. (1928), 10–11, 29–30.

23. *Cong. Rec.,* 69 Cong., 2 Sess., 4536–37, 4742–58. The Senate Muscle Shoals debate as well as the hearings held before the House Military Committee during this session took place while Chester Gray was bombarding Congress with a virtual shower of Farm Bureau letters warning that members of Congress from agricultural areas would be expected to support the cyanamid bid because

no one group was yet sufficiently strong to gain the whip hand in the Muscle Shoals controversy. Perhaps the Norris plan benefited from this Senate debate because the supporters of the two principal contenders, the cyanamid company and the power combine, ignored the Norris bill while attempting to discredit each other's measure.

In the second session of the Sixty-ninth Congress, Senator Norris, realizing the apparent impossibility of securing an adoption at this time of a comprehensive plan for the unified development of the Tennessee River, introduced a compromise plan in the form of a joint resolution. The Nebraska Senator waited until February 17, about three weeks before adjournment, before introducing the resolution. In this new Norris measure plans for further construction of dams were abandoned and consideration was confined to the Muscle Shoals project only. The resolution authorized the Secretary of War to complete and operate the power installations at Muscle Shoals, the proceeds from the sale of power to be made available to the Secretary of Agriculture for fertilizer research. The Norris measure also called for public construction of transmission lines and the granting of preferences to public agencies in the sale of power. The fertilizer provisions of the resolution were practically identical to those proposed by the Department of Agriculture during this session.[24] The Senate Agriculture Committee reported favorably on the Norris plan on February 26, but it failed to reach the Senate floor before the

of the alleged benefits that it held for farmers. Gray's work was partially offset by the Southern States Republican League which attempted to carry out a publicity program in favor of the power companies' offer. Gray to members of Congress (form letters), Jan. and Feb., 1927, Norris Papers; *Report of the Muscle Shoals Committee of the Southern States Republican League* (Feb. 21, 1927), Correspondence of the Secretary of Agriculture, Muscle Shoals, National Archives.

24. *Cong. Rec.*, 69 Cong., 2 Sess., 4022; *Muscle Shoals*, Senate Hearings, 69 Cong., 2 Sess., 1–2; Joseph S. Ransmeier, *The Tennessee Valley Authority* (1942), 57. At the beginning of the second session of the Sixty-ninth Congress, Norris turned over the chairmanship of the Agriculture Committee to Senator McNary. Norris said that the reason for this move was his belief that the Oregon Senator, who was considered to be more of a party regular than Norris, would be able to secure better co-operation from the Republican administration with respect to agricultural and Muscle Shoals legislation. Richard L. Neuberger and Stephen B. Kahn, *Integrity* (1937), 251; New York *Times*, Dec. 12, 1926.

adjournment on March 4.[25] During this session Norris did not seem to be particularly energetic in pressing his plan for Muscle Shoals. He did not publicly reveal why he waited until late in the session before introducing his resolution. Perhaps he was waiting for the new Congress to meet before making another wholehearted effort to obtain public operation of Muscle Shoals.

The apparent failure of private bids in the post-Ford era of the controversy up to March, 1927, had resulted in turning more members of Congress toward the Norris plan for Muscle Shoals.[26] By the end of the session on March 4, some pro-Underwood Southerners in both houses of Congress began to voice a sentiment for public operation of Muscle Shoals. None of this group, however, would go so far as to advocate public construction of transmission lines, although there appears to have been at this time no awareness of the fact, later revealed, that the public transmission feature was the very heart of the Norris plan. These new exponents of public operation advocated that the power be sold at the switchboard.[27]

The Norris scheme for a comprehensive development of the Tennessee River had been given an unqualified endorsement by the *Progressive Farmer* in January, approximately a month before the Nebraska Senator introduced his compromise plan. This publication was probably the most influential farm publication in the South. The editor of this magazine opposed the offer of the power companies because he had concluded that the theory of public regulation of private utilities had failed, leaving public power as the only alternative. He questioned the sincerity of

25. *Completion of Dam No. 2 and Steam Plant at Muscle Shoals,* Senate Report 1633, 69 Cong., 2 Sess. (1927), 1–3.

26. It was apparent that a feeling prevailed to some extent within the electrical power industry that the Muscle Shoals problem already had been solved because the Alabama Power Company had gained control of Muscle Shoals power through its contract with the War Department. The contract which that company had signed with the War Department in 1925 for the disposal of test power at Wilson Dam had been renewed, giving the power company access to Muscle Shoals power on a more permanent basis. "New Muscle Shoals Idea Falls Flat," in *Electrical World,* LXXXIX (April 9, 1927), 771.

27. *Cong. Rec.,* 69 Cong., 2 Sess., 359, 2029, 3683, 3881, 5759.

those making the cyanamid bid by declaring that it made a "gesture at promising cheaper fertilizers." [28]

Following the adjournment of Congress on March 4, 1927, Norris attempted, in an article in the *New South,* to refute two of the principal arguments which the private power industry had been using against public power projects: first, that public power held an unfair competitive advantage because it was tax-free and, second, that government operation of business was impossible because of political interference. Norris held that the taxation theory of the power companies was a "myth" in that the companies themselves did not pay taxes but were, in reality, tax collectors that gathered the tax money from consumers. In answer to the second argument, the Nebraska Senator asserted that private power companies were actively engaged in politics in all parts of the country. [29]

After March, 1927, the position of Muscle Shoals as a fertilizer proposition was subjected to a heavy attack by opponents of the cyanamid bid. In June, in an address at the annual convention of the National Fertilizer Association, Charles J. Brand, executive secretary of that organization, made a vigorous attempt to refute the arguments of the supporters of the cyanamid offer. He attempted to show that Muscle Shoals could not be utilized profitably for fertilizer production and that the fertilizer industry was already on the brink of ruin as a result of overproduction and excessive competition. In his article in the *New South* in July, Senator Norris attempted to prove conclusively that the cyanamid process was obsolete by reviewing the accumulated scientific evidence with respect to fertilizer processes. Norris concluded that the attempt to promote commercial fertilizer production at Muscle Shoals had been "propaganda to deceive the farmers of America." A few months later, in an article in the *Annalist,* Benjamin Baker, a political commentator, called Norris's article in the *New South* a frank treatment of the "farmers' nitrate illusion." Baker felt that Norris's article had

28. *Progressive Farmer,* Jan. 15, 1927, quoted *ibid.,* 3016.
29. *New South,* July, 1927, quoted in *Cong. Rec.,* 70 Cong., 1 Sess., 801–4,

prepared the way for a "complete abandonment of the nitrate hoax." [30]

As the first session of the Seventieth Congress approached, the advocates of the offer of the power companies made a desperate effort to revive that proposal and defeat the cyanamid bid. In October, 1927, the Southern Appalachian Power Conference, a meeting dominated by power company supporters, declared that Muscle Shoals was no longer of any value as a possible fertilizer plant because of technological advances in the fertilizer industry. The conference report demanded that the offer of the power companies be accepted to relieve an alleged acute power shortage in the South.[31]

In November, Samuel S. Wyer, a publicist for the private power industry, issued a pamphlet which he claimed was an independent study of the nation's fertilizer problem. The study was conducted under the auspices of the Fuel-Transportation-Education Foundation of Columbus, Ohio, an organization which was created and controlled by the Ohio State Chamber of Commerce. In this pamphlet Wyer attempted to show that the cyanamid process was obsolete for fertilizer production and that Muscle Shoals could not be profitably operated as a fertilizer enterprise. The publication, which included a statement by Secretary of Agriculture William M. Jardine endorsing Wyer's views on the fertilizer problem, constituted a vigorous attack on the cyanamid offer.[32]

In the same month, Herbert Hoover, in answer to an inquiry from President Coolidge concerning the future supply of nitrogen for national defense, informed the President that the productive capacity of the private nitrate and fertilizer industries had increased to such an extent that Muscle Shoals was no longer

30. *Cong. Rec.*, 70 Cong., 1 Sess., 804; National Fertilizer Association, *Proceedings of the Third Annual Convention of the National Fertilizer Association, June 6–9, 1927* (Washington, D.C., 1927), 38–52; Benjamin Baker, "Muscle Shoals Plans and Issues Before Congress," in *Annalist*, XXXI (March 9, 1928), 445.

31. *Report of the Southern Appalachian Power Conference* (Oct. 15, 1927), Bureau of Plant Industry, Fertilizer, National Archives.

32. Samuel S. Wyer, *Fundamentals of Our Fertilizer Problem* (1927); New York *Times*, May 12, 1929.

needed for national defense. Also, wide circulation was given to a letter by Senator Norris, which the Senator made public, condemning the cyanamid offer and questioning the motives behind the Farm Bureau support of it. Response to the Norris letter disclosed the fact that Chester Gray had not yet secured complete subordination of state Farm Bureau leaders to his Muscle Shoals policy. This incident revealed that some state Farm Bureau presidents outside the South had either deserted Gray or failed to join him because of the belief that Muscle Shoals held out little, if any, hope for the benefit of agriculture in their states.[33] Despite this determined drive against the cyanamid offer, Cully A. Cobb, president of the American Agricultural Editors' Association and editor of the *Southern Ruralist,* made an unrelenting effort to keep the fertilizer issue alive in the agricultural press.[34]

The climax to the campaign against Muscle Shoals as a fertilizer plant came on December 6 when President Coolidge, in his message to Congress, completely reversed his position on Muscle Shoals. He stated that

The last year has seen considerable changes in the problem of Muscle Shoals. Development of other methods shows that nitrates can probably be produced at less cost than by use of hydroelectric power. Extensive investigation made by the Department of War indicates that the nitrate plants on this project are of little value for national defense and can probably be disposed of within two years. . . . This leaves this project mostly concerned with power.[35]

This message as originally written left the matter at this very definite point, but an advance copy of the document fell into the hands of Chester Gray who was greatly dismayed because the President apparently had deserted his position of supporting fertilizer production at Muscle Shoals. Thereupon, Gray wired Coolidge, reminding him that less than a week before he, the President, had (according to Gray) solemnly vowed to support the Farm Bureau position. Gray requested that the President

33. Hoover to Coolidge, Nov. 28, 1927, Coolidge Papers; letters to Norris concerning his letter to C. A. Cobb of Nov. 18, 1927, Dec., 1927, Norris Papers.
34. Harry Slattery to Norris, Feb. 14, 1928, Norris Papers.
35. New York *Times,* Dec. 7, 1927; *Cong. Rec.,* 70 Cong., 1 Sess., 106.

change that section of his message to make it more favorable
to the Farm Bureau's stand on the Muscle Shoals issue. In an
apparent attempt to placate Gray, Coolidge added another
sentence in the message as sent to Congress recommending that
in disposing of Muscle Shoals "preference should be given to
proposals to use all or part of it for nitrate production and fertilizer
manufacturing," a statement which was completely contradictory
to his other statements on Muscle Shoals.[36] There could be little
doubt, however, that the President favored the point of view of
the power companies on the project.

As the Seventieth Congress, which assembled for the first
session on December 5, 1927, settled down to work, prospects
for the bid of the power companies seemed bright for the first
time since the spring of 1926. The *New Republic*, believing that
the supporters of the power companies were about to make a big
push in Congress in the hope of gaining a quick victory for their
bill, declared that the principal goal of the power industry was
the establishment of a decisive congressional policy in favor of
private power.[37]

Strangely enough, during this session the bill to accept the offer
of the power companies was not reintroduced in Congress, thus
apparently leaving the cyanamid and Norris groups as the leading
competitors in the Muscle Shoals controversy. The Department of
Agriculture, however, did sponsor a bill in the House which
seemed to have been an attempt to combine Norris's views on
fertilizer with provisions for production of power which would
have given the power companies access to power at Muscle
Shoals. This bill, which was introduced by Representative John
M. Morin, was very similar to the Norris Muscle Shoals resolution in its fertilizer provisions, which authorized the Secretary
of Agriculture to conduct a program of fertilizer research to be
financed by sales of Muscle Shoals power. Unlike the Norris
measure, the Morin bill authorized the Secretary of War to lease
the Muscle Shoals power plants to private operators. In the event

---

36. *Cong. Rec.*, 70 Cong., 1 Sess., 106; Chester Gray and Edward O'Neal
to Coolidge, Dec. 1, 1927, Coolidge Papers.
37. "Fooling the Farmers Again," in *New Republic*, LIII (Dec. 7, 1927), 60.

no suitable lessee could be found, the War Department would operate the power plants, selling the power at the switchboard where it would be divided equitably between local industries and the power companies.[38]

The cyanamid bid was reintroduced in the House by Representative Martin B. Madden and in the Senate by Senator Frank B. Willis of Ohio. The consideration of the Willis-Madden bill during the Muscle Shoals hearings before the Senate Agriculture Committee in January, 1928, consisted primarily of a verbal tug of war between Senator Norris and Chester Gray. Norris reiterated his stand that the cyanamid proposal was merely an attempt to gain access to a large source of cheap power by soliciting the sympathy of the farm population through an insincere promise of cheap fertilizer. Gray, who at this time considered the cyanamid bid superior to the Ford offer, contended that not only did the proposal contain an adequate guarantee of fertilizer production, but that under the cyanamid proposal, farmers in every section of the nation could purchase fertilizer economically at Muscle Shoals. Despite the fact that Norris marshaled an enormous amount of scientific evidence indicating beyond a reasonable doubt that in the production of fertilizer the cyanamid process, when compared to the Haber process, was obsolete, Gray continued to maintain that the cyanamid process was the only method of fertilizer production that could be operated successfully at Muscle Shoals.[39]

Norris scolded Gray severely for allegedly using the Farm Bureau to distribute propaganda in favor of the cyanamid bid. The Nebraska Senator speculated that perhaps vested interests

38. *Muscle Shoals*, Hearings, U. S. House of Representatives, on H. R. 8305, 70 Cong., 1 Sess. (1928), 301–2; William M. Jardine to Morin, March 3, 1928, Bureau of Plant Industry, Soils, National Archives. Perhaps the reason for the failure of the power companies to make a formal effort to acquire Muscle Shoals during this session of Congress was that the power and chemical interests at this juncture were apparently attempting to negotiate a compromise deal involving the project. See *Lobby Investigation*, Hearings, U. S. Senate, pursuant to S. Res. 20, 71 Cong., 2 Sess. (1930), 3089–91, 3248–51. This episode is discussed further in Chapter X.

39. *Disposition of Muscle Shoals*, Hearings, U. S. Senate, on S. 2786, 70 Cong., 1 Sess. (1928), 51–69; Baker, "Muscle Shoals Plans and Issues before Congress," *loc. cit.*, 445.

had defrayed the expenses of the Farm Bureau's Muscle Shoals publicity program. He stated that several state Farm Bureau leaders had written to him expressing concern lest Gray abuse his position by permitting special interests to exert control over the Muscle Shoals policy of the Farm Bureau. Norris characterized the Farm Bureau publicity on Muscle Shoals as being composed of half-truths designed to deceive the public. Gray solemnly averred that the entire expense of this campaign was being defrayed by the Farm Bureau, and he accused Norris of attempting to destroy that organization. Gray boldly challenged Norris to investigate the Farm Bureau, but Norris abruptly changed the subject.[40]

In the report of the Senate Agriculture Committee, which recommended passage of the Norris compromise plan, the cyanamid offer was emphatically rejected. This report, which was adopted by the committee by a vote of 9 to 3, reviewed the available scientific information regarding the relative merits of the cyanamid and Haber processes and concluded that the cyanamid method of fertilizer production was entirely out of date, rendering the acceptance of the cyanamid proposal impractical and uneconomical.[41]

During the Senate hearings, Senator Norris attempted to prove conclusively that the fertilizer provisions in the offer of the American Cyanamid Company had not been made in good faith but were intended as a ruse to aid in gaining control of a tremendous source of cheap water power. Norris offered to support a bill which would provide that nitrate plant no. 2 be leased to the cyanamid company, or to the Farm Bureau, free of any rental charges or taxes, for a period of fifty years provided the lessee would agree to manufacture fertilizer to the capacity of the plant during the entire term of the lease. Power would be furnished to the lessee at cost. Although Gray and William B. Bell, president of the cyanamid company, protested that Norris had no authority to make such an offer, they realized that to

40. *Disposition of Muscle Shoals,* Senate Hearings, 70 Cong., 1 Sess., 70–89.
41. *Disposition of Muscle Shoals,* Senate Report 228, 70 Cong., 1 Sess. (1928), 1–2; Minutes of the Senate Agriculture Committee, Feb. 1, 1928, Senate Records, National Archives.

permit the Norris proposal to go unanswered would give the
Nebraska Senator a potent political weapon. Consequently, a few
days afterward, they informed Chairman McNary of the Agriculture Committee that the Norris proposal could not be accepted
for two reasons: first, contrary to established policy, no profit
limitation on fertilizer production was provided and, second, to
accept this offer would constitute an endorsement of public operation of the Muscle Shoals power plants, a policy which Gray
declared the Farm Bureau could not condone. Norris agreed to
write in a profit-limitation clause, but he denied that the proposal
could be construed as affecting any form of government operation. Thereupon, Gray admitted that the Norris proposal could
not be accepted because it did not provide compensation to the
cyanamid company in the form of electric power.[42]

After the hearings, Norris continued his devastating attack on
Chester Gray and the Farm Bureau's Muscle Shoals policy. In
addition to his repeated charges that Gray was deceiving the
nation's farmers, he further accused the farm leader of purchasing
support of southern farm magazines for the cyanamid bid.[43] For
his part, Gray continued to flood Congress and the country with
pro-cyanamid literature under the masthead of the Farm Bureau.
He asserted that government scientists, in testifying before congressional committees, had described the cyanamid process as the
most feasible method of fertilizer manufacture and that they
had shown that opponents of the cyanamid offer had grossly
exaggerated the amount of power that the company would obtain
under the terms of the proposal. In reply, two of these experts,
Oscar C. Merrill and Dr. Frederick G. Cottrell, asserted that Gray
had quoted them out of context.[44]

42. *Disposition of Muscle Shoals*, Senate Hearings, 70 Cong., 1 Sess., 61–68,
103–4; *Muscle Shoals*, House Hearings, 70 Cong., 1 Sess., 35, 72–74; *Cong. Rec.*,
70 Cong., 1 Sess., 2310, 2507.

43. *Cong. Rec.*, 70 Cong., 1 Sess., 3516, 3525–30, 3692–97. The latter charge
was probably based on a letter from a friend of Norris containing a report that
the cyanamid company was purchasing support of farm magazines through
lucrative advertising accounts and that the American Agricultural Editors' Association had been organized by the cyanamid company. Harry Slattery to Norris,
Feb. 14, 1928, Norris Papers.

44. Form letters of the American Farm Bureau Federation, Jan. 16 and Feb.
16, 1928, Norris Papers; Dr. Frederick G. Cottrell to Henry Knight, Jan. 31,

The House Military Committee, which continued to adhere to the policy that any lease of Muscle Shoals must be based on the assumption that the project was primarily a potential source of cheap fertilizer, held hearings on the Muscle Shoals question intermittently from late January to March, 1928. At these hearings William B. Bell made a desperate effort to convince the committee of the merits of his company's bid. He admitted that the rental payments proposed in the offer were low but asserted that this defect would be more than counterbalanced by the vast benefits which he said would accrue to farmers from the fertilizer provisions. Bell also admitted that the offer contained no guarantee of fertilizer production, but he pleaded with the committee to accept the prestige of the American Cyanamid Company in lieu of such a warranty. Furthermore, he made it plain that, because of uncertain market conditions, his company would not under any circumstances legally blind itself to produce fertilizer.[45]

Apparently realizing that the cyanamid plan was receiving a cool reception by the Military Committee, Representative Madden made a personal appeal to President Coolidge for administration support.[46] The President's failure to respond to Madden's call for help, together with the anti-cyanamid attitude of two administration Republicans on the committee, Reece and Morin, made it obvious that there was to be no administration support for the Willis-Madden bill.[47] Furthermore, the Muscle Shoals plan of the Secretary of Agriculture, which had been introduced as a bill by Representative Morin, who had become chairman of the Military Committee, seemed to conform more closely to the President's December message to Congress than did the cyanamid bid. Thus, the House Military Committee again rejected the cyanamid offer. The committee's report was primarily concerned with an analysis of the Morin bill, which

1928, Bureau of Plant Industry, Soils, National Archives; Merrill to Norris, Feb., 20, 1928, Norris Papers.

45. *Muscle Shoals*, House Hearings, 70 Cong., 1 Sess., 20–31, 77, 85, 117, 197–200, 211–12.

46. Madden to Coolidge, Feb. 13, 1928, Coolidge Papers.

47. *Muscle Shoals*, House Hearings, 70 Cong., 1 Sess., 122–24, 185–88, 257–59.

was being reported favorably, and merely stated that the cyanamid bid was unsatisfactory.[48]

William B. Bell's lengthy testimony before the House Military Committee inadvertently dealt the cyanamid bid a death blow. According to the *Annalist*, Bell's statements succeeded in convincing the committee that "the cyanamid company's bid was aimed at securing government-provided power for its own private purposes, among which President Bell . . . explicitly admitted that the manufacturing of fertilizer occupied a very minor place." [49] Representative John J. McSwain of South Carolina, a member of the Military Committee, in discussing in the House the defects of the cyanamid offer, came to practically the same conclusions.[50] Thus the cyanamid bid, though it lingered like a ghost throughout the remainder of the controversy, was no longer a serious competitor for Muscle Shoals.

The cyanamid proposal was the last important private bid for Muscle Shoals. According to the *New Republic*, the private Muscle Shoals proposals during the period 1925–28 had two characteristics in common. The bidders did not believe Muscle Shoals to be suitable for a successful venture in fertilizer manufacturing but instead depended on the sale or use of surplus power for their prospective profits. Furthermore, they were not interested in Muscle Shoals alone but based their bids on a wider development of the Tennessee River which would not only bring new sites into the production of power but would convert much of the vast secondary power at Muscle Shoals to primary power. Consequently, the value of Wilson Dam alone would be greatly increased.[51]

48. *Muscle Shoals,* House Report 1095, 70 Cong., 1 Sess. (1928), 16. During the hearings, Representative Lister Hill of Alabama, a member of the Military Committee, was working behind the scenes with Chester Gray in a desperate attempt to obtain a favorable report on the cyanamid bid. Hill warned Gray that unless Bell consented to a legal guarantee of fertilizer production, the committee would reject the bid. *Lobby Investigation,* Senate Hearings, 71 Cong., 2 Sess., 3037.

49. Benjamin Baker, "Political Forces in the Muscle Shoals Struggle," in *Annalist,* XXXI (March 2, 1928), 405.

50. *Cong. Rec.,* 70 Cong., 1 Sess., 5795.

51. "Muscle Shoals in Crisis," in *New Republic,* LV (May 30, 1928), 33–34.

Therefore, the term "Muscle Shoals" came to designate a mighty stream of energy rather than a surplus war plant, and the project was more and more losing its appeal as a fertilizer proposition. Perhaps the only state in the South during the period 1927–28 in which there was a statewide demand for fertilizer production at Muscle Shoals as opposed to water-power distribution was Florida, where the fruit and vegetable industries were experiencing a rapid growth.[52] By 1928, moreover, the weight of scientific opinion definitely appeared to indicate the obsolescence of the cyanamid process, a condition which minimized the importance of cheap water power in the fixation of nitrates.[53] Although Chester Gray and his colleagues managed to keep the fertilizer issue alive, the Department of Agriculture continued vigorously to oppose the use of the cyanamid process at Muscle Shoals for fertilizer production. In August, 1928, Secretary of Agriculture Jardine apparently attempted to end the fertilizer controvery by endorsing, in the name of the Department of Agriculture, a magazine article containing separate essays on this subject by Senator Norris and Dr. Robert Stewart, a professor of chemistry at the University of Nevada. Norris and Stewart, by a review of scientific evidence with respect to fertilizer processes, attempted to show that the cyanamid process was obsolete and that economical fertilizer production did not depend on cheap water power.[54]

In the meantime, the true status of the cyanamid bid was revealed by the fact that Congress had turned its attention to the Norris proposal.

52. *Cong. Rec.*, 70 Cong., 1 Sess., 139, 4321.
53. See R. O. E. Davis, "Muscle Shoals, Nitrogen and Farm Fertilizers," in *Annals of the American Academy of Political and Social Science*, CXXXV (January, 1928), 157–65.
54. "The Problem of Muscle Shoals," in *Current History*, XXVIII (Aug., 1928), 724–33. Introduction by William M. Jardine, Part I by Robert Stewart, and Part II by George W. Norris.

IX

The First Norris Victory
and the Coolidge Veto

O N DECEMBER 15, 1927, very early in the first session of the
Seventieth Congress, Norris again introduced the compromise plan he had offered near the end of the previous session.
This plan, which contained no provisions for the unified development of the Tennessee River, called for public operation of the
Muscle Shoals project for power production and fertilizer research and for public distribution of the surplus power produced
at the project. In reintroducing this joint resolution, Norris informed his colleagues that he had not wavered in the least from
his desire for a unified development of the Tennessee River but
that he still believed it to be impossible to obtain congressional
sanction of such a program at this time.[1] The rejection of the
Willis-Madden bill by the Senate Agriculture and House Military committees in February and March, respectively, left the
Norris Muscle Shoals joint resolution and the Morin bill as the
principal plans for Muscle Shoals.

On February 3, 1928, the Senate Agriculture Committee, in the
same report rejecting the cyanamid bid, endorsed the Norris
compromise plan. The committee reported that the principal
object of the Norris resolution was to ascertain the most efficient
method of fertilizer production. The report declared that the
Norris measure would carry out as nearly as possible the original
intension of the National Defense Act as properly interpreted in
the light of later scientific developments. This was an obvious
attempt to justify the construction of a new Haber experimental
plant as provided in the resolution. The committee defended the

1. *Cong. Rec.*, 70 Cong., 1 Sess., 3441.

provisions of the resolution which authorized governmental construction and operation of transmission lines. Such a proposal, the committee reported, was justified because of the monopoly of electrical distribution held by the Alabama Power Company in the Muscle Shoals area, a situation which, the report alleged, would prevent municipalities and other public agencies from acquiring the surplus Muscle Shoals power on reasonable terms.[2]

As in the previous session, the fertilizer provisions in the Norris compromise plan were endorsed by the Secretary of Agriculture, William M. Jardine, who praised these features as having "the flexibility which is necessary if efficient work is to be done in this field, where changes come so rapidly." Nevertheless, the Secretary pointed out that the policy of the administration was to lease the power facilities at Muscle Shoals to private operation rather than to follow a policy of public operation, as provided by the Norris measure.[3]

In addition to having the limited support of Secretary Jardine, the Norris Muscle Shoals measure of 1928 was endorsed by the National League of Women Voters which appears to have conducted an extensive campaign in an attempt to popularize the Norris plan.[4] On the other hand, the Farm Bureau continued its campaign against public operation of Muscle Shoals.[5] Chester Gray, who refused to distinguish between the Norris and Morin bills, protested in a message to state Farm Bureau leaders that

The Norris-Morin resolution does not guarantee fertilizer production, but simply a fund for experimenting in fertilizer manufacture. Furthermore, the Norris resolution separates the fertilizer manufacture

2. *Disposition of Muscle Shoals,* Senate Report 228, 70 Cong., 1 Sess., 1–4.

3. Jardine to Norris, March 3, 1928, Norris Papers.

4. Letters and telegrams to Senator McNary urging passage of the Norris Muscle Shoals joint resolution, March, 1928, McNary Papers; Juliette Sessions to Norris, Feb. 28, 1928, Norris Papers. From 1921 to 1924, the League of Women Voters advocated the use of Muscle Shoals primarily for the production of fertilizer, but in 1925 distribution of water power was given equal rank with fertilizer in the League's platform. In 1926, water-power distribution forged ahead to become the chief tenet of the League's Muscle Shoals policy while the fertilizer recommendations were reduced to mere advocacy of research. Water power was also dominant in the League's Muscle Shoals policy of 1928. Julia M. Hicks, *Facts about Muscle Shoals* (1928), 26–28.

5. J. Carl Laney to Senator Wesley L. Jones, Feb. 13, 1928, Norris Papers.

from the power and thus destroys our surest guaranty of production, namely, that failure to carry out guaranties means a loss of the power.[6]

Benjamin Baker, a political commentator writing in *Annalist,* saw in the fertilizer provisions of the Norris and Morin bills a plot to deceive farmers by implying, through provisions for fertilizer research, that cheap fertilizer would be produced. Baker, who credited Norris with having refuted the argument that Muscle Shoals should be devoted to fertilizer production, declared the Nebraska Senator to be guilty of political hypocrisy for continuing to associate Muscle Shoals with fertilizer.[7]

In mid-February, 1928, approximately a week before debate on the Norris plan began in the Senate, a short but stormy clash between the exponents and opponents of public power was precipitated in the upper house. This episode was occasioned by a resolution, which had been introduced by Senator Thomas J. Walsh of Montana at the beginning of the session in December, to investigate the alleged power trust. The Walsh resolution proposed a general investigation by a Senate committee of the nation's power industry, particularly methods of financing, the relationships between various utility corporations, contributions by power companies to election campaigns, and alleged attempts to turn public opinion against public power projects.[8]

Senator Walsh was a strong supporter of Norris on Muscle Shoals and doubtless he was aware that his resolution probably would create a favorable political atmosphere for the consideration of the Norris Muscle Shoals resolution upon its arrival on the Senate floor. According to the press, however, the Walsh resolution was inspired by the first report of the Federal Trade Commission on its investigation of the General Electric Company pursuant to Senator Norris's resolution of 1925. The commission submitted its first report in February, 1927, absolving the General Electric Company of charges of monopoly in the

6. Gray "to all State Farm Bureaus," Feb. 9, 1928, reprinted in *Cong. Rec.,* 71 Cong., 2 Sess., 6373.

7. Benjamin Baker, "Some Hope for Some Action on Muscle Shoals," and "Muscle Shoals Plans and Issues before Congress," in *Annalist,* XXXI (Feb. 14, March 9, 1928), 363, 445.

8. New York *Times,* Jan. 15 (IX), 1928; *Cong. Rec.,* 70 Cong., 1 Sess., 788.

public utility business. Nevertheless, the report warned Congress
of the "extreme degree" to which pyramiding of holding companies in the public utility business was being practiced and
recommended congressional legislation looking to regulation
and control of this problem. In January, 1928, the Federal Trade
Commission submitted a second report in which it again
declared that no unlawful monopoly had been found in the
power business, but the commission also repeated its warning
about the "speculative pyramiding" of public utility holding
companies. Moreover, the commission severely criticized various
publicity methods which were being employed by the National
Electric Light Association, the principal trade organization of
the electrical power industry. According to the commission,
this organization had been engaged in attempts to mold public
opinion through devices that appeared to be somewhat unethical and which were sometimes "lacking in frankness toward
the public." [9]

On February 1 the Senate Interstate Commerce Committee
reported the Walsh resolution with amendments limiting the
investigation to power companies engaged in interstate commerce and limiting the political campaigns that could be
investigated to those related to presidential and congressional
elections. In the committee session, Senator James E. Watson of
Indiana, an administration Republican leader, unsuccessfully
attempted not only to limit further the scope of the investigation
but to hand the investigatory role to the Federal Trade Commission rather than a Senate committee. Senator Burton K.
Wheeler of Montana led the defense of the Walsh resolution in
committee.[10]

When the Walsh resolution reached the floor of the Senate,
a lively debate ensued as the result of an administration-spon-
sored amendment offered by Senator Walter F. George to

9. New York *Times*, Jan. 15 (II), 1928; Federal Trade Commission, *Control of
Power Companies*, Senate Doc. 213, 69 Cong., 2 Sess. (1927), xii–xvi; Federal
Trade Commission, *Electrical Equipment and Competitive Conditions*, Senate
Doc. 46, 70 Cong., 1 Sess. (1928), xviii–xix.

10. *Investigation of Public Utility Corporations*, Senate Report 225, 70 Cong.,
1 Sess. (1928), 1–2; New York *Times*, Feb. 2, 1928.

delegate the proposed investigation to the Federal Trade Commission. Despite Norris's assertions that acceptance of the George amendment would mean that no real investigation could be carried out, it was adopted by a vote of 46 to 31, through a coalition of administration Republicans and southern Democrats. Several Southerners followed the lead of McKellar in supporting the Norris group. Significantly, Senator Hugo L. Black, who had replaced Underwood in the Senate at the beginning of this session, not only supported the Norris group but was the author of a successful amendment requiring the investigation to be open to the public. The Walsh resolution, as finally agreed to, directed the Federal Trade Commission to report to the Senate monthly during the entire investigation.[11]

During the Senate debate, the Republican administration made an attempt to limit the investigation. The Attorney General's office ruled that the Trade Commission could not legally investigate the political activities of power companies. After the passage of the Walsh resolution and following an accusation by Norris that the commission was seeking to avoid its responsibility, that agency announced that it did have the authority to execute the resolution in full.[12]

In the Senate debate on the Norris Muscle Shoals resolution, an unusual turn of events occurred—those attacking the measure most vigorously were Southerners who had been allied with the Norris group, principally McKellar, Smith of South Carolina, and Black. Since the Norris resolution provided that Muscle Shoals power not purchased by public agencies could be sold to private power companies, Black and McKellar professed concern that the power industry would be able to acquire most of the Muscle Shoals power. They asserted that most munici-

11. *Cong. Rec.*, 70 Cong., 1 Sess., 2942–51, 3029, 3053–54.

12. New York *Times*, Feb. 15, 18, 1928. The insistence by Norris and his supporters that political activities of power companies be investigated was prompted by the revelations made before a special election investigating committee under the chairmanship of Senator James A. Reed of Missouri which in January, 1928, developed proof that the Insull interests had contributed almost $500,000 to recent political campaigns. *Senatorial Campaign Expenditures*, Senate Report 603, 70 Cong., 1 Sess. (1928), Part 2, 5–46.

palities in the Tennessee Valley would not be able to take advantage of the government's offer to sell power within the immediate future because of existing contracts with power companies and other legal difficulties. Although Norris denied that this contention possessed any merit, he finally agreed to amendments designed to give greater protection to the public agencies in this respect. Senator Smith also demanded a guarantee of fertilizer production rather than a mere experiment and practically accused Norris of having completely abandoned the idea of actually producing fertilizer at Muscle Shoals. Norris refused to agree to such a guarantee.[13]

The desire of many Mississippians that Muscle Shoals power be made available to their communities was voiced by Senator Harrison who accused the people of northern Alabama of attempting to concentrate that power in the Muscle Shoals area for their own selfish benefit. Harrison, who declared the cyanamid process to be obsolete, emphasized water power rather than fertilizer. He offered an unsuccessful amendment to require that Muscle Shoals power be sold at the switchboard to private power companies. Senator Heflin, on the other hand, attempted to delete the equitable distribution provision from the Norris resolution in order to prevent the transportation of Muscle Shoals power from Alabama. Senator Black did not openly oppose equitable distribution. He declared, however, that Alabama was entitled morally, if not legally, to share in the proceeds from the sale of Muscle Shoals power, and he offered a resolution, which was decisively defeated, authorizing the Secretary of War to pay the state 5 per cent of the proceeds of such sales.[14]

Senator Black revealed that he was much less opposed to public power than had been his predecessor, Oscar W. Underwood. Although Black paid lip service to the principle of private operation of Muscle Shoals, he was clearly not opposed to public operation of the project. With respect to the issue of public versus private power at Muscle Shoals, Senator Norris denied

13. *Cong. Rec.*, 70 Cong., 1 Sess., 3434-37, 3527, 4085-91, 4180-84.
14. *Ibid.*, 3438-39, 4263, 4522-23, 4540-44, 4623.

that in operating the project the government would be competing with private power companies in the area, the Nebraska
Senator contending that it would be merely supplementing
private power. He added, however, that public operation of
Muscle Shoals would force private power companies in the
area to lower their rates.[15]

Senator Duncan U. Fletcher of Florida, who emphasized the
growing need for fertilizer in his state, saw no promise of fertilizer
relief in the Norris resolution, and he joined Heflin in demanding
that nitrate plant no. 2 be put to work producing fertilizer.
Senator La Follette, in reply to Fletcher and Heflin, prefaced a
lengthy speech on public power with the assertion that one of
the chief values of the Norris resolution was that it would prevent
the "power trust" from exploiting Muscle Shoals while the government was ascertaining which fertilizer process was most feasible.
Senator Fletcher's appeal for fertilizer was almost like a voice
out of the past. By this time only a few senators, principally
Fletcher, Heflin, and Caraway, continued to press for commercial
production of fertilizer at Muscle Shoals.[16]

On March 13, 1928, the Norris resolution passed the Senate by
a vote of 48 to 25. It was significant that only two senators from
the former Confederate States, Pat Harrison of Mississippi and
Cole L. Blease of South Carolina, opposed it. The eight other
Democrats opposing the measure were about equally divided
among the East, the border states, and the West. In addition,
fifteen administration Republicans, mostly from the East, opposed
the resolution, while twenty Republicans, mostly from the West,
joined twenty-eight Democrats in supporting the measure. It was
a victory by a reunited farm bloc of southern and western
senators. The Norris resolution emerged from the Senate without
any important alterations.[17]

After seven years of persistent effort, George W. Norris had
gained his first significant victory in his fight for public operation of Muscle Shoals, although his resolution did not include the

15. *Ibid.*, 3435–36, 3438–39, 3527.
16. *Ibid.*, 4256, 4308–22, 4326–33.
17. *Ibid.*, 4635.

Norris scheme for unified development of the Tennessee watershed. The Norris joint resolution was still far from final victory, and in many quarters it was doubted that it could get through the House. Nevertheless, the Senate victory meant that the Norris plan would loom large in the formulation of a permanent policy for Muscle Shoals. The editor of the *Nation* felt that should the Norris measure be defeated in the House, his Senate victory was "a guaranty at least that Muscle Shoals will not be surrendered to the power companies just now, and every new delay is a gain to the campaign for public ownership." [18]

Some of the leading newspapers in Tennessee expressed general approval of the Norris resolution which they recognized as a repudiation of the Muscle Shoals fertilizer proposition in favor of water-power distribution.[19] On the other hand, the Birmingham *News,* long a supporter of the power companies' bid, predicted that final victory for the Norris bill would mean the retardation and devitalization of progress and industry in the South.[20]

Following the acceptance of the Norris resolution by the Senate, the measure was assailed by the Farm Bureau because it failed to provide for commercial production of fertilizer and because it contained the principle of public power. On the other hand, the National Fertilizer Association protested that the resolution sought to put the government in the fertilizer business in competition with private industry.[21]

Several days prior to the passage of the Norris resolution by the Senate, the House Military Committee had begun hearings on the Morin bill. At these hearings, important scientists from the Department of Agriculture testified in behalf of the Morin bill, the gist of their testimony being that fertilizer prices could not

18. "Norris' Power Fight," in *Nation,* CXX (March 26, 1928), 338.

19. Nashville *Banner,* March 14, 1928; Nashville *Tennessean,* March 15, 1928; Memphis *Press-Scimitar,* March 14, 1928.

20. Birmingham *News,* March 11, 1928, quoted in *Cong. Rec.,* 70 Cong., 1 Sess., 5026.

21. Memorandum, American Farm Bureau Federation, March 16, 1928, Coolidge Papers; National Fertilizer Association, *Muscle Shoals and Fertilizer* (1928).

be lowered until technological processes could be improved, a
goal that could be accomplished through the provisions for
research in the Morin and Norris plans. They described the
cyanamid process as obsolete and predicted that future success
lay with the Haber method. The Secretary of War was even more
definite. He notified the committee that in view of recent improvements in the Haber process by private industry, Muscle
Shoals was no longer needed for national defense.[22]

Representative Lister Hill, a member of the committee who
was fighting desperately for the ill-fated cyanamid bid, produced
documentary evidence indicating that the Department of Agriculture had consulted the National Fertilizer Association in drawing
up the Morin bill. Dr. Albert F. Woods, scientific director for the
entire department, admitted that such consultation had taken
place but denied any intention of collusion. He declared it to be
the policy of the department to consult all interested parties in
formulating legislation.[23]

After the passage of the Norris resolution in the Senate, it was
referred to the House Military Committee which held a brief
hearing on the measure, the only witnesses being Senators Norris
and McKellar. Realizing apparently that this committee had
consistently advocated the dedication of Muscle Shoals to
fertilizer production, Norris emphasized the fertilizer benefits
that his resolution allegedly would produce. He also attempted to
placate the conservatives, who had been dominating the committee, by declaring that he would not have advocated public
operation of Muscle Shoals had not the government already
invested such a large sum of money there. He hastened to add,
however, that public operation of the project would be justified
on the basis of either flood control or navigation. Norris also told
the committee that private enterprise was too absorbed in day-
by-day profits to conduct an effective research program such
as that embodied in his resolution. Senator McKellar, who appeared before the committee to endorse the Norris resolution,
devoted most of his time to extolling the merits of the fertilizer

22. *Muscle Shoals*, House Hearings, 70 Cong., 1 Sess., 303–28, 373–74.
23. *Ibid.*, 359–60, 388–90.

aspects of the Norris measure. According to the Tennessean, its chief value lay in its plan definitely to settle the issue regarding the relative virtues of the various fertilizer processes.[24]

The House Military Committee adopted a plan which was a compromise between the Norris and Morin bills. It recommended that the whole Muscle Shoals project be operated by a federal corporation, primarily for the purpose of manufacturing fertilizer. The corporation would be required to earn a 4 per cent profit on fertilizer operations less the cost of a limited research program. Use of the cyanamid process would be required in the beginning but the corporation would be permitted to use another method if necessary. In addition, the committee bill laid down the policy that all members of the board of directors "shall be persons that profess a belief in the feasibility and wisdom . . . of producing fertilizer under this act." The power provisions of the Norris resolution, including the construction of public transmission lines, were adopted almost intact except that proceeds from the sale of power would be used to liquidate the government's investment in the project and public agencies were not specifically given preference in the sale of power. A provision for construction of a dam at Cove Creek was also included in the committee bill.[25]

In reporting the Military Committee bill to the House, Chairman Morin, who apparently was the chief architect of the measure, pointed out that the bill did not commit the government to permanent operation of the project, which he said could be leased at any time without violating the terms of the measure. He declared that the purpose of the bill was to give the production of fertilizer at Muscle Shoals a fair test under the management of

24. *Muscle Shoals,* Hearings, U. S. House of Representatives, on S. J. Res. 46, 70 Cong., 1 Sess. (1928), 5–9.

25. *Muscle Shoals,* House Report 1095, 70 Cong., 1 Sess., 1–10. The requirement that members of the board of directors profess faith in the wisdom of the act, a concept which later was to become an issue, particularly after the establishment of the Tennessee Valley Authority, apparently made its first appearance in the Morin bill.

The committee justified the inclusion of Cove Creek in the bill on the ground that the General Electric "power combine" was on the verge of gaining control of it. *Muscle Shoals,* House Hearings on S. J. Res. 46, 70 Cong., 1 Sess., 17–20.

persons friendly to the proposal.[26] A minority report on the new Morin bill by some of the most conservative Republicans on the committee objected strenuously to the use of Muscle Shoals in competition with the private fertilizer industry.[27]

Representative Morin reported the committee bill to the House on March 27, and debate on it occurred intermittently in April and May. The bill was supported by a coalition of midwestern Republicans and southern Democrats. The opposition came principally from eastern Republicans, particularly New Englanders, who attempted to block consideration of the bill and who termed it a "socialistic" measure. Representative James P. Glynn of Connecticut called the bill the "most dangerous and vicious" piece of legislation reported by any committee during the decade in which he had been in Congress. The eastern Republicans attempted unsuccessfully to amend the bill so that the power would be sold to power companies at the switchboard. They also attempted, without success, to require the Secretary of Agriculture to conduct extensive experiments before commencing quantity production of fertilizer.[28]

As usual, the southern Democrats endeavored to avoid the issue of private versus public operation, but on this subject, Representative LaGuardia met the attack of the New England Republicans without hedging. He said:

I believe, and I do not hesitate to say so, in Government or State operation of water power for generating electricity. I believe that this gift of God . . . belongs to all of the people. . . . As between the cost of Government operation and the cost to the people of excessive, exorbitant rates imposed by public utility corporations the people of the country will save hundreds of millions of dollars under Government operation.[29]

Some Tennessee congressmen, who were the only Southerners to oppose the bill, vigorously protested against the inclusion of Cove Creek in the Muscle Shoals project. In fact, on April 6 the House Military Committee assembled to hear complaints from

26. House Report 1095, 70 Cong., 1 Sess., 17–18.
27. *Ibid.*, Part 2, 1–2.
28. *Cong. Rec.*, 70 Cong., 1 Sess., 8221–23, 8232–33, 8555–56, 8872.
29. *Ibid.*, 8879.

the Tennessee delegation about this matter. Porter Dunlap, a
member of the Tennessee Railroad and Public Utilities Commission and chief spokesman for the Tennessee delegation, asserted
that Tennessee's rights to the Cove Creek site were superior to
those of the federal government. Moreover, he offered a compromise proposal by which the federal government would build
Cove Creek dam and turn it over to the State of Tennessee free
of cost within about seven years. The committee gave the
compromise proposal an exceedingly cool reception. Cordell Hull,
in testifying before the committee, again assailed the Water
Power Act and suggested that the committee formulate a water-
power policy which would be more equitable to the states. It was
evident that the principal purpose of the Tennessee delegation
was to persuade the committee that the water-power resources
of the upper Tennessee ought to be developed immediately in
order to prevent the subordination of Cove Creek to Muscle
Shoals. The Tennessee delegation was accompanied by General
Edgar Jadwin, Chief of Engineers, who recommended that the
waters of the upper Tennessee River system be leased entirely
to power companies.[30]

Back in the House, Tennessee representatives, led by Joseph
W. Byrns and Cordell Hull, declared that the inclusion of Cove
Creek in the committee bill would violate the constitutional
rights of Tennessee and hamper power development in the state.
They advanced the claim that the states had a right to levy and
collect taxes on federal water-power projects. LaGuardia of
New York and Hill of Alabama denied the validity of this
contention, the latter repudiating the Bibb Graves claim of the
previous year.[31]

Opponents of the new Morin bill did manage to alter sub-

30. *Muscle Shoals*, House Hearings, 70 Cong., 1 Sess., Part 2, 1–26.
31. *Cong. Rec.*, 70 Cong., 1 Sess., 8222, 8874–76. Senator Norris endorsed the
inclusion of Cove Creek in the House bill. In reply to E. B. Stahlman, publisher
of the Nashville *Banner*, who had showered Congress with messages protesting
this feature of the House Muscle Shoals bill, Norris stated that Cove Creek's
principal value lay in its use for flood and stream control and that it should be
operated in conjunction with Muscle Shoals. Stahlman to Norris, March 29, 1928,
and Norris to Stahlman, April 1, 1928, Norris Papers.

stantially the fertilizer provisions. They secured the adoption of
an amendment by Representative Thomas S. McMillan of South
Carolina which stipulated that fertilizer activities at Muscle
Shoals must be confined to the production of nitrates, no complete commercial fertilizer to be manufactured. Leading supporters of the bill declared that the McMillan amendment meant
no cheap fertilizer for the farmers and that it was the work of the
"fertilizer trust." [32] During the debate on the McMillan amendment, the New York *Times* reported that "scores" of fertilizer
manufacturers had gone to Washington to attempt at least to
weaken the fertilizer provisions of the new Morin bill.[33] The
League of Women Voters, which was an enthusiastic supporter
of the new Morin bill, was jubilant over the victory of the Mc-
Millan amendment, the League's leaders asserting that elimination of fertilizer production would mean more water power for
general distribution.[34]

The new Morin bill, as altered by the McMillan amendment,
was accepted by the House on May 17 by a vote of 251 to 165.
Its passage represented another victory for the farm states in
Congress.[35]

In the conference, the Senate was represented by Norris,
McNary, and Ellison D. Smith, and the House by Morin, James,
Reece, Quin, and Wright. The principal differences to be recon-
ciled involved these questions: Should the project be operated
by separate agencies or by a single government corporation,
should Cove Creek be included, and what should be the character
of the nitrogen or fertilizer products to be manufactured? Inas-
much as Norris tended to favor the House provisions for a
government corporation and Cove Creek, the Senate conferees
conceded on these points at once. The House conferees, in turn,

32. *Cong. Rec.*, 70 Cong., 1 Sess., 8553–55, 8876–80.
33. New York *Times*, May 17, 1928. Preceding the adoption of the McMillan
amendment, the New York *Sun* predicted that passage of the House Muscle
Shoals bill "would mean the ultimate ruin of the private fertilizer business in
the United States." New York *Sun*, May 11, 1928, quoted in *Cong. Rec.*, 70 Cong.,
1 Sess., 8614.
34. Bulletin, League of Women Voters, May 17, 1928; Norris Papers.
35. *Cong. Rec.*, 70 Cong., 1 Sess., 8883.

accepted the Senate provisions for preference to public agencies in the sale of power. As for fertilizer, the conferees agreed to both a large-scale research program and the production of commercial fertilizer, and it was further provided that the process to be used would be determined by experimentation. The last provision constituted a major surrender for the ardent cyanamid-process advocates who had long dominated the House Military Committee.[36]

In the Senate, a group of conservative Democrats, including Royal S. Copeland of New York, Carter Glass of Virginia, and Millard E. Tydings and William C. Bruce of Maryland, protested vigorously against the conference report, asserting that the provision guaranteeing fertilizer production would ruin the private fertilizer industry. Glass and Copeland declared that they had voted for the Norris resolution with the understanding that only fertilizer research would be undertaken. Norris replied that he had never opposed fertilizer production at Muscle Shoals but merely the use of the cyanamid process. For the first time the Nebraska Senator hurled the charge of "fertilizer trust" at his opponents. He averred that fertilizer and power trusts were working hand-in-hand to prevent the development of Muscle Shoals. Bruce and Tydings, who represented one of the leading fertilizer-producing states, warned that the conference bill was the first step toward government confiscation of all private property in the country. Having become convinced that the conference bill could not pass the Senate because of this opposition to its fertilizer provisions, Norris had it recommitted to conference.[37]

The only substantial change made in the Muscle Shoals legislation in the second conference was that all manufacture of commercial fertilizer, except for experimental purposes, was prohibited. This new accord on fertilizer appeared to restore the original Norris-Morin fertilizer research program.[38]

36. Conference Committee, *Disposition of Muscle Shoals*, Senate Doc. 118, 70 Cong., 1 Sess. (1928), 1–8; *Cong. Rec.*, 70 Cong., 1 Sess., 9344, 9466–67.
37. *Cong. Rec.*, 70 Cong., 1 Sess., 9466–78, 9542.
38. *Ibid.*, 9692.

The second conference bill precipitated one of the most colorful events of the entire Muscle Shoals controversy—the McKellar filibuster.[39] Although other members of the Tennessee delegation in Congress had been openly opposing the proposed subordination of Cove Creek to Muscle Shoals for several months, McKellar hitherto had not commented on the subject publicly. When the second conference bill reached the Senate, however, he immediately protested against the Cove Creek provision, which had not been changed by the second conference. He also vigorously assailed the fertilizer provisions of the second conference bill, his contention being that the revised measure would make it virtually impossible to use Muscle Shoals to lower the price of fertilizer and that the research program contemplated by the bill would benefit fertilizer manufacturers instead of farmers. Oddly enough, McKellar's principal supporters in his filibuster against the bill were avowed enemies of any fertilizer production at Muscle Shoals, mainly Bruce and Tydings of Maryland, and Blease of South Carolina, all of whom opposed the second conference bill on the ground that it would permit the government unduly to project itself into the fertilizer business.

In his filibuster, Senator McKellar devoted comparatively little time to fertilizer; it was the Cove Creek provision that attracted most of his attention. Until this time he had hardly committed himself on the Cove Creek matter, but apparently the growing clamor of Tennessee business interests prompted him to take action. He repeated all of the claims and supporting arguments which the Tennessee congressional delegation had developed; that is, that Tennessee held sovereign constitutional rights over the Cove Creek site and should the federal government construct a dam there it would unlawfully deprive the state of two sources of taxes—the land to be inundated or otherwise included in the project and the water power. Senator Black reminded McKellar that in 1927 the latter had subscribed to exactly the opposite position with regard to Alabama's claims to Muscle Shoals, but McKellar replied that the case of Muscle Shoals was different

39. For the highlights of this event see *Cong. Rec.*, 70 Cong., 1 Sess., 9692–9705, 9724, 9796, 9809, 9838–42.

because Alabama had induced the federal government to build a dam there without having imposed conditions.

The McKellar filibuster continued for about twenty-one hours, May 24 and 25, before collapsing because of the lack of sufficient support from other senators. Thereupon, southern Democrats combined with midwestern and far western Republicans in both houses to approve the second conference bill, the Senate passing it 43 to 34 and the House adopting it by a vote of 211 to 147. Preceding the final vote in the House, New England Republicans combined with Tennessee Democrats to oppose the bill but they were completely overwhelmed. Representative Reece of Tennessee, a Republican, supported the bill.[40]

McKellar's break with Norris boded ill for the future of unified development of the Tennessee River, for the Tennessee Senator had been one of the essential cornerstones of the Progressive Republican–southern Democratic alliance which had prevented the disposal of Muscle Shoals to private parties. McKellar's anger appeared to be intense; he assailed Norris personally, accusing the Nebraska Senator of betraying the faith which had held together the Norris-McKellar Muscle Shoals team. He solemnly predicted that all of the good work Senator Norris had done for Muscle Shoals "will come to naught, not only for this session, but probably for all time." [41]

Edward B. Stahlman, in the Nashville *Banner*, gave high praise to McKellar for his fight against the "Tennessee Robbery":

No more gallant, courageous, able fight was ever made on the floor of the United States Senate in defense of the rights of the several states than that led by Senator McKellar . . . when over his almost prostrate form the Senate, confirming what had been done in the House, ruthlessly robbed and plundered Tennessee of natural resources having an undoubted value in excess of $100,000,000. . . . McKellar battled as bravely for the sovereign and property rights of Tennessee as Andrew Jackson fought for the preservation of the rights of the whole United States at New Orleans.[42]

Although the ultra-conservative press saw in Norris's first

40. *Cong. Rec.*, 70 Cong., 1 Sess., 9842, 9953–58.
41. *Ibid.*, 9838.
42. Nashville *Banner*, May 26, 1928.

Muscle Shoals victory something outrageously socialistic, a surprisingly large number of more moderate publications endorsed the victorious Muscle Shoals measure which was largely the handiwork of Senator Norris. These editors, in leaning toward the Norris camp, appear to have been greatly influenced by the revelations with respect to the power industry that were being made by the Federal Trade Commission. The St. Louis *Post-Dispatch*, for instance, citing the investigation by the Trade Commission, asserted that it was now clear why the Muscle Shoals controversy had been so bitter: "Muscle Shoals has been the main test of strength between Congress and the power combine." [43]

The Muscle Shoals bill was presented to President Coolidge on May 26, three days before the adjournment of Congress. It was well known that the President disliked this Muscle Shoals legislation because of its provisions for government operation as well as the requirements for additional outlays of federal funds, but it was not known definitely what he intended to do about the bill. Upon receipt of the measure, he announced that he would subject it to a thorough study, creating the impression that perhaps he had not yet reached a decision on the matter. Richard V. Oulahan, veteran New York *Times* correspondent, believed that in view of the weakened fertilizer provisions in the bill there was a good chance that the President would sign it. J. W. Worthington, the executive secretary of the Tennessee River Improvement Association, confidentially informed Chester Gray that he was fearful that the President would sign the bill and suggested that Gray personally request Coolidge to veto the measure.[44]

No sooner had the bill passed Congress than pressure from proponents and opponents of the measure began to be applied to

43. St. Louis *Post-Dispatch*, May 26, 1928. Other important publications examined include the New York *World*, May 18, 1928; Hartford *Courant*, May 18, 1928; Toledo *News-Bee*, May 18, 1928; New York *Times*, May 18, 1928; San Francisco *Chronicle*, May 18, 1928; Rocky Mountain *News*, May 26, 1928; Washington *Post*, May 26, 1928; Pittsburgh *Press*, May 28, 1928. The Hartford *Courant*, San Francisco *Chronicle*, and Washington *Post* opposed the Norris Muscle Shoals bill.

44. New York *Times*, May 29, June 3 (III), 1928; Worthington to Gray, June 2, 1928, Coolidge Papers.

the White House. Senator William E. Borah went to the President and personally urged him to sign it. Borah assured Coolidge that the bill did not establish or violate any basic economic principles but was merely an attempt to salvage a government investment. The League of Women Voters also urged the President to sign the bill. Among those who emphatically advised the Chief Executive to veto the measure were Representative Joseph W. Byrns of Tennessee, Edward B. Stahlman, publisher of the Nashville *Banner,* the Secretary of War, the chiefs of the Corps of Engineers and Ordnance, and important figures in the chemical industry. Although Secretary of Agriculture Jardine did not officially approve the bill, he nevertheless told the President that it was as good a Muscle Shoals measure as was likely to be obtained.[45]

After the adjournment of Congress, President Coolidge allowed the constitutional time limit to expire without taking action on the Muscle Shoals bill, thus subjecting it to a pocket veto. Senator Norris severely arraigned the President for resorting to this device which permitted him to kill the bill without explaining the nature of his objections to it. Norris accused Coolidge of obeying the dictates of the "power trust" and sarcastically declared:

To have offended this great trust by approving the Muscle Shoals bill would have dried up the sources of revenue that we must have in the great campaign just ahead of us.

The failure of this bill may disappoint American farmers interested in cheaper fertilizers; it may drive away from the Administration candidate a large number of progressive, thinking citizens; but it will give us money in unlimited profusion and will enable us to win the election by controlling . . . the sources of publicity.

The power trust has received a black eye recently in the terrible exposures made by the Federal Trade Commission, and no doubt the managers of that great monopoly have been considerably disturbed; but the failure of the Muscle Shoals legislation will give them new

45. New York *Times,* May 29, 1928; copy of letter from Belle Sherwin, president of League of Women Voters, to Coolidge, May 26, 1928, Norris Papers; Joseph W. Byrns to Coolidge, May 31, 1928, Coolidge Papers; War Department Memorandum, May 28, 1928, Judge Advocate General, National Archives; Jardine to Coolidge (undated), Bureau of Plant Industry, Soils, and Agriculture Engineering, Fixed Nitrogen Laboratory and Research Reports, Muscle Shoals, National Archives.

courage and will open up their financial chest with a freedom that will be illuminating and startling.[46]

In general, the press attributed Coolidge's veto to his inherent dislike of economic principles contained in the bill, particularly the provisions permitting govermental distribution and sale of power directly to municipalities. In some quarters of the press where the veto had resulted in keen disappointment, it was asserted that Coolidge vetoed the bill to prevent the Muscle Shoals "yardstick" from revealing the excessive nature of private power price rates.[47]

Norris and LaGuardia challenged the legality of the Coolidge pocket veto. They interpreted that part of the United States Constitution which permits the President to void a bill in this manner as applying only to adjournments sine die and not to an ad interim adjournment as was the case in this instance. Many legal authorities felt that the Norris-LaGuardia contention possessed merit. Since the Okanogan Indians, whose claims had been embodied in a bill which also had received a pocket veto at this time, were carrying their case to the courts on this constitutional point, Norris held out hope that the Muscle Shoals bill would become law. But the United States Supreme Court, which finally handed down a decision on the Okanogan Indian case in May, 1929, held that the Coolidge pocket vetoes were legal.[48]

The congressional victory of the Norris compromise bill in 1928 is somewhat surprising in view of the strong anti–public-power sentiment which had prevailed in Congress up through 1927. The tarnished reputation sustained by the private power companies as a result of the Federal Trade Commission investigations, the acrid debate on the Walsh resolution authorizing that investigation, and the revelations of the Reed special committee investigating elections, contributed to the passage of the Muscle Shoals bill. The effect of the investigation of the power industry was perhaps intensified, with respect to members of Congress, by the fact

46. New York *Times,* June 9, 1928.
47. "The Troublous Muscle Shoals Veto," in *Literary Digest,* XCVII (June 23, 1928), 11–12.
48. New York *Times,* June 9, Dec. 23, 1928, Jan. 22, 1929,

that 1928 was an election year. Undoubtedly, the principal reason for the passage of the bill was that the great majority of southern Democrats in both houses, many of whom had previously supported only private leasing bills, finally came to accept the Norris plan as the only feasible solution. The strength of a solid southern Democracy, combined with the farm bloc Republicans, was overwhelming. It must not be overlooked that a large group of midwestern Republicans in the House supported Norris on this issue for the first time.

In the Presidential campaign of 1928, the power question for the first time became a national issue. This turn of events came to pass not as a choice of the principal participants, Herbert Hoover and Alfred E. Smith, both of whom sought to evade the issue, but because of other factors. Among these were the tremendous expansion of the interstate power business which had been taking place throughout the country and the accompanying evils which were being disclosed by the Federal Trade Commission. Moreover, the Progressive Republicans, led by Norris and Gifford Pinchot, set out deliberately to make power an issue in the campaign. In fact, Norris, who offered his political endorsement to any candidate who would subscribe to the Progressive creed regardless of party affiliation, named Muscle Shoals and Boulder Dam, along with the lame duck issue, as among the key questions to be considered in determining whether a candidate was a Progressive.[49]

On the power issue in general, the gulf between Hoover and Smith was greatly exaggerated by the political animosities permeating the campaign. Smith advocated public control of public-owned water power, a meaningless position which Hoover did not reject, but the Happy Warrior refused to take a definite stand on public operation of power projects though he definitely rejected public transmission and sale of power away from the switchboard. Specifically, he avoided taking a definite stand on Muscle Shoals. The charges and countercharges during the campaign with respect to the power issue made it appear that there was a radical difference between the two candidates on this issue. The

49. Memorandum by Senator George W. Norris, Oct. 2, 1928, Norris Papers.

Republicans called Smith's power proposals "socialistic" and accused him of being a champion of government ownership of power utilities. Smith declared that Hoover was a friend of the "power trust" and attempted to connect the Republican administration with the power scandals being uncovered by the Federal Trade Commission.[50]

Hoover made his most definite commitment on the power issue in his Elizabethton, Tennessee, speech of October 6. The choice of Tennessee as the place for an important power statement was thought to have been part of a major Republican effort to win the electoral votes of that state where water power was a vital issue. In Elizabethton, Hoover declared:

I do not favor any general extension of the Federal Government into the operation of business in competition with its citizens. . . . [but] There are local instances where the Government must enter the business field as a by-product of some great major purpose such as improvement in navigation, flood control, scientific research, or national defense.[51]

Following this speech, Hoover told Edward J. Meeman, editor of the Knoxville News-Sentinel, that the "local instances" referred to in his address applied to Muscle Shoals. Meeman thereupon concluded, in the News-Sentinel, that Hoover was in favor of government operation of Muscle Shoals. When Hoover confirmed Meeman's account of their conversation, which also had been published in the News-Sentinel, it appeared that the Knoxville editor had made a fair interpretation of Hoover's position. Hoover accompanied this confirmation, during the same interview, with other statements which completely confused the subject for many people. He stated that Muscle Shoals should be devoted to agriculture and national defense with the surplus power being utilized in a manner that would serve the national welfare; but

50. New York Times, Sept. 23, 24, Oct. 4, 10, 20, 23, 1928. Despite Smith's confused and indefinite stand on the power issue, Edward A. O'Neal, president of the Alabama Farm Bureau, wrote to Chester Gray late in October that he feared that if Smith should win "we might as well forget about the cyanamid offer for the Democrats in this country believe at least that he is a Government operationist." O'Neal to Gray, Oct. 20, 1928, quoted in Lobby Investigation, Hearings, U. S. Senate, 71 Cong., 2 Sess., 3551.

51. New York Times, Oct. 7, 1928.

he refused to specify whether this project should be operated publicly or privately.[52] As the New York *Times* put it:

When Mr. Hoover got back to Washington [from Tennessee] he found that he had become a Scripps-Howard man instead of a Coolidge man, and the task was to make a Coolidge man out of him again. Hours followed of wrestling with another explanatory statement which, when issued, although it does not further deal with the only controverted point—operation—sufficiently skirts it to afford a measure of dry ground for the New York *Telegram* to jump on, and yet keeps that ground annexed to the Coolidge reservation.[53]

On October 27, in a speech in Omaha, Senator Norris endorsed the Smith candidacy, his decision allegedly being made on the basis of Smith's stand on water-power development. Norris called on all Progressives to come to the aid of the Democratic candidate who, according to Norris, had embraced the Rooseveltian water-power principles. Norman Thomas, who felt that Norris had exaggerated the importance of Muscle Shoals during the campaign, called the Nebraskan's attention to the fact that Smith had not taken a definite stand on a single one of the vital power issue. It was Smith's ringing denunciation of the "power trust" together with his previous fights against private power companies in New York, which involved water-power development, that probably led Norris to support Smith.[54]

In Pennsylvania, Gifford Pinchot, ostensibly on a speaking tour for Hoover, devoted most of his time to attacking the Republican presidential candidate on the water-power and other issues. Consequently, the Republican National Committee invited the noted conservationist to cease his alleged efforts in Hoover's behalf. The New York *Times* referred to Pinchot, who commended Smith's position on power and other issues, as "a Hoover-ite, two-thirds for Smith." [55]

The disclosures being made by the Federal Trade Commission

52. *Ibid.*, Oct. 9, 1928.
53. *Ibid.*, Oct. 10, 1928. The Scripps-Howard chain of newspapers, which included the New York *Telegram*, was supporting public operation of Muscle Shoals at this time.
54. Thomas to Norris, Oct. 26, 1928, Norris Papers; New York *Times*, Oct. 28, 30, Nov. 1, 1928.
55. New York *Times*, Oct. 17, 18, 1928.

as a result of its investigations of the power industry came at a time to affect the presidential campaign. Carrying out the directives imposed by the Walsh resolution, the commission began conducting hearings in early March, 1928.[56] As the investigation got under way, Senator Norris charged that the public utilities industry was endeavoring to control the press in various areas in order to influence public opinion against public-owned utilities. He requested the commission to direct its inquiry in this direction. The commission complied and found evidence that the utilities were influencing the press in various ways. Newspaper editors, lured by fat advertising contracts, were printing power propaganda as news stories. Other methods of influencing the press were revealed, such as the distribution to newspapers of paid statements by prominent people, which endorsed the principle of private utilities, on the pretense that they were legitimate news stories.

More dramatic charges were made by Senators Hiram Johnson and Thomas J. Walsh. Johnson asserted that the public utilities industry was conducting a large-scale campaign to collect a fund with which to influence public utilities legislation. Walsh charged that public utility associations were subsidizing lecturers and college professors throughout the country in order to influence students, as well as the public, in favor of the private utilities industry. Subsequent investigations by the commission in 1928 indicated that the Johnson-Walsh charges possessed much validity.

In addition to finding that the utilities industry had attempted to influence education, the commission revealed that the industry had expended large sums in financing lobbyists to work against the Walsh resolution and had financed extensive publicity campaigns with respect to Muscle Shoals and Boulder Dam legislation. The most startling revelation was that Mrs. John D. Sherman, while serving as president of the Federation of Women's Clubs, had been paid by the National Electric Light Association to

56. For the highlights of the Federal Trade Commission investigation of the power industry in 1928 see *ibid.*, March 17, 20, 23, April 12, 25, May 11, 13, 29, June 2, 3, 6, 13, 14, 16, Oct. 4, 5, 11, 28, 1928. See also Stephen Raushenbush, *High Power Propaganda* (1928), 1–89.

write magazine articles. The commission also heard testimony to
the effect that the Appalachian Power Conference, which was
purportedly a group of southern businessmen and political leaders
studying the water-power problem in the South, was merely a
publicity arm of the southern power companies, which they had
been utilizing to help mold public opinion against public operation of Muscle Shoals. Disclosures before the commission showed
that two professors of engineering, John A. Switzer of the University of Tennessee and Thorndyke Saville of the University of
North Carolina, were instrumental in conducting the pro–private-
power publicity of the power conference.

Norris declared that these revelations proved that the "power
trust" was exerting political influence from the White House to
the school district. The conservative New York *Times* condemned
these activities of the utilities industry as being highly unethical.[57]
Gifford Pinchot said of the Federal Trade Commission investigation of 1928:

> The Federal Trade Commission has already proved that the power
> monopolists have resorted to unprecedented uses of corruption funds
> to poison the fountains of all public information—not only our news-
> papers, our public lecture platforms, and our periodical publications
> but even our universities and grammar schools.
>
> Testimony before the Federal Trade Commission has disclosed
> subsidized reporters, subsidized editors, subsidized professors, sub-
> sidized governors, subsidized ex-governors, and ex-Senators, even a
> subsidized ambassador. . . .
>
> Never in the history of America has there been another so wide-
> spread, so bold, and so unscrupulous plot to corrupt all sources of
> public information and public education.[58]

Despite the investigation of the power industry by the Federal
Trade Commission, the conservative Republicans won a sweeping
victory in the election of 1928, a fact which would give little
comfort to Norris and his fellow advocates of public power. There
were signs, however, that the investigation, by affecting the
thinking of influential people, was creating a political environment favorable to the growth of sentiment for public power.

57. New York *Times*, Oct. 13, 28, 1928.
58. Gifford Pinchot, *The Power Monopoly* (1928), 13.

X

Between Norris Victories, 1929–30

IN PRESIDENT COOLIDGE's last annual message to Congress on December 4, 1928, he made a brief reference to Muscle Shoals. In this message, the President receded somewhat from his Muscle Shoals position of the previous year when he had rejected the project as a fertilizer enterprise. While reasserting that new developments in methods of nitrate production had rendered the Muscle Shoals project less useful for fertilizer production than formerly, he nevertheless recommended that nitrate plant no. 2 be utilized for that purpose. The President declared that the Muscle Shoals fertilizer plant was not yet completely obsolete and that it still provided a "practical method" for producing fertilizer for farmers and nitrates for national defense. He recommended that Congress, the House in particular, yield its long-held position that Muscle Shoals should remain intact as a unit and that it should provide for separate leases of the power and nitrate facilities. The argument for separate leases had been supported by the power company adherents who had opposed the use of Muscle Shoals primarily for fertilizer production. On the other hand, Coolidge promised that he would approve a bill for leasing "the entire property for the production of nitrates." With respect to the development of the Tennessee River, he declared that he was opposed to further construction of dams at government expense, but he added that, should the power companies be required to repay the government the cost of such construction at the prevailing rates of interest, "this difficulty will be considerably lessened." [1]

1. *Cong. Rec.*, 70 Cong., 2 Sess., 24.

There was practically no action on Muscle Shoals in the Senate during the second session of the Seventieth Congress (December, 1928, to March, 1929). The failure of the Senate to take action on the Muscle Shoals question at this time was perhaps the result of the shortness of the session, which was a lame duck session. Early in January, 1929, Senator Norris asserted that there would not be sufficient time to take up a new proposal and push it through both houses of Congress before the final adjournment on March 4. Moreover, Norris contended that no new Muscle Shoals bills should be presented until the Supreme Court had acted on the legality of the Coolidge veto of the Muscle Shoals bill of the previous session. On the same day that Norris stated his reasons for not introducing a Muscle Shoals bill during this session, Senator McKellar introduced a Muscle Shoals measure. In fact, Norris's statement of his policy of delay was made as a protest against the McKellar measure.

The McKellar bill authorized the Secretary of War to sell the power from Wilson Dam to municipalities and other public agencies, any surplus power to be made available to private parties. Senator Heflin, who had become one of the most ardent defenders of the Norris plan, also protested against McKellar's action. Heflin declared that there should be no further action on Muscle Shoals until the legal dispute over the Coolidge veto was settled. Nevertheless, for the first time since 1924, the great gulf separating Heflin and McKellar on Muscle Shoals seemed to be disappearing. Heflin warmly praised McKellar's criticism of the Alabama Power Company with respect to the waste of power at Wilson Dam, and promised that should the Coolidge veto be sustained by the courts, he would support the Tennessee Senator's bill.[2] The McKellar bill failed to reach the floor for consideration.

McKellar's action in introducing a Muscle Shoals bill appeared to be a protest against the failure of Norris to present his Muscle Shoals plan at this time. According to the Tennessee Senator, however, the purpose of his measure was to stop the waste of power at Wilson Dam and to frustrate the possible designs of

2. *Ibid.*, 1173–74.

the Alabama Power Company with respect to Muscle Shoals. Currently, a variable portion of the available power at Wilson Dam was being sold to that power company with the remainder going to waste through the spillways. McKellar offered evidence from the Corps of Engineers to show that the Alabama Power Company was decreasing its use of Wilson Dam power as it expanded its own hydroelectric facilities. Yet the surplus power at Wilson Dam could not be sold elsewhere because the Alabama Power Company owned all of the transmission lines leading out of the area. Senator McKellar probably would have been even more perturbed about the power situation at Wilson Dam had he known that at this very time the War Department was trying to negotiate a five-year contract for the sale of Wilson Dam power to the Alabama Power Company. This proposed contract was revocable at not less than an eighteen-month notice whereas the existing contract stipulated a ninety-day notice.[3]

In bringing the matter to a head at this time, the Tennessee Senator was influenced by J. L. Meeks, editor of the Florence, Alabama, *News-Times*. Meeks had been warning McKellar and Norris that the Alabama Power Company was attempting to gain control of Muscle Shoals by encircling the area with additional transmission lines with the view of preventing Congress from disposing of the project in a manner contrary to the interests of that company. Meeks also had been publishing daily reports on the amount of power that was going to waste at Wilson Dam.[4] Moreover, Judson King, director of the National Popular

3. *Ibid.*, 1173–74; Memorandum, War Department, to Coolidge, Aug. 28, 1928, Judge Advocate General, National Archives.

4. *Cong. Rec.*, 70 Cong., 1 Sess., 1738–39, 7145; Meeks to Norris, April 21, 1928, Norris Papers. The Alabama Power Company covertly was making other moves to aid in securing its position at Muscle Shoals. First, the company was making an effort to lure New England cotton mills into the Tennessee Valley so that the company would have a stronger claim to a right to distribute Muscle Shoals power because of increased industrialization in the area. Second, the power company was in the process of attempting to negotiate a deal with the American Cyanamid Company which would prevent the latter from distributing Muscle Shoals power in competition with the power company. In fact, the proposal called for a much reduced power development on the Tennessee River as compared to that contemplated in the cyanamid bid. W. C. Adamson to Coolidge, Nov. 21, 1928, Coolidge Papers; Memorandum, Alabama Power Company, Dec. 18, 1928, *ibid.*

Government League, asserted that the power company was netting fantastic profits from the sale of Wilson Dam power, a contention that was stoutly denied by the company's president, Thomas W. Martin.[5] In addition the application of the town of Muscle Shoals, Alabama, for a share of the wasted Wilson Dam power thus far had been unsuccessful.[6]

Despite the hostile reception given the cyanamid bid by Congress in 1928, the American Cyanamid Company had by no means given up hope of acquiring control of Muscle Shoals. Chester Gray informed Samuel H. Thompson, president of the Farm Bureau, in late November, 1928, that he believed, on the basis of deference shown him at the White House, that President Coolidge was in sympathy with the cyanamid bid. At the same time the president of the American Cyanamid Company opened negotiations with the War Department in an effort to gain that department's approval of his company's proposal.[7]

In February, 1929, William B. Bell again appeared to plead his cause before the House Military Committee, which was holding hearings on Muscle Shoals. Pointing out that the chief objection which the committee had previously voiced against his offer was the absence of a recapture clause in case of failure to produce fertilizer, Bell offered a concession in this matter. In fact, he stated that he would agree to a provision permitting the government to have such recapture privileges, but his seemingly generous offer had conditions attached. In the first place, in the event of recapture, the company would be compensated for its equity in the project, an amount to be determined by a complicated process of arbitration which appeared to the committee to be decidedly favorable to the company. Secondly, the government could not move to recapture the project until after the passage of the first fifteen years of the lease period. Bell in-

5. Martin to King, Nov. 26, 1928, OCE, Alabama Power Company, National Archives; *Cong. Rec.*, 70 Cong., 2 Sess., 5035.

6. Captain C. N. Iry to General John A. Hull, July 12, 1928, Judge Advocate General, National Archives.

7. Gray to Thompson, Nov. 24, 1928, quoted in *Lobby Investigation*, Hearings, U.S. Senate, 71 Cong., 2 Sess., 3041; W. B. Bell to General John A. Hull, Nov. 22, 1928, Judge Advocate General, National Archives.

advertently revealed the motive behind this provision—the belief that after fifteen years the government would not be prone to enforce the fertilizer provisions of the contract. Moreover, the government would not be able to initiate condemnation proceedings until there had been a complete suspension of fertilizer production for a total of eighteen months within any period of three years. As one committee member pointed out, this provision would enable the company to hold possession of the project by manufacturing one sack of fertilizer every eighteen months. In addition, Bell stipulated that the government could not move to retake the project until sixty days after the adjournment of Congress. Chairman Morin protested that this provision would permit the company to exert pressure on the administration in the absence of Congress.[8]

Charles J. Brand, president of the National Fertilizer Association, was the principal witness opposing the cyanamid bid. In general, he attempted to show that fertilizer production at Muscle Shoals was not needed and that it would further depress conditions within the fertilizer industry which, he declared, was faced with excessive competition and a saturated market. Brand denied Representative Frank James's charge that he was the author of the original Morin bill of the past year. At the beginning of this session, Brand had suggested to the Department of Agriculture that it sponsor a bill which would provide for disposal of Muscle Shoals to the power industry.[9]

On the House floor, meanwhile, North Alabama congressmen were speaking fervently in favor of the cyanamid proposal. They reaffirmed their faith in the efficiency of the cyanamid process and declared that the attempt to prove its obsolescence was merely false propaganda by the power and fertilizer interests. They asserted that despite the statements of Chairman Morin and others to the contrary, the cyanamid plan did contain an absolute guarantee of fertilizer production, and they pointed to

8. *Muscle Shoals,* Hearings, U.S. House of Representatives, on H. R. 8305, 70 Cong., 2 Sess. (1929), 1–6, 20–22, 89, 119.

9. *Ibid.,* 34–64; Brand to Dr. H. G. Knight, Nov. 28, 1928, Correspondence of the Secretary of Agriculture, Muscle Shoals, National Archives.

the opposition of the National Fertilizer Association as evidence in support of their assertion. Representative Almon declared that the power which the Alabama Power Company had permitted to escape through the spillways at Wilson Dam would have saved the farmers many millions of dollars in reduced prices of fertilizer if it had been used in the operation of nitrate plant no. 2.[10]

During this session, Representative Reece of Tennessee became the sponsor of a bill calling for acceptance of the cyanamid bid, despite the fact that previously he had been vigorously opposed to that offer. Reece's first attempt to secure a favorable report on the bill by the Military Committee was defeated. Then on February 14 Reece called a "rump" meeting of the committee without informing Chairman Morin and other known opponents of the cyanamid bid such as Frank James of Michigan. Controlling a majority in this "rump" body, the Reece faction reported the cyanamid bill favorably. When the report reached the House, its legality was challenged by Morin who claimed that, according to House rules, a meeting of a committee could only be called by the chairman. Morin also charged that the bill had been reported without a quorum's being present. Moreover, Reece was accused of using proxy votes in an illegal manner in reporting the bill. The Tennessee Republican denied all charges of irregularity and contended that House committees legally met by schedule rather than by the call of a chairman. Representative Nicholas Longworth, the Speaker of the House, upheld Reece's theory regarding committee meetings and ruled that the cyanamid bill had been reported in the presence of a quorum. Oddly enough, the Reece "rump" revolt served further to democratize Congress for it appeared to eliminate one-man rule of committees.[11]

The Reece report contained fifty-seven "perfecting" amendments to the original cyanamid bid, none of which altered in the least its fundamental meaning. The alleged guarantee of fertilizer

10. *Cong. Rec.,* 70 Cong., 2 Sess., 1738–40, 5094–95.
11. *Ibid.,* 988, 3601–7; New York *Times,* Feb. 15, 1929.

production which William B. Bell had outlined to the Military Committee was included in these amendments. Reece assured his colleagues that the lessee's obligation to produce fertilizer was now definite and enforceable. Like many Southerners, Reece characterized cheap fertilizer as the most feasible form of farm relief, and he attempted to refute the arguments by opponents of fertilizer production at Muscle Shoals that increased use of fertilizer would only lead to further overproduction and lower prices for farm products. In reply to charges that acceptance of the cyanamid bid would amount to a government subsidy to the American Cyanamid Company, Reece reported that because of the profit limitation on fertilizer operations which was contained in the offer, the advantage of any subsidy would have to be passed on to the farmers.

Despite the furor which had been raised in Tennessee over the inclusion of Cove Creek in the Muscle Shoals project, the Reece report sought to justify that plan since the cyanamid offer provided for it. Reece declared that the whole of the river basin should be developed as a unit in order that everyone in the area might receive maximum benefits. He denied that federal construction of a dam at Cove Creek would interfere with the rights of Tennessee since, he averred, the power distributed from there would be subject to state regulation. Furthermore, he endorsed the theory that most of the power developed on the Tennessee River should be concentrated and used directly in the electrochemical industry. According to Reece, the development of such an industry at Muscle Shoals would be more important to national defense than would be the production of nitrates.[12]

In a minority report, Representative Morin forcefully assailed the Reece report. In particular, he criticized the cyanamid bid for not providing for the distribution of the surplus power, and he ridiculed Reece's claim that the offer contained a guarantee of fertilizer production. He pointed out that the cyanamid bid had been rejected five times by congressional committees and that the Reece report was an expression of a minority of the

12. *Muscle Shoals*, House Report 2564, 70 Cong., 2 Sess. (1929), 1–35.

Military Committee. He saw no legal equity for the government in the cyanamid bill:

> Under the bill as drafted the rights of the Government and the lessee are in sharp contrast. The obligations of the Government are fixed and determined, the obligations of the lessee are vague and shadowy. There are no provisions protecting the rights and interests of the Government, while the rights and interests of the lessee are fixed and determined.[13]

Morin urged the adoption of his original bill of the previous session which he said was still supported by Secretary of Agriculture Jardine.[14] No further action was taken on Muscle Shoals in the House during this session.

On March 7, 1929, three days following the final adjournment of the Seventieth Congress, President Hoover called a special session of the Seventy-first Congress which assembled on April 15, 1929, and did not adjourn until late in the following November. The President declared that the purpose of the special session was to consider legislation on farm relief and the tariff. In his message to Congress on April 16, 1929, Hoover did not mention Muscle Shoals, but the fact that the project had been associated with farm relief made it likely that the Muscle Shoals controversy would be considered during the session.[15]

Immediately following the decision of the Supreme Court in the Okanogan Indian case in May, 1929, in which the legality of the Coolidge pocket vetoes was upheld, the Senate Agriculture Committee reported favorably a new Norris Muscle Shoals joint resolution. The Norris measure was identical with that vetoed by Coolidge except for the inclusion of a provision intended to mollify the Alabama and Tennessee delegations in Congress with respect to the rights they claimed in Muscle Shoals and Cove Creek, respectively. Perhaps the principal purpose behind the new provision was to win Senator McKellar back to the Norris camp. It provided that the states of Alabama and Tennessee would receive 5 per cent of the gross proceeds from the sale

13. *Ibid.*, Part 2, 2.
14. *Ibid.*, 2, 17–18.
15. *Cong. Rec.*, 71 Cong., 1 Sess., 19, 43.

of power at Muscle Shoals and Cove Creek, respectively. Moreover, each of the two states would receive 2½ per cent of the gross value of the additional power at Wilson Dam resulting from the construction and operation of a Cove Creek dam. Norris asserted that the inclusion of this compensatory feature did not mean that he endorsed the principles of the claims advanced by these two states, but he declared it to be only fair that in cases where states were being deprived of taxable resources by reason of federal enterprises, the states should be compensated.[16]

At the request of Senator Norris, no public hearings on the Norris bill were held by the Senate Agriculture Committee, the Nebraska Senator averring that more than enough hearings had already been held on the Muscle Shoals problem. The most significant objection to the Norris bill in the closed committee session came from Senator Heflin who earlier in the year had praised the measure. At this point Heflin had praise only for the cyanamid bid which had suddenly skyrocketed to renewed prominence as a result of the Reece "rump" revolt. Heflin again raised the question about the most efficient process, the cyanamid versus Haber issue, but Norris asserted that the latter process already had succeeded in cutting the price of nitrates in half. Chairman McNary reminded Heflin that the provisions for research in the Norris measure would ferret out the best process. Despite Heflin's objections to the Norris resolution, he voted for committee approval of the measure.[17]

The Agriculture Committee's report, written by Norris and submitted on June 3, declared that in so far as fertilizer was concerned, Muscle Shoals should be used only for experimental purposes and not for quantity production. Thus, for the first time, Norris openly rejected the idea of producing commercial fertilizer at Muscle Shoals. In regard to Cove Creek, he described that huge reservoir as the key to successful development of the Tennessee River, and he warned that should private power com-

16. *Muscle Shoals,* Hearings, U.S. Senate, on S. J. Res. 49, 71 Cong., 1 Sess. (1929), 1–11.

17. *Ibid.,* 11–12; Minutes of the Senate Agriculture Committee, May 29, 1929, Senate Records, National Archives.

panies be permitted to gain control of it "we would commit a sin of negligence against future generations." [18]

In the report Norris claimed that the investigation of the power industry by the Federal Trade Commission had already proved the existence of a power trust. He declared that:

It has been developed that aggregations of capital and combinations of utility companies have a nation-wide organization. They have undertaken, through the intricate and secret control of the most human activities, to build up a public sentiment in favor of their viewpoint and in opposition to the retention by the Government of Muscle Shoals and other similar properties. . . .

Day after day the country has been shocked with new developments coming from the Federal Trade Commission. Millions of dollars have been spent, as shown by that investigation, for the purchase of newspapers, for the employment of college professors and school-teachers, and in the election of public officials. From the unimportant school director to the highest office in the land nothing has been overlooked.

Norris noted the importance of Muscle Shoals in the matter:

Muscle Shoals is one important element which has brought about this great combination of power companies. It is one of the key positions. These companies did not want the government to operate Muscle Shoals. They did not want an illustration given to the country as to just how cheap electric current could be supplied to the homes and to the factories.[19]

No further action was taken on the Norris resolution during this session. Senator McKellar reintroduced his bill authorizing the Secretary of War to distribute and sell Muscle Shoals power to public agencies, but it received no consideration.[20]

During this special session President Hoover was subjected to some pressure to support the bid of the American Cyanamid Company for the sake of farm relief. Part of this pressure came from New England, an area where agriculture was relatively unimportant. The commissioners of agriculture of five New England states, joined together in the New England Muscle Shoals Committee, appealed to Hoover to endorse the cyanamid

18. *Disposition of Muscle Shoals*, Senate Report 19, 71 Cong., 1 Sess. (1929), 7–11.

19. *Ibid.*, 2.

20. *Cong. Rec.*, 71 Cong., 1 Sess., 628.

bid, asserting that its acceptance was necessary to relieve an acute fertilizer shortage in the country. An almost identical appeal was made by the Muscle Shoals Committee of the Illinois Farm Institute, former Congressman John C. McKenzie being the chairman of this organization. In April, 1929, Representative Lister Hill of Alabama denounced Hoover roundly for not approving the cyanamid offer. Hill asserted that Hoover's refusal to do so constituted typical Republican discrimination against the South where large amounts of fertilizer were used. Representative Gordon Browning of Tennessee described the cyanamid bid as the most feasible measure for farm relief "yet proposed to the Congress." [21]

On the other hand, the League of Women Voters issued a large pamphlet endorsing the Norris Muscle Shoals plan.[22]

The attitude of Representative Browning, whose constituency was located in West Tennessee, was perhaps influenced by a preliminary report of the Corps of Engineers in February, 1928. Previously, West Tennessee had joined with Mississippi and other neighboring sections in expressing a fear that it would be prevented from sharing in the use of cheap Muscle Shoals power because of the probability that large industries, such as envisaged by the cyanamid supporters, would be located in the Muscle Shoals area. This fear was intensified by the apparent lack of fuel or hydroelectric resources in West Tennessee. The preliminary report of the Corps of Engineers, which was a partial report of a comprehensive survey of the entire Tennessee River system in progress intermittently since 1922, showed that it was feasible to develop approximately 500,000 horsepower at each of two sites on the lower Tennessee River in the West Tennessee area. One of these proposed power sites was located at Pickwick Landing above Savannah, Tennessee, and the other was at Aurora, Kentucky, just across the Kentucky-Tennessee border.

The discovery of the possibility of a million horsepower in this area set the imagination of the people of West Tennessee on fire. Alabama could keep its power; in fact, West Tennesseans

21. *Ibid.*, 323–24, 459–60, 501, 2978–79.
22. Marguerite Owen, *Muscle Shoals and the Public Welfare* (1929).

were anxious at this point to settle the Muscle Shoals controversy on terms suitable to Alabama and the cyanamid company. In the first place, such a settlement would permit the Federal Power Commission to lift its ban on further development of the Tennessee, thus giving West Tennessee a chance to begin water-power developments on its sector of the river. Moreover, since the cyanamid bid contemplated the concentration of Muscle Shoals power in North Alabama, West Tennesseans, using Muscle Shoals as a precedent, might keep their power at home to attract industry.[23] Thus Congressman Browning became a supporter of the cyanamid bid.

During 1929 the Federal Trade Commission continued its investigation of the power industry, and Norris and his allies continued to draw from the investigation ammunition which could be used against proposals to dispose of Muscle Shoals to private interests.[24] The commission followed the same line of inquiry in the first quarter of 1929 as they had followed in the previous year. During this period the reputation of the private power industry undoubtedly continued to suffer because of disclosures before the commission which either revealed or indicated unethical practices in the industry. The refusal of the Electric Bond and Share Company to honor the commission's subpoena to produce the company's records was perhaps more damaging to the power industry than any other incident. Officers of the holding company asserted that it was not engaged in interstate commerce and therefore was outside the commission's jurisdiction by the terms of the Walsh resolution, but Robert E. Healy, chief counsel for the commission, declared that this company controlled over 150 utility holding companies affecting a thousand American communities.[25]

23. Jackson (Tenn.) *Sun*, April 26, 1929, quoted in *Cong. Rec.*, 71 Cong., 1 Sess., 760; War Department, *Tennessee River and Tributaries*, House Doc. 185, 70 Cong., 1 Sess. (1928), 73.

24. For the highlights of the Federal Trade Commission's investigation of the electric power industry in 1929 see New York *Times*, Jan. 9, 12, 26, March 1, 14, April 13, 14 (II), 15, 21, 27, 30, May 1, 2, 5, 7, 11, 16, 17, 18, 21, 22, 23, June 5, 6, 13, 20, 21, 1929.

25. *Ibid.*, Jan. 9, Feb. 17, 1929

The investigation established that Mrs. John D. Sherman, former president of the General Federation of Women's Clubs, not only had received payments from the National Electric Light Association while serving as president of the Federation, but that the Federation itself had been partially financed by this public utility organization. In other instances, evidence was uncovered which indicated that the power industry had exerted itself, financially and otherwise, to influence elections of public utility commissioners and to defeat public ownership of utilities in referendums.[26]

These revelations, which were made early in 1929, were capped in February by Gifford Pinchot's charge that over one-third of the $8,000,000,000 invested in utilities stocks in the country was "water." Pinchot asserted that the interest on this watered stock was taken from the pockets of the American people in the form of higher power rates. He claimed that household consumers paid two-thirds of the total electric bill in the nation but used only one-fifth of the power. Although he would not go so far as to advocate public ownership of power utilities, he called for drastic control of the "power monopoly" which, he said, "attempts to run the political affairs of the States and the nation." [27]

The second phase of the Federal Trade Commission's investigation in 1929 began in April when Senator Norris asked the commission to direct its inquiry toward the relationships existing between the power and newspaper industries. Norris's request preceded the introduction of the Norris Muscle Shoals plan in the first session of the Seventy-first Congress by only a few days. Norris's specific complaint was that the purchase of control of two Boston newspapers, the *Herald* and the *Traveller,* by the International Paper and Power Company, which controlled the New England power system, represented a move by power interests to control public opinion. The Federal Trade Commission's investigation revealed that the power company had heavy invest-

26. *Ibid.,* Jan. 12, 26, 1929. Mrs. Sherman testified that the payments which she received from the utility association were put in the revolving fund of the Federation and that the utility association did not influence the substance of the magazine articles which she wrote. *Ibid.,* Jan. 12, 1929.

27. *Ibid.,* March 1, 1929.

ments in a large number of daily newspapers in the East, Midwest, and South. Company officials claimed that their purpose was to secure outlets for the newsprint which the company manufactured rather than to influence public opinion. They denied that they had influenced the editorial policies of these papers. It was also found that this company had made unsuccessful attempts to purchase other newspapers, including the Cleveland *Plain Dealer,* the Atlanta *Constitution,* the Kansas City *Star,* the Detroit *Free-Press,* and the Memphis *Commercial-Appeal.*[28]

Evidence that other power companies, the Insull interests in particular, were attempting to enter the newspaper field was bared by the commission. The commission investigated charges that the Mobile *Press,* which began publication on May 5, 1929, had been financed by the Alabama Power Company. Although no direct connections between the power company and the newspaper were established, it was discovered that officials of the power company had made a "personal" loan with which to establish the Mobile publication.[29] To Norris this evidence constituted a confirmation of the charges that the Mobile *Press* had been founded by the "power trust." He said:

Other evidence has almost daily startled the country in the magnitude of the investment of the trust in newspapers in various parts of the country, but the investigation of the Mobile newspaper situation discloses that, where the trust could not buy a newspaper it did not hesitate to establish a newspaper.

In this particular instance, the trust took extraordinary precautions to cover its tracks. Another illustration of the secret methods that have been employed by the trust all over the United States, in order to carry out its program . . . to control every avenue of human activity.[30]

Before its adjournment for the summer on June 26, the Federal Trade Commission elicited other information which was highly

28. *Ibid.,* April 14, (II), 30, May 1, 11, 16, 1929. Newspapers in which the International Paper and Power Company held an interest, directly or indirectly, included the Brooklyn *Daily Eagle,* Albany *Knickerbocker Press,* Chicago *Journal,* Chicago *Daily News,* Augusta (Ga.) *Chronicle,* Columbia (S.C.) *Record,* Spartanburg (S.C.) *Chronicle,* Tampa *Tribune,* and Greensboro (N.C.) *Record.*

29. New York *Times,* May 17, 18, 21, 22, June 20, 21, 1929.

30. *Ibid.,* June 21, 1929.

embarrassing to the power industry. It found documentary evidence that utility organizations had expended much time and money in an attempt to turn public opinion and Congress against public operation of Muscle Shoals and Boulder Dam. It was discovered that these organizations had played an influential hand in getting the Walsh resolution to investigate the power industry referred to the Interstate Commerce Committee instead of the Judiciary Committee. The chairman of the former was Senator Watson of Indiana, an adamant foe of public power, while the chairman of the latter was Senator Norris.[31]

The commission threw some light upon the activities of Samuel S. Wyer and his relationship with the Smithsonian Institution. Wyer admitted that he had been paid by the private power industry for making the survey of the Ontario, Canada, public power system in 1925, an allegedly independent study under the auspices of the Smithsonian Institution. According to Wyer, the survey was instigated by the National Electric Light Association which had been frightened by the prospects of the growth of public power in the United States. The public relations committee of that association gave the Wyer study much publicity, describing it as a product of the Smithsonian. Wyer further disclosed that in early 1925, Chauncey W. Walcott, the director of the Smithsonian Institution, asked him to conduct a survey of Muscle Shoals. Wyer said that he protested that he could not get the necessary co-operation from the Corps of Engineers, but that Walcott assured him that he had made the necessary arrangements with the President, who had approved of the project. Upon arriving in Chattanooga, Wyer went into consultation with members of the Corps of Engineers, but a newspaper reporter heard the conversation and wrote a news article about the affair. This event frightened Walcott, Wyer said, resulting in the withdrawal of the Smithsonian as the sponsor of the Wyer survey. Wyer, however, continued in his work and prepared the report, the financial burden of which was borne by the Duquesne Light and Power Company. Later Wyer conducted another survey of

31. *Ibid.*, April 21, June 13, 15, 1929.

Muscle Shoals for an organization under the control of the Ohio State Chamber of Commerce.[32]

As a result of the disclosures made before the Federal Trade Commission in the first half of 1929, Norris, Walsh of Montana, and LaGuardia called for congressional legislation to control the power industry's relationships with the press. Nothing with respect to this subject was accomplished at this time. Norris called it imperative that this alleged threat against a free press be checked lest the following generation become economic slaves as a result of controlled public opinion.[33]

The Federal Trade Commission's power investigation, by the late summer of 1929, greatly intensified the power issue as well as the Muscle Shoals controversy. At this time Governor Franklin D. Roosevelt of New York called for public operation of Muscle Shoals, the St. Lawrence power project, and Boulder Dam as yardsticks with which to determine fair power rates. In September, 1929, Senator Clarence C. Dill of Washington, in a nationwide radio address, declared that the struggle in Congress over the disposition of Muscle Shoals had been motivated by the private power industry in order to prevent the government from demonstrating how cheaply power could be supplied to consumers. In November, William Madgett, a former president of the Nebraska League of Municipalities, stated that the "power trust" was already laying plans to defeat Norris in the election of 1930 because of his fight for public operation of Muscle Shoals. Madgett declared that the power interests were engaged in "a life and death struggle" to prevent the public development of Muscle Shoals.[34]

The Federal Trade Commission resumed its power investigation in October, 1929. Before the proceedings were well under way, another investigation had been launched by the Senate which overshadowed the commission's work for a time and proved to be exceedingly pertinent to the Muscle Shoals controversy. This was the investigation of lobbying activities in the District

32. *Ibid.*, May 12, 1929.
33. *Ibid.*, May 5, 7, 21, 23, June 5, 6, 1929.
34. *Ibid.*, Sept. 15, Oct. 14, Nov. 20, 23, 25, 1929.

of Columbia by a subcommittee of the Judiciary Committee headed by Senator Caraway of Arkansas. Senator Norris was chairman of the full committee. The resolution authorizing this investigation, which was adopted on October 1, provided primarily for an inquiry into tariff lobbying, but at the request of Senator Black, Muscle Shoals was placed on the agenda. Hearings on Muscle Shoals lobbying were held intermittently from January to April, 1930.[35] These hearings were marked by ill temper on the part of both witnesses and committee members. The principal interrogators, Thaddeus Caraway, Thomas J. Walsh, and Hugo Black, treated some of the witnesses in a rather brusque manner.

The most important aspect of the Muscle Shoals phase of the Caraway lobby committee's investigations dealt with the activities of Chester Gray, the Washington representative of the Farm Bureau. The committee's inquiry into this subject was greatly aided by documentary materials subpoenaed from Gray's office. As the committee probed into the matter, it was disclosed that several thousand dollars' worth of publicity material promoting the cyanamid bid had been provided and distributed at the expense of the American Cyanamid Company but under the name of the Farm Bureau. Gray testified that since the Farm Bureau had endorsed the cyanamid bid, he saw no moral wrong in working in such close harmony with the cyanamid company. It was found that the funds provided by this company for the Farm Bureau publicity campaign had been shuttled through a third party, Oliver M. Kile, a former assistant Washington representative of the Farm Bureau, who operated an agricultural publicity service in Washington. Kile testified that for a period of two years, 1928–1929, he had been paid some $44,000 by the American Cyanamid Company for directing its Muscle Shoals publicity. W. B. Bell, president of the cyanamid company, admitted that his firm had spent approximately $180,000 in its efforts to acquire Muscle Shoals.[36]

35. *Ibid.*, Oct. 14, 1929; *Cong. Rec.*, 71 Cong., 1 Sess., 4115. Senator Black was not a member of the Caraway committee but was permitted to sit with it because of his vital interest in Muscle Shoals.

36. *Lobby Investigation*, Senate Hearings, 71 Cong., 2 Sess., 2823, 2841, 2895, 3062, 3067, 3083, 3237–38. Later Gray changed the official committee records,

The committee probed into Gray's political activities in behalf of the cyanamid proposal. Confronted with evidence from his own files, the Farm Bureau representative admitted having used his organization as a means of exerting pressure on various members of Congress with regard to Muscle Shoals legislation. It was found that Gray had exerted Farm Bureau pressure to secure membership on Muscle Shoals committees—the House Military Committee, the Senate Agriculture Committee, and the Joint Muscle Shoals Committee of 1926—for various members of Congress who favored the cyanamid proposal.[37]

The Caraway committee found that Gray had assisted Senator Frederic C. Walcott of Connecticut, a member of the Agriculture Committee, in writing a minority report against the Norris Muscle Shoals resolution in May, 1929. This report was never submitted to the Senate because Gray became apprehensive lest the fact that Senator Walcott was a director of the Union Carbide Company, an associate of the American Cyanamid Company in the latter's Muscle Shoals bid, cause an unfavorable public reaction toward the cyanamid offer.[38]

The committee also inquired about Gray's relationship with President Coolidge. It found that the farm leader had indeed carried his fight for the cyanamid bid to the White House, but, with the possible exception of one instance, nothing was uncovered that could really be classed as unethical. The one exception was the fact that Gray had persuaded President Coolidge to change his message to Congress, in December, 1927, so that it would contain something favorable to the cyanamid bid. The country learned for the first time why the Coolidge message had been so contradictory in nature. It was revealed that though Gray

without permission of the committee, to state that the expenses of promoting the cyanamid offer had been borne "cooperatively" between the American Cyanamid Company and the Farm Bureau. Senator Norris declared that this action meant that Gray had perjured himself in his original testimony, but the farm leader escaped legal prosecution because the committee had neglected to put him under oath when he had testified. *Ibid.*, 2993–95; Stephen Raushenbush, *The Power Fight* (1932), 195.

37. *Lobby Investigation*, Senate Hearings, 71 Cong., 2 Sess., 2896, 2929–35, 2997–98, 3016–20, 3042, 3046.

38. *Ibid.*, 2891–95.

was not particularly pleased with the sentence added by the President, he boasted that it "at least made a beautiful straddle out of the Muscle Shoals paragraph." [39]

The lobby committee found that Gray went to the White House early in 1928 to protest personally to President Coolidge against the Morin Muscle Shoals bill which was being prepared by the Department of Agriculture. Gray believed that the Morin measure was designed to deliver Muscle Shoals to the power companies, and he was greatly alarmed lest sufficient strength be mustered in Congress to pass it. The farm leader declared that President Coolidge was not then aware of the existence of the Morin bill and that upon being informed of the matter, the Chief Executive ordered the Department of Agriculture to suspend preparation of the measure until he could study it. Gray was pleased by this step, interpreting it to mean that the President was in favor of the cyanamid bid. [40]

Among Gray's other contacts with the White House was a letter the Farm Bureau representative sent to the President in April, 1928, again soliciting his support for the cyanamid bid. He assured Coolidge that a presidential endorsement would mean certain victory for the cyanamid plan. He pleaded with the President to veto the Norris Muscle Shoals resolution should Congress adopt it, and warned that the Norris plan constituted a "direct dole to agriculture." Publicly, Gray had criticized the Norris measure on the ground that it would result in no fertilizer production. In his letter, Gray informed Coolidge that American farmers opposed the Norris plan because it would confront the fertilizer industry with unfair competition by providing below-cost fertilizer for farmers. [41]

Gray's activities in the campaign of 1928 were another subject of investigation by the lobby committee. It developed that Gray had worked closely with J. W. Worthington and Claudius H. Huston, both of whom were associated with the Tennessee River Improvement Association, in attempts to influence the platforms

39. *Ibid.*, 3035–36.
40. *Ibid.*, 2968.
41. Gray to Coolidge, April 2, 1928, quoted *ibid.*, 2902–3, 2907.

of the major parties with regard to Muscle Shoals. In reality, it appeared that Worthington was the director of these political operations. Fearing that the Democrats might endorse the Norris Muscle Shoals bill, they decided to concentrate their efforts on the Democratic platform to prevent such an endorsement. Furthermore, they hoped to obtain Democratic approval of some plan favorable to the cyanamid bid. On the eve of the Democratic convention, Gray urged Governor Smith to endorse the cyanamid proposal. Failing in this effort, the Farm Bureau official went to the convention, which was held in Houston, Texas, bearing a proposed Muscle Shoals plank, which had been prepared by Worthington, for the Democratic platform. Worthington's plank proposed a solution for the Muscle Shoals problem which would have been very favorable to the bid of the cyanamid company. Upon his arrival in Houston, Gray received a message from Worthington stating that he had learned from a contact in the "inner temples" of the Hoover group that the Republicans were hoping that the Democratic convention would approve the Norris position on Muscle Shoals, thus giving the Republicans an opportunity to go to the country on the issue of socialism. Worthington warned Gray that if party lines became drawn in this fashion, the cyanamid proposition would have less chance of passing Congress.[42]

The lobby committee failed to determine whether or not Gray was able to influence the writing of the Democratic platform of 1928. He may have helped to prevent an endorsement of the Norris plan, but in view of Governor Smith's stand on the matter, it appears unlikely that the Democratic party would have advocated public operation of Muscle Shoals in any event. On the other hand, it is certain that Gray did not succeed in writing into the platform a plan favorable to the cyanamid bid.

Later in the summer of 1928, Edward A. O'Neal, president of the Alabama Farm Bureau, informed Gray that Worthington's fears that the Norris Muscle Shoals plan had been about to

42. *Lobby Investigation,* Senate Hearings, 71 Cong., 2 Sess., 2708, 2954–55, 2961–63.

capture the affections of the Democratic party were groundless. O'Neal stated that the southern senators who were supporting the Norris bill were doing so for political reasons and predicted that many of them would return to the support of the cyanamid company after the election.[43]

Some other incidents uncovered by the lobby committee with respect to the activities of Chester Gray tended to embarrass the Farm Bureau. It was discovered that Gray had been working covertly to prevent municipalities in northern Alabama from being permitted to purchase power directly from the War Department's switchboard at Wilson Dam, and that he had at times worked closely with the National Fertilizer Association and the National Electric Light Association, which were ostensibly inveterate enemies of the cyanamid offer, in fighting the Norris Muscle Shoals plan. It was also disclosed that Gray had attempted to have Russell F. Bower listed as a field agent of the Alabama Farm Bureau in order that the latter could utilize Farm Bureau prestige in a publicity campaign for the offer of the American Cyanamid Company which, together with the Union Carbide Company, would pay Bower's salary. But Edward A. O'Neal, though active in support of the cyanamid bid, refused to accede to Gray's request.[44]

It was found, however, that Bower had been engaged in an extensive publicity campaign for the cyanamid bid, under the auspices of the Washington office of the Farm Bureau but secretly in the pay of the cyanamid-carbide partnership. In this campaign, in which Bower traveled to several states equipped with official Farm Bureau credentials, including a letter of introduction from Chester Gray, he seemed to have an affinity for those congressional districts which were the constituencies of the members of the House Military Committee. His principal function in this campaign appears to have been to encourage local Farm Bureau leaders to exert pressure on Congress for the cyanamid bid. Senators Black and Caraway criticized Gray severely, asserting

43. *Ibid.*, 2981.
44. *Ibid.*, 2864–79, 2974–75, 3035.

that he and Bower were guilty of misrepresentation, but Gray
professed to see nothing morally offensive about the matter.[45]

The lobby committee was particularly interested in the activities of J. W. Worthington, the executive secretary of the Tennessee River Improvement Association. Despite a committee
subpoena, Worthington, pleading ill health, refused to appear
before the committee to testify. Instead, he hurriedly disposed of
his files in his Washington office and fled to the Ford Hospital in
Detroit where he remained throughout the hearings. Caraway
flatly accused Worthington of feigning sickness in order to
escape the hearings but decorum forced him officially to accept
the statements of the Detroit doctors to the effect that the Muscle
Shoals promoter was seriously ill. The chief reason that the
committee desired the presence of Worthington was to force
him to disclose the whereabouts of his records so that they could
be subpoenaed. Despite the great wrath displayed by Caraway,
Black, and Walsh, Worthington's subordinates steadfastly asserted
that they knew nothing about the location of his records. Caraway
declared that Worthington had misappropriated association
funds, but no evidence supporting this contention was discovered,
Worthington's subordinates testifying that all financial records of
the association were kept by the executive secretary himself.[46]

The committee subpoenaed the files from the office of W. G.
Waldo, Worthington's assistant and consulting engineer to the
association. The subsequent examination of Waldo with the
support of these records revealed that the Worthington group, in
co-operation with the Farm Bureau, had conducted an extensive
campaign at the local level, particularly in the South, against
members of Congress who had not supported the cyanamid proposal. Perhaps the most important revelation resulting from the
examination of Waldo was the discovery that he and Worthington
were the authors of the cyanamid bid.[47]

Another controversial figure involved in the Caraway com-

45. *Ibid.*, 3588–89; *Lobbying and Lobbyists*, Senate Report 43, 71 Cong.,
2 Sess., Part 7, 1–2.
46. *Lobby Investigation*, Senate Hearings, 71 Cong., 2 Sess., 225–26, 2552,
2604–7, 3225–26.
47. *Ibid.*, 2619, 2629–30, 2643, 2655, 2670–75, 2709.

mittee hearings was Claudius H. Huston, formerly an associate of Worthington but at that time the chairman of the Republican National Committee. Huston, whose name appeared frequently in the testimony and evidence before the committee, had been close to the Hoover circle in the Republican administrations throughout the 1920's. Upon Hoover's election to the Presidency in 1928, Huston was chosen to head the Republican committee.

According to evidence uncovered by the Caraway committee, Huston was bending every effort to avoid an appearance before Caraway and his colleagues. When Caraway openly accused the Republican leader of such tactics, there followed a verbal war in which Huston protested that he was being defamed by the committee. Upon Huston's appearance before the committee, it was found that in 1929, while acting in an official capacity for the Tennessee River Improvement Association, of which he was then president, Huston had solicited a contribution of $36,000 from the Union Carbide Company for the purpose of promoting the cyanamid bid. Instead of using the money for that purpose, Huston placed it with his stock broker to finance speculative purchases of stock. He could offer no substantial proof that the funds were ever used for their original purpose, but he asserted that he regarded this money as payment for debts owed to him by the association. In addition, Chester Gray testified that Huston was expected to use his position as chairman of the Republican National Committee to gain administration support for the cyanamid bid.[48]

The lobby committee found that various attempts had been made to harmonize the power and chemical interests in regard to Muscle Shoals. Secret conferences were held in 1925 and 1926 at which representatives of the power interests, including Owen D. Young of the General Electric Company, and the cyanamid-carbide companies were brought together at the instigation of Herbert Hoover and the Farm Bureau. In 1927 Chester Gray again attempted to lead these interests to a compromise on Muscle Shoals. No accord could be reached. Finally, President

Coolidge took a hand in the matter. In 1928 he called William B. Bell, president of the American Cyanamid Company, to the White House on two different occasions to urge him to agree to a compromise with the power companies. The President explained to Bell that the power companies were alarmed because of the great amount of power to be produced under the terms of the cyanamid bid, their principal fear being that the chemical company would enter the power distribution business. Bell promised the President that he would agree to a compromise whereby the amount of power to be produced by his company in the Tennessee Valley would be radically reduced, thereby insuring the power companies against competition from that source. Nevertheless, Bell and the Alabama Power Company were never able to reach an agreement on the matter even though Bell offered a compromise proposal which faithfully embodied his promise to the President. Whether these attempts at a compromise caused the power companies to drop their bid in 1928 was not revealed.[49]

Senators Caraway and Walsh made a determined effort to show that the cyanamid company itself was owned by the "power trust." William B. Bell admitted that as late as 1922 the Duke power interests of North Carolina were the principal stockholders in the company, but he insisted that the Duke people had disposed of their cyanamid stock. He denied that any power interests then held stock in the company, but he refused to make public a list of the company's stockholders.[50] Although Caraway and Walsh may have been successful in convincing the public that there was a connection between the American Cyanamid Company and the power companies with which it supposedly had been competing for the acquisition of Muscle Shoals, they failed to turn up any evidence to that effect.

In the majority report to the Senate on May 31, 1930, Senator Caraway singled out J. W. Worthington and Claudius H. Huston as the chief villains in Muscle Shoals lobbying. Caraway concluded that Chester Gray had been the naïve but innocent victim

49. *Lobby Investigation*, Senate Hearings, 71 Cong., 2 Sess., 2809–10, 2914, 2949, 3006, 3089–91, 3231, 3248–51.
    50. *Ibid.*, 2714, 3077–79.

of the charms of Worthington and Huston, who had enticed the Farm Bureau leader into using the Farm Bureau as a tool of the American Cyanamid Company. Since Caraway felt that Gray was the only major national official of the Farm Bureau who was deeply involved in the matter, he concluded that the honor of that organization itself had not been seriously impaired.[51]

Senator Arthur R. Robinson of Indiana, a member of the Caraway committee and an administration Republican, stoutly defended Huston and accused his colleagues of having attacked the Republican leader merely to embarrass the Republican party. Robinson denied that Huston's activities were either unethical or dishonest. Nevertheless, the committee's disclosures regarding Huston precipitated a heated debate within the ranks of the Republican party with the result that in August, 1930, the Republican national chairman was forced to submit his resignation. He was ruined politically.[52]

The lobby committee hearings unquestionably had an important effect on the Muscle Shoals controversy. In the first place, they destroyed any hopes for acceptance of the cyanamid bid that might have been raised by the Reece "rump" revolt. It was felt in some quarters that the hearings had demonstrated that all of the persons connected with the cyanamid bid had acted primarily in the interest of the American Cyanamid Company rather than in that of the farmers.[53] The hearings further emphasized the power aspect of Muscle Shoals at the expense of fertilizer. More important, these hearings, coupled with the revelations by the Federal Trade Commission, served to brighten the prospects for public operation of Muscle Shoals.[54]

51. Senate Report 43, 71 Cong., 2 Sess., Part 7, 1–4. One recent authority on the Farm Bureau, Grant McConnell, feels that the lobby investigation cast doubts upon Farm Bureau activities in connection with Muscle Shoals, but he concluded that it would be a mistake to place great emphasis on this episode in evaluating the merits of the organization. Grant McConnell, *The Decline of Agrarian Democracy* (1953), 159.

52. *Cong. Rec.*, 71 Cong., 2 Sess., 9269–76; New York *Times*, April 28, 30, June 7, 28, 30, July 24, Aug. 8, 1930.

53. Duff Gilfond, "The Muscle Shoals Lobby," in *New Republic*, LXII (April 16, 1930), 234–36.

54. *Electrical World*, which generally reflected the attitude of the power industry, held that most of the evidence uncovered by the Caraway lobby com-

No doubt Senator Norris and his allies greatly exaggerated the substance of the findings of both the Trade Commission and the lobby committee. In the case of the former, it was not definitely shown that the power companies were acquiring newspapers with the intent to control public opinion, although it was demonstrated that they intended to influence public thinking by other methods. In the case of the lobby investigation, the committee did not reveal evidence that any of the major principals involved possessed a dishonest intention in desiring the acceptance of the cyanamid bid, and, with the possible exception of Huston, it was not shown that any of the major principals profited personally or had expectations of such a profit.

Nevertheless, the general impression that resulted from both investigations caused an unfavorable public reaction toward both the power and chemical interests, thus leaving the field open for the Norris forces. In fact, while the lobby committee hearings were in progress, the Norris plan for Muscle Shoals was meeting with great success in Congress.

mittee "is political in bearing and will not materially affect the final disposition of Muscle Shoals." See the article entitled "Gray, Coolidge, Norris and Muscle Shoals," in *Electrical World*, XCV (March 1, 1931), 423.

XI

The Second Norris
Congressional Victory

I N PRESIDENT HOOVER'S MESSAGE to Congress on December 3, 1929, he apparently attempted to placate both the power and chemical interests that were endeavoring to acquire control of Muscle Shoals. The President advocated the lease of power and fertilizer facilities at Muscle Shoals, as a unit or separately, and recommended that the revenues therefrom be used to promote fertilizer research. Hoover's sanction of separate leases of the power and fertilizer facilities and his emphasis on fertilizer research conformed to leasing principles advocated by the power companies. But he did not mention water-power distribution. Instead he spoke of the possible utilization of the project to develop a chemical industry in the Tennessee Valley. The President also recommended that, because of the technical nature of the Muscle Shoals problem, Congress should create a commission endowed with authority to negotiate a lease of the project without further interference from the legislative branch of the government.[1]

At the time President Hoover sent this message to Congress, Chester Gray entertained high hopes for the success of the cyanamid bid during the session which had just opened. Hoover had shown Gray an advance copy of his message and had discussed its Muscle Shoals section with the farm leader. Gray apparently was well pleased with the message; afterward, he expressed a strong hope that should Congress create a commission as recommended in Hoover's message, the President would use it to dispose of the project on terms similar to those contained in the cyanamid

1. *Cong. Rec.*, 71 Cong., 2 Sess., 25–26.

bid. Moreover, Gray was jubilant because Secretary of Agriculture
Arthur M. Hyde had promised him that he would not issue any
official statements disparaging the cyanamid process.[2]

Gray's hopes were dashed by the subsequent hearings held by
the Caraway lobby committee. The thorough discrediting of the
cyanamid bid by the lobby investigation, coupled with the embarrassment of the power companies as a result of the Federal
Trade Commission probe, enabled the Norris plan to reach the
floor of the Senate in early April, 1930, under auspicious circumstances. Apparently there was little doubt that the Norris Muscle
Shoals joint resolution, which was identical to that of the
previous session, would soon pass the Senate.[3]

Unlike the debates on past Muscle Shoals bills, the senatorial
deliberation on the Norris resolution at this session was a colorless
affair, apparently the result of the prevailing feeling that Norris
held a comfortable majority in the Senate. Norris, who defended
his resolution against a half-hearted administration attack based
on the issue of public versus private power, dominated the discussion. The debate produced little that was new except refer-
ences to the Caraway committee and Federal Trade Commission
investigations, which were then in progress and which were
utilized extensively in the debate by the Norris group. Senator
Norris delivered a slashing attack on the cyanamid bid and declared that the Caraway committee, by discrediting that proposal,
had completely eliminated the only remaining opposition to the
Norris proposal.[4]

Apparently as a result of the revelations being made by the
lobby committee, Senator Heflin withdrew his support from the

2. Gray to Hyde, Dec. 2, 1929, Correspondence of the Secretary of Agriculture, Muscle Shoals, National Archives; *Lobby Investigation*, Hearings,
U.S. Senate, 71 Cong., 2 Sess., 3541–44. It is interesting to note that one
of the papers presented at a meeting of the American Electrochemical Society
in September, 1929, was a condemnation of Muscle Shoals as a fertilizer venture
as well as of the cyanamid process as a method of fertilizer production. Farley
G. Clark, "Muscle Shoals Relative to Conservation," in *Transactions of the
American Electrochemical Society*, LVI (Sept., 1929), 89–95.

3. New York *Times*, April 1, 3, 1930; *Cong. Rec.*, 71 Cong., 2 Sess., 6357,
6367.

4. *Cong. Rec.*, 71 Cong., 2 Sess., 6363–67, 6700.

cyanamid bid. His colleague, Senator Hugo Black, who had never definitely committed himself to the proposal of the American Cyanamid Company, roundly denounced that offer. Neither of the Alabama senators was entirely pleased with the Norris measure despite its provisions for compensating the state of Alabama. Both senators attempted unsuccessfully to add private leasing provisions to the Norris resolution, evidently in an attempt to wring further concessions from the Nebraska Senator. One of Black's complaints was the failure of the Norris measure to provide for construction of dam no. 3. Black also wanted the Norris resolution strengthened in the section providing for preference to municipalities in the sale of power, a desire which led to a conflict with Senator Walter F. George of Georgia who accused Black of plotting to sell all of the Muscle Shoals power to towns in northern Alabama. The Georgia Senator was apprehensive lest the Alabama towns, which he believed would be given first access to the power because of their proximity to the source, should contract for large supplies of power in anticipation of obtaining new industries. The Senate accepted a compromise amendment designed to pacify George on this matter.[5]

Norris's provision to compensate the states of Alabama and Tennessee was successful in bringing Senator McKellar back to the Norris camp but at the expense of displeasing other Norris supporters, particularly Alben W. Barkley of Kentucky and Arthur H. Vandenberg of Michigan. The compensatory provision was especially unattractive to Vandenberg, who described it as an undeserved subsidy to the two states and asserted that they would be compensated adequately by virtue of the flood control, navigational, and power benefits that would result from the Norris plan.[6]

On April 4, 1930, the Norris joint resolution on Muscle Shoals passed the Senate without any significant changes. Supporting

5. *Ibid.*, 6427–39.
6. *Ibid.*, 6400, 6404, 6430–31, 6495–96, 6500, 6506. McKellar's defection from the Norris cause in 1928 led Chester Gray to believe that the Tennessee Senator could be won over to the support of the cyanamid bid. Consequently, in 1929 Gray attempted to convert McKellar to the cyanamid cause but without success. *Lobby Investigations*, Senate Hearings, 71 Cong., 2 Sess., 3561.

the measure were twenty-six Democrats and eighteen Republicans, and opposing it were two Democrats and twenty-one Republicans. No senator from the former Confederate states, except Ransdell of Louisiana, who was paired against the measure, voted against it. It was a clear-cut victory for the southern-western farm bloc.[7]

Some newspapers asserted that the easy Norris victory in the Senate, following the embarrassment of the private power companies and the chemical interests as a result of the investigations, meant a turning point in the country's policy that was more favorable to public power. These newspapers also pointed out that Muscle Shoals definitely had become the focal point on which the nation's power policy was being determined.[8] Mark Sullivan, noted newspaper correspondent, stated:

Muscle Shoals as treated in the Norris bill means . . . a beginning toward undermining and embarrassing the manufacture of electricity by private corporations. . . .
The result of repeated disclosures is a psychological condition in which Senators and Representatives are voting, not on Muscle Shoals, but on the activities of the private power corporations.[9]

An editorial in the New York *Times* put it this way:

Lately Muscle Shoals has become almost a symbol. Advocates of the [Norris] bill regard it as a blow at the "power trust," now a more lively political issue than ever. The revelations with regard to Mr. Huston and his connections with the Muscle Shoals lobby have not made it any easier for the opponents of the bill in Congress or for the President.[10]

On the other hand, *Outlook and Independent* saw little popular support for the Norris bill outside Congress, and *Business Week* declared that the Muscle Shoals issue was merely a convenient tool with which the farm bloc hoped to gain farm votes.[11]

7. *Cong. Rec.*, 71 Cong., 2 Sess., 6511.
8. "Muscle Shoals Nearing Its Climax," in *Literary Digest*, CV (April 19, 1930), 11.
9. Quoted *ibid.*
10. New York *Times*, April 7, 1930.
11. "Muscle Shoals," in *Outlook and Independent*, CLIV (April 23, 1930), 656–57; "Muscle Shoals May Yet Be Leased to Highest Bidder," in *Business Week*, No. 34 (April 23, 1930), 40.

Meanwhile, the House Military Committee was conducting hearings on the Muscle Shoals problem. During the hearings, which were held intermittently from February 6 to April 11, 1930, William B. Bell appeared to make another plea for the cyanamid bid. The cyanamid company president was subjected to a barrage of embarrassing questions regarding the revelations by the lobby committee of the activities of various persons engaged in assisting the American Cyanamid Company in its quest for control of Muscle Shoals. Bell denied that his company had been unethical in its relations with the Farm Bureau, the Tennessee River Improvement Association, or the power companies. He acknowledged that the cyanamid company had helped to defray the expenses of the Farm Bureau's campaign for the cyanamid bid, but he declared that such a transaction conformed to the accepted standards of the business world.[12]

A group of experts from the War and Agriculture Departments appeared before the committee for the purpose of demonstrating that because of rapid advances in the development of the Haber process Muscle Shoals was no longer an important factor in either fertilizer production or national defense. They recommended that any plans for operating the Muscle Shoals nitrate plants be abandoned and that the plants be salvaged for scrap. The Department of Agriculture officials who formerly had sponsored the plan of fertilizer research which had been embodied in the Norris bill of 1928, now rejected that scheme. They declared that the private fertilizer industry had reached such a stage of development that further fertilizer research could be readily financed by the industry. In short, these official representatives of the federal government sought to deal a death blow to any further association between Muscle Shoals and fertilizer. They were aided in this work by Charles J. Brand, representing the National Fertilizer Association, who assured the committee that the nation's fertilizer industry could adequately serve the American farmers and that production of fertilizer at Muscle Shoals was not feasible. Added to this was a report on Muscle Shoals released during the hearings

12. *Muscle Shoals,* Hearings, U.S. House of Representatives, 71 Cong., 2 Sess. (1930), 1–34.

by the United States Chamber of Commerce which purported to prove that the project was no longer a practical fertilizer proposition.[13]

Early in April, following a charge by Representative Lister Hill of Alabama that Representative Harry C. Ransley of Pennsylvania, a stanch administration Republican who was acting chairman of the Military Committee, was using the hearings to delay action on the Norris bill, the hearings were terminated. A subcommittee headed by Carroll Reece was appointed to draft a bill, which, after its approval by the full committee by a vote of 11 to 5, was reported to the House on May 12.[14]

The Reece bill apparently was an attempt to carry out President Hoover's recommendation that the Muscle Shoals problem be referred to a commission. It authorized the President to appoint a commission of three "eminent citizens" and endowed the commission with the authority to lease the Muscle Shoals properties for fifty years, subject only to the approval of the President. The bill fixed certain stipulations under which the lease could be made. First, the lessee would be required to manufacture commercial fertilizer, the amount to be determined by market demands, but with the lessee not being required in any case to produce in excess of the existing capacity of the Muscle Shoals project. Second, the lessee would be limited to an 8 per cent profit on fertilizer operations, the cost factors to be determined by agreement between the President and the lessee. Although the Reece bill declared the principle of equitable distribution of surplus Muscle Shoals power to be the established policy, it stipulated that none of the surplus power was to be sold to private power companies until the demands of municipalities and other public agencies and "manufacturing industries" in the Muscle Shoals area had been satisfied. The "manufacturing industries" were not identified.

The bill also required the lessee to construct a dam at Cove

13. *Ibid.*, 170–243, 253–55, 276–93; U.S. Chamber of Commerce, National Water Power Policies Committee, *Muscle Shoals: A Groundwork of Facts* (1930).
14. New York *Times*, April 10, May 7, 1930; *Cong. Rec.*, 71 Cong., 2 Sess., 8818.

Creek under the terms of the Federal Water Power Act and permitted him to construct dam no. 3 under the same terms, the value of navigational and flood control benefits of such dams to be determined by the President and paid by the federal government. The Reece bill, violating a long-established policy of the House Military Committee, would permit separate leases of the power and nitrate plants.

The intent of the authors of the Reece bill was not clear. Since it was a bill to establish a commission, perhaps the authors had not speculated on any action beyond that point. In many respects it appeared to be the cyanamid bill in disguise. Since there was no designation of a time limit within which public agencies would be protected in their preference to purchase power, it would be possible for a large industry to contract for a considerable share of the power before local public agencies could prepare themselves legally to purchase the electricity produced by the project. Apparently, the House Military Committee had reverted to its former policy of favoring the lease of Muscle Shoals to an electrochemical firm. The bill provided an opportunity for the lessee to escape fertilizer production should it prove to be unprofitable.[15] Before the measure was reported from the committee, it was approved by the War Department, a fact which appears not to have been made public.[16] Thus, it apparently had administration backing despite the fact that experts from the War and Agriculture departments had argued at the hearings that Muscle Shoals should not be used for fertilizer production.

In the House debate, the Reece bill was defended mainly by administration Republicans. There appeared to be confusion as to the meaning of the bill. Representative Lewis W. Douglas of Arizona, a Democrat who aided in the defense of the measure, asserted that the House Military Committee had concluded that to approve public operation of Muscle Shoals, as it did in 1928, without completely exhausting all possibilities for a private lease would be to violate the policy of the committee. While Reece, in

15. *Muscle Shoals,* House Report 1430, 71 Cong., 2 Sess. (1930), 1–8.
16. Lieutenant Colonel Joseph I. McMullen to Acting Secretary of War F. T. Davidson, April 15, 1930, Judge Advocate General, National Archives.

his report, had declared the bill to be in harmony with the long-established policy of the Military Committee that Muscle Shoals should be devoted to fertilizer production, Douglas said that in drafting the bill, there had also been an attempt to mollify those who felt that the project was primarily a power proposition. Douglas further declared that rapid advances in science had rendered Muscle Shoals unfit for fertilizer production. Representative Harry M. Wurzbach, a Texas Republican and member of the Military Committee, also declared that the Reece bill embodied a "spirit of compromise" between the fertilizer and power aspects of Muscle Shoals. On the other hand, Representative William H. Stafford of Wisconsin, an ardent administration Republican, implied, like Reece, that the purpose of the Reece bill was to devote Muscle Shoals to the cause of cheap fertilizer.[17]

Representatives Quin of Mississippi and Hill of Alabama led a group of militant southern Democrats in opposing the Reece bill. Hill and Quin were members of the Military Committee, and both charged that the primary purpose of the Reece bill was to delay action on the Norris plan with the secondary goal of placing Muscle Shoals under the control of the "power trust." Most of the southern Democrats who participated in the debate praised the Norris resolution.[18]

The House passed the Reece bill on May 28, 1930, by a vote of 197 to 114, thus reversing its position of two years before when it adopted a public operation bill. The decisive vote, however, was on the motion to substitute the Reece bill for the Norris resolution which brought the two measures into direct conflict. The Reece bill carried, 187 to 135. In this vote, the principal opposition to the Reece bill came from a combination of southern Democrats, who constituted the largest bloc of opposition votes, and midwestern Republicans. Although the vote showed that the farm bloc in the House was still functioning, there were too many

17. *Cong. Rec.*, 71 Cong., 2 Sess., 9671, 9675, 9682–83. While the Reece bill was under consideration by the House, it received the endorsement of the American Engineering Council. L. W. Wallace to Representative W. Frank James, May 22, 1930, Senate Records, National Archives.

18. *Cong. Rec.*, 71 Cong., 2 Sess., 9679–80, 9684–85, 9741–42.

defections to prevent passage of the Reece bill.[19] Although the Norris resolution lost in the House vote, it was clearly shown that the Norris plan had definitely established itself in the South as the most popular plan for the development of Muscle Shoals.

Early in June, 1930, House and Senate conferees met to attempt to bridge the vast gulf that separated the Norris and Reece bills. Neither side was willing to compromise and the result was a deadlock that was not broken until February, 1931.[20]

On March 4, 1930, the final report of the Corps of Engineers on its comprehensive survey of the Tennessee River and tributaries was submitted to Congress. The report contained conclusive evidence that tremendous power, navigational, and flood control benefits could be achieved by a unified development of the Tennessee River and its principal tributaries. It declared that the Tennessee River system, with the aid of a reasonable amount of auxiliary steam power, was capable of producing approximately 4,000,000 primary horsepower at a very low cost. In addition, the same network of dams would create some 1,800 miles of navigable waters as well as provide a large annual saving through control of destructive floods. The engineers also reported that such a plan would result in the improvement of sanitary and health conditions in the Tennessee Valley.

In its recommendation to Congress, the Corps of Engineers did not contemplate an immediate execution of its rather ambitious program for the Tennessee River. Instead, Congress was advised that the river should be developed gradually by a "proper combination of private enterprise and public works" under the provisions of the Federal Water Power Act.[21]

19. *Ibid.*, 9766–67. Southern Democrats supporting the Reece bill included the entire Tennessee delegation. A majority of Democrats from outside the South joined with a majority of the Southerners in opposing the bill.

Apparently the Tennessee delegation believed that the Reece bill was designed to dispose of Muscle Shoals to the power companies in some fashion, since most Tennessee congressmen probably would have opposed any proposition, such as the cyanamid bid, that they thought would have subordinated Cove Creek to Muscle Shoals as the chemical interests desired.

20. New York *Times*, June 8, 17, 20, 25, 1930.

21. War Department, *Tennessee River and Tributaries, North Carolina, Tennessee, Alabama, and Kentucky*, House Doc. 328, 71 Cong., 2 Sess. (1930), 1–7, 91–100.

The engineers' report vindicated, to a great extent, Senator Norris in his fight for a multiple-purpose development of the Tennessee River which he had been waging with varying degrees of intensity since 1922. Despite the fact that the program recommended in the report was tantamount to a plan for development of the river by private power companies, it gave Norris potent ammunition in his struggle for public operation of Muscle Shoals.

Another important sidelight of the Muscle Shoals controversy was a quarrel between Senator Black and the War Department which reached a climax in the summer of 1930. This dispute began in September, 1929, when the Tennessee Electric Power Company announced plans to acquire power from Wilson Dam. This development, coupled with the fact that the town of Muscle Shoals, Alabama, had been unable to acquire power from Wilson Dam, thoroughly provoked the Alabama Senator.[22] In December, Senator Black protested to Secretary of War Patrick J. Hurley that it seemed "very strange" for the War Department to sell power to the Tennessee power company while denying this privilege to the town of Muscle Shoals. Secretary Hurley replied that the Tennessee power company would have no contract with the War Department but would purchase Wilson Dam power directly from the Alabama Power Company. Hurley also informed Black that the request of the town of Muscle Shoals had been denied because the amount of power required would not be sufficient to justify the additional costs that would accrue as a result of supplying the town with power.[23]

Black's letter showed that the Alabama Senator objected to the sale of Wilson Dam power to the Tennessee Electric Power Company for two reasons—he feared that such a development would strengthen the hold of the Alabama Power Company on Muscle Shoals and that the Tennessee power company's transmission line would remove power from North Alabama to the detriment of industrial development there. Black undoubtedly believed that

22. *Cong. Rec.*, 71 Cong., 2 Sess., 11648, 11754; New York *Times*, Sept. 29 (II), 1929.

23. Black to Hurley, Dec. 17, 1929, and Hurley to Black, Jan. 8, 31, 1929, quoted in *Cong. Rec.*, 71 Cong., 2 Sess., 11968–69.

under the Norris bill Alabama municipalities would have the first opportunity to acquire Muscle Shoals power.

In June, 1930, the town of Muscle Shoals, which had been trying to purchase power from Wilson Dam since June, 1927, placed another application with the Secretary of War. The town officials agreed to pay a higher rate than that being paid by the Alabama Power Company.[24] Then they dispatched the following message to Senator Black:

Telegram [containing copy of the application] you received from Muscle Shoals this morning framed by city fathers, in City Hall by light of kerosene lamps, though within 2 miles of tremendous power tumbling to waste over Wilson Dam with administration's consent.[25]

Senator Black thereupon accused the administration of refusing to sell power to Muscle Shoals in order to discourage municipally owned power systems. He secured the adoption of a resolution declaring it to be the sense of the Senate that the Secretary of War should sell Wilson Dam power to municipalities applying for it and upon the same terms under which it was being sold to the Alabama Power Company. On the same day, June 26, Secretary Hurley rejected the application of Muscle Shoals. This time he informed the town officials that to sell power to their municipality would violate the terms of the contract with the Alabama Power Company. Thereupon, Senator Black denied that such would be the case unless the War Department held a secret contract with the power company. Senator Robert B. Howell of Nebraska obtained the adoption of a resolution directing the Secretary of War to forward to the Senate all written materials on which the contract with the power company was based. At the same time the Senate passed a joint resolution offered by Senator Norris requiring the Secretary of War to sell Muscle Shoals power to municipalities that applied for it. This measure died in the House.[26]

24. *Cong. Rec.*, 71 Cong., 2 Sess., 11069; A. W. Sharpton to Major General Edgar Jadwin, June 14, 1927, Judge Advocate General, National Archives.

25. Quoted in *Cong. Rec.*, 71 Cong., 2 Sess., 11177.

26. *Cong. Rec.*, 71 Cong., 2 Sess., 11069, 11648, 11764, 11965–70, 12037, 12384, 12511–12.

The Secretary of War did not comply with the Howell resolution until the following December, the delay resulting in a heated protest by Black. The documents which finally were submitted gave no evidence of an exclusive agreement with the Alabama Power Company and, therefore, did not sustain the Secretary's contention that approval of the application of Muscle Shoals would violate the contract.[27]

Secretary Hurley consistently refused to confirm Black's assertion that the Muscle Shoals application for power was being rejected because of administration opposition to public power. Whether Hurley's contention that such a sale of power would be too costly to the government was based on facts was not made clear. In June, 1928, Dwight F. Davis, who was then secretary of War, informed President Coolidge that he had not approved the Muscle Shoals application because he feared that it would set a precedent of putting the government in the power business contrary to administration policy. *Electrical World,* immediately following the original application of Muscle Shoals in 1927, declared the event to be a test between private and public power advocates.[28]

In January, 1931, Black unsuccessfully sought to obtain legislation requiring the Secretary of War to sell Muscle Shoals power to municipalities.[29] Thus Black was beaten in his fight with the War Department.

Another important factor which indirectly affected the Muscle Shoals controversy in 1930 was the Federal Trade Commission's inquiry into the public utility industry, which continued intermit-

27. *Ibid.,* 12382; War Department, *Surplus Hydroelectric Power Generated at Wilson Dam, Ala., Sold to Alabama Power Company,* Senate Doc. 222, 71 Cong., 3 Sess. (1930), 1–6. According to a memorandum prepared in the Judge Advocate General's office, the statement by Secretary Hurley that sale of power to Muscle Shoals, Alabama, would violate the War Department's contract with the Alabama Power Company was included by mistake in Hurley's message rejecting the application. The memorandum, which admitted that there was no justification for such a statement, was not made public. Memorandum by Lieutenant Colonel Joseph I. McMullen, July 8, 1930, Judge Advocate General, National Archives.

28. Davis to Coolidge, June 23, 1928, Coolidge Papers; Paul Wooton, "Muscle Shoals City's Plea for Power," in *Electrical World,* XC (July 9, 1927), 82.

29. *Cong. Rec.,* 71 Cong., 3 Sess., 3307, 3385, 3476.

tently through 1930 though at a much slower pace. The commission's hearings proved to be somewhat less embarrassing to the power industry because the power companies defended themselves more energetically than in 1928 and 1929. In fact, the utilities industry staged a counteroffensive by attempting to prove that a concerted effort to promote public ownership of private property was being made nationally by the same groups that were supporting public power. When the Federal Trade Commission refused to accept as evidence a large collection of materials which was supposed to constitute proof of this conspiracy against private property, the National Electric Light Association published the rejected matter in a pamphlet which also purportedly proved that a group of "radicals" and "socialists" were motivating the Trade Commission's investigation.[30] Despite the partial recovery of the utilities industry from the initial shocks of the investigation, a spokesman for the industry stated in the summer of 1930 that "all signs point to a political offensive on an extended scale against the . . . electric industry." [31]

As previously stated, no progress toward agreement was made in the Senate-House conference on Muscle Shoals legislation before the 1930 elections. The House conferees, led by Representative Reece, rejected a Norris compromise proposal whereby the power facilities at Muscle Shoals would be operated by the federal government and the nitrate plants would be leased to private operation. Norris asserted that the rejection of the compromise proved that the House conferees were not really desirous of producing cheap fertilizer.[32]

Thereupon, Norris, Black, and their allies attempted to connect the Republican administration with the "power trust" and blame this combination for the delay on Muscle Shoals. They were aided

30. The materials rejected by the commission consisted of publicity by various organizations advocating public power. These organizations included the National Popular Government League, the Public Ownership League of America, and the League for Industrial Democracy. New York *Times,* Jan. 9, 11, 16, 19, Feb. 28, April 17, 18, 22, 24, 1930.

31. Henry C. Spurm, "Will the Public Utilities Be a Major Political Issue?" in *Public Utilities Fortnightly,* VI (July 10, 1930), 3.

32. New York *Times,* July 7, 8, 1930.

in this task by the Federal Trade Commission which disclosed at this time that Claudius H. Huston, the chairman of the Republican National Committee and close friend of Hoover, had, while serving with the Tennessee River Improvement Association, accepted contributions from power companies ostensibly to promote their Muscle Shoals plans.[33] Moreover, an attempt by the administration at this time to remove the New River in Virginia from the jurisdiction of the Federal Water Power Act, at the request of the Appalachian Electric Power Company, aided the Norris group in putting the "power trust" label on the Hoover administration. In this case, the administration's own actions which appeared to constitute an attack upon the Federal Water Power Act, put the President in an embarrassing position on the power issue.[34]

While attempting to tie the Hoover administration to the "power trust," Senators Norris and Black declared that the Reece bill was an administration measure and charged that the role of Reece in the conference was merely to execute the orders of President Hoover. Senator Black, in fact, set out to make the President personally responsible for the deadlock in the conference; he asserted that Hoover had complete control over the House conferees. Black reminded the President of his Elizabethton address in 1928 in which, according to the Alabama Senator, Hoover promised public operation of Muscle Shoals.[35] The St. Louis *Post-*

33. *Ibid.*, June 17, 1930; *Cong. Rec.*, 71 Cong., 2 Sess., 10995, 11672.

34. In the New River case, the Federal Power Commission consistently had refused to grant the request of the Appalachian Electric Power Company to exempt the New River from the provisions of the Federal Water Power Act. Asserting that the New River was not navigable, the power company contended that the stream was not subject to federal jurisdiction. In the summer of 1930 the power company appealed to President Hoover who responded by asking Attorney General William D. Mitchell for an opinion on the matter. In September, 1930, Mitchell ruled that the New River was not navigable and, therefore, not subject to federal jurisdiction. The Federal Power Commission immediately appealed to the federal courts, but the case was not settled until 1940. In that year, the United States Supreme Court ruled that the New River was navigable and that private power developments on the stream would have to conform to the provisions of the Federal Water Power Act. Stephen Raushenbush, *The Power Fight* (1932), 167–68; Amos Pinchot, "Hoover and Power," in *Nation*, CXXXIII (Aug. 12, 1931), 151–53; New York *Times*, Dec. 17, 1940.

35. *Cong. Rec.*, 71 Cong., 2 Sess., 11070–71, 11551, 11672.

Dispatch and the Washington *Daily News* agreed with Black that the deadlocked conference was now Hoover's personal responsibility, the press assertion being that the President could end the conference merely by ordering the House conferees to accept the Norris compromise proposal.[36]

The deadlocked Muscle Shoals conference committee was directly involved in the elections of 1930. The work of the committee was completely suspended in early July when the chief House conferee, Carroll Reece, returned to Tennessee to wage his campaign for renomination in the Republican primary election. At the time there was much bitterness toward Reece in East Tennessee because of his fight against the Norris bill, which had become popular in that area as a result of the Cove Creek provisions that promised to bring some $45,000,000 of federal money into the section. East Tennesseans tended to blame Reece for delaying the fruition of the project. Although the Reece bill contained a plan for the construction of a Cove Creek dam, many people in the area had little faith in the future of that measure.[37]

Before Reece's departure to the political battlefield, his campaign had already attracted wide interest. His campaign manager had been circulating throughout his district a letter from John Q. Tilson, the Republican leader in the House, to Guy L. Smith, a prominent East Tennessee newspaper publisher, the burden of which was that Reece was so important to the Hoover administration that the President had entrusted to him the important job of drafting and managing a Muscle Shoals bill. It was also stated in the letter that:

The Alabama Power Company is the only company that has transmission lines to Muscle Shoals, and therefore it has no competitor in bidding for this power and will not have as long as the operation at Muscle Shoals is under the influence of a political oligarchy who have an interest in the Alabama and Tennessee Power companies.

The Tilson letter identified Reece's opponents as the "Alabama Power Trust and the red radicals." It also praised Reece for his

36. Washington *Daily News*, June 20, 1930 and St. Louis *Post-Dispatch*, June 17, 1930, quoted *ibid.*, 11313, 11551.
37. *Cong. Rec.*, 71 Cong., 2 Sess., 12351; New York *Times*, July 20 (III), 1930.

refusal to agree to the proposals of the Senate conferees in the conference committee on Muscle Shoals. In the letter, Tilson declared that the Tennessee Congressman would have been a "traitor" to his party had he accepted the Senate proposals and thereby shifted the responsibility for this controversial question to the "Republican House" and to the President.[38]

Since the operation of Muscle Shoals obviously was under the control of the Hoover administration, Senator Black professed to see in the Tilson letter conclusive proof that the Reece bill was intended to convey Muscle Shoals to the Alabama Power Company and that President Hoover was responsible for the delay on Muscle Shoals legislation.[39]

In Reece's campaign for renomination, Muscle Shoals became an important issue. Reece's opponent, Samuel R. Price, severely criticized Reece for having opposed the Norris Muscle Shoals plan. In turn, Reece subjected the Norris plan to vigorous criticism, describing it as a socialistic measure. It soon became evident that the Tennessee Congressman was in trouble politically, and, consequently, he called on President Hoover for help. Although the President had just rejected a similar appeal from New Jersey, he considered the re-election of Reece of such vital importance that he was willing to risk the perils of open interference in a primary election. Thus, on July 24, President Hoover publicly endorsed Reece's candidacy, urging Reece's constituents to send the Congressman back to Washington. In the primary election, Reece barely won. In the general election, he was opposed by an independent Republican, Oscar B. Lovette, who ran on a platform favoring the Norris Muscle Shoals bill. In the absence of Democratic opposition, Lovette soundly defeated Reece.[40]

In Nebraska in 1930, Norris, who was a candidate for renom-

38. Tilson to Smith, June 4, 1930, quoted in *Cong. Rec.*, 71 Cong., 2 Sess., 12382.

39. *Ibid.*, 12383–85.

40. New York *Times*, July 20 (III), 29, 30, Aug. 9, 11, Oct. 24, 1930; editorial in *Nation*, CXXXI (Nov. 19, 1930), 539. Although some leading Tennessee newspapers expressed surprise at Hoover's endorsement of Reece's candidacy since such an act meant open interference in a primary campaign, nevertheless these publications asserted that Hoover's action would have little effect on the

ination in the Republican primary there, faced a determined effort by conservative Republicans to defeat him. They discovered an obscure grocery clerk named George W. Norris and sponsored him as a candidate against the Senator in the Republican primary. Fortunately for Senator Norris, the grocery clerk was disqualified because of a technical error in filing his candidacy. After the primary, which Norris won handily, an election investigating committee headed by Senator Gerald P. Nye investigated the "Grocer George" plot, exposing it as an unethical attempt to unseat Senator Norris. "Grocer George" and Victor Seymour, manager of the Republican western congressional campaign were convicted of perjury before the Nye committee. The fact that a public utilities magnate, Walter W. Head, chairman of the board of directors of the Nebraska Power Company and president of the Boy Scouts of America, had helped to finance this attempt to defeat Norris gave the Nebraska Senator more ammunition, which he used extensively in his attack on the "power trust" and in his fight to push his Muscle Shoals plan to final victory.[41]

It is impossible to ascertain the extent to which the power question influenced the voters in the election of 1930. The overriding factor was the economic depression, but the power issue was certainly one of the factors in the election, and the power companies suffered a severe setback at the hands of the electorate.[42] The New York *Times* observed:

Tuesday [election day] was a bad day for the utilities. They had been under fire in a dozen states, and in almost every case electoral victory perched on the banners of their severest critics. . . .

One would have to search with a microscope to find a successful candidate for high office who defended the utilities, or even had a kind word to say for the regulatory process.[43]

According to the *Nation:*

The failure of the power trust to defeat a single one of the candidates

outcome of the election. The Chattanooga *News* predicted that Reece would be defeated. Chattanooga *News,* July 26, 1930, Knoxville *News-Sentinel,* July 27, 1930, Memphis *Press-Scimitar,* July 28, 1930, and Chattanooga *Times,* July 29, 1930.

41. Richard L. Neuberger and Stephan B. Kahn, *Integrity* (1937), 234–48.
42. New York *Times,* Nov. 30 (X), Dec. 7 (X), 1930.
43. *Ibid.,* Nov. 7, 1930.

who have been fighting for public control of the country's power resources was the most immediately satisfying result of the elections.[44]

On the eve of the short session of the lame duck Congress following the elections of 1930, Norris, fresh from another election triumph in Nebraska, said:

The results of the election have shown that the Power Trust which has been standing in the way of human progress has been overthrown and defeated in all sections of the country. It shows that the people are not only alive to the issue but they are going to demand through their public servants that this vital element [electrical energy] . . . must be placed within the reach of all classes of our people. . . .

There is no reason why Muscle Shoals legislation should be longer delayed, and if the Power Trust that has been standing in the way of governmental use of governmental property at Muscle Shoals persists in continuing its opposition to the proper development of this great national asset, the probabilities will be that public sentiment will demand the convening of the new Congress, which to a great extent has been elected on the power issue.[45]

As the lame duck Congress settled down to business, Richard V. Oulahan, a veteran political commentator, observed:

Outstanding in the first week's sittings of the reassembled Congress was the emphasis given to the Muscle Shoals project as a national issue. The undertaking has assumed an importance far beyond the benefits expected to come to [the Muscle Shoals area]. . . . It involves principles of the deepest political significance to the whole country—principles which may become a foremost issue in the Presidential struggle of 1932. . . .

Thus, to a considerable degree the political importance of the power question approximates the old-time contest over the regulation of the trusts and the common carriers. The Muscle Shoals controversy furnishes the means of testing the issue on a national scale.[46]

Despite the setback suffered by the administration in the elections of 1930, Republican leaders in the House indicated that they intended to fight the Norris bill to the end. Nevertheless, by mid-January the House conferees on the Muscle Shoals bills had conceded to the Senate on all important points, including governmental operation of the Muscle Shoals power facilities, save one—

44. Editorial in *Nation*, CXXXI (Nov. 19, 1930), 539.
45. New York *Times*, Nov. 30 (X), 1930.
46. *Ibid.*, Dec. 7 (X), 1930.

the construction and operation of transmission lines by the government. In return, Norris agreed to a private lease of the nitrate plants, but this, in reality, was no concession on his part for he repeatedly had made the offer before. Moreover, he had never been enthusiastic about the use of Muscle Shoals in connection with fertilizer; consequently, he was willing to give up his proposal for fertilizer research on the slightest pretext. By this time it had become apparent that the transmission line question was one of the most important issues involved, for without means of transporting the power a public authority operating Muscle Shoals could neither control consumer power rates nor establish an effective yardstick. House conferees were particularly critical of the fact that the Norris resolution would permit construction of transmission lines from a revolving fund without reference to Congress. Reece demonstrated that he could easily adjust his economic philosophy to government operation of the power plants, providing that the lessee had control of the bulk of the power.[47]

The transmission line issue caused the conference committee to become tightly deadlocked again, and in late January Norris walked out of the conference. Since he was confident that the newly elected Congress would adopt his Muscle Shoals measure intact, he made it plain that there would be no concessions on the transmission line issue. At this time Senator Heflin delivered a violent attack on the Norris provisions for transmission lines, protesting that construction of such lines would result in the transportation of part of Alabama's power to Tennessee and other states. He also declared that such action would be tantamount to confiscation of transmission lines already built by the Alabama Power Company. On the other hand, Alabama's junior Senator, Hugo L. Black, apparently had become convinced that Alabama would profit by passage of the Norris measure, for he conducted a short but unsuccessful filibuster aimed at forcing action on the Norris bill.[48]

The deadlocked Muscle Shoals conference committee was subjected to heavy pressure, much of it directed against the Norris

47. *Ibid.*, Nov. 11, 27, 30, Dec. 13, 1930, Jan. 7, 8, 9, 11, 1931.
48. *Ibid.*, Jan. 14, 28, 29, Feb. 18, 1931; *Cong. Rec.*, 71 Cong., 3 Sess., 3291–92.

bill. Besides the perennial Farm Bureau opposition, the Norris measure was violently denounced by various important economic organizations, including the National Association of Manufacturers, the United States Chamber of Commerce, and the Merchants' Association of New York. In late December, 1930, the Chamber of Commerce announced the results of a survey of American businessmen regarding Muscle Shoals in particular and public power in general. According to the figures released by that organization, businessmen voted overwhelmingly either to lease or sell Muscle Shoals and to turn the problem of control of waterpower development over to the states. In January, 1931, William S. Lee, president of the American Institute of Electrical Engineers, in an address at a convention of that organization, described the Norris Muscle Shoals bill as an example of "socialism." [49]

At the same time some pressure was directed against one of the declared purposes of the Reece bill—the production of fertilizer for agriculture and nitrates for national defense. Despite administration support of the Reece bill, Major General Samuel Hof, Chief of Ordnance, asserted to the War Department at this time that Muscle Shoals was no longer of any value to either national defense or agriculture. The United States Chamber of Commerce apparently opposed the Reece bill, as well as that of Norris, by declaring Muscle Shoals to be obsolete from the standpoint of fertilizer. Believing that the Reece bill was not intended to produce fertilizer, Judson King, director of the National Popular Government League, accused President Hoover of being a friend of the "fertilizer trust" as well as the "power trust." [50]

The Senate-House conference on Muscle Shoals remained deadlocked until after the middle of February. On February 17, 1931, in a speech in the House, Carroll Reece declared that the real issue involved was whether Congress should abandon the idea of utilizing the Muscle Shoals nitrate plants for national defense and cheap fertilizer in order to subject the power facilities there

49. New York *Times,* Dec. 11, 27, 1930, Jan. 13, 19, 27, 1931.
50. Memorandum by Major General Samuel Hof, Jan. 9, 1931, Judge Advocate General, National Archives; Washington *Star,* Jan. 17, 1931; Bulletin No. 43, National Popular Government League, Jan. 14, 1931.

to an ill-advised experiment in governmental generation and distribution of power. On the next day, Reece's fellow House conferees cut the ground from under him by reaching a compromise with the Senate conferees, including Norris, who had returned to the conference. The compromise measure contained all of the power provisions of the Norris resolution, including public operation of the power facilities and public-owned transmission lines. In return, the Senate conferees agreed to the private leasing of the nitrate plants, with the further concession that the lessee would be permitted to purchase from the government not only sufficient power for fertilizer purposes but an additional amount equal to 15 per cent of that used in fertilizer production which the lessee would have at his own disposal. Should the President fail to find a satisfactory lessee within a year, the entire Norris resolution would become law.[51]

The New York *Times* and some of the Tennessee newspapers saw in the compromise measure a complete victory for Norris. Among the Tennessee publications, satisfaction over the outcome was generally expressed. The Nashville *Banner* endorsed the provisions authorizing public production, distribution, and sale of power, but condemned the bill as a whole for including the Cove Creek site with the Muscle Shoals project. Unlike Senator McKellar, the *Banner* editor was not satisfied with the Alabama-Tennessee compensatory features of the Norris measure; he described them as a "mere gesture" which did not sufficiently compensate the state of Tennessee for the loss of Cove Creek.[52]

The conference bill was submitted to the House on February 20, with the assurance that

... the leasing language is so liberal as that the President will be able to effectuate a lease, thus consuming all of the power distributable at Muscle Shoals, leaving little, if any, power for sale, or sale and distribution. . . . They [the House conferees] believe further that if a lease is made, and if not quite all of the power is thus consumed, that a minor part for distribution will be taken by municipalities, willing

51. *Cong. Rec.*, 71 Cong., 3 Sess., 5219–25, 5549–53.

52. Chattanooga *News*, Feb. 19, 1931; Nashville *Banner*, Feb. 19, 1931; Knoxville *News-Sentinel*, Feb. 20, 1931; Memphis *Press-Scimitar*, Feb. 20, 1931; New York *Times*, Feb. 20, 1931.

to build their own transmission lines and thus prevent, by making wholly unnecessary, at least the construction of any transmission lines. . . .[53]

Carroll Reece sent the House a separate report in which he reluctantly endorsed the conference bill as "the best that could be obtained in view of the situation." He also expressed hope that practically all of the available power would be absorbed by the lessee so that government transmission lines would be rendered unnecessary.[54]

In the House a group of administration Republicans, chiefly from the East, made a determined effort to defeat the conference bill. They branded it as "socialistic" and "communistic." Representative Quin, who led a solid southern contingent in support of the bill, characterized the opposition as "predatory wealth," which he said was selfishly organized against the masses of the American people. He called on the Republican members of the farm bloc for aid and many responded to the call. As a result, the conference bill passed the House by a vote of 216 to 153.[55]

When the conference bill reached the Senate on February 23, Senator Hiram Bingham, a stanch New England conservative, warned that its acceptance would lead to the stifling of individual initiative throughout the country and lead to national inefficiency and "tyranny." On the other hand, Senators Hiram Johnson and Clarence Dill described the measure as a victory over the "power trust." Senators Black and William J. Harris had glowing praises for it because of its fertilizer provisions. They expressed confidence that it would greatly lower fertilizer prices.[56]

After a very brief debate, the Senate adopted the conference bill by a vote of 55 to 28. The bill was opposed by twenty-six Republicans and two Democrats, Millard E. Tydings of Maryland and William H. King of Utah. Senator Ransdell of Louisiana, a Democrat, was paired against it. It was a complete victory for the

53. *Completion of Dam No. 2, etc., at Muscle Shoals,* House Report 2747, 71 Cong., 3 Sess., 12.
54. *Ibid.,* 14.
55. *Cong. Rec.,* 71 Cong., 3 Sess., 5553–70. As usual, a majority of Democrats from the eastern cities supported the Norris group.
56. *Ibid.,* 5707–16.

coalition of southern Democrats and Progressive Republicans.[57]

The passage of the conference report represented a personal victory for George W. Norris. A conservative publication commented at the time:

As far as Congress is concerned, Senator Norris won a decisive victory in his fight for government operation at Muscle Shoals. The bill . . . passed by Congress has been called a compromise. . . . It would have been closer to the facts to call it the Norris proposal with comparatively slight modifications.[58]

Nevertheless, the victory was not yet complete; before that final goal could be achieved, the conference bill would have to hurdle the President's desk where, in view of President Hoover's known economic philosophy, it was likely to receive a cool reception.

57. *Ibid.*, 5716.
58. "The Muscle Shoals Bill," in *Outlook and Independent*, CLVII (March 4, 1931), 328.

XII

The End of the Controversy

IMMEDIATELY FOLLOWING THE PASSAGE of the Norris Muscle
Shoals bill by the Senate in April, 1930, there was much speculation as to whether President Hoover would veto the measure
should it be accepted by the House as was expected in most quarters. On the eve of Senate action on the bill, the opposition had
asserted that it would be futile to pass the measure because it
was certain to meet the same fate as the Muscle Shoals bill of 1928.
At that time, friends of the Norris measure demanded that Hoover
declare himself on the issue, but the President remained silent.
Less than a week after the Senate passed the Muscle Shoals bill
in 1930, George Fort Milton, editor of the Chattanooga *News*,
optimistically predicted that the President would sign the
measure. Milton, who had supported Hoover in 1928, based his
prediction on Hoover's Elizabethton campaign speech of October,
1928. In his letter endorsing the candidacy of Carroll Reece in
July, 1930, however, the President stated explicitly that he would
not approve the Senate Muscle Shoals bill. As the deadlock in the
Muscle Shoals conference continued, predictions of a Hoover
veto were used by administration forces in the House in an attempt to force the Senate conferees to accede to the House bill.[1]

Upon passage of the conference bill in February, 1931, friends
of the measure were active in seeking to persuade President
Hoover to approve it. A delegation of southern congressmen
visited Hoover at the White House to urge him to sign the bill,
and the Alabama state legislature adopted a resolution urging

1. New York *Times*, April 3, July 29, 1930, Jan. 9, 1931; Chattanooga *News*,
April 8, 1930; "Mr. Hoover Defies the Senate on Muscle Shoals," in *Literary
Digest*, CVI (Aug. 9, 1930), 8.

approval of the legislation. Governors of various southern states as well as the Democratic members of the New York legislature requested the President to assent to the bill. On the other hand, the National Association of Manufacturers made a last minute appeal for a veto.[2]

In a statement to the press on February 28, President Hoover seemed to hint that a veto was forthcoming. This statement was intended by Hoover to be a reply to the many Southerners who had urged him to approve the Muscle Shoals bill. The President said:

> To be against Senator Norris's bill appears to be cause for denunciation as being in league with the power companies. It appears also to be emerging as the test of views upon government operation and distribution of power and government manufacture of commodities. In other words, its adaptation to the use of the people of the Tennessee Valley and to the farmers generally is now enmeshed in an endeavor to create a national political issue. . . .
>
> This happens to be an engineering project and so far as its business merits and demerits are concerned is subject to the cold examination of engineering facts. I am having these facts exhaustively determined by the different departments of the government and will then be able to state my views upon the problem.[3]

On the next day, March 1, Norris ridiculed Hoover's efforts to shift Muscle Shoals from a political to a technical basis. The Nebraskan said:

> The President, being an engineer, it would seem he would have no difficulty in solving the problem and, therefore, it is rather surprising to learn from his statement that he is referring the matter to the heads of his departments, none of whom is an engineer.
>
> The great engineer is asking advice on an "engineering project" from those who are not engineers, and when those who are not engineers tell the engineer what to do with "an engineering project" the engineer will know whether to sign or veto the bill.
>
> It reminds me of the New England country justice who, at the close of a law suit, said he would take it under advisement for three days, at which time he would render judgment for the plaintiff.[4]

2. New York *Times*, Feb. 22, 27, March 1, 3, 1931.
3. *Ibid.*, March 1, 1931.
4. *Ibid.*, March 2, 1931.

On the following day Norris made President Hoover a proposal which must have sorely tempted the Chief Executive. The Nebraska Senator offered to resign from the Senate if Hoover would sign the Muscle Shoals bill and force the Republican leadership in Congress to accept the Norris lame duck bill. On the same day, Senator Clarence Dill of Washington, in a speech on the Senate floor, severely arraigned Hoover for his attitude on the power question in general. Dill declared that public regulation of private power had failed and should be replaced with a public yardstick.[5]

President Hoover, on March 3, 1931, vetoed the conference Muscle Shoals bill. Since Congress adjourned on March 4, the President had the alternative of letting the bill die by means of a pocket veto after the adjournment. Instead he chose to meet the issue forthrightly by frankly stating his opinion on the matter. In his veto message, Hoover stated numerous reasons why the bill had not received his approval. He cited estimates of the Corps of Engineers which purported to show that the measure would result in a net loss of $2,000,000 annually on power operations. These figures had been prepared by the Corps of Engineers to aid the President in his study of the bill. He declared also that the provisions of the bill authorizing a private lease of the nitrate plants were of "no genuine importance" because of the limitations placed on the lessee. Furthermore, he stated that nitrate plant no. 2 was obsolete and would be of no value as either a source of fertilizer or for national defense. The President criticized the provisions of the bill requiring that members of the governing board profess a belief in the feasibility and wisdom of the aims of the project as set forth in the conference bill. He expressed fear that this type of qualification would lead to appointments based on politics rather than on competence.[6]

Despite the great amount of emphasis placed on technical as-

5. *Ibid.*, March 3, 1931; *Cong. Rec.*, 71 Cong., 3 Sess., 6604–5.

6. President of the United States, *Veto Message Relating to Disposition of Muscle Shoals*, Senate Doc. 321, 71 Cong., 3 Sess. (1931), 1–8. The President's veto message undoubtedly left the impression that the profession-of-faith qualification in the Muscle Shoals bill was an original product of the Norris public power group. In reality, it first appeared in the Morin bill of 1928 and was proposed by a group of moderately conservative members of the House Military Committee.

pects, the President's veto message clearly revealed that his principal reason for rejecting the bill was the underlying political and economic philosophy involved. He said:

This bill raises one of the most important issues confronting our people. That is squarely the issue of Federal Government ownership and operation of power and manufacturing business not as a minor by-product but as a major purpose. Involved in this question is the agitation against the conduct of the power industry [the Federal Trade Commission investigation]. The power problem is not to be solved by the Federal Government going into the power business. . . . The remedy for abuses in the conduct of that industry lies in regulation. . . . I hesitate to contemplate the future of our institutions, of our government, and of our country if the preoccupation of its officials is to be no longer the promotion of justice and equal opportunity but is to be devoted to barter in the markets. That is not liberalism, it is degeneration.[7]

The President also professed to see in the bill a violation of state rights in that it would allegedly deprive the states of authority to regulate the distribution and sale of power, as well as sources of tax revenue. He insisted that the development of the Tennessee Valley could only be accomplished by the people of the valley themselves, and, as a means of implementing a practical application of this theory, he recommended that the states of Alabama and Tennessee be permitted to establish a joint commission with "full authority to lease the Muscle Shoals properties in the interest of the local community and agriculture generally." He also recommended that the Corps of Engineers and the farm organizations have representation on the proposed commission. In suggesting the Alabama-Tennessee commission, Hoover implied that Congress, through its failure to bring an end to the Muscle Shoals controversy, had proved itself incompetent to handle the problem. He also implied that the existence of rivalry between private groups seeking control of Muscle Shoals as well as the presence of a strong public power sentiment in Congress constituted evidence of congressional ineptness.[8]

Later, the same day, Senate supporters of the Muscle Shoals

7. *Ibid.*, 6.
8. *Ibid.*, 7–8.

bill attempted to pass the measure over the President's veto. The
vote to pass the bill was 49 to 34, less than the necessary two-
thirds majority. There was no attempt in the House to override
the veto. In the Senate debate on the veto, the Norris group
demonstrated much bitterness toward Hoover. Senator Black accused the President of having deliberately misled the people of
the Tennessee Valley in his Elizabethton campaign speech of
1928 in which, the Alabama Senator asserted, Hoover promised to
support governmental operation of Muscle Shoals. According to
Black, thousands of people in that area voted for Hoover on the
basis of that promise. Black criticized Hoover's statement that
nitrate plant no. 2 was obsolete and asked why, if this were true,
the President thought the proposed Alabama-Tennessee commission could lease an obsolete plant. He scoffed at the idea of
such a commission, declaring it to be merely an attempt by the
power companies to delay action on Muscle Shoals. The Alabama
Senator accused the Corps of Engineers of mixing politics with
mathematics in its report to the President on the Muscle Shoals
bill.[9] He asked:

Now, which Army engineer will we get [for the proposed Alabama-
Tennessee Muscle Shoals commission]? Will we get the Army engineer
who reported that power at Muscle Shoals cost 9 mills or will we get
the engineer who reported that power at Muscle Shoals cost 1.36
mills?[10]

9. *Cong. Rec.*, 71 Cong., 3 Sess., 7070-75.
10. *Ibid.*, 7075. Dr. John Bauer, formerly consultant to the St. Lawrence Power
Development Commission, also sharply criticized the estimates of the Corps of
Engineers used by Hoover to support his contention that public operation of
Muscle Shoals would be a losing proposition. According to Dr. Bauer, the
engineers' figures contained the following serious "errors": the allocation of
$5,000,000 to navigation was $11,000,000 short; the allocation of $40,000,000
to transmission lines was $34,000,000 too large; the interest estimates were five
times too high; the allocation to amortization was excessive by 50 per cent; and
the estimated production of primary power was short by 50 per cent. In addition, Dr. Bauer averred that there was absolutely no justification for Hoover's
statement that the secondary power at Muscle Shoals had no practical value.
Dr. Bauer estimated the cost of power production at Muscle Shoals to be 3.75
mills per kilowatt hour as compared to 9 mills in the Hoover veto message, and
he also estimated that the project would realize, on power operations, a profit
of $3,500,000 annually. Dr. John Bauer, "Muscle Shoals and the President's
Veto," in *National Municipal Review*, XX (April, 1931), 231-4.

Senator Norris accused President Hoover of deliberately misrepresenting the facts of the Muscle Shoals problem in his veto message, and he described Hoover's disapproval of the Muscle Shoals bill as a great victory for the "power trust." He was highly provoked by the President's statement that the bill would deprive the states of Alabama and Tennessee of tax revenue because this section of the veto message was not accompanied by any reference to the provisions in the measure for compensating these states. The Nebraska Senator referred to the President's rejection of the Muscle Shoals bill as "his cruel, his unjust, his unfair, his unmerciful veto." [11]

According to the conservative *Review of Reviews*, the nation's leading newspapers outside the South, and many leading publications in the South, "in general" endorsed the Hoover veto.[12] A closer examination reveals that there was considerable opposition to the veto among the nation's large dailies.[13] In the pro-Hoover press, the point stressed most often by the editors was that the President had struck a mighty blow for fundamental American economic principles by keeping the government out of business. Most of these editors felt that Hoover had proved beyond a doubt that public operation of Muscle Shoals was economically unsound, and this conclusion was doubly reinforced by the fact that Hoover was an engineer of high reputation. In addition, they lauded the President's recommendation for the establishment of an Alabama-Tennessee commission as being wise and sound, and many of them predicted that Muscle Shoals would be an issue in the presidential campaign in 1932.

The opposing editors agreed with their pro-Hoover colleagues

11. *Cong. Rec.*, 71 Cong., 3 Sess., 7085–89.

12. "The Unsolved Problem of Muscle Shoals," in *Review of Reviews*, LXXXIII (April, 1931), 53.

13. "Muscle Shoals to Plague the 1932 Campaign," in *Literary Digest*, CVIII (March 14, 1931), 7. In addition some newspapers were examined individually, including the Hartford *Courant*, March 4, 1931; Milwaukee *Journal*, March 4, 1931; New York *Herald-Tribune*, March 4, 1931; New York *World-Telegram*, March 4, 1931; Sacramento *Union*, March 4, 1931; Chicago *Daily News*, March 5, 1931; Philadelphia *Record*, March 5, 1931; *Rocky Mountain News*, March 5, 1931; Spokane *Spokesman-Review*, March 5, 1931; St. Louis *Post-Dispatch*, March 5, 29, 1931; Toledo *News-Bee*, March 5, 1931; Washington *Post*, March 5, 1931; Portland *Oregonian*, March 6, 1931.

on only one point—that Muscle Shoals would be a campaign issue in 1932. Otherwise, those editors who criticized the veto asserted that Hoover had broken his Elizabethton campaign promise and that the President's desire to continue public regulation as the sole means of controlling power rates was unreasonable in view of the revelations of the Federal Trade Commission, which had raised serious questions regarding the regulatory system. Hoover was criticized for allegedly assuming a contradictory position on fertilizer, the editors' contention being that his statement in his veto message condemning Muscle Shoals as a fertilizer project conflicted with his first message to Congress in which he recommended that Muscle Shoals be devoted to agriculture. The most serious charge raised by these editors against the veto message was that the President's figures which showed that public operation of Muscle Shoals would be unprofitable were unreliable and questionable. With respect to this subject, the Baltimore *Sun* stated:

We think some risk of loss might be taken, though we remain unconvinced that there would be loss, as compared with other offers. For on Mr. Hoover's detailed figures on the financial aspects of the proposed Muscle Shoals legislation one must reserve judgment. If the President proves no sounder on these figures than he has been on many others—for example his statistics when he defended the signing of the Smoot-Hawley tariff law—a reasonable reserve will have been abundantly warranted.[14]

The President, in his veto message, presented a solution for the Muscle Shoals problem by proposing an Alabama-Tennessee commission. But Congress already had established a definite policy for Muscle Shoals by providing for public operation in the vetoed Muscle Shoals bills of 1928 and 1931. Although these bills did not provide for the comprehensive multiple-purpose development of the Tennessee River basin that Norris desired, they did include the important Cove Creek reservoir site. Through control of Cove Creek and Muscle Shoals, the keys to the utilization of the waters of the river, a federal authority would be able to con-

14. Baltimore *Sun*, March 4, 1931, quoted in *Cong. Rec.*, 71 Cong., 3 Sess., 7318.

trol, if not design, the pattern of further development of the river. In reality, this congressional policy had its origin in late 1927 when Southerners in Congress as a whole began to veer toward the Norris idea, and it took definite form when the Republican members of the farm bloc in the House joined hands with the Southerners. By 1930 the congressional policy of public operation had gained additional support because of the economic depression and because of the investigations by the Caraway lobby committee and the Federal Trade Commission.

In the Muscle Shoals area, the disappointment over the veto was particularly keen, and the President's plan for an Alabama-Tennessee commission was not well received. There was speculation as to whether the plan necessarily excluded state operation of the project or whether it was merely another administration plan to transfer the Muscle Shoals properties to private capital. There also was considerable discussion as to the possibility of another Ford offer for Muscle Shoals, but Ford soon put a stop to this talk by endorsing the Hoover veto and declaring that "Muscle Shoals should be, and eventually will be, the property of privately owned electrical companies." [15]

President Hoover and the governors of Alabama and Tennessee established a joint Muscle Shoals Commission in July, 1931. The President chose as his appointees Edward A. O'Neal, formerly president of the Alabama Farm Bureau and at the time president of the Farm Bureau's national organization, and two army officers, Colonel Joseph I. McMullen of the Judge Advocate General's office and Colonel Harley B. Ferguson, Corps of Engineers. The Governor of Alabama, Benjamin M. Miller, appointed W. F. McFarland of Florence, J. N. Duncun of Auburn, and Sam F. Hobbs of Selma; the Governor of Tennessee, Henry H. Horton, appointed Mercer Reynolds of Chattanooga, Vance J. Alexander of Nashville, and W. A. Caldwell of Jackson. All of the appointees of the two governors were either businessmen or members of the legal profession. Hobbs was named permanent chairman. The function of the commission was to formulate, in conformity with the

15. New York *Times,* March 15, 1931.

recommendations in the President's veto message, a plan for the disposal of Muscle Shoals which would be presented to the President and Congress.[16]

As soon as the organization of the new commission was complete, Secretary of War Hurley held a conference with it at which he stated that the Muscle Shoals plants were obsolete in so far as the production of nitrates for defense was concerned, but he recommended that the commission devise a plan to utilize these plants for the benefit of agriculture. It was not made clear to the public whether Hurley explicitly advised the use of the plants for the production of agricultural nitrates, but the press account of the conference left the implication that the Secretary was referring to nitrates when he asked the commission to find a way to use the plants for the benefit of agriculture. Hurley's approach to the subject seemed to be contradictory in nature since the same nitrates used for fertilizer were also used in munitions.[17]

When the commission, acting on Hurley's advice, adopted as one of its recommendations the lease of the Muscle Shoals project for the production of fertilizer, W. A. Caldwell, one of the Tennessee representatives on the commission, resigned. Caldwell declared that he had been convinced that the project was obsolete for the purpose of producing fertilizer and that he did not desire to be a party to the leasing of Muscle Shoals for that alleged purpose. Caldwell also objected to the commission's failure to consider the possibility of multiple-purpose development of the Tennessee River with the main object being the production and

16. *Ibid.*, July 15, 1931. Judson King, Director of the National Popular Government League, protested that all nine appointees were known to be opposed to public operation of Muscle Shoals, eight of them having been active in this opposition. Bulletin 150, National Popular Government League, July 22, 1931, quoted in Joseph S. Ransmeier, *The Tennessee Valley Authority* (1942), 53*n*.

Since President Hoover stated in his veto message that the proposed Alabama-Tennessee Muscle Shoals commission should be vested with full authority to lease the Muscle Shoals project, it appears that he was suggesting immediate congressional action on that matter. Congress adjourned on the following day, March 4, without further consideration of the problem. Therefore, when the commission was set up, it possessed no authority actually to dispose of the Muscle Shoals properties.

17. New York *Times*, July 17, 26, 1931.

distribution of cheap electric power to rural and urban consumers in the Tennessee Valley.[18]

In September, the Department of Agriculture received a special request from the commission to examine the possibility of utilizing Muscle Shoals in the production of phosphoric acid as a fertilizer ingredient. Dr. Henry C. Knight, Chief of the Bureau of Chemistry and Soils, promised to look into the matter, but he warned that Muscle Shoals was antiquated as far as nitrogen production was concerned.[19]

The commission invited some 130 large corporations to submit bids for Muscle Shoals. Although the commission had no authority to lease the properties, it felt offers submitted would be helpful in formulating a plan for Congress. By September 1, the deadline for submission of bids, seven proposals were received, of which five were from power and chemical firms. Two of the bidders were the Alabama Power Company and the Tennessee Electric Power Company.[20]

A majority of the members of the Hoover Muscle Shoals Commission desired to include Cove Creek in the Muscle Shoals project, but Mercer Reynolds, one of the Tennessee representatives on the commission, objected strenuously and insisted that this was merely a scheme to deprive Tennessee of her water power for the benefit of the Muscle Shoals area. After Congressman Oscar B. Lovette, J. Will Taylor, and Sam D. McReynolds, of the first three congressional districts of Tennessee, respectively, urged the commission to include Cove Creek in the project, Reynolds relented and agreed to support the idea.[21]

President Hoover made public the report of the Muscle Shoals Commission on November 19, 1931. In this report, the commission reached two general conclusions: that it was "economically feasible and desirable" to utilize the Muscle Shoals properties primarily for the production of concentrated fertilizer, or fertilizer ingredients, and secondarily for fertilizer research and the manu-

18. *Ibid.*, Aug. 23, 1931; Stephen Raushenbush, *The Power Fight* (1932), 201.

19. Knight to Arthur M. Hyde, Sept. 22, 1931, Correspondence of the Secretary of Agriculture, Muscle Shoals, National Archives.

20. New York *Times*, Aug. 13, 23, Sept. 2, 1931.

21. *Ibid.*, Aug. 3, 23, Oct. 31, 1931.

facture of chemicals; that public interest would best be served by
a lease of the project to private operation. The commission recommended that Congress enact legislation empowering the President to lease the properties under the following general conditions: that a minimum amount of fertilizer production by the
lessee be stipulated, any increases to depend on market demands;
that the fertilizer produced be sold to farmers under conditions of
equitable distribution and reasonable profits; that those parts of
the nitrate plants found to be serviceable be used in the production of fertilizer; and that the power necessary for the manufacture
of fertilizer and chemicals be guaranteed to the lessee. It recommended that surplus power be sold at the switchboard with public agencies and chemical companies having equal preference in
buying it. The commission advised that the lessee be charged a
fair rental which should be applied to the amortization of the
construction costs of a Cove Creek dam and to help defray the
expenses of the fertilizer program. The commission reported that
none of the bids received were sufficiently satisfactory to warrant
endorsement by the commission.[22]

The Muscle Shoals Commission also reported that at its request
Colonel Max C. Tyler, Corps of Engineers, had conducted a survey to determine the feasibility of governmental operation of
Muscle Shoals for the production and distribution of power. The
Tyler report showed that such a program would result in an annual loss of $2,644,000. In arriving at this estimate, Colonel Tyler
charged 100 per cent of the proposed Cove Creek investment to
power operations, despite the great flood control and navigational
benefits that would result from the construction of a dam there.
The Tyler report was also based on an assumption that there
would be a poor market for power in the Tennessee Valley area.[23]

The commission's specific conclusions and recommendations
concerning fertilizer production implied that nitrate plant no. 2
would be used for the production of nitrates. It developed further

22. Muscle Shoals Commission, *Muscle Shoals: A Plan for the Use of the
United States Properties on the Tennessee River by Private Industry for "the
Manufacture of Fertilizers and Other Useful Products"* (1931), 16–20.
23. *Ibid.*, 61–94.

in the report that the commission had depended solely on the Department of Agriculture experts for advice on fertilizer, and a report by Dr. P. E. Howard of that department was included in the commission's published brochure. Here, Dr. Howard reiterated the Agriculture Department's stand against the use of nitrate plant no. 2 because of alleged obsolescence of the cyanamid process. Instead, he recommended that the project be employed in the production of phosphoric acid for fertilizer. The Howard report, which by its context in the commission's brochure appeared to have the sanction of that body, left the impression that the commission contemplated the abandonment of plans for nitrate production at Muscle Shoals altogether.[24] The document that reached Congress as the official report of the commission contained neither the Howard report nor the accompanying comments which had appeared in the original brochure.[25]

Senator Norris and his Progressive colleagues in the Senate delegated to Judson King the task of replying to the Hoover commission. In response, King prepared a counter report in which he questioned the honesty and integrity of everyone connected with the commission's report, the White House not being spared. He charged that the report constituted an attempt by President Hoover, in cooperation with the Farm Bureau and the "power trust," to keep alive a fiction of cheap fertilizer in order to deceive the farmers on the Muscle Shoals issue and to justify the granting of the project to the special interests.

24. *Ibid.*, 22–43. *Electrical World* interpreted the report of the Muscle Shoals Commission to mean that the commission had concluded that as far as fertilizer was concerned Muscle Shoals should be used for the production of phosphoric acid rather than nitrates. The editor of this publication, which generally reflected the viewpoint of the electrical power industry, was pleased with the report because he felt that at last the fertilizer element which had been confusing the Muscle Shoals issue for so long apparently was being removed by the commission. "Muscle Shoals Rededicated to Fertilizer and Power Production," in *Electrical World*, XCIX (Jan. 23, 1932), 184.

Secretary of Agriculture Arthur M. Hyde informed Samuel S. Wyer in December, 1931, that Dr. Howard's report to the Muscle Shoals Commission represented the policy of the Department of Agriculture. Hyde's letter apparently was not made public. Hyde to Wyer, Dec. 1, 1931, Correspondence of the Secretary of Agriculture, Muscle Shoals, National Archives.

25. Muscle Shoals Commission, *Report of Muscle Shoals Commission*, Senate Doc. 21, 72 Cong., 1 Sess. (1932).

King noted the apparent conflict in the commission's report in regard to nitrate production at Muscle Shoals and charged it to hypocrisy. He pointed out that the commission, while adopting the report of Colonel Tyler, had ignored the comprehensive report on the Tennessee River made by the Corps of Engineers in 1930 which had indicated that either public or private development of that stream would be a tremendously profitable venture. The Popular Government League director ridiculed the Tyler report and contended that it perverted engineering facts. He pointed out that Tyler had not allocated any of the proposed investment at Cove Creek to navigation and flood control. King also charged that Tyler, while serving as chief engineer for the Federal Power Commission, had helped power companies to evade the regulations imposed by the Federal Water Power Act. King's analysis of the commission report was publicly endorsed by Norris.[26]

The report of the Hoover commission appeared to represent a victory for the chemical interests in that it contemplated the use of Muscle Shoals for chemical production rather than as a source of power for distribution to the public. Nevertheless, the power industry endorsed the report. The New York *Times* attributed this changed attitude on the part of the power companies to their apparent readiness to accept any plan that would preclude competition from the federal government. Since the commission's plan apparently provided for the development of industry in North Alabama, it was popular with a great many people there. According to the Birmingham *News,* no Muscle Shoals proposal ever had been so "unanimously" and "enthusiastically" supported by all economic groups in Alabama as the Hoover commission plan.[27]

The Seventy-second Congress, which assembled for its first session in December, 1931, was even less friendly to Hoover than the previous Congress which had passed the Norris Muscle Shoals bill. Supporters of public operation of Muscle Shoals had gained

26. Richard L. Neuberger and Stephan B. Kahn, *Integrity* (1937), 223. King's analysis of the Hoover commission's report was reprinted in *Cong. Rec.,* 72 Cong., 1 Sess., 3490–96.

27. New York *Times,* Feb. 7, 1932; Birmingham *News,* Jan. 24, 1932, quoted in *Cong. Rec.,* 72 Cong., 1 Sess., 9575.

additional strength as a result of the elections of 1930. Thus it seemed unlikely that the report of the Hoover commission on Muscle Shoals would be received favorably by the new Congress. Nevertheless, President Hoover submitted the report of the commission to Congress on December 16, 1931, without further recommendations. In January, 1932, the House Military Committee held hearings on two Muscle Shoals bills, a bill by Representative Edward B. Almon of Alabama which contained the recommendations of the Hoover commission and a bill by Representative W. Frank James of Michigan which was identical to the Muscle Shoals measure vetoed by President Hoover. A large delegation of Alabama congressmen and political leaders testified in behalf of the Hoover commission plan, stressing the importance of the production of cheap fertilizer at nitrate plant no. 2. On the other hand, the two Republican congressmen from Tennessee, Oscar B. Lovette and J. Will Taylor, appeared in behalf of the James bill; they declared that the people of Tennessee were "almost unanimous" in favor of the Norris plan for Muscle Shoals.[28]

Several members of the Hoover Muscle Shoals Commission were called before the Military Committee to testify regarding the commission's report on Muscle Shoals. The committee was particularly anxious to question these witnesses with respect to the apparent conflict in the fertilizer features of the Muscle Shoals Commission's report. The committee found that all of the members of the commission except two, Hobbs and McFarland of Alabama, interpreted the commission's report as recommending the abandonment of plans for nitrogen production at Muscle Shoals in favor of the manufacture of phosphoric acid. McFarland and Hobbs insisted that the report recommended the manufacture of nitrates at nitrate plant no. 2 for fertilizer. The House committee discovered that the commission had signed only the specific conclusions and recommendations, which implied the production of nitrates, and that Colonel McMullen, the President's chief representative on the commission, had later attached the other ma-

28. *Muscle Shoals*, Hearings, U. S. House of Representatives, 72 Cong., 1 Sess. (1932), 1–3, 136, 140–42, 461–77.

terials, some of it written in language suggesting it to be the opinion of the commission.

The attached material, which included a preface, various comments, and the report of the Department of Agriculture, implied that no nitrates should be produced at Muscle Shoals. One member of the commission stated that Colonel McMullen had appended the materials with the knowledge and consent of the whole commission; others denied that such was the case. Despite the confusion as to the meaning of the report, all commission members remained loyal to it.[29]

The examination of the Hoover commission members by the Military Committee revealed definitely that the power companies involved in the Muscle Shoals controversy were pleased with the commission's report, even though it apparently meant victory for the chemical industry, because it proposed to eliminate the prospect of governmental competition. The passage of the Norris bills of 1928 and 1930, together with a growing public distrust of private power companies, had greatly frightened the power industry. The members of the commission failed to explain why the Corps of Engineers report of 1930 on the Tennessee River had been ignored. Colonel Tyler, who, the committee found, had supplied the engineering data for both the Hoover veto message and the Hoover commission's report, admitted that he had derived the data from the general inspection of a map.[30]

Some members of the House Military Committee had been highly provoked by a newspaper story which appeared in September, 1931, stating that the Hoover commission had discovered that the President had authority under either the National Defense Act or the Federal Water Power Act to lease Muscle Shoals without

29. *Ibid.*, 4–5, 98, 108, 133, 177–81, 206–7, 234–35, 250–57, 266, 322. The National Fertilizer Association opposed the use of Muscle Shoals for the manufacture of either nitrates or phosphoric acid. *Ibid.*, 172–73; Charles J. Brand to George W. Norris, April 25, 1932, Norris Papers.

30. *Muscle Shoals*, House Hearings, 72 Cong., 1 Sess., Part 1, 154-55, 248, 344–65, 507–8. At these hearings, the engineering data used by President Hoover in his veto message were vigorously assailed by Colonel J. Edward Cassidy, a construction engineer who aided in the building of Wilson Dam. According to Colonel Cassidy, Hoover's estimates of the cost of producing power at the Muscle Shoals project were much too high. *Ibid.*, 621.

reference to Congress. It appeared that the commission was seriously considering the possibility of disposing of the project in this
manner. One of the principal objects of the committee in interrogating the members of the Hoover commission was to learn more
of this matter. The committee found that the commission members had discussed the possibility of taking such action, but
Colonel McMullen, who had initiated this movement, denied that
such a plan was ever seriously considered and acknowledged the
undisputed right of Congress to solve the Muscle Shoals problem.
The basis for the commission's discussion of this possible alternative was Colonel McMullen's theory that the Muscle Shoals project was merely war surplus material and could be disposed of as
such by the President under the National Defense Act. Moreover,
he had concluded that the President had the authority to lease
Wilson Dam to a private power company just as he was empowered by the Federal Water Power Act to lease any other
water-power site which was under federal control.

This consideration of the possibility of leasing Muscle Shoals
without the permission of Congress apparently was motivated by
some unidentified chemical firms which had notified McMullen
that they would like to bid for Muscle Shoals but were deterred
from doing so because of fear of becoming embroiled in politics
and being interrogated by congressional committees. Thereupon,
Colonel McMullen began to discuss the possibilities of removing
the problem from Congress. He had chosen a very inappropriate
time to propose such a maneuver because of the growing unpopu-
larity of the Hoover administration and because relations between
Hoover and Congress already were strained as a result of congressional criticism of the way in which the President was handling the problem of the economic depression.[31]

The House Military Committee purportedly attempted to compromise between the Norris and the Hoover commission plans.
The committee reported a bill, which had been drafted by a sub-

31. *Ibid.*, 163; New York *Times*, Sept. 20 (II), Dec. 7, 13 (IX), 1931;
"Smoke Screen over Muscle Shoals," in *New Republic*, LXVIII (Oct. 21, 1931),
249; "Three Honest to Goodness Bidders Startle Muscle Shoals Board," in
Business Week, No. 109 (Sept. 30, 1931), 20.

committee headed by Representative Lister Hill of Alabama, providing for governmental operation of the Muscle Shoals power plants and a private lease of the nitrate plants. Authority for leasing the latter would be delegated to a Muscle Shoals Board composed of three men appointed by the President with the advice and consent of the Senate. Preference in selecting a lessee would be given to nonprofit organizations, the implication being that the nitrate plants might be leased to the Farm Bureau or some other farm organization. The lessee would be required to produce fertilizer containing 10,000 tons of nitrates and 15,000 tons of phosphoric acid annually, with periodic increases according to market demands, up to the capacity of the plants. As usual the lessee would be limited to a profit of 8 per cent on fertilizer operations, and all fertilizer would be sold directly to farmers or their agents.

The Muscle Shoals Board, which would operate the power plants, would furnish the lessee with adequate power for fertilizer operations. Instead of constructing transmission lines, the Muscle Shoals Board would sell the surplus power at the switchboard, preference to be granted to public agencies and chemical companies. In fact, the Hill bill conformed closely to the recommendations of the Hoover commission in both its power and fertilizer features except for public operation of the power plants and a provision for the manufacture of nitrates for fertilizer. These exceptions brought administration disapproval of the bill.[32]

The Hill bill was a compromise in name only. Since its proposed governmental operation features would give the federal government no authority beyond the switchboard, little of the essence of the Norris plan was embodied in the measure. The bill was, in reality, the plan set forth by the Hoover commission with the interpretation that the commission had recommended the production of nitrates at Muscle Shoals.

32. *Leasing of Muscle Shoals Properties*, House Report 1005, 72 Cong., 1 Sess. (1932), 1–8; Patrick J. Hurley to Charles L. McNary, May 11, 1932, Judge Advocate General, National Archives. The report of the Hoover commission was opposed by Percy Quin of Mississippi, who was the new chairman of the Military Committee. But Quin, who was fighting for a share of cheap Muscle Shoals power for Mississippi, died suddenly during the hearings; thus Quin's death made it less difficult for Hill to obtain a favorable report on his bill. *Cong. Rec.*, 72 Cong., 1 Sess., 4404.

The House debate on the Hill bill began on May 4, 1932. Southern Democrats were practically unanimous in supporting the measure, the Southerners affirming that its acceptance would result in greatly reduced fertilizer prices. Despite the fact that the Hill bill proposed to subordinate Cove Creek to Muscle Shoals, the entire Tennessee congressional delegation supported it. Since that delegation remained silent during the debate, its motives were not revealed, but the fact that the bill did not contemplate construction of a dam at Cove Creek until the Muscle Shoals Board deemed it necessary for expanding operations at Muscle Shoals, might have been the motivating factor. On the other hand, the growing acuteness of the economic depression had stimulated a growing sentiment in Tennessee for construction of the Cove Creek dam under any terms in order to bring federal money to the state.

The House debate on the Hill bill was dominated by stanch administration Republicans from the East who bitterly denounced the measure because of its provisions for federal control of the power plants and production of nitrates. Representative Harry C. Ransley of Pennsylvania, who led the administration forces, described the bill as "un-American" and declared that its acceptance would take the country "a long stride toward socialism." The southern Democrats, as usual, attempted to avoid a clash on economic principles, substituting instead a plea for expediency and a claim that Muscle Shoals was above and beyond common economic philosophies. Midwestern Republicans gave the Southerners lukewarm support.[33]

Perhaps some of the Southerners, in supporting the Hill bill, followed the policy adopted by Representative LaGuardia. The New York Congressman and some of his liberal colleagues in the House, though they opposed the Hill bill, voted for it in order to get it before the Senate where the Norris bill would be substituted for the Hill measure. Some of LaGuardia's colleagues were criticized severely by constituents who preferred the Norris plan, the belief being that these congressmen had supported the Hill

33. *Cong. Rec.*, 72 Cong., 1 Sess., 9568–9608, 9647–70.

bill in principle. LaGuardia requested Norris to clarify the issue and put the congressmen back in the good graces of their displeased constituents. Norris complied by writing a letter to one of these congressmen, Representative Ralph Horr of Washington, in which the Nebraska Senator explained the strategy which had been employed by LaGuardia and the other House supporters of public power. Norris intended that his letter to Horr should be made public in the constituencies of all of those congressmen who were faced with political trouble because of their support of the LaGuardia strategy.[34]

In the voting on the Hill bill, the farm bloc Republicans joined the Southerners with the result that the measure was passed by a vote of 183 to 132.[35]

In the Senate early in this session, Norris reintroduced his joint Muscle Shoals resolution which had passed the Senate in 1930. Only brief hearings were held on the measure. The Agriculture Committee heard representatives of Alabama coal and Tennessee phosphate interests testify in behalf of the Hoover commission plan. The coal interests were opposed to the manufacture of nitrates at Muscle Shoals. Their hope was that under the Hoover commission plan, which they interpreted as a condemnation of nitrate production at Muscle Shoals, the use of that project as a place to mix commercial fertilizers would stimulate an expansion of the coke-oven by-product industry in the Alabama coal regions. In short, they hoped to supply Muscle Shoals with nitrates. The Tennessee group hoped Muscle Shoals could be used exclusively for the manufacture of phosphoric acid in order to provide a market for Tennessee phosphates.[36]

The Senate Agriculture Committee reported the Norris resolution favorably, but it was not considered further by the Senate.[37] This measure, along with the Hill bill, died upon the adjournment of Congress in July, 1932. Norris does not appear to have

34. LaGuardia to Norris, June 13, 1932; Norris to Horr, June 27, 1932; and Horr to Norris, June 29, 1932, Norris Papers.

35. *Cong. Rec.*, 72 Cong., 1 Sess., 9670.

36. *To Create Muscle Shoals Corporation of the United States*, Hearings, U. S. Senate, 72 Cong., 1 Sess. (1932), 50, 67–106.

37. *Cong. Rec.*, 72 Cong., 1 Sess., 6884.

made any great effort to obtain action on his bill; in all probability, he was awaiting the outcome of the election of 1932.

There was little doubt, in the early summer of 1932, that the power issue would be even more important in the coming presidential campaign than it had been in the elections of 1930. The power industry had continued to be the object of unfavorable publicity as a result of the Federal Trade Commission investigation, which was still in progress. During 1931 and the first half of 1932 there were more disclosures that were embarrassing to the public utilities business. The Trade Commission was forced to seek additional authority from Congress as a result of resistance to the investigation by some power companies. The failure of these companies to co-operate with the commission increased public skepticism as to the ethics of the power industry. On the eve of the 1932 presidential campaign, Senator Norris charged that President Hoover was attempting to curb the investigation of the Trade Commission.[38]

The failure of the Hoover administration to deal effectively or tactfully with the power problem had greatly intensified the issue. The New River case of 1930 had opened the way for accusations that the administration was bent on sabotaging the Federal Water Power Act. In addition, in 1931 the President became engaged in a quarrel with Congress over the Federal Power Commission which reacted unfavorably toward the administration. This episode grew out of the passage of a bill by Congress in 1930 which created a new Federal Power Commission. The original Federal Power Commission, which had been created by the Federal Water Power Act of 1920, was composed of the secretaries of War, Agriculture, and Interior. By 1930 many members of Congress had become dissatisfied with the commission because of its failure to enforce adequately the provisions of the Water Power Act. Consequently, in June, 1930, Congress passed a bill, sponsored by

38. New York *Times*, May 31, Dec. 14, 1931, June 15, 16, 18, July 2, 15, 1932. Norris did not document the charge that Hoover was attempting to stop the Trade Commission's investigation. In late November, 1929, Morris L. Cooke, a consulting engineer and champion of public power, informed Norris that he had received confidential information that Hoover was going to attempt to stop the investigation. Cooke to Norris, Nov. 28, 1929, Norris Papers.

Senator James Couzens of Michigan, which replaced the original
commission with a new independent commission of five full-time
members. Some of the President's appointees to the new governmental body had been closely identified with the electric power
industry, giving rise to the charge that the Power Commission
would be dominated by the "power trust." Soon after Hoover's
appointees were confirmed by the Senate, the new commission
dismissed two key employees of the old commission, Charles A.
Russell and William V. King, solicitor and accountant, respectively. Some members of Congress, particularly Senator Thomas J.
Walsh, charged that Russell and King had been dismissed because they had offended power interests by attempting to enforce
the water-power law.

Thereupon, the Senate, led by Senator Walsh, recalled the
chairman of the Power Commission, Otis Smith, early in 1931,
but Hoover refused to acknowledge the Senate's action, the
President's assertion being that presidential appointees were not
subject to recall after they had been confirmed. The fight was
carried to the courts, and in May, 1932, the United States Supreme Court sustained the President's point of view. It was indeed
a hollow victory because this quarrel with Congress left an impression with the public that Hoover's primary concern in the
episode was the protection of the interests of the power companies.[39]

Increasingly, Muscle Shoals had become the focal point of the
power issue, and by 1932 that much-publicized place on the
Tennessee River symbolized the struggle between private and
public power exponents. Indeed, the New York *Times,* in early
1931, declared that Muscle Shoals had long been the principal
bone of contention between these two forces:

Politically, Muscle Shoals long ago became a symbol . . . [of the]
extreme progressives. . . . Their end is not the best utilization of a war
heritage [Muscle Shoals itself], but government ownership of electric
utilities generally. In their hands Muscle Shoals is only a fulcrum, the

39. New York *Times,* May 13, June 10, 25, 1930, Jan. 10, 11, 24, 28, Feb. 5, 6,
Dec. 6, 1931, May 3, 1932; Raushenbush, *The Power Fight,* 159–66; Thomas J.
Walsh to Otis Smith, Dec. 23, 1930, Norris Papers.

"Power Trust" a lever. . . . It is well to have this understood, for without such an interpretation of the deeper significance of the Norris plan as Mr. Hoover's veto message affords, rates and nitrates might leave the ordinary mortal confused.[40]

Charles Merz, veteran political commentator for the New York *Times,* speculated that Muscle Shoals "affords the most obvious point on which a national 'power issue' could be raised in 1932." [41] In other areas of the press, the Muscle Shoals controversy was interpreted as the synonym of the principal points of dispute in the power fight, which seemed destined to play an important role in the coming campaign.[42] President Hoover, in his message vetoing the Norris bill, noted that Muscle Shoals had made the struggle between exponents of public and private power "one of the most important issues confronting our people." [43]

In March, 1932, the National Popular Government League, under the direction of Judson King, conducted a survey of the leading presidential candidates in the two major parties to determine which candidate had been the most zealous in protecting the public's interest from the "power trust." The survey consisted of an analysis of the official acts and speeches of each candidate. When this work was concluded, the name of Governor Franklin D. Roosevelt of New York far outranked the rest. The completed survey was endorsed by thirty-seven members of Congress, twenty-one Democrats, fourteen Progressive Republicans, and two members of the Farm-Labor party, among whom were such veterans of the Muscle Shoals controversy as Senators Norris and McKellar and Representative LaGuardia.[44] In endorsing the Popular Government League's survey, this congressional group signed and attached to the survey a memorandum which stated that

We regard the power question in its economic, financial, industrial and social aspects as one of the most important issues before the American people in the campaign of 1932.

Its political significance cannot be overestimated and must challenge

40. New York *Times,* March 5, 1931.
41. *Ibid.,* June 14 (IX), 1931.
42. "Muscle Shoals to Plague the 1932 Campaign," *loc. cit.,* 7.
43. Senate Doc. 321, 71 Cong., 3 Sess., 6.
44. New York *Times,* March 21, 1932.

the attention of those interested in any progressive movement or measure. The reason is plain. The combined utility and banking interests, headed by the power trust, have the most powerful and widely organized political machine ever known in our history. . . . It is strenuously working to control the nominations for the Presidency and the Congress of both dominant political parties.[45]

Governor Roosevelt refused to comment on the National Popular Government League's survey. Nevertheless, public power advocates recognized Roosevelt as a friend of public power because of his attitude toward the power question in New York. The New York Governor was at this time waging a fight for public development of water-power resources in his home state. After being nominated by the Democrats in 1932, the New Yorker pledged, in his acceptance speech, a policy of rigid regulation of public utility holding companies. He did not mention, however, the subject of public power in this address. The platform adopted by the Democratic party in 1932 called for a stringent regulation of the private power industry and "conservation, development and use of the nation's water power in the public interest." [46]

Early in August, 1932, on the eve of the presidential campaign, Roosevelt sought the advice of Judson King, director of the National Popular Government League, on the power question. The New York Governor invited King to his home at Hyde Park, New York, where they discussed the power problem. The Popular Government League director long had been fighting for the cause of public power.[47]

Early in the campaign, Roosevelt forced the power issue to the front. On September 21, 1932, at Portland, Oregon, deep in the heart of a water-power conscious region, the New Yorker chose to outline his power policy. It consisted of two principal parts—the use of public power projects such as Muscle Shoals as yardsticks to regulate power rates, and rigid federal regulation of the electric power industry as a whole. Roosevelt insisted that "as a broad

45. *Ibid.;* Bulletin No. 153, National Popular Government League (March 18, 1932), 1.
46. New York *Times,* Jan. 7, Feb. 16, June 30, July 3, 1932; Raushenbush, *The Power Fight,* 203–10.
47. New York *Times,* Aug. 6, 1932.

general rule, the development of utilities should remain with certain exceptions a function for private initiative and private capital." But the exceptions were important. One exception would be determined by the "birch rod" principle; any community in the nation that was not satisfied with the service rendered or the rates charged should have the right to establish its own power system. He called this right the "birch rod" which would be used to force the private power companies to perform efficient service at reasonable rates.

A second exception was Roosevelt's contention that all water-power sites belonging to the federal government should be developed and operated by that agency. In most cases, he would grant the private power companies the privilege of distributing the power developed by the government with the understanding that should there be abuses by these companies, the federal government would assume that function also. Since the federal government held title to most of the nation's water-power resources, the Governor's water-power doctrine threatened the Federal Water Power Act. Four important water-power projects would receive his special attention, Roosevelt promised; these major developments would be Muscle Shoals, Boulder Dam, the Columbia River, and the St. Lawrence project.[48]

President Hoover failed to take a definite stand on the power issue. On the whole, he defended the policy of federal and state regulation as provided in the Federal Water Power Act, but this position was somewhat compromised by his strong emphasis on state rights in the matter of regulating public utilities.[49]

The issue of private versus public power continues to be a subject of political strife, but the Muscle Shoals controversy itself came to an end in November, 1932. The solution for this vexatious problem was found, not in the halls of Congress, but at the ballot box. The overwhelming victory of Franklin D. Roosevelt and the Democratic party in the election of 1932 assured victory for the Norris plan—not the Norris compromise plan of 1928 and 1930 but the original Norris program for a comprehen-

48. *Ibid.*, Sept. 22, 1932.
49. *Ibid.*, Sept. 23, 24, 25, 1932.

sive multiple-purpose development of the waters of the Tennessee
Valley.

Interpreting the election as a clear mandate for the acceptance
of his comprehensive Muscle Shoals plan, Norris did not introduce a Muscle Shoals bill in the lame duck session of 1932-33.
He announced that he would wait until after March 4 when
President-elect Roosevelt was scheduled to call an extra session
of Congress.[50] If there were any doubts in Norris's mind regarding this matter, they were dispelled in late January, 1933, when
Roosevelt said to him, as the two stood watching the waters of
the Tennessee swirl through the flood gates of Wilson Dam:
"This should be a happy day for you, George." "It is, Mr. President," replied the Nebraska Senator, "I see my dreams come
true." [51]

In early February, 1933, a few days after his visit to Muscle
Shoals, President-elect Roosevelt announced a plan for the comprehensive development of the Tennessee River basin which satisfied Norris's expectations in every respect. The Roosevelt proposal called for a co-ordinated program of flood control, reclamation of flood lands, power development, improvement of navigation, and stimulation of industry in the region. Roosevelt told
the press that his scheme for the Tennessee Valley would probably be "the widest experiment ever conducted by a government." Gifford Pinchot called the Roosevelt proposal "a practical
application of the Theodore Roosevelt conservation policy." [52]

Immediately following Roosevelt's visit to Muscle Shoals, where
he had confided to some members of Congress his plan for
the Tennessee Valley, Senator McKellar, in a radio address, declared that the election of the New York Governor had "virtually
settled" the Muscle Shoals question. He foresaw speedy action in
the forthcoming special session of Congress on Roosevelt's program for development of the Tennessee River, with which the
Tennessee Senator said he was "perfectly delighted." More important, Senator McKellar expressed his appreciation to Senator

50. *Ibid.*, Jan. 21, 1933.
51. *Ibid.*, Jan. 22, 1933.
52. *Ibid.*, Feb. 3, 4, 1933.

Norris for having fought so long and so vigorously for development of the Tennessee Valley. McKellar said:

The entire Tennessee Valley, and indeed the entire South, owes to George W. Norris a deep debt of gratitude for the wonderful fight that he has made for the last 10 years to keep Muscle Shoals in the hands of the Government to use it for the benefit of the people. . . . As a Southerner and as a representative of the Tennessee Valley, I want to express my great debt of gratitude for the splendid fight that Senator Norris has made.[53]

When, in May, 1933, the new Congress enacted Roosevelt's recommendations for the development of the Tennessee River into law through the Tennessee Valley Authority Act, more than a decade of strife and uncertainty as to the future of Muscle Shoals, and indeed the entire Tennessee River system, had come to an end.

53. *Cong. Rec.*, 72 Cong., 2 Sess., 3181–82.

Bibliography

PRIMARY MATERIALS

Manuscripts

Library of Congress (Division of Manuscripts)
    Papers of William E. Borah.
    Papers of Calvin Coolidge.
    Papers of Charles L. McNary.
    Papers of George W. Norris.
    Papers of Gifford Pinchot.
    Papers of Thomas J. Walsh.

National Archives
    General Records of the Department of Agriculture, Correspondence of the Secretary of Agriculture, Muscle Shoals Nitrate Plant.
    Records of the Bureau of Plant Industry, Soils, and Agricultural Engineering: Correspondence of the Bureau of Soils, Muscle Shoals; Fertilizer Investigations, Muscle Shoals; Fixed Nitrogen Laboratory Research Reports, Muscle Shoals.
    Records of the Office of the Chief of Engineers, Alabama Power Company, Correspondence A, Muscle Shoals.
    Records of the Office of the Judge Advocate General, Muscle Shoals Correspondence File.
    Records of the United States Senate.

Publications, United States Congress

General
    Congressional Directory, 66 Cong. through 72 Cong. (1918–1933).
    Congressional Record, 66 Cong. through 72 Cong. (1918–1933).
    United States Statutes at Large, XXXIX (1915–1917), XLI (1919–1921).

Documents, United States House of Representatives
    War Department, *The Henry Ford Muscle Shoals Offer,* House Doc. 167, 67 Cong., 2 Sess. (1922).
    War Department, *Offer Made by the Alabama Power Company Proposing to Complete Wilson Dam,* House Doc. 192, 67 Cong., 2 Sess. (1922).

War Department, *Offer of Union Carbide Company for Muscle Shoals,* House Doc. 166, 68 Cong., 1 Sess. (1924).

War Department, *Additional Offer Made by the Tennessee Electric Power Company to Manufacture Nitrogen and Fertilizer at Muscle Shoals,* House Doc. 173, 68 Cong., 1 Sess. (1924).

Muscle Shoals Inquiry, *Majority and Minority Reports of the Muscle Shoals Inquiry,* House Doc. 119, 69 Cong., 1 Sess. (1925).

War Department, *Tennessee River and Tributaries,* House Doc. 185, 70 Cong., 1 Sess. (1928).

War Department, *Tennessee River and Tributaries, North Carolina, Tennessee, Alabama, and Kentucky,* House Doc. 328, 71 Cong., 2 Sess. (1930).

Documents, United States Senate

Department of Commerce, *A General Review of the Nitrogen Situation in the United States,* Senate Doc. 88, 68 Cong., 1 Sess. (1924).

Conference Committee, *Muscle Shoals,* Senate Doc. 196, 68 Cong., 2 Sess. (1925).

War Department, *Muscle Shoals,* Senate Doc. 189, 69 Cong., 2 Sess. (1927).

Federal Power Commission, *Revised Offer for Muscle Shoals,* Senate Doc. 209, 69 Cong., 2 Sess. (1927).

Federal Trade Commission, *Control of Power Companies,* Senate Doc. 213, 69 Cong., 2 Sess. (1927).

Department of Justice, *Legal Rights of the United States and Alabama in Muscle Shoals Project,* Senate Doc. 31, 70 Cong., 1 Sess. (1928).

Federal Trade Commission, *Electrical Equipment and Competitive Conditions,* Senate Doc. 46, 70 Cong., 1 Sess. (1928).

Conference Committee, *Disposition of Muscle Shoals,* Senate Doc. 118, 70 Cong., 1 Sess. (1928).

Conference Committee, *Disposition of Muscle Shoals,* Senate Doc. 142, 70 Cong., 1 Sess. (1928).

War Department, *Surplus Hydroelectric Power Generated at Wilson Dam, Ala., Sold to Alabama Power Company,* Senate Doc. 222, 71 Cong., 3 Sess. (1930).

Conference Committee, *Disposition of Muscle Shoals,* Senate Document 272, 71 Cong., 3 Sess. (1931).

President of the United States, *Veto Message Relating to Disposition of Muscle Shoals,* Senate Doc. 321, 71 Cong., 3 Sess. (1931).

Muscle Shoals Commission, *Report of Muscle Shoals Commission,* Senate Doc. 21, 72 Cong., 1 Sess. (1932).

Hearings, United States House of Representatives

Atmospheric Nitrogen, Hearings before the Committee on Military Affairs on H. R. 10329, 66 Cong., 2 Sess. (1920).

Sundry Civil Appropriations Bill for 1922, Hearings before the Committee on Appropriations, 66 Cong., 3 Sess. (1920).

Sundry Civil Appropriations Bill for 1922, Supplement to the Hearings before the Committee on Appropriations, 66 Cong., 3 Sess. (1921).

Muscle Shoals Propositions, Hearings before the Committee on Military Affairs, 67 Cong., 2 Sess. (1922).

Nitrate, Hearings before the Committee on Agriculture, Series HH, 67 Cong., 4 Sess. (1923).

Nitrate, Hearings before the Committee on Agriculture, Series HH, 1st. Supplement, 67 Cong., 4 Sess. (1923).

Nitrate, Hearings before the Committee on Agriculture, Series HH, 2nd. Supplement, 67 Cong., 4 Sess. (1923).

Muscle Shoals Propositions, Hearings before the Committee on Military Affairs, 68 Cong., 1 Sess. (1924).

Muscle Shoals, Hearings before the Committee on Military Affairs on H. R. 16396 and H. R. 16614, 69 Cong., 2 Sess. (1927).

Muscle Shoals, Hearings before the Committee on Military Affairs on H. R. 8305, 70 Cong., 1 Sess. (1928).

Muscle Shoals, Hearings before the Committee on Military Affairs on S. J. Res. 46, 70 Cong., 1 Sess. (1928).

Muscle Shoals, Hearings before the Committee on Military Affairs on H. R. 8305, 70 Cong., 2 Sess. (1929).

Muscle Shoals, Hearings before the Committee on Military Affairs, 71 Cong., 2 Sess. (1930).

Muscle Shoals, Hearings before the Committee on Military Affairs, 72 Cong., 1 Sess. (1932).

Hearings, United States Senate

Atmospheric Nitrogen, Operation of Muscle Shoals Nitrate Plants, Hearings before the Committee on Agriculture and Forestry on S. 3390, 66 Cong., 2 Sess. (1920).

Sundry Civil Appropriations Bill for 1922, Hearings before the Committee on Appropriations on H. R. 15422, 66 Cong., 3 Sess. (1921).

Muscle Shoals, Hearings before the Committee on Agriculture and Forestry on S. 3420, 67 Cong., 2 Sess. (1922).

Muscle Shoals, Hearings before the Committee on Agriculture and Forestry on S. 139, S. 2372, S. 3214, and H. R. 518, 68 Cong., 1 Sess. (1924).

Newspaper Charges Against Senator Underwood in Connection with the Muscle Shoals Project, Hearing before the Committee of the Judiciary, 68 Cong., 2 Sess. (1925).

Muscle Shoals, Hearings before the Committee on Agriculture and Forestry on H. Con. Res. 4, 69 Cong., 1 Sess. (1926).

To Suspend the Jurisdiction of the Federal Power Commission, Hearings before the Committee on Agriculture and Forestry on S. J. Res. 35, 69 Cong., 1 Sess. (1926).

Muscle Shoals, Hearings before the Committee on Agriculture and Forestry on S. J. Res. 163, 69 Cong., 2 Sess. (1927).

Disposition of Muscle Shoals, Hearings before the Committee on Agriculture and Forestry on S. 2786 and S. J. Res. 46, 70 Cong., 1 Sess. (1928).

Muscle Shoals, Hearing before the Committee on Agriculture and Forestry on S. J. Res. 49, 71 Cong., 1 Sess. (1929).

Lobby Investigations, Hearings before the Committee of the Judiciary pursuant to S. Res. 20, 71 Cong., 2 Sess. (1930).

To Create Muscle Shoals Corporation of the United States, Hearings before the Committee on Agriculture and Forestry on S. J. Res. 15, 72 Cong., 1 Sess. (1932).

Hearings, Joint Committees

Leasing of Muscle Shoals, Hearings before the Joint Committee on Muscle Shoals, 69 Cong., 1 Sess. (1926).

Reports, United States House of Representatives

War Expenditures—Ordnance, House Report 998, 66 Cong., 2 Sess. (1920).

Muscle Shoals Propositions, House Report 1084, 67 Cong., 2 Sess. (1922).

Muscle Shoals, House Report 143, 68 Cong., 1 Sess. (1924).

Muscle Shoals Commission, House Report 1627, 68 Cong., 2 Sess. (1925).

Disposition of Muscle Shoals, House Report 2303, 69 Cong., 2 Sess. (1927).

Muscle Shoals, House Report 1095, 70 Cong., 1 Sess. (1928).

Muscle Shoals, House Report 2564, 70 Cong., 2 Sess. (1929).

Muscle Shoals, House Report 1430, 71 Cong., 2 Sess. (1930).

Completion of Dam No. 2, Etc., at Muscle Shoals, House Report 2747, 71 Cong., 3 Sess. (1931).

Leasing of Muscle Shoals Properties, House Report 1005, 72 Cong., 1 Sess. (1932).

Reports, United States Senate

Muscle Shoals, Senate Report 831, 67 Cong., 2 Sess. (1922).

Muscle Shoals, Senate Report 678, 68 Cong., 1 Sess. (1924).

Investigation of Editorial Charges Against Senator Underwood, Senate Report 823, 68 Cong., 2 Sess. (1925).

Muscle Shoals, Senate Report 672, 69 Cong., 1 Sess. (1926).

Completion of Dam No. 2 and Steam Plant at Muscle Shoals, Senate Report 1633, 69 Cong., 2 Sess. (1927).

Investigations of Public Utility Corporations, Senate Report 225, 70
Cong., 1 Sess. (1928).

Disposition of Muscle Shoals, Senate Report 228, 70 Cong., 1 Sess.
(1928).

Senatorial Campaign Expenditures, Senate Report 603, 70 Cong., 1
Sess. (1928).

Disposition of Muscle Shoals, Senate Report 19, 71 Cong., 1 Sess.
(1929).

Lobbying and Lobbyists, Senate Report 43, 71 Cong., 2 Sess. (1930).

Disposition of Muscle Shoals, Senate Report 423, 72 Cong., 1 Sess.
(1932).

Executive Publications, United States Government

War Department Report No. 2041, United States Ordnance Department, *Report on the Fixation and Utilization of Nitrogen* (1922).

Muscle Shoals Commission, *Muscle Shoals: A Plan for the Use of the
United States Properties on the Tennessee River by Private Industry
for "the Manufacture of Fertilizers and Other Useful Products"*
(1931).

Publications, State Governments

Legislative Doc. 28, State of Alabama, Session of 1927.

Contemporary Periodicals

"A Contemptible Effort to Arouse Hatred in New England to the
South," in *Manufacturers' Record,* XC (Sept. 2, 1926), 75.

"A. E. C. Wants Muscle Shoals Under Water-Power Act," in *Electrical
World,* LXXXIII (May 3, 1924), 895.

"Again the Bugaboo of a Power Trust," in *Electrical World,* LXXXV
(Jan. 10, 1925), 83–84.

"Alabama Power's Muscle Shoals Offer Makes Favorable Impression,"
in *Electrical World,* LXXIX (Feb. 25, 1922), 399–400.

Baker, Benjamin, "Muscle Shoals Plans and Issues Before Congress,"
in *Annalist,* XXXI (March 9, 1928), 445–46.

———, "Political Forces in the Muscle Shoals Struggle," in *Annalist,*
XXXI (March 2, 1928), 404–5.

———, "Some Hope for Some Action on Muscle Shoals," in *Annalist,*
XXXI (Feb. 14, 1928), 363–64.

Bauer, John, "Muscle Shoals and the President's Veto," in *National
Municipal Review,* XX (April, 1931), 231–34.

"Bill Leasing Muscle Shoals to Ford Strongly Backed," in *Electrical
World,* LXXXIII (Dec. 22, 1923), 1284.

"City All Main Street," in *Literary Digest,* LXXIII (April 8, 1922),
72-74.

Clark, Farley G., "Muscle Shoals Relative to Conservation," in *Transactions of the American Electrochemical Society*, LVI (Sept., 1929), 89-95.

"Committee for Ford Offer," in *Electrical World*, LXXXIII (Feb. 2, 1924), 248.

"The Conference Report on Muscle Shoals Should Be Defeated," in *Manufacturers' Record*, LXXXVII (Feb. 19, 1925), 62.

"Congressman Quin Still Favors Muscle Shoals Bill," in *Electrical World*, LXXXVIII (Oct. 30, 1926), 339.

"Consideration of Muscle Shoals Deferred," in *Electrical World*, LXXXIV (Dec. 6, 1924), 1219.

Dakin, Edwin, "Henry Ford—Man or Superman?" in *Nation*, CXVIII (March 26, 1924), 336-38.

"The Dance on Muscle Shoals," in *Outlook*, CXXXIX (Jan. 28, 1925), 129-31.

Davis, R. O. E., "Muscle Shoals, Nitrogen and Farm Fertilizers," in *Annals of the American Academy of Political and Social Science*, CXXXV (Jan., 1928), 157-63.

"Deadlock in Congress Over Muscle Shoals," in *Electrical World*, LXXIX (April 8, 1922), 697-98.

"Defenders of Water-Power Act Attack Ford Plan," in *Electrical World*, LXXXI (Feb. 17, 1923), 411.

"Developing the Tennessee," in *Electrical World*, LXXXV (May 2, 1925), 940.

Editorial in *Nation*, CXXXI (Nov. 19, 1930), 539.

Editorial in *Wallace's Farmer*, Dec. 29, 1922.

"Editorial Views on the Ford Offer," in *Congressional Digest*, II (Oct. 1922), 22.

"Effort to Report Ford Bill Fails," in *Electrical World*, LXXXIII (May 24, 1924), 1099.

"Facing a Dilemma with Very Sharp Horns," in *Electrical World*, LXXVI (March 12, 1921), 577.

"Facts and Fancies About Muscle Shoals," in *Outlook*, CXLII (Feb. 3, 1926), 165-66.

"Farm Bureau Federation Decries Muscle Shoals Bill," in *Electrical World*, LXXXVII (May 22, 1926), 1159.

"Farmers' National Council," in *Nation*, CVIII (March 15, 1919), 400.

"Fooling the Farmers Again," in *New Republic*, LIII (Dec. 7, 1927), 59-60.

"Ford Mesmerism and Muscle Shoals," in *Current Opinion*, LXXVI (May, 1924), 626.

"Ford Politics in Muscle Shoals," in *Literary Digest*, LXXIX (Oct. 27, 1923), 14-15.

"Ford Winning Muscle Shoals," in *Literary Digest*, LXXX (March 29, 1924), 10–12.

"Ford Withdraws Offer for Muscle Shoals," in *Electrical World*, LXXXIV (Oct. 18, 1924), 827.

"Ford's Muscle Shoals Offer and Public Policy," in *Electrical World*, LXXVIII (Aug. 20, 1921), 353.

Gilfond, Duff, "The Muscle Shoals Lobby," in *New Republic*, LXII (April 16, 1930), 234–36.

"Government Moves Slowly on Muscle Shoals Offer," in *Electrical World*, LXXVIII (Aug. 13, 1921), 337.

"Gray, Coolidge, Norris and Muscle Shoals," in *Electrical World*, XCV (March 1, 1930), 423.

Greenwood, Ernest, "The Myth of Muscle Shoals," in *Independent*, CXIV (Feb. 28, 1925), 230–32.

Hard, William, "Mr. Ford Is So Good," in *Nation*, CXVIII (March 26, 1924), 340–41.

"Hearings on Muscle Shoals Concluded," in *Electrical World*, LXXIX (March 25, 1922), 595.

"Henry Ford and Muscle Shoals," in *Manufacturers' Record*, LXXXIII (March 1, 1923), 80–81.

"Henry Ford's Bid for Muscle Shoals," in *Literary Digest*, LXXII (Jan. 28, 1922), 10–11.

"Henry Gets Right at Last," in *Independent*, CXIII (Oct. 25, 1924), 300.

Ladd, Edwin F., "Why I Am for Henry Ford's Offer for Muscle Shoals," in *Saturday Evening Post*, CXCVII (Nov. 22, 29, 1924), 22, 30.

Lane, Alfred P., "Muscle Shoals—Bonanza or White Elephant?" in *Scientific American*, CXXXII (May, 1925), 293–95.

McClung, Littel, "Building of the World's Largest Monolith," in *Scientific American*, CXXIX (July, 1923), 8–9.

——, "The Seventy-Five Mile City," *ibid.*, CXXVII (Sept. 22, 1922), 156–57.

McMurray, K. C., "The Geographic Setting of Muscle Shoals," in *Bulletin of the Geographical Society of Philadelphia*, XXII (July, 1924), 10–23.

"Merrill on Muscle Shoals," in *Electrical World*, LXXXVI (July 4, 1925), 31.

Merz, Charles, "Muscle Shoals," in *Century Magazine*, CVIII (Sept. 1924), 615–21.

Milton, George F., Jr., "The South and Muscle Shoals," in *Independent*, CXII (Jan. 19, 1924), 39–41.

"Mr. Hoover Defies the Senate on Muscle Shoals," in *Literary Digest*, CVI (Aug. 9, 1930), 8.

"Muscle Shoals," in *Outlook and Independent*, CLIV (April 23, 1930), 656–57.

"Muscle Shoals: A Scandal in the Making?" in *New Republic*, XXXVIII (April 23, 1924), 220–21.

"Muscle Shoals Again," in *New Republic*, XLVI (March 10, 1926), 60.

"Muscle Shoals as a Hot Air Plant," in *Current Opinion*, LXXVIII (Feb. 1925), 141–43.

"The Muscle Shoals Bill," in *Outlook and Independent*, CLVII (March 4, 1931), 328.

"Muscle Shoals Commissioners Confer Informally," in *Electrical World*, LXXXV (May 9, 1925), 992.

"Muscle Shoals in Crisis," in *New Republic*, LV (May 30, 1928), 33–34.

"Muscle Shoals May Yet Be Leased to Highest Bidder," in *Business Week*, No. 34 (April 23, 1930), 40.

"Muscle Shoals Nearing Its Climax," in *Literary Digest*, CV (April 19, 1930), 11.

"Muscle Shoals Open for Bids," in *Literary Digest*, LXXXVIII (March 27, 1926), 11–12.

"Muscle Shoals—Ours," in *Nation*, CXIX (Dec. 17, 1924), 668.

"Muscle Shoals Power Soon a Reality," in *Electrical World*, LXXXV (March 28, 1925), 651.

"Muscle Shoals Rededicated to Fertilizer and Power Production," in *Electrical World*, XCIX (Jan. 23, 1932), 184–88.

"The Muscle Shoals Situation," in *Manufacturers' Record*, LXXXI (March 2, 1922), 75.

"The Muscle Shoals Situation Again," in *Manufacturers' Record*, LXXXI (March 9, 1922), 62.

"The Muscle Shoals Situation as Viewed in Mississippi," in *Manufacturers' Record*, LXXXVII (Feb. 19, 1925), 70–71.

"Muscle Shoals to Plague the 1932 Campaign," in *Literary Digest*, CVIII (March 14, 1931), 7.

"New England and the South's Interest in Muscle Shoals," in *Manufacturers' Record*, XC (Sept. 23, 1926), 53–56.

"New Muscle Shoals Idea Falls Flat," in *Electrical World*, LXXXIX (April 9, 1927), 771.

Norris, George W., "Shall We Give Muscle Shoals to Henry Ford?" in *Saturday Evening Post*, CXCVI (May 24, 1924), 30-31.

———, "Why Henry Ford Wants Muscle Shoals," in *Nation*, CXVII (Dec. 26, 1923), 738–39.

"Norris' Power Fight," in *Nation*, CXX (March 26, 1928), 338.

"Officials Not Backing Ford," in *Electrical World*, LXXXII (Sept. 22, 1923), 618.

"One Million Primary Horsepower Could Be Developed at Muscle Shoals," *Manufacturers' Record*, LXXXIII (May 3, 1923), 81–82.

Pinchot, Amos, "Hoover and Power," in *Nation*, CXXXIII (Aug. 12, 1931), 151–53.

"President Gives a Free Hand to Muscle Shoals Commissioners," in *Electrical World*, LXXXV (April 11, 1929), 781–82.

"The Problem of Muscle Shoals," in *Current History*, XXVIII (Aug., 1928), 724–33. Introduction by William M. Jardine, Part I by Robert Stewart, and Part II by George W. Norris.

"The Rejection of Ford's Muscle Shoals Offer," in *Electrical World*, LXXX (July 22, 1922), 161.

"The Rival Bids for Muscle Shoals," in *Literary Digest*, LXXXI (May 10, 1924), 10–11.

"The Senate Navigating the Shoals," in *Outlook*, CXXXIX (June 21, 1925), 86–88.

"Senator Harrison Optimistic on Muscle Shoals Bills," in *Electrical World*, LXXXVIII (Aug. 14, 1926), 339.

"Smoke Screen Over Muscle Shoals," in *New Republic*, LXVIII (Oct. 21, 1931), 249.

"Snell and Garrett to Confer," in *Electrical World*, LXXXVI (Dec. 26, 1925), 1321.

Spurm, Henry C., "Will the Public Utilities Be a Major Political Issue?" in *Public Utilities Fortnightly*, VI (July 10, 1930), 3–10.

Switzer, John A., "The Muscle Shoals Question," in *Manufacturers' Record*, XCI (Jan. 13, 1927), 64–66.

"Three Honest to Goodness Bidders Startle Muscle Shoals Board," in *Business Week*, No. 109 (Sept. 30, 1931), 20.

"The Troublous Muscle Shoals Veto," in *Literary Digest*, XCVII (June 23, 1928), 11–12.

"The Unsolved Problem of Muscle Shoals," in *Review of Reviews*, LXXXIII (April, 1931), 53.

Welliver, Judson C., "The Muscle Shoals Power and Industrial Project," in *American Review of Reviews*, LXV (April, 1922), 381–94.

Wells, Philip, "Our Federal Power Policy," in *Survey Graphic*, LI (March, 1924), 572–73.

"What Next at Muscle Shoals?" in *Literary Digest*, LXXXIII (Nov. 8, 1924), 10–11.

"Whole Country Should Back Ford-Edison Scheme for Muscle Shoals Development," in *Manufacturers' Record*, LXXXI (Jan. 19, 1922), 53.

"Why Henry Ford Wants the Muscle Shoals Property," in *Current Opinion*, LXXII (Feb., 1922), 262–64.

Wooton, Paul, "Chances for Muscle Shoals Bill Improve," in *Electrical World*, LXXXVII (May 8, 1926), 1019.

———, "Cyanamid and Farmers' Bids Rejected," *ibid.*, LXXXIX (April 9, 1927), 771.

———, "Muscle Shoals City's Plea for Power," *ibid.*, XC (July 9, 1927), 82.

———, "Tennessee Senator's Views," *ibid.*, LXXXVII (June 12, 1926), 1309.

Newspapers

Atlanta *Constitution*, 1925.
Birmingham *Age-Herald*, 1921, 1924.
Boston *Herald*, 1925.
Chattanooga *News*, 1921, 1923, 1924, 1925, 1930, 1931.
Chattanooga *Times*, 1924, 1930.
Chicago *Daily News*, 1925, 1931.
Chicago *Tribune*, 1921, 1924.
Cleveland *Plain Dealer*, 1925.
Detroit *Free-Press*, 1931.
Hartford *Courant*, 1928, 1931.
Kansas City *Star*, 1925.
Knoxville *News-Sentinel*, 1930, 1931.
Macon *Telegraph*, 1922.
Memphis *Commercial-Appeal*, 1922, 1924.
Memphis *Press-Scimitar*, 1928, 1930, 1931.
Milwaukee *Journal*, 1931.
Minneapolis *Tribune*, 1931.
Nashville *Banner*, 1922, 1924, 1925, 1928, 1931.
Nashville *Tennessean*, 1921, 1922, 1924, 1928.
New York *Herald Tribune*, 1925, 1931.
New York *Times*, 1919–1933, 1940.
New York *World*, 1928.
New York *World-Telegram*, 1931.
Philadelphia *Record*, 1921, 1931.
Pittsburgh *Press*, 1928, 1931.
Portland *Oregonian*, 1931.
Rocky Mountain News (Denver), 1928, 1931.
Sacramento *Union*, 1931.
St. Louis *Post-Dispatch*, 1928, 1931.
St. Paul *Pioneer-Press*, 1923, 1925.
San Francisco *Chronicle*, 1928.
Spokane *Spokesman-Review*, 1931.
Toledo *News-Bee*, 1928, 1931.
Washington *Daily News*, 1932.
Washington *Post*, 1927, 1928, 1931.
Washington *Star*, 1931.

Bulletins and Pamphlets

American Farm Bureau Federation, *Report of the Muscle Shoals Committee of the American Farm Bureau Federation* (Chicago, May 31,
1921), in General Records of the Department of Agriculture, Correspondence of the Secretary of Agriculture, Muscle Shoals Nitrate
Plant, National Archives.

American Farm Bureau Weekly News Letter (Feb. 1, 1923), in General Records of the Department of Agriculture, Correspondence of
the Secretary of Agriculture, Muscle Shoals Nitrate Plant, National
Archives.

Bulletin, League of Women Voters (May 17, 1928), in Papers of
George W. Norris, Division of Manuscripts, Library of Congress.

Bulletin No. 43, National Popular Government League (Jan. 14, 1931),
in Papers of George W. Norris, Division of Manuscripts, Library of
Congress.

Hicks, Julia A., *Facts About Muscle Shoals.* Washington, D. C.: National League of Women Voters, 1928.

King, Judson, *Power Records of the Presidential Candidates,* Bulletin
No. 153, National Popular Government League (March 18, 1932),
in Papers of George W. Norris, Division of Manuscripts, Library of
Congress.

————, *Shall Coolidge and Congress Railroad the Underwood
Bill and Deliver Muscle Shoals to the Power Trust?* Bulletin No. 96,
National Popular Government League (Jan. 20, 1925), in Papers of
George W. Norris, Division of Manuscripts, Library of Congress.

Mississippi Valley Association, *Report of the Special Committee of
the Mississippi Valley Association* (May 28, 1921), in General
Records of the Department of Agriculture, Correspondence of the
Secretary of Agriculture, Muscle Shoals Nitrate Plant, National
Archives.

National Fertilizer Association, *Proceedings of the Third Annual
Convention of the National Fertilizer Association.* Washington, D.
C.: National Fertilizer Association, 1927.

Owen, Marguerite, *Muscle Shoals and the Public Welfare.* Washington, D. C.: National League of Women Voters, 1929.

Southern Appalachian Power Conference, *Report of the Southern
Appalachian Power Conference* (Oct. 15, 1927), in Records of the
Bureau of Plant Industry, Soils, and Agriculture Engineering,
Fertilizer Investigations, National Archives.

Southern States Republican League, *Report of the Muscle Shoals
Committee of the Southern States Republican League* (Feb. 21,
1927), in General Records of the Department of Agriculture, Cor-

respondence of the Secretary of Agriculture, Muscle Shoals Nitrate Plant, National Archives.

Tennessee Manufacturers' Association, *The Muscle Shoals Situation as Viewed by the Press of America* (Nashville, Tenn., 1924), in General Records of the Department of Agriculture, Correspondence of the Secretary of Agriculture, Muscle Shoals Nitrate Plant, National Archives.

United States Chamber of Commerce, *Muscle Shoals: A Groundwork of Facts.* Washington, D. C.: U. S. Chamber of Commerce, 1930.

Wyer, Samuel S., *Fundamentals of Our Fertilizer Problem.* Columbus, Ohio: Fuel-Power-Transportation-Educational Foundation, 1927.

————, *Niagara Falls: Its Power Possibilities and Preservation.* Washington, D. C.: Study of Natural Resources 2820, Smithsonian Institution, 1925.

————, *Power Possibilities at Muscle Shoals* (Reprint of paper presented at Annual Convention of American Institute of Electrical Engineers, June 22–26, 1925), in Papers of Calvin Coolidge, Division of Manuscripts, National Archives.

Memoirs

Norris, George W., *The Fighting Liberal: The Autobiography of George W. Norris.* New York: The Macmillan Company, 1945.

SECONDARY MATERIALS

Books

Davidson, Donald. *The Tennessee.* 2 Vols. New York: Rinehart and Company, Inc., 1946–1948.

Garrett, Garet. *The Wild Wheel.* New York: Pantheon Books, 1952.

Kerwin, Jerome G. *Federal Water-Power Legislation.* New York: Columbia University Press, 1926.

Loeb, Carl M. Rhoades and Company, *Aluminum: An Analysis of the Industry in the United States.* New York: Carl M. Loeb, Rhoades and Company, 1950.

McKay, Kenneth C. *The Progressive Movement of 1924.* New York: Columbia University Press, 1947.

Neuberger, Richard L. and Stephan B. Kahn, *Integrity: The Life of George W. Norris.* New York: The Vanguard Press, 1937.

Pinchot, Gifford, *The Power Monopoly: Its Make-Up and Its Menace.* Milford, Pa., 1928.

Pritchett, C. Herman, *The Tennessee Valley Authority: A Study in Public Administration.* Chapel Hill, N. C.: The University of North Carolina Press, 1943.

Ransmeier, Joseph S., *The Tennessee Valley Authority: A Case Study in the Economics of Multiple Purpose Stream Planning.* Nashville, Tenn.: The Vanderbilt University, Press, 1942.

Raushenbush, Stephen, *High Power Propaganda.* New York: New Republic, Inc., 1928.

———, *The Power Fight.* New York: New Republic, Inc., 1932.

Richards, William C., *The Last Billionaire: Henry Ford.* New York: Charles Scribner's Sons, 1948.

Sinclair, Upton B., *The Flivver King: A Story of Ford-America.* Pasadena, Calif.: Upton Sinclair, 1937.

Articles

"More Power for Bomber Production," in Engineering *News-Record,* CXXVIII (Feb. 26, 1942), 334.

Index

Agricultural publications, 44, 209, 213n
Agriculture: question of importance of continuance of Muscle Shoals project to, 12–13, 145, 155–56, 171, 198, 209, 237–38, 250–51, 298; *see also* Fertilizer
Agriculture, Department of, *see* Department of Agriculture, U. S.
Air Nitrates Corporation, 9–10, 45, 55, 69
Alabama: real estate boom in northern, 40; attitude toward Alabama Power Company in, 57–58 (*see also* Alabama Power Company); attitude toward Muscle Shoals offers, 120, 222, 248, 251–52, 269
Alabama Farm Bureau, 58
Alabama Muscle Shoals Commission, 203
Alabama Power Company: War Department contract with, 3, 9, 14, 18–19, 55, 69–70, 98, 101, 108, 206n; Wilson Dam and, 22–23, 174, 243, 246, 276, 281–82; opposition to Ford offer, 54–56, 66–71 *passim;* bid made by, 56–60, 77, 92, 96, 109–10, 119–20, 147, 299; question of foreign ownership, 57–58; Norris bill and, 80; Gorgas plant sold to, 99; alleged political influence of, 159n, 160, 181; alleged influence on Mobile *Press,* 254; *see also* Martin, Thomas W.
Alabama Public Service Commission, 159, 189, 190
Alabama-Tennessee Commission, 293, 297, 308
Alexander, Vance J., 297
Almon, Edward B., 21; on feasibility of fertilizer production at Muscle Shoals, 22, 60, 246, 303; in favor of Ford offer, 94, 109–10, 117
Aluminum, 32, 46, 70, 93
Alunite, 93
American Agricultural Editors' Association, 209, 213n
American Cyanamid Company: War Department contract with, 3, 9, 55;

opposition to government operation of Muscle Shoals, 8, 17, 19; bid by, 174, 184, 193–214 *passim,* 244, 247, 250, 257, 264–65
American Electrochemical Society, 268n
American Engineering Council, 124–25, 131–32, 274n
American Farm Bureau Federation, 8; *see also* Farm Bureau
American Federation of Labor, 75, 97, 172, 180
American Institute of Electrical Engineers, 64, 132n, 171, 286
American Legion, 97
American Society of Civil Engineers, 132n
American Society of Mechanical Engineers, 132
Annalist, cited, 207, 215, 219
Anti-Semitism, Ford's, 37, 119, 142
Appalachian Electric Power Company, 280
Appalachian Power Conference, 240
Arkansas, 198, 199
Armour Fertilizer Company, 54
Associated Power companies, 109, 134
Atlanta *Constitution,* 254
Atmospheric Nitrogen Association, 14

Baker, Benjamin, 207–8, 219
Baker, Newton D.: instigator of Wadsworth-Kahn bill, 5, 6–8, 12–13, 25–26; opposition to Ford offer, 120–21, 145; for Norris bill, 128, 133
Baltimore *Sun,* quoted, 296
Bankhead, William B., 22, 79
Barkley, Alben W., 269
Barrett, Charles S., 95
Baruch, Bernard, 9–10, 12, 82
Bauer, John, 294n
Bauxite deposite, 93
Beach, Lansing H., 28, 42, 51, 55, 81
Bell, William B., 174, 212–15; before House Military Committee, 244, 247, 271; before Federal Trade Commission, 257; Coolidge and, 264
Bethel, Walter A., 99

Index

AMERICAN HISTORY TITLES IN THE NORTON LIBRARY